Brazilian Popular Music

and Citizenship

D0768023

Brazilian Popular Music and Citizenship

: : :

Edited by Idelber Avelar
and Christopher Dunn

Duke University Press

Durham & London

2011

© 2011 Duke University Press
All rights reserved
Designed by Amy Ruth Buchanan
Typeset in Scala by Tseng Information
Systems, Inc.
Library of Congress Cataloging-in-
Publication Data appear on the last
printed page of this book.

For Ana and Ladee

: : :

For Alexandre, Laura,

Luango, Isa, and Joaquin

contents

acknowledgments

This book has been over five years in the making, and along the way we have benefited from the support and assistance from many people and institutions. Home to one of the largest Latin American research libraries in the country, Tulane University served as an ideal place to develop this project. We are grateful to the Stone Center for Latin American Studies and its executive director, Tom Reese, for early financial support to translate chapters from Portuguese to English. (In general, the translations were done by Idelber Avelar, Christopher Dunn, and Aaron Lorenz; in the other chapters, translations of Portuguese-language quotations are the works of the respective authors.) We appreciate the good work of Michael Bernstein, provost and senior vice president for academic affairs, and Carole Haber, the dean of the School of Liberal Arts, who have shown a keen interest in Brazilian studies at Tulane University. We are also grateful to our colleagues in the Department of Spanish and Portuguese, for the wonderful atmosphere and the continuing support. We would not have been able to complete this book without the help of Claudia de Brito, our executive secretary. In 2008, Tulane University hosted the IX Congress of the Brazilian Studies Association, which gave further impetus to the research and teaching of Brazilian studies on campus. In an indirect way, this book is a product of this favorable intellectual environment.

We have benefited from the work of several scholars of Brazilian music who didn't participate directly in this volume, but whose work is central to our concerns, including Charles Perrone, José Miguel Wisnik, George Yúdice, Byran McCann, Marta Ulhôa, Marcos Napolitano, Herom Vargas, Paulo César de Araújo, Paulo Henrique Caetano, Fred Góes, Júlio Tavares, Jason Stanyek, and Ana María Ochoa. We appreciate the efforts of two anonymous evaluators, who provided insightful commentary and useful suggestions.

We are grateful to several individuals who were instrumental in researching and acquiring authorization to publish the photos that appear in this book, including Pedro Belchior of the Museu Villa-Lobos, Carol Brasil of CUFA (Central Única das Favelas; Unified Center of Favelas), Valeria Cysneiros of the Divisão de Música e Arquivo Sonoro of the Biblioteca Nacional, Márcia Cláudia Figueiredo of FUNARTE (Fundação Nacional de Artes; National Foundation for the Arts), and Henrique Gandelman of the Academia Brasileira de Música.

Finally, we would like to thank Reynolds Smith and Sharon Torian of Duke University Press. We are especially grateful to have worked with Reynolds on one of his last projects with Duke. He was an early enthusiast for this book and guided it through several keys stages in the editorial process before handing it off to Valerie Millholland. We can't think of a better home for this book.

Music as Practice of Citizenship in Brazil

Idelber Avelar and Christopher Dunn

In Brazil music has been both an instrument through which disenfranchised groups have asserted claims to citizenship, as well as a tool in the formulation of disciplinary or repressive state policies. While music brought
mixed-race and black people into the urban public sphere for the first time
in the late nineteenth century with maxixe, it also encoded messages of
obedience in the pedagogy of choral singing concocted by the authoritarian
state of the 1930s and 1940s. Music allegorized hopes and anxieties like
no other art during the military dictatorship of the 1960s and 1970s, but it
also provided upper and middle classes with the paradigm for an exclusionary conception of taste, based on the imaginary belonging to a community
of enlightened, sophisticated aesthetic consumers—an operation that imposed a considerable stigma of "bad taste" upon the preferences of poorer
populations (Araújo, 2002). Music has played a decisive role in reconstruct-
ing the self-esteem of numerous communities in Brazil, from the rebirth
of the Candeal neighborhood in Salvador, Bahia, to Recife's definitive entrance into a national and international pop scene. On the other hand, music
has been the primary currency in the corrupt industry of the *jabá* ("payola,"
record company bribes to radio stations), a practice as pervasive and politically decisive in Brazil as anywhere in the world. Popular music has been,
therefore, an essentially contradictory phenomenon in Brazil, one that invariably produces multiple political effects. This book compiles essays that
focus both on popular music as an agent and image of citizenship, as well as
essays that detail music's imbrication in the foreclosure of citizenship. Our
chapters do, in fact, often study both movements simultaneously, thereby
offering the dynamic picture of a cultural practice whose political meaning
is never given in advance. This is the first English-language collection of
essays that focuses on the political dimensions of Brazil's most fecund form

of popular art; it is also one of the first books to address specifically the question of citizenship in Brazilian popular music.

Scholars have usually distinguished between a liberal school and a civic republican school in the interpretation of citizenship: the former emphasized rights while the latter stressed duties (Heater 1999: 4–79). The liberal tradition is the more recent, but it has been the decisive force in shaping the ways in which citizenship has been conceptualized in the West for the past two centuries. For Thomas Hobbes (1588–1679), the major concern was the securing of order rather than the establishment of civic rights, but he can be seen as a precursor to the liberal tradition insofar as he shifts the medieval understanding of rights and liberties as belonging to groups and estates toward a system where the individual enjoys a direct relationship with the state (Faulks 2000: 22). John Locke (1632–1704) later systematized the liberal conception of citizenship in *The Two Treatises of Civil Government* (1690). The second treatise, particularly, presented a theory of individual natural rights, stating that every man should have the right to "preserve . . . his life, liberty, and estate" (1988: 323), a formula later adapted by the American and the French revolutionaries. As noted by Derek Heater, "Liberal citizenship was the offspring of the liaison between revolutionary upheaval and contractarian natural rights theory, Great Britain playing the role of midwife" (1999: 4). The liberal conception of citizenship is predicated, then, on Hobbes's individualization and on Locke's naturalization of the concept of rights.

The civic republican tradition can be said to hark back to Book III of Aristotle's *Politics*, which concerns itself with the definition of the citizen. The emphasis here is definitely on the requirements for citizenship, *aretē* (virtue) foremost among them. As one of us has shown in earlier work (Avelar 2004: 33–36), Aristotle's attempts to establish an ontological rationale for the contingent Athenian requirements for citizenship (maleness, adulthood, ownership of property, etc.) endowed his politics with an essentially unstable nature. After all, Aristotle's ontologizing efforts notwithstanding, today's citizens could be the noncitizens of tomorrow due to, for example, a defeat in war. Aristotle inaugurated a long tradition in which the thrust to naturalize the qualifications for citizenship clashed against the essentially contingent nature of those qualifications. The Aristotelian emphasis on virtue continued with Marcus Tullius Cicero's *De Officiis* (*On Duties*; 44 BCE), which makes a strong argument, grounded on the Stoic ethic, about the citizen's responsibility to the polis. Niccolò Machiavelli would later toughen those requirements even more. The modern version of the civic republican tradition would be inaugurated by Jean-Jacques Rousseau's *Social Contract* (1762), which, as Derek Heater points out, sets itself the task of answering a thorny question: "How can men subject themselves to government, which is necessary for security, while, at the same time, retaining their freedom, which is their moral right? His solution was the General Will" (1999: 50).

Although the civic republican tradition would continue with the likes of Georg Hegel and Alexis de Tocqueville, the liberal tradition would undoubtedly become the dominant one in the nineteenth and twentieth centuries. Standard accounts of citizenship have, in fact, inherited the Kantian belief in perfectibility visible in works such as *To Perpetual Peace* (1795), a short essay in which Kant addressed the possibility of a universally sustainable state of peace. The most canonical and foundational of these accounts of citizenship remains T. H. Marshall's essay "Citizenship and Social Class" (1950), which distinguishes three forms of citizenship: civil, political, and social. By civil citizenship Marshall alluded to rights such as free speech, the liberty of the person, and the right to property and to justice, while political citizenship encompasses the right to participate in the exercise of state power through voting and other means. Finally, social citizenship represents a "whole range from the right to a modicum of economic welfare and security to share to the full in the social heritage" (Marshall and Bottomore 1992: 8). Implied in all its variants is the notion of "rights held by individuals and protected by a state whose authority is exercised within explicit boundaries that cannot be exceeded without violating a state's legitimacy" (Mitchell and Wood 1998: 1003). None of these classical theories, however, endow culture with any independent valence as an agent of citizenship. Only in past decades, propelled by new realities such as global migration, has a discourse around cultural citizenship consolidated itself (such discourse being, of course, *one* of the ways in which the relation between culture and citizenship can be posed). Cultural citizenship most often refers to the "maintenance and development of cultural lineage through education, custom, language, and religion and the positive acknowledgment of difference in and by the mainstream" (Miller 2001: 2). We will place our emphasis less on lineage and maintenance than on processes of recodification and transformation of available cultural materials. More than the questions regarding lineage and preservation raised by the term *cultural citizenship* in the contexts of migration in relation to which the term arose, this book will resort to notions such as recoding and mixing, rather than preservation, as better terms to describe how music has acquired citizenship dimension in Brazil.

In a landmark book on the current expediency of culture as a mediator in a growing field of social and political circumstances, George Yúdice notes music's increasingly relevant role for practices of citizenship in Latin America. Speaking of a cultural turn in citizenship, Yúdice highlights how practices of popular culture have opened up spaces of citizen representation not previously available. Located in the "turn to a politics of interpretability and representation in the 1980s and 1990s," a transformation "from what was traditionally deemed properly political to cultural mediation" (2003: 164), these new forms of citizenship ask

> not who count as citizens but how they are construed; not what their rights and duties are, but how these are interpreted; not what the channels of participation in opinion formation and decision making are but by what tactics they can be intervened on and turned around to the interests of the subordinated. (ibid.)

Claims to citizenship have, then, progressively moved from relying on an ontology of political beings to something like a semiotics of political representation. Whereas previous historical moments often saw a dichotomy between, on the one hand, a musician's career and, on the other hand, his/her "real" political action, in recent years it has become patent that the political dimension is to be sought in the cultural artifact itself. In other words, the argument on the expediency of culture does not simply note the increasingly broad political scope that culture has acquired as a mediator that provides access to areas not usually deemed cultural. The argument goes further, implying a redefinition of the very border that separated the political from the cultural. In fact, some of the most innovative interventions by musicians in the field of production, distribution, exchange, and consumption of popular music in Brazil have effected precisely this form of agency of culture upon politics. This is not to say, of course, that Yúdice and other scholars who have observed the cultural turn in citizenship are not attentive to the ways in which these practices can also be reabsorbed and cushioned by hegemonic power formations. It is undeniable, however, that from politicized musical groups such as AfroReggae to the ever-so-popular funk dances of the impoverished north zone of Rio de Janeiro the last two decades have seen an exponential growth in the citizenship dimension of popular cultural practices in Brazil. Studies of these musical phenomena, compiled in this book, will shed unique light on the scope and limits of popular music's role in the ongoing redefinition of citizenship in Brazil.

A venerable tradition of Brazilian social scientists has noted how much Brazil's experience distances itself from standard accounts of citizenship. Anthropologists such as Roberto DaMatta have shown how the traditional sequence of acquisition of those rights in Europe was not followed in Brazil, with social dimensions of citizenship often appearing before civil or political rights existed as such. Political scientists such as Wanderley dos Santos have noted how the Brazilian state has functioned as a true obstacle to the universalization of citizenship, adding that the figure of the citizen still tends to imply privilege and state sponsorship (1979). Not necessarily in contradiction with Santos, DaMatta has observed that the word *citizen* tends to appear in situations in which individuals are fundamentally diminished before the law, as in "O cidadão não tinha seus papéis em ordem" (The citizen, i.e., the individual, did not have his/her papers in order). That subject can only hope to have a privileged treatment if he or she can mobilize relations that would allow him/her to subvert the universality with which the law should presumably treat the case. This is the context where one sees the emergence of the question "Você sabe com quem está falando?" (Do you know whom you're talking to?), as individuals attempt to claim a special and privileged position vis-à-vis the law (1997: 65–95). Whereas the status of the citizen in advanced industrial nations implies at least a basic level of impersonality and universality, the very status of the notion in Brazil has often presupposed a relational, familial, uneven, and heterogeneous order.

More recent scholarship on Brazil has noted the country's uniqueness in conceiving of citizenship as a comparatively more universal, more inclusive process than was the case either in the United States or in Europe: "Neither the denial of national citizenship for racial or religious reasons nor the imposition of local definitions of membership on national citizenship ever occurred" (Holston 2008: 63). At the same time, citizenship in Brazil has always been marked by pronounced inequalities in the actual access to rights. With colonization limited to urban settlements, Brazil's vast rural areas never really counted on the presence of the state. The particular alliance, known as *coronelismo*, between private local powers and public office represented, for all intents and purposes, a privatization of the public. Formal distinctions among citizens were always drawn with the language of nationality (and until 1934, gender), not race. Miscegenation, however, was assumed to offset legal disability. In his excellent *Insurgent Citizenship: Dis-*

junctions of Democracy and Modernity in Brazil, James Holston has studied these remarkable paradoxes of civil society in Brazil, a country where incorporation into citizenship "was at the same time based on dependency, deference, and deceit, as well as their correlates of exploitation, paternalism, and ambiguity" (2008: 81). For Holston, contemporary, insurgent forms of claiming citizen status are visible in the renewed emphasis on the language of citizenship among new organizations of Brazilian civil society. These are markers of an extension of democracy that is real and undeniable, yet at the same time plagued with insufficiency, ambiguities, and contradictions. Music has not been indifferent to these processes.

Given music's social importance and representativeness for Brazil's self-understanding, even the most seemingly "apolitical" genres of Brazilian music have played a role in defining how subjects have situated themselves politically in the country. In fact, the very distinction between "alienated," "individualistic," or "nonpolitical" music, on the one hand, and musics with "political content," on the other, is now more false than it has ever been. As several chapters of this book attest, from romantic ballads to popularesque accordion-based dance music to new electronic, hybrid forms, popular music has been inherent in the struggles around who gets to count as a citizen in Brazil and how. Music has often been, in fact, one of the primary arenas in which those struggles have taken place. No rigorous understanding of the history of Brazilian democracy, for example, can dispense with a study of popular music's interaction with it. This book offers a set of critical glimpses into selected moments of the relationship between musical practices and the construction of citizenship from the early twentieth century to our present. After reading this volume, the reader will hopefully have gained a complex, nuanced understanding of why this relationship has been so intense and indispensable in Brazil. Indeed, the essays collected here share more than the thematic focus on citizenship. Although we have built on the considerable amount of recent scholarship on Brazilian popular music, we have also staked out some of our differences with it. We share with a collection such as *Decantando a República* (Cavalcante et al. 2004) the premise that Brazilian music is shot through with questions related to the polis and the nation. The essays collected here, however, depart from many of the chapters in those volumes in not limiting themselves to seeing citizenship as an already given content later to be studied as something that gets represented in lyrics or in performance. We have, instead, attempted to advance arguments that look at music as a practice constitutive of what we understand as citizenship itself.

This collection of essays is also in dialogue with *Brazilian Popular Music and Globalization* (edited by Charles Perrone and Christopher Dunn, 2001), a project that involved both editors and some contributors present here. While many of the contributors featured there address globalized or diasporic cultural practices informed by the international circulation of musical styles and identity discourses, our project is resolutely grounded in local and national contexts. In this sense, our project is positioned as a counterpoint to the "postnational turn" in music studies, best exemplified by the recent collection of essays *Postnational Musical Identities: Cultural Production, Distribution, and Consumption in a Globalized Scenario.* In their introduction, the editors suggest that a "postnationalist approach" to music scholarship is a necessary corrective to "univocal nationalist discourses" that have excluded or otherwise victimized citizens of various countries (Corona and Madrid 2008: 6). While recognizing that postnational perspectives can indeed serve to critique narrow nationalisms, we are also interested in the ways in which discourses of nationhood and national belonging have been used to claim or expand citizenship rights. Our premise is that the construction of citizenship in all of its dimensions takes place primarily within national boundaries even as it is informed by international and postnational discourses and practices.

Although the contributions to this volume address modern and contemporary cultural contexts, our introductory overview has a wider temporal scope in order to historically situate the musical practices and critical debates that would later emerge. In the colonial context of a slaveholding society, masters, slaves, and impoverished free people had different, if not conflicting, cultural affinities and different ways of imagining home. In what sense can we say that African slaves had or acquired a feeling of belonging to a place called Brazil? The history of Brazil is rife with examples of enslaved and brutalized Africans who fled to the hinterlands to establish maroon communities, or *quilombos*. Of all of the New World societies, Brazil also had the largest number of freed slaves who chose to return to West Africa. It's worth noting, however, that these transatlantic *retornados* typically constructed privileged cosmopolitan identities in the Anglo and Francophone African colonies to which they returned in the nineteenth century. Several popular musical genres, most notably juju music of Yoruba-speaking people of Nigeria, are historically connected to musical practices introduced by diasporic retornados from Brazil (Waterman 1990: 31–32).

But the overwhelming majority of Africans and their descendants remained in Brazil and contributed profoundly to cultural practices identified with the country both before and after independence. More important from the perspective of Afro-Brazilians, both slaves and free alike, was the role of music in creating spaces of sociability and cultural agency separate from dominant white society. Various forms of collective music-making, based largely on West African polyrhythms and produced with a variety of percussion instruments (and occasionally marimbas and strings), served to bring people together in both sacred and secular settings. These events were typically described using the generic term *batuque*, which could refer to a wide range of African and Neo-African musical practices and dances. Local authorities during the time of slavery and following abolition regarded these gatherings with ambivalence. On the one hand, there is evidence to suggest that some slave owners saw batuques as a convenient weekly ritual for mitigating tensions inherent in a slave economy, just as modern authorities have seen popular festivals as a form of social control in which the lower classes could have some fun and "blow off steam." The count of Arcos (the governor of Bahia, 1810–18) saw these gatherings as a useful way to promote group identities, thereby fomenting rivalries among the various African ethnicities (Reis 1993: 157). On the other hand, these gatherings also posed a threat to plantation owners and government officials, who feared large congregations of black people and frequently imposed measures to inhibit or prevent them. Stuart Schwarz recovered a fascinating document that had served as a negotiated settlement between slaves and their owner following a slave revolt in rural Bahia in 1789. The accord highlights the key role of music in the struggle for cultural rights long before citizenship was even imaginable for Afro-Brazilians. As one of the conditions for returning to the plantation, the rebel slaves stipulated: "We shall be able to play, relax and sing any time we wish without your hindrance, nor will permission be needed" (Schwartz 1992: 62; Fryer 2000: 87). Within the context of slavery and the postabolition period, when Afro-Brazilians were socially marginalized, batuque gatherings provided alternative spaces to cultivate communities.

Afro-diasporic music would also have a decisive impact on the music of Brazilians of all colors and social classes, serving in many ways as the primary terrain for various forms of cultural exchange. Of particular significance was the *modinha*, a love song form accompanied by a traditional guitar, called a *viola*, that emerged in the late eighteenth century. Modinha was influenced by the Portuguese *cantigas*, by the Italian arias, and by Afro-diasporic rhythmic patterns. José Ramos Tinhorão has suggested that the modinha was intimately linked to an incipient modern urban imaginary that allowed for greater contact between men and women (1998: 117). The greatest proponent of Brazilian modinhas, Domingos Caldas Barbosa (ca. 1740–1800), born to a Portuguese father and Angolan mother in Rio de Janeiro, popularized the song form in Lisbon, most notably at court functions. There is some debate about the class origins of the modinha, with some arguing that it "was composed for, and first heard, in the salon" (Fryer 2000: 143), and others arguing that it was a popular form that was "made erudite" (Tinhorão 1998: 118) after its success in Portugal. What is clear is that the modinha was the first song form from the colony to gain popularity in the metropolis, becoming well known internationally as a distinctively Brazilian genre. More than a century after Caldas Barbosa's death, the Brazilian writer Lima Barreto would reference the modinha in his acclaimed novel *Triste Fim de Policarpo Quaresma* (1911) as a touchstone for cultural nationalism. The main protagonist, an earnest patriot, scolds his sister for criticizing his relationship with a guitarist-singer who plays modinhas: "The *modinha* is the most genuine expression of national poetry and the *violão* [guitar] is its required instrument. We have abandoned the genre, but it was honored in Lisbon last century when Father Caldas played for noblemen" (2006: 21).

In nineteenth-century Rio de Janeiro, European ballroom dances represented key spaces for the performance of citizenship among the upper classes. As often is the case, these dances were popular in their origins and were later appropriated by other social groups. Social life in Rio changed dramatically with the arrival of the Portuguese royal family in 1808, fleeing the Napoleonic wars. This occasioned the transfer of the Portuguese empire's headquarters to Brazil, the opening of the country's ports, the lifting of the banning of print culture, and a host of cultural transformations, including the introduction of the waltz, solidified with the presence of composers such as Sigismund von Neukomm, an Austrian musician who resided in Rio between 1816 and 1821. In the first half of the nineteenth century, the waltz consolidated itself as the dance of preference amongst the country's elites, particularly during the fifteen-year period in which the performance of operas was suspended in Rio (1830–45). Even though in its European context the waltz was originally associated with plebeian and peasant subjects, in Rio it quickly acquired the status of a metropolitan icon. In contrast with previous genres—such as minuets, polonaises, or quadrilles—waltz dancers move about while remaining in each other's arms. Written in ternary (3/4) time, the waltz's condition as a pioneer dance of embraced bodies explains the furious and misogynistic reactions it generated. In Brazil, the waltz is undoubtedly connected with a new image of female pleasure, an ascension by women to spaces of sociability hitherto closed to them. A socially restricted dance such as the waltz, limited at that moment to the upper classes, represented a true opening of possibilities of cultural citizenship for bourgeois and aristocratic women, as registered by a number of Machado de Assis's characters, such as Eugênia, in *Helena* (1874), or Flora, a truly obsessed pianist, in *Esaú e Jacó* (1904).

The introduction of the polka in Brazil in 1845 inaugurated a cycle of closer contact between European ballroom dances and Afro-Brazilian musical practices, an encounter that would produce profound effects on the production and performance of citizenship. Interpreted for the first time in Rio on 3 July 1845 in the São Pedro Theater, the polka was quickly and enthusiastically received in city's ballrooms. By 1846 a "Polka Constant Society" had been constituted in Rio; the genre would soon displace the waltz in the elite's preferences. According to José Ramos Tinhorão, the polka's 2/4 time in allegretto, with its hopping movements, was more apt at expressing the period's social sensibility of euphoria with political stability and economic prosperity, unattainable by the waltz's more cadenced pace. As noted by José Miguel Wisnik (2004: 48), there is a significant difference between the polka in the strict sense and the "Brazilianized" form of playing it that developed in Rio after 1860 and that has received various names: *polca-tango*, *polca-lundu*, *polca-cateretê*, or, yet, *polca maxixada*. Whereas in its classic form, the polka reiterates redundancy (a basic principle of binary accentuation is repeated), its contact with popular and particularly Afro-Atlantic musical practices in Brazil made way for a principle of uneven, contrametric accentuation patterns. It was this long and complex process that gave rise to Brazil's first distinctly national urban musical genre, the maxixe. It emerged in the late nineteenth century, which witnessed the abolition of slavery in 1888, the end of the monarchy, and the foundation of the First Republic in 1889. During this period, the question of citizenship became a topic of debate in literary circles and political fora as Brazilian elites pondered the role of former slaves, immigrants, and other communities that were socially and politically excluded (Valente 2001: 13).

It would not be an exaggeration to claim that the maxixe represented the first sustained entrance into cultural and musical citizenship by the masses of urban Afro-Brazilians. Evolving in the 1870s from the contrametric, or "syncopated," Brazilian style of playing the polka, the maxixe was disseminated, fed by the enthusiasm for dance generated by the waltz and the polka. Throughout the last decades of the nineteenth century, the name *maxixe* is directly associated with the notions of lasciviousness and indecency. Widely considered a "dangerous" dance of libidinal and racialized nature, maxixe is an interesting case in which a way of dancing progressively constitutes a musical genre, one that cannot, however, be named without provoking considerable scandal. A heavy social censorship weighed over the very word *maxixe* in the latter half of the nineteenth century, to the point of leading the foremost Brazilian composer of the time, Ernesto Nazareth, to call his own maxixes with the evasive and safer name of "Brazilian tangos." Evoking a popular, Afro-Brazilian, and sexualized body, the maxixe traveled a long road toward acceptance. On 6 March 1885, when the word was still taboo, the playwright Arthur Azevedo incorporated the maxixe into the *teatro de revista* (vaudeville theater) in the play *Cocota*, performed in the Santana Theater in Rio. Throughout the 1890s we find references to the dissemination of maxixe in other cities of Brazil, and in 1905 the genre reached Europe with the acclaimed dancer Duque. In the first couple of decades of the twentieth century, the maxixe was still widely popular in Rio and would constitute the basis for the emergence of Brazil's national genre: the samba.

Modern samba emerged from predominantly black and mixed-race downtown neighborhoods, working-class suburbs, and hillside favelas of Rio de Janeiro during the early twentieth century. One Bahian migrant, known as Tia Ciata (Aunt Ciata), became especially famous for hosting late-night samba sessions in her home on the square called Praça Onze. In 1917, a young musician, Donga, took the song "Pelo Telefone," which had been composed collectively at Tia Ciata's home, and registered it as his own at the National Library. It is unlikely that "Pelo Telefone" was the "first samba" as Donga liked to claim. One of his rivals, Ismael Silva, even pointedly remarked that it wasn't a samba at all, but rather an old-time maxixe (Tinhorão 1998: 294). It was, however, the first known song to be registered as a samba. The recording of "Pelo Telefone" is emblematic of samba's modern urban sensibility, as it makes reference to this new technology of mass communication. The recording also coincided with a massive general strike in São Paulo, involving native-born and immigrant workers, a milestone in modern Brazilian labor history that can be understood as the beginning of the end for the First Republic (1889–1930).

Modern samba would reach a larger audience after 1922, when the first commercial radio station of Brazil began operations in Rio. This year also saw the first major military revolt against the republican regime, the founding of the Brazilian Communist Party, and the Modern Art Week of São Paulo. Several artists and intellectuals connected to Brazilian modernism, most notably the composer Heitor Villa-Lobos, celebrated the emergent musical form, at a time when police still arrested or beat samba musicians under spurious vagrancy charges (H. Vianna 1999: 6–11). The emergence of modern samba was related, in direct and indirect ways, to profound social, cultural, technological, and ultimately political transformations that brought the populist leader Getúlio Vargas to power in the Revolution of 1930.

The rule of Getúlio Vargas went through distinct phases, both authoritarian and democratic, during his nearly twenty years as president (1930–45, 1951–54). Between 1937 and 1945, during the Estado Novo regime, state policies were particularly repressive. Throughout his terms, Vargas consistently pursued politics of corporatism and populism designed to co-opt urban labor and forming a base of loyal working-class support, while suppressing efforts to produce radical change in Brazilian society. During this period, the Vargas regime advanced forms of urban social and cultural citizenship, often as a way to control or curtail any efforts to advance political and civic rights. To this day, he is revered by sectors of the nationalist Left, who cite his legacy in education and social welfare, and reviled by antipopulist leftists, who denounce his legacy of authoritarianism and clientelism. Above all, Vargas was a nationalist, committed to forging a sense of national unity and identity in a vast, culturally heterogeneous, and socially segmented country that had been ruled by regional interests. The Vargas period coincided with the rise of samba as Brazil's national popular music, aided by the expansion of the recording and mass communication industries throughout the country. Populist politics and cultural nationalism were evident in Rio, then still the federal capital, which was home to the most famous *sambistas*. Rio was also the base of operation for large, commercial radio stations, such as Rádio Nacional, which supported the government's nation-building efforts through musical programming with a broad appeal (McCann 2004: 21). As the mass appeal of samba extended across geographical, social, and racial lines, a new generation of middle-class artists such as

Francisco Alves, Mario Reis, Aracy de Almeida, and Carmen Miranda came to dominate the airwaves. They were artists from the "city," or in common parlance, the *asfalto* ("asphalt," i.e., where streets were paved) as opposed to the *morro*, the hillside slums with little or no urban infrastructure, known as favelas. Tensions arose over the symbolic value of samba. Was it an essentially "black" music appropriated opportunistically by privileged "white" (or light-skinned) artists? Or was it a form that could and should be rightly claimed by all Brazilians regardless of race and social class? This symbolic dispute was dramatized in a series of dueling sambas composed by Wilson Batista (1913–68), a self-fashioned "real sambista," or *bamba*, and Noel Rosa (1910–37), a white composer from Vila Isabel, a middle-class neighborhood in the city's north zone. Rosa had composed a song that was critical of Batista's celebration of the streetwise hustler, or *malandro*, in an earlier samba. Batista was black, but he was not from the morro. He was the son of a police officer from a provincial town in Rio State who moved to the capital with his family as an adolescent. Batista responded with "O Mocinho da Vila" (The Little Boy from Vila) that instructed Rosa to "look after your microphone," an ironic reference to successful radio singers, and "don't mess with the *malandros*." Rosa responded with "Feitiço da Vila" (The Spell of Vila), in which he celebrates his neighborhood as a great producer of samba, akin to other regions of Brazil known for agricultural production:

Lá, em Vila Isabel,	There in Vila Isabel
Quem é bacharel	Those who go to college
Não tem medo de bamba.	Are not afraid of *bambas*
São Paulo dá café,	São Paulo produces coffee
Minas dá leite,	Minas produces milk
E a Vila Isabel dá samba.	And Vila Isabel produces samba

Rosa died young, leaving behind hundreds of compositions, many of which have become standards of the Brazilian songbook. Batista would later find modest success on the radio and helped to found the Brazilian Composers' Union, created to defend the rights of composers, although he always affirmed an outsider identity as a malandro. The episode of the dueling sambas was short lived, but the songs were later compiled in a 1956 recording. It has remained over the years as a point of reference for debates around the symbolic meaning of samba in relation to race and class.

Rio's famous Carnaval also experienced a sea change in the 1930s with the rise of the *escolas de samba* (samba schools), predominantly black, working-

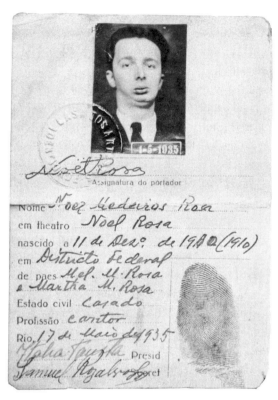

National identity card of Noel Rosa, 1935
(Biblioteca Nacional).

class parading organizations located in the hillside favelas and suburban periphery of Rio's north side. During much of the First Republic, Rio's Carnaval was dominated by the *grandes sociedades*, elite parading organizations that often represented rival political factions that used Carnaval as a platform for political satire. Under the Vargas regime, political satire became increasingly difficult to stage during Carnaval due to official censorship (Raphael, 1980: 96). The grandes sociedades also became anachronistic in the context of the nationalist and populist politics because they belonged to the symbolic economy of the First Republic.

Meanwhile, the theme songs to samba schools became sources of reflection on Brazilian history. As Luiz Antonio Simas and Alberto Mussa (2010) have pointed out, sambas de enredo constitute the only epic form genuinely created in Brazil. Samba schools were required to select celebratory themes, or "allegories," related to Brazilian history and culture to present during Carnaval. A logic of quid pro quo defined the relationship between working-class blacks and political elites: populist leaders would gain a co-operative mass constituency, and poor Afro-Brazilians would gain more access to public space and be recognized as an intrinsic part of Brazilian society. The Estado Novo regime curtailed or limited civil and political rights, but also promoted incipient forms of social and cultural citizenship for the urban working class.

The surrogate logic, or what Joseph Roach calls the "three-sided relationship of memory, performance, and substitution" (1996: 2), has been central to the symbolic economy of carnivals all over the world. Ersatz figures of lost royalty and nobility are especially common in Carnaval performance, exemplified in Rio's Carnaval by the crowning of Rei-Momo (King Momus), a tradition started in 1931. In a curious act of substitution, a group of journalists proposed to stage a coup against the carnivalesque monarch and replace him with the first Cidadão-Momo (Citizen-Momus). In 1935 they elected the popular singer Sílvio Caldas as the first Cidadão-Momo. In an ironic reference to the 1930 Revolution, they proclaimed that "one of our greatest singers, one of the best promoters of our popular music was a citizen who, in the name of our revolutionary armies of spontaneous melodies, victoriously arrived on the main avenue surrounded by songs and drums" (Silva and Santos 1979: 89). Finally, in 1937, the Union of Samba Schools established guidelines for the election of a Cidadão-Samba, stipulating that he "must be a familiar face in the favela," "must prove his good behavior," and, among other criteria, "must know how to play the *pandeiro*, *cuíca*, *tamborim*, and *surdo* and dance in a samba circle" (90). Unintended irony accompanied this process of carnivalesque substitution in a context of authoritarian rule: just as Vargas curtailed citizenship rights in proclaiming the Estado Novo, which was modeled after the Portuguese fascist state, Paulo da Portela (named after his samba school) was elected the first Cidadão-Samba.

As several of these chapters make clear, the Vargas regime may have been authoritarian, but during his rule the field of cultural production was rife with conflict, debate, contradiction, and even sly subversion. In the specific field of music, the state made efforts to censor *sambistas* and encourage them to reject the ethos and myths of the malandro, the urban street hustler romanticized in countless sambas. Many composers duly created "regenerated" sambas that promoted Brazilian patriotism, hard work, and a stable family life. Yet as Adalberto Paranhos shows in his contribution to this volume, sambistas also created alternative discourses that rejected the

Ballot published in the daily newspaper *A Rua* on 4 January
1937 to vote for the "samba-citizen" of Rio de Janeiro.
From Silva and Santos, 1979: 78.

ideology of Vargas's Estado Novo, composing songs that critiqued the false
promises of labor populism and celebrated malandros and other figures of
marginality. As samba was consecrated as Brazil's national popular music
and was backed by record companies and radio stations, the Vargas regime
promoted an ambitious agenda for musical education in the primary and
secondary schools. As Flávio Oliveira's chapter shows, the use of patriotic
choral singing in state-sponsored "civilizing campaigns" began in the late
nineteenth century, but was significantly expanded during the first Vargas
presidency. Mass educational programs in *canto orfeônico*, or (collective) orpheonic singing, were promoted as civilizing endeavors, often tied to the
racialized discourse of eugenics. Even as some agents of the Vargas regime
endorsed the escolas de samba during Carnaval and tolerated composers of
patriotic or "regenerated" sambas, others underwrote music education programs that explicitly opposed these Afro-Brazilian forms of popular music,
which they regarded as a corrupting influence on Brazilian youth. Cultural
policy under the Vargas regime was not as much contradictory as it was contingent and situational. In the realm of mass culture, the state tolerated and
even endorsed forms of sanitized popular music, but a program of choral
music, with roots in European tradition, prevailed in the schools. The case
of the world-renowned modernist composer Heitor Villa-Lobos is emblem-

atic in this context. In the mid-1920s, he was an early elite champion of samba as an authentic expression of Brazilian musical nationality, a position that he maintained throughout his life. Yet in the 1930s and 1940s, he also organized and directed massive performances of orpheonic singing among school children of Rio and São Paulo.

The Vargas years represented a historical watershed that would have profound and lasting impact on Brazilian political, social, and cultural life. The now familiar notions of national identity, popular culture, the *povo* (people), and *brasilidade* (Brazilianness) remain central, albeit contested, terms in the national discussion. It was also during this period that the analytic category and commercial moniker "popular music" began to circulate to refer to mass-mediated urban music as opposed to rural folklore. This distinction was accentuated in the 1940s, often regarded as the golden age of Brazilian radio singers, who popularized stylized and orchestrated sambas throughout the country. Samba gained mass international projection in the voice and image of Carmen Miranda, who achieved fame and fortune in Hollywood with performance and sartorial styles that drew heavily from Afro-Brazilian culture, most notably from Bahia (Davis 2008: 148–51).

In the late 1950s, Brazilian popular music entered a period of remarkable innovation with the emergence of bossa nova, which combined the 2/4 rhythm of samba with complex harmonies inspired by cool jazz and modernist art music. The new style was invented by a small cohort of artists, including the composer Antonio Carlos Jobim, the poet Vinícius de Moraes, and the performer João Gilberto, the last of whose unique finger-picking technique and breathy, understated vocal delivery defined the aesthetic values of bossa nova. Emerging during the presidency of Juscelino Kubitschek, a democratic populist committed to state-driven development, bossa nova is associated with a utopian national imaginary tied to the project of modernization (Mammí 1992: 63–64). Bossa nova belongs to the same high modernist cultural logic that guided the design and rapid construction of Brasilia (1956–60) and the mid-century concretist avant-garde that flourished in poetry and visual arts. Developed and performed primarily by white, affluent artists of Rio's south zone, bossa nova expressed a kind of domestic intimacy with lyrics that addressed themes of natural beauty, existential contemplation, and romantic love (Treece 1997: 10). By the early 1960s, a culture of left-wing nationalism emerged in Brazil, spurred on by an economic crisis and its attendant social effects at home as well as revolutionary, anti-imperialist struggles abroad, especially in Cuba. Progressive artists and intellectuals embraced the notion that culture could be, indeed must be, a vehicle for raising mass consciousness and inspiring radical political and social transformations. Young musicians began to eschew the quiet complacency of bossa nova, turning to themes of social protest, anti-imperialism, and popular revolution. Although not articulated in terms of citizenship as such, this music was concerned with issues of social equality, economic opportunities, and political rights for the urban and rural poor.

The political meanings of popular music came into focus especially after the military coup of 1964, which installed a authoritarian right-wing regime backed by the United States. In his contribution to this volume, Carlos Sandroni traces this history of Música Popular Brasileira as a concept, with special attention to its implications for national identity debates, social struggles, and political conflicts. Beginning in 1965, artists and critics began to use the acronym MPB to refer to a particular acoustic style of modern Brazilian popular music as opposed to international pop styles, especially rock 'n' roll, that had attracted large segments of urban youth. In general, the production and consumption of MPB were associated with what Sandroni calls republican ideals—democracy, liberty, and social equality. In the early days of the acronym's use (1965–66), the nationalist and acoustic content evoked by it was more prominent than it would be later, after the Tropicalist rebellion of 1967–68, led by the young Bahians Caetano Veloso and Gilberto Gil, showed that Brazilian popular music could embrace rock music and electric instruments, while remaining engaged in regional and national musical practices.

Given that MPB was closely associated with left-wing artists, intellectuals, and students who opposed the regime, some of its leading artists were persecuted and censored by the regime. Veloso and Gil were exiled to London between 1969 and 1972. Chico Buarque de Hollanda lived in Italy in 1970. The most strident protest singer, Geraldo Vandré, escaped to Chile in the late 1960s before moving to France. By 1973, however, most of the leading names in MPB were living and working in Brazil, where they were targets for surveillance, especially by agents of the Department of Public Order and Security, the secret police responsible for some of the worst human rights abuses during the military period (Napolitano 2004). Most MPB artists opposed the military regime and some recorded songs that denounced authoritarian rule, but like the malandros of samba during the Vargas dictatorship, their critiques were typically subtle and sly. In an essay originally published in 1980, the musician and literary critic José Miguel

Wisnik described these critiques as oblique *recados*, or messages that could pass muster with the censors while still communicating dissent to a large audience (1980: 25–26). Where the agents of repression looked for strident protest, they often found irony, subterfuge, and double-entendre. The most famous example is Chico Buarque's "Apesar de Você" (In Spite of You), a rousing Carnaval samba with an irresistible chorus proclaiming "in spite of you tomorrow will be another day," which could be read a shrill protest of a spurned lover, was widely interpreted as a message to the generals that the military's days in power were numbered.

With the gradual *distensão*, or relaxation of authoritarian politics, the late 1970s saw the rekindling of a lively debate around culture and politics that revisited controversies of the previous decade. A central question for artists who opposed the regime related to the role of popular music and other arts in promoting social and political transformation. This question had been hotly debated in the 1960s between artists who attempted to use popular music to denounce social ills and raise consciousness among the masses and others who emphasized the importance of formal experimentation and invention that over time could have liberating effects. The former Tropicalist Tom Zé stands out as an artist who has produced trenchant social critique, while also relentlessly pursuing formal experimentation in his music. As Christopher Dunn shows, Tom Zé's work is particularly relevant to this volume of essays, since he has consistently reflected on the meaning of citizenship in Brazil since the 1960s. In the 1970s, the figure of the citizen appears in his work either as a privileged subject who is complicit with the authoritarian state or as a hapless victim of modern consumer society who is ultimately punished for good behavior. With the reemergence of civil society and slow redemocratization in the 1980s, Tom Zé's work reveals a more affirmative notion of citizenship premised on the notion of self-representation among working-class people who demand participation in the political process. His most recent work references insurgent forms of citizenship involving historically marginalized and impoverished urban communities within the context of neoliberal globalization.

Rock music has been an integral part of most debates on popular music in Brazil since the 1960s, but the genre really coalesced as a movement in the 1980s, producing multiple political effects. The campaign for direct elections, launched in 1984, counted on ample support from MPB singer-songwriters such as Milton Nascimento and Chico Buarque de Hollanda, who regularly appeared in massive popular marches delivering speeches and singing political songs, shoulder to shoulder with major leaders of the movement. Their model of citizen participation for artists was, in that sense, still inherited from the 1960s: the politically committed singer was either a demiurge or a mouthpiece, a representative of a broader community that is endowed with a presumably unified voice. Brazilian rock music in the 1980s (known as *rock nacional* or *BRock*) would rely on a vision of politics that contrasted with the institutional channels privileged by successful MPB artists. The latter were, by then, fortysomethings still at their creative pinnacle, but they had undoubtedly been somewhat absorbed by the remarkable entertainment industry developed in Brazil in the 1970s. In contrast, a host of grass-roots rock movements—from more pop forms such as RPM to the theatrical, cartoon-influenced Blitz, in Rio de Janeiro; postpunk bands such as Brasilia's Legião Urbana, Plebe Rude, and Os Paralamas do Sucesso (the latter evolving to incorporate Caribbean forms); avant-gardist rockers such as Fellini, in São Paulo; or heavy-metal bands such as Sepultura and Sarcófago, in Belo Horizonte—staked out a rather different way of linking music and citizenship. Seeing traditional, ventriloquist forms of politicizing popular music with a high degree of skepticism, many of those bands, however different they were from each other musically, opted for strategies such as those described by Angélica Madeira's chapter on São Paulo hard rock / punk octet Titãs. Rather than offering long-winded, discursive allegories of oppression or political violence like MPB often did, Titãs *enacted violence* in the music, resorting to minimalist, "dirty," and direct lyrics; powerful percussion; a solid wall of electric guitars; and an intelligent use of samplers. The format of the band—an octet with several singers taking turns in the lead—further distanced them from the singer-songwriter-centered model of MPB. Madeira's chapter shows how Titãs' critiques of institutions such as the police, the church, and the family—along with the band's frequent references to scatological themes—constitute a particular entrance of Brazilian youth into politics in the transition between dictatorship and democracy that took place in the 1980s.

Several chapters in this volume focus on music practices since the end of the military dictatorship in 1985, when the first civilian president was elected indirectly by Congress. The first directly elected president, Fernando Collor, assumed power in 1990, but when he became mired in a serious corruption scandal Brazilians demanded and achieved his impeachment. In the 1990s, Brazilians elected for two terms the renowned sociologist Fernando Henrique Cardoso, a key figure in the prodemocracy opposition during the sixties and seventies, who forged a Center-Right coalition under the banner of neoliberal modernization in the 1990s. In 2002, Brazilians went to the polls to elect Luiz Inácio Lula da Silva, a former metalworker and leader of the leftist PT (Partido dos Trabalhadores; Workers' Party), who has pursued a politics of caution, implementing moderate though effective social reforms while also accommodating international capital interests. Teresa Caldeira and James Holston have described postauthoritarian Brazil as a "disjunctive democracy" that combines high levels of democratic participation and relatively low levels of electoral fraud (if compared, e.g., with the 2000 and 2004 presidential elections in the United States) with durable forms of exclusion and state-sponsored violence that victimize the poor (1999: 715–16).

When Lula came to power, he appointed Gilberto Gil, the Tropicalist musician, activist, and public intellectual, to serve as minister of culture. Appointed in 2003, Gil remained in the government well into Lula's second term. Stepping down in 2008, Gil was succeeded by Juca Ferreira, his former chief of staff. More than any of his predecessors, Gilberto Gil has promoted the idea that culture plays a central role in economic development, combating social ills, and promoting citizenship rights. The Cultural Points program of his Ministry of Culture was oriented toward providing the financial and technological means for artists from poor communities to produce their own cultural interventions. Frederick Moehn's chapter discusses this program, taking into account its skeptics, in relation to an array of artists and cultural organizations that use music as a means for critiquing forms of social exclusion and promoting citizenship rights in a profoundly unequal class society.

In dialogue with some of Moehn's concerns, Malcolm K. McNee's chapter offers an in-depth look at the role of music in the most significant and radical social movement to emerge in Brazil in the past decades, the MST (Movimento dos Trabalhadores Rurais Sem Terra; Landless Rural Workers' Movement). In collections that relied heavily on accordion-based *forró* or traditional *sertaneja* (country) music, the Movement of the Landless mobilized music extensively to advance their political agenda, often oscillating, on the one hand, between the idyllic view of an authentic, lost, and past rurality and, on the other hand, a cruel depiction of the bloody realities of contemporary rural conflicts in Brazil. While McNee's chapter deals with the realities of internal migration, Shanna Lorenz's chapter addresses the musical production of an important and unique immigrant community in Brazil — the Japanese Brazilians of São Paulo. She analyzes the band Zhen Brasil

(1998–2003) and its strategies for renegotiating racial stereotypes both in Brazil and in Japan, offering yet another example of how popular music has engaged claims to citizenship in complex, multiethnic, and multinational contexts.

Aaron Lorenz's chapter gives testimony to the continuing presence of a contestatory, oppositional form of samba in Rio de Janeiro by addressing the music of Bezerra da Silva, a black composer and singer heavily identified with the shantytowns and with the critique of police violence. His improvisational and satirical style has long been recognized by some of the samba luminaries as a legitimate representative of the tradition. By featuring the world of drugs, prostitution, and a myriad of other problems facing Rio's poorer populations (including racial discrimination), Bezerra's work is a rich case study in the continuing dimension of samba as a tool in the claiming of citizenship.

The hip-hop movement in Brazil provides a particularly striking example of the use of culture to achieve concrete social and political objectives in marginalized, primarily black urban and peripheral communities. In one of the earliest studies on the hip-hop phenomenon in São Paulo, Elaine Nunes de Andrade noted, "As a social movement, hip-hop allows young people to develop a political education and, consequently, the direct exercise of citizenship. In the social history of the country, there has never been such an expressive movement produced by black youth" (1999: 89). Brazil is not unique in this regard, as hip-hop has proven to be a useful tool for integrating, educating, and politicizing youth globally. A contemporary musical form that emerged in working-class African American and Afro-Caribbean communities of New York in the late 1970s, hip-hop has often been closely associated with expressions of black power and pride in Brazil. Many rappers are vocal in denouncing forms of racial discrimination and violence directed at Afro-Brazilians and have partnered with NGOs and state agencies dedicated to antiracist struggles. In their analysis of rap lyrics in this volume, Wivian Weller and Marco Aurélio Paz Tella demonstrate that hip-hop in São Paulo has emerged with particular force as a movement representing the vast *periferia*, the socially and spatially marginalized area outside of the city. Derek Pardue's chapter focuses more on the discourse of hip-hop activists in relation to citizenship rights and their interactions with the state and NGOs. He shows that the implications of the terms *cidadão* (citizen) and *cidadania* (citizenship) have transformed significantly in the decades since the end of military rule and are now being used to make claims about rights, instead of simply connoting duty and obligation. Both of these chapters show that hip-hop has developed into a complex social movement in São Paulo that has been quite effective in representing the interests of their communities.

Unlike the hip-hop that is so representative of the peripheral youth of São Paulo, the funk movement of Rio de Janeiro does not often highlight politics; rather, the music and the events surrounding it have been insistently politicized by what João Freire Filho and Micael Herschmann call "moral panic" in their contribution to this book. It should be noted that what is called "funk" in that specific context of the north zone of Rio—an area associated with the primarily black, poor, and lower middle class—bears little resemblance to what is understood by the term in the African American tradition, exemplified by groups such as the Meters, Parliament-Funkadelic, or the Ohio Players. Composed of rapping lyrics recited over a sparse, electronically produced rhythmic base, Brazilian funk has been paradigmatic of a development mapped out by Hermano Vianna's chapter: the dissemination of an informal market of MP3s produced by musicians themselves and sold at concerts and by street vendors. Vianna focuses largely on *technobrega* of Belém, which finds analogues in other contemporary musical practices that flourish outside of conventional channels of distribution and consumption in Brazil. The phenomenon, in which Vianna sees liberating potential, imposes a true transformation in the reality of musical production, circulation, and consumption in Brazil, as ample sectors of the population have come to form their tastes in spheres that completely bypass the major media and the official market of CDs.

In Brazil, the northeast occupies a place in the national imaginary somewhat akin to the deep South in the United States. In the early twentieth century, these regions were configured as spaces of economic and social decadence in both national contexts, but were also imagined as places of cultural effervescence and tradition. Within the region defined as northeast, the state of Bahia—and especially its capital city, Salvador—has been particularly prominent in the national imaginary, primarily due to Afro-Brazilian sacred and secular cultural practices. In the 1930s and 1940s, the singer-songwriter Dorival Caymmi enjoyed national acclaim and success with his utopian songs about Salvador that described the city as a place of magic and sensuality removed from the stressful process of industrial modernization taking place in the major cities of the center-south (Risério 1993: 108–9). Although Salvador is more than 80 percent black, the city has been dominated politically and economically by a small white elite. Historically, the Afro-Bahian community has in general pursued a politics of negotiation rather than confrontation, developing clientelistic networks with privileged white (or light-skinned) patrons.

During the last three decades, Salvador has been a privileged site for various forms of black cultural activism associated with neighborhood-based Carnaval clubs and musical groups. In 1975, a group of young working-class Afro-Brazilians from the Liberdade neighborhood founded the first *bloco afro*, Ilê Aiyê. Inspired by anticolonial struggles in Africa, the Black Power movement in the United States, and Afro-Bahian history and culture, the founders of Ilê Aiyê sought to use Carnaval as an occasion to express black pride and protest against racial inequality. Within a few years, other blocos afro—such as Olodum, Muzenza, and Malê Debalê—formed in primarily black, poor neighborhoods throughout the city, leading to a burst of Afro-Bahian musical creativity in the 1980s. At the same time, several blocos afro embarked on ambitious community development and education projects designed to provide job training for and instill self-esteem in youth. Activists and scholars have criticized these organizations for their culturalism, suggesting that their symbolic gestures of racial pride had little impact on actual social relations. Osmundo Pinho argues in his chapter, however, that the blocos afro provided new models of community organization and black subjectivity that have begun to transform the social landscape of Salvador. He argues that black musical subcultures in Bahia (including reggae, soul, rap, funk, and pagode) have had significant effects on identity formation and political attitudes among young Afro-Bahians. Ari Lima's contribution focuses specifically on samba in Bahia, which was historically removed from the processes that led to the nationalist consecration of the genre in Rio. Although elite intellectuals celebrated samba as a mixed-race, or *mestiço*, Brazil in the 1930s, there were many places where the variants of the genre were confined to spaces of black leisure and sociability, which were often regarded with suspicion by local authorities. Lima focuses on contemporary *pagode baiano*, a distinct style of samba related to the traditional *samba-de-roda* of Bahia, which has attracted thousands of poor, predominately black youth to weekly dances on the periphery of Salvador. Lima's piece offers an insight into the unique ways in which relations between race, gender, and sexuality have been coded the denizens of pagode dances.

The popular music field in Salvador, which ranges from groups that function essentially as NGOs to the most blatantly commercial pop bands, has also provided a means for social ascension for many Afro-Brazilians in the last couple of decades. One of the most successful musical enterprises in Salvador is Carlinhos Brown's group Timbalada, a percussion-based troupe inspired by the blocos afro, but generally avoiding explicit social protest. In her study of Carlinhos Brown's work in the community of Candeal, Goli Guerreiro analyzes the successes and limits of several educational programs designed to provide local youth with marketable skills in the entertainment industry. In many ways, Salvador has become one of the models of cultural expediency in Brazil, with a wide variety of groups and organizations, primarily from poor black communities, that have redefined the parameters of political action and economic development through popular music.

Pernambuco, the northeastern state that rivals Bahia in the depth and variety of its contribution to the popular music of Brazil, is the object of two chapters in this volume. Known as the home of the foremost manifestation of Afro-Brazilian coronation dances (the percussion-based *maracatu*) as well as one of the most popular forms of Carnaval music (the modern, electrified marchlike *frevo*), Pernambuco has also boasted for decades a rich scene of forró, the accordion dance genre heavily identified with the northeast but virtually national in its execution. Pernambuco's musical tradition further includes various forms of verbal arts such as *embolada* and the particularly northeastern, rich dialogue between voice and clapping (or percussion) known as *coco*. In the 1950s, following the boom of frevo, Pernambuco became a major center for record production, with labels such as Rosenblitz sending a diverse selection of local music to the national market. As the popular music canonized as national in the center-south evolved from Tropicália to the acoustic forms sanctioned under the acronym MPB in the 1960s and 1970s, Pernambuco troubadours such as Alceu Valença and Zé Ramalho (the latter Paraíba-born) occupied a somewhat unique position, partly through the legitimation bestowed on MPB artists and through appealing mostly to the alternative, hippie fringe of the popular music map. At that moment and certainly into the 1980s, there was an overwhelming sense of crisis and decadence in the state capital of Recife, emblematized by choice of the Population Crisis Committee, a Washington-based Institute, which in the early 1990s ranked Recife as one of the five worst urban areas in the world.

Both Idelber Avelar's and Daniel Sharp's chapters deal with different facets of the extraordinary rebirth that has taken place in the city of Recife and the state of Pernambuco in the fifteen years or so since that low point, thanks in large part to the politicized influence of popular music. The re-birth has been such that many would agree that in the past decade and a half the most diverse and fruitful combinations of pop ideas and genres in Brazil have taken place precisely there. Avelar studies the cultural interven-tion of the musical movement that sparked that Renaissance, mangue beat (*mangue* being Portuguese for swamp), arguing that its considerable impact had to do with the ways in which it bridged the gap between national music and popular music visible in Brazil since the crisis of legitimation of MPB artists among the youth. By the time the first generation of the national rock movement came of age in the mid-1980s, that gap was consolidated, as most rockers manifested a decided refusal to engage what Caetano Veloso (Barbosa et al. 1966: 378) had called the *linha evolutiva* (evolutionary line) of Brazilian popular music, preferring instead models taken from rock music from Britain and the United States. In the 1980s, the popularity of genres identified as regional (e.g., percussion based or accordion based) was at a particularly low point among youth. It was in Recife that some of these en-trenched binaries (youth music vs. national music, regional influences vs. international influences) would definitely be imploded. Fueled by the re-markable musical intelligence of the lyricist, performer, and singer Chico Science and the band he fronted, Nação Zumbi, mangue beat would find amazing avenues of dialogue between regional languages—maracatu, em-bolada, coco, and so on—and international youth genres not immediately recognized as part of the mainstream of pop—hip-hop, heavy metal, and various forms of soul or funk music. Science's music takes as its motto a metaphor of resonances between the global and the local, "the satellite dish stuck in the mud," a reference point in relation to which the "crabs with brains"—images of the musical subjects of the swamp—combine regional traditions with the latest international information. Although limited to a two-CD output, as his career was interrupted by his tragic death in 1997, Science has had an impact that is difficult to overestimate. A full decade since his death, the movement he inspired continues to intervene musi-cally and culturally in a myriad of forms such as, for example, battles over digital inclusion (particularly important for Science's fellow *recifenses*, the rock-samba combo Mundo Livre S/A, who have been going strong for over two decades now). An entire volume could be written on the various combi-nations of northeastern and international musics sparked by mangue beat since its emergence in the early 1990s.

Daniel Sharp's chapter addresses another facet of this musical rebirth in

Pernambuco, the town of Arcoverde, situated right where the dry lands of the *sertão* start. In the quite different context of a small town in the backlands, where forms such as samba de coco are particularly popular, Sharp finds an emblematic case of dialogue between local and global forms, as a host of autochthonous traditions have been engaged and transformed by bands that took their inspiration from mangue, such as Cordel do Fogo Encantado, an experimental pop group that relies heavily on hallucinatory, dramatic singing over percussion and features a frontman, Lirinha, in a variety of roles, from a marionette tied with strings to a popular storyteller inspired by fire. In the various ways in which the rebirth of Pernambuco music has impacted how music is produced, circulated, and consumed in Brazil, we find instances of creative interventions of popular music into the production of cultural citizenship.

This book is not, or course, an exhaustive catalogue of Brazil's rich musical traditions. It is not even a full compendium of all the important moments in the relations between popular music and citizenship in the country. The editors feel, however, that some of the most relevant contemporary scholarship on the subject is compiled here, and the book as a whole documents and contributes to a facet of the cultural studies of popular music that has gained increasing importance. As diverse as the approaches represented in the volume are, they testify to a common tendency to observe the mutual constitution between musical practice and the processes of citizenship. Whereas scholarship was once dominated by the study of how certain contents were represented in the music, the simultaneity and the intertwining of political and music processes have recently been more emphasized. Our intent has been to deepen that promising tendency, while also offering an entryway into the diverse body of Brazil's contemporary musical production.

::: Dissonant Voices under a Regime of Order–Unity

Popular Music and Work in the Estado Novo

Adalberto Paranhos

The cadaver / of the indigent
It's clear / he died
And still / He moves
As proves / Galileo
—Chico Buarque, Ópera do malandro, 1978

In the 1930s, the Brazilian state emerged as a great agent of historical transformation. It is as if the spotlight of national thought had been projected onto a dominant protagonist who condemned other social actors to supporting roles. Resigned to the condition of mere extras, the working masses filled the ranks of the chorus, a place reserved in the Greek tragedy for slaves, women, children, the old, the homeless, and the sick.[1] It may seem surprising, at first glance, that the Brazilian tradition to which I refer is sufficiently broad to harbor contributions of the most distinct origins, both from the Right and the Left of the nation's politicoideological spectrum.[2] In this analytical framework, the brilliance of the state obscures the presence of other social actors. The audience enters the stage—when it enters at all—either disfigured or without a face.

We see this pattern emerge in the relations between authoritarian Estado Novo under Getúlio Vargas and the working classes. The ring of silence built around practices and discourses that deviated from institutionalized norms has led many, for quite a long time, to believe in the triumph of a supposed "chorus of national unanimity" under a regime of order and unity (Paoli 1987: 87–90, 1989: 57–65; Paranhos 1999a: 201–14). It would be as if Brazilian society had been a mere echo chamber for a state ideology that employed countless means of coercion and of consensus production in order to impose itself. The musical realm could obviously not deviate from the rule. Judging from most studies of the industrialized popular music of the Estado

Novo period, the popular composers were duly framed within new codes of behavior, sidelining the traditional praise of street smarts (or "street hustling"), known as *malandragem* and embodied by the figure of the *malandro*. In other words, they allowed themselves to be caught up in the populist cult of labor.[3]

Working against this analytical current, this chapter seeks to lift the veil that covers manifestations outside the harmony of the "chorus of the contented" during the Estado Novo. Supported initially by the DIP (Departamento de Imprensa e Propaganda; Department of Press and Propaganda), the dictatorship sought to inaugurate a new type of disciplinary society, while simultaneously constructing a certain identity profile of the Brazilian worker as someone docile to capitalist domination. Its action, via the ideology of laborism, based on the co-optation of workers, was far, however, from attaining the claimed unanimity. Once we delve beneath the superficiality of the facts that inflate appearances and undertake an empirical investigation of the phonographic production of the period, the situation shifts dramatically. Despite the tight censorship of the DIP, there is a strong presence of "struggles of representations" revolving around opposing definitions of "labor" and of "the worker."

On the one hand, there was a high number of popular compositions and composers in tune with the Estado Novo regime and the valuing of work. On the other hand, in alternative discourses, there emerged songs (sambas, in the majority) which sketched lines of flight away from state ideology. At least until 1943 or 1944 open contestation of official ideological dogmas was not immediately audible, but images and concepts that deployed other values continued to circulate socially. By intervening in the set of discourses around labor, the field of industrialized popular music was not reduced to a mouthpiece of hegemonic discourse.[4] There is a broad consensus with regard to relations between the state and popular music under the Estado Novo. I distance myself from a consensus in order to explore a more nuanced view of capitalist society marked by conflicts (Chartier 1990: 17).

::: History's Side B

One of the primary goals of the Estado Novo was the model citizen, adjusted to the principles of citizenship encouraged by the state (Gomes 1982). It became imperative to exorcise once and for all the ghosts of unproductive leisure or opposition to the reigning labor system. Attuned to this standard,

Article 136 of the Constitution promulgated on 10 November 1937 prescribed that "work is a social duty." Article 139 categorized the strike as an "antisocial measure," a criminal act punishable by three to eighteen months of prison, in addition to other punishments stipulated by Article 165 of the Penal Code. Disciplined work was the rule by which social responsibility of citizens was measured, particularly for the popular classes. Furthermore, it also suggested that workers should cultivate a feeling of gratitude in recognition of the "gift" of social legislation mandated by the "statesman genius" who governed Brazil. As one of the main ideologues of the administration claimed, "With the labor laws of Getúlio Vargas, the Brazilian worker felt for the first time in our history true citizenship" (Amaral 1941: 116).[5]

The DIP from 1940 onward, intended to disrupt the relationship that historically linked samba with malandragem, that refused regimented work. The DIP's anti-malandragem campaign embraced certain discourses available in the very realm of popular Brazilian music in the 1930s. Various defenders of "the poetic hygiene of samba," or "the healthy and thematic rehabilitation" of popular song made themselves heard at the time (Paranhos 1999b). The intervention of the DIP tightened the straitjacket imposed on composers, under siege by conservative forces in the Vargas administration. These forces, operating either through clientelism or censorship, sought to attract composers to official ideology. This led to a shift in *samba-exaltação* (i.e., samba in praise of the nation) toward "paraphrase," a trope that fundamentally acted to support and celebrate collective identity. As a consequence, paraphrase should be distinguished from parody, since parodic approaches emphasize difference, when not outright inversion.

The governmental strategy was seemingly successful. One of the most cited studies on the period claims that "the DIP had absolute control over all that was related to popular music" (Gomes 1982: 159), blocking all channels through which a counterdiscourse could develop. Did things effectively happen that way? After hearing hundreds of original recordings of 78 RPM records released between 1940 and 1945, I concluded that these notions about the monopoly of state power needed to be revised. It became a question of listening to the "B sides" of the history of the Estado Novo. Without denying that many popular composers, either coerced or self-interested, adhered to the monotony of state-sponsored themes, dozens of phonographic recordings reveal a diversity of perspectives.

A preliminary observation is necessary. Since I don't limit myself to working within the binary of conformity and resistance, the sambas examined here are not necessarily characterized as counterdiscourses. The majority of the recordings deviate, in part or entirely, from the chorus of Estado Novo, and are concrete expressions of alternative modes of thought and action. They do not directly confront the established disciplinary order, but convey instead alternative values rooted in the lived experiences of the samba composers. There is a broader range of options between conformity and resistance.

For example, subtlety is not missing from the recording of "Onde o Céu Azul É Mais Azul" (Where the Blue Sky is Bluer; 1940), a samba-exaltação by João de Barro, Alberto Ribeiro, and Alcir Pires Vermelho that proclaims "my Brazil, so great and happy" where one "works a lot in order to dream later." What is remarkable are the metalinguistic possibilities of sound in this recording. The master arranger Radamés Gnattali sketches a notable critical counterpoint to a patriotic conception in the literal message of the song. The introduction recalls North American big bands in their gathering of brass, bass, and drums. With a harmonization that makes strong use of brass instruments, the arrangement moves the listener towards a rhythm and timbre beyond the borders of Brazil,[6] notably at the end of the song, which foreshadows the Tropicalist approach nearly three decades later.[7]

While working with musical expression, we will see that it is important not to become enthralled with the literal meaning of song lyrics. Instead, we must take into account that lyrics do not have autonomous status within a song, and that it's important to pay attention to musical discourse articulated in a nonliteral manner (Paranhos, 2004). "O Amor Regenera o Malandro" (Love Rehabilitates the Malandro; 1940) serves as another example. Similar to so many other sambas from this period, this song claims that

Sou de opinião	I am of the opinion
de que todo malandro	that all *malandros*
tem que se regenerar	must rehabilitate themselves
se compenetrar	convince themselves
e ainda mais [breque]	and furthermore [break]
que todo mundo deve ter	that everyone should have
o seu trabalho para o amor merecer	a job in order to be worthy of love

The first impression, nevertheless, is undone once we accompany the performance of singers Joel and Gaúcho at the end of the second stanza:

Regenerado	Rehabilitated
ele pensa no amor	he thinks of love

mas pra merecer carinho	but to be worthy of affection
tem que ser trabalhador	he must be a worker
que horror! [breque]	how awful! [break]

The use of the rhythmic break in both instances announces a critical distance and undermines the Estado Novo jargon that appeared, at first glance, to have informed the recording. We can understand their interpretation as another form of composition, as the performer reconfigures the piece, dismantles and puts back together the composition, thereby investing it with meanings not imagined by its author. It is not enough to take a composition abstractly, reduced to the verses of the lyrics or the sheet music. Its sound, from the arrangement to the vocal interpretation, is also a vehicle for meaning.[8]

By only examining the lyrics or researching the magazines of the time, in which lyrics of popular songs were published, one would not capture the main thrust of the recording. To restrict the analysis of a song exclusively to its lyrics results in the reduction of it to a mere written document, narrowing its field of meanings and emptying it of its sonority.[9] In this particular case, not even sheet music would register the essential fact of the breaks that were later incorporated.[10] Naturally, the final verse was not part of the text submitted to the approval of the censors. Joel's and Gaúcho's syncopated performance interrupts the seemingly harmonious feel established by the lyrics, thereby subverting their original content. In a typically malandro attitude, there is a seemingly accepting position vis-à-vis institutionalized rules, but it is a strategy of survival (Vasconcellos and Suzuki 1984: 520).

Another composer who adeptly used malandragem in his music was Assis Valente, a *mulato* of humble origin who split his time between the arts of making dentures and composing. His song "Recenseamento" (Census; 1940) illustrates ways of subverting official censors. As a musical chronicler of daily life, Assis Valente tackled a prominent issue, the 1940 Census. The song narrates the climbing up of the hillside ghetto by a nosy census agent who wants to probe into the lives of an unmarried couple. Among other things, the agent "asked if my *moreno* was decent / and if he was a worker / or if he was a bohemian [*da folia*]." Faced with this interpellation, the woman — who declares herself to be "obedient to all that is the law" — responds:

| O meu moreno é brasileiro | My *moreno* is Brazilian |
| é fuzileiro | is a marksman |

e é quem sai com a bandeira	he is the flag bearer too
do seu batalhão . . .	in his battalion . . .
A nossa casa não tem nada de grandeza	Our house is not grand
mas vivemos na pobreza	but we live in poverty
sem dever tostão	without owing a dime
Tem um pandeiro,	We have a pandeiro,
tem cuíca e um tamborim	a cuica and a tamborim,
um reco-reco, um cavaquinho	a reco-reco, a cavaquinho,
e um violão	and a guitar
Fiquei pensando	I was thinking
e comecei a descrever	and began to describe
tudo, tudo de valor	everything, everything of value
que meu Brasil me deu . . .	that my Brazil has given me . . .
Um céu azul	A blue sky
um Pão de Açúcar sem farelo	a Sugarloaf without crumbs
um pano verde-amarelo	a green and yellow rag
Tudo isso é meu!	All this is mine!
Tem feriado	There are holidays
que pra mim vale fortuna . . .	that are worth fortunes to me . . .

While seemingly reproducing the dominant discourse of the "great and industrious Brazil" by the Estado Novo apologists, the piece perceptively deconstructs official arguments, ironically spicing up the woman's speech in her response to the Census agent. Her words point to the fact that her moreno could not be included in the regular army of the "workers of Brazil." Rather, he was probably the flag bearer or even the lead dancer of a samba school. In contrast with the "New Brazil" produced by government propaganda, their shack lacks everything except, of course, samba instruments. After all, what had Estado Novo given them?

At first glance the woman is quite happy. As we have seen, however, within the codes of malandragem the art of dissimulation is a matter of honor. For that reason, it is not a sign of intelligence to offer oneself as prey to the hunter. Noel Rosa and Ismael Silva, who understood this, had already declared in "Escola de Malandro" (School for the Malandro; 1933) that "by faking, you gain an advantage / yes that / is what malandragem is." Another important detail is that "Recenseamento" is a *samba-choro* and the accompaniment creates musical atmosphere typical of the *gafieiras* (samba dance halls).[11] Assis Valente subtly demonstrated how a discourse and counterdis-

Assis Valente and Bando Carioca, ca. 1937 (FUNARTE).

course became intertwined, creating a song that subtly conflicted with the Vargas government's propaganda.

There were also those who went straight to the bitter world of the worker. Without glamorizing his daily life, Ciro de Souza, a samba composer from Vila Isabel, describes the "Vida Apertada (Tough Life; 1940) of a longshoreman:

Meu Deus, que vida apertada	My God, what a tough life
trabalho, não tenho nada	work, I have none
vivo num martírio sem igual	I live in unequaled martyrdom
A vida não tem encanto	Life has no enchantment
para quem padece tanto	for the one who suffers so
desse jeito eu acabo mal	this way, I'll end badly
Ser pobre não é defeito	To be poor is not a defect
mas é infelicidade	but unhappiness
nem sequer tenho direito	without a single right
de gozar a mocidade	to enjoy youth
Saio tarde do trabalho	I leave work late
chego em casa semimorto	and get home half-dead
pois enfrento uma estiva	because I'm a stevedore

todo dia lá no 2	everyday there on number 2
no cais do porto	on the docks of the port
tadinho de mim [breque]	poor me [break]

Like in other compositions from the period, we are far from the exaltation of labor (Paranhos 1999b: 141–67). Nothing appeals to the greatness and the grandiloquence trumpeted by the regime.[12] Even in the strictly musical aspects of the song, it is possible find these registers. The accompaniment is entrusted to a regional band, in contrast to the orchestral adornments which embellished the sambas-exaltação. It swings and is punctuated by breaks, a pattern established by the piano at the beginning. The colloquial tone of the singer, Ciro Monteiro, can be clearly distinguished from the more imposing, grandiose interpretations by, for example, Francisco Alves in "Onde o Céu Azul É Mais Azul."

As noted by Santuza Cambraia Naves, the Brazilian avant-garde and popular music of the time went hand in hand, even if across oblique paths. Presiding over that encounter, intuitively, was the "aesthetic of simplicity"— closer to the literary modernism of Oswald de Andrade, Mário de Andrade, and Manuel Bandeira than to the "aesthetics of monumentality" that traverses the musical modernist project of a Heitor Villa-Lobos.[13] If we associate *modernism*, among other things, with "the thematization of aspects of modern life," implying the "valorization of the vulgarity of life and of the description of daily reality" (Sant'Anna 1986: 131), we can see its relation to Brazilian popular music.

On the other hand, realism and dream go together in the *samba-de-breque* (break-samba) "Acertei no Milhar" (I Won the Lottery; 1940) by Wilson Batista and Geraldo Pereira, composers who showed little inclination for regular work. What is the first thought of the character of the song, a "vagabond" who wins big in the animal lottery?

"Etelvina, minha filha!	"Etelvina, my dear!
Acertei no milhar	I won the lottery
ganhei 500 contos	I won 500 *contos*
não vou mais trabalhar."	I'll work no more."

Euphoric, he begins to make miraculous plans of "buying a blue plane / to tour South America." Suddenly, however, the alarm rings; "Etelvina called me," he narrates. "It's time to work / . . . it was a dream, my people."[14] The moment of the dream has dissipated, and reality has demanded attention.

The morality of the story tramples upon habitual formulations that justified social domination and class inequalities. As a general rule, social ascension through work is never more than a chimera.

::: Laments

The flurry of criticism of malandragem impacted Brazilian popular music strongly during the Estado Novo. The "unproductive bohemian" was walking a tightrope: based on constitutional articles, the dictator Getúlio Vargas proclaimed during the 1 May festivities in 1943 that "laziness should be considered a crime against the collective good."[15] Even so, often in subtle ways, social types who lived more or less on the margins of society continued to appear in numerous compositions.

It is impressive how many songs expressed the anguish of unsatisfied women exploited by their abusive partners. Frequently composed by men and performed by women, those songs, despite the duplicitous interpretations they may suggest, continued to portray the survival of masculine figures who turned their backs on the world of work. A case in point is "Não Admito" (I Don't Condone; 1940) composed by Ciro de Souza and Augusto Garcez and recorded by Aurora Miranda. Irritated, the feminine voice of this samba doesn't mince words:

Eu digo e repito que não acredito	I say and repeat that I don't believe
que você tenha coragem	that you have the courage
de usar malandragem	to deceive me
pra meu dinheiro tomar	to take my money
Se quiser vá trabalhar, oi	If you want to go work, hey
vá pedir emprego na pedreira	go ask for a job at the construction site
que eu não estou disposta	because I'm not in the mood
a viver dessa maneira	to live this way
Você quer levar a vida	You want to carry on
tocando viola de papo pro ar	playing guitar and chatting
e eu me mato no trabalho	while I kill myself at work
pra você gozar	so you can have fun

Another rebellious woman speaks out in "Inimigo do Batente" (Enemy of Work; 1940), a samba performed by Dirchinha Batista. Composed by Wilson Batista and Germano Augusto (a malandro who was notorious for stealing other composers' work), this song exposes the complaints of a laundress, tired of suffering in the "grind, killing myself":

Eu já não posso mais	I can't do it anymore
a minha vida não é brincadeira	my life is no game
É, estou me desmilingüindo	It's true, I'm dissolving
igual a sabão	just like the soap
na mão da lavadeira	in the hand of the laundress
Ele diz que é poeta	He says he is a poet
Ele tem muita bossa	He's got a lot of talent
e compôs um samba e quer abafar	and composed a hot samba
é de amargar! [breque]	it's enough to get bitter! [break]
Não posso mais	I can't do it anymore
em nome da forra	in the name of revenge
vou desguiar	I'm taking off
Se eu lhe arranjo trabalho	If I get him a job
ele vai de manhã	he goes in the morning
de tarde pede a conta	by the afternoon, he asks for his wages
Eu já estou cansada de dar	I'm tired of
murro em faca de ponta	punching the blade of a knife
Ele disse pra mim	He told me
que está esperando ser presidente	that he's waiting to become president
tira patente do sindicato	to get his union papers
dos inimigos do batente	from the enemies of the clock

There is a rather significant aspect of this samba that should not go unnoticed. As the song turns to slang with words such as "batente" (hard work) and "abafar" (be successful), it shows the proximity of certain genres of popular music to "spoken Brazilian" as opposed to "written Portuguese"—as Mário de Andrade called the "two languages of the motherland" (Andrade 1972: 115). It contrasts with the sambas-exaltação, such as the famous "Aquarela do Brasil" (Watercolor of Brazil; 1939), by Ary Barroso, a song dominated by an official and grandiloquent tone and by the use of supercilious expressions, which are loved by those "guardians of grammar" and "repressors of popular music lyricists" as the writer Marques Rebelo notes (2002: 179).[16] I could cite many more examples of malandro types that emerged here and there in recordings released between 1940 and 1945. "Já que Está Deixa Ficar" (As Long as It's Here, Let It Stay), by Assis Valente, recorded by Anjos do Inferno; "Não Vou pra Casa" (I'm Not Going Home), by Antonio Almeida and Roberto Ribeiro, with Joel and Gaúcho; "Quem Gostar de Mim" (Whoever Likes Me), by Dunga, with Ciro Monteiro; "Batatas Fritas" (French Fries), by Ciro de Souza and Augusto Garcez, with Aurora Miranda; and "Fez Bobagem" (You Did a Stupid Thing), by Assis Valente, with Aracy de Almeida, are but a few of these songs.

One should not see the representation of gender relationships in Brazilian popular music only through the lens of the victimization of women (Paranhos 2005). The women portrayed in many songs of the time were not "poor wretches" willing to "perish in paradise." This would be a unilateral and distorted image. A better-adjusted lens would be songs also including women who broke with institutionalized standards of behavior. Furthermore, it is noteworthy that popular music was and is a field of expression—whether dissimulated or evident—of the fragility of the "strong sex" (Oliven 1987). Indeed, the laments, the complaints, and the pains of the male cuckold found a fertile ground in popular music. "Oh! Seu Oscar" (Oh, Mr. Oscar!) by Ataulfo Alves and Wilson Batista, recorded in the second half of 1939, illustrates this well. The interesting extra detail is that in addition to being a tremendous success in the 1940 Carnaval, it was the winning composition of the samba competition held by the DIP in Rio de Janeiro.

What is this samba about? Oscar, "tired from work," barely arrives home, when his neighbor delivers a note from his wife that reads: "Não posso mais / eu quero é viver na orgia" (I can't stand it / I want have some fun). Faced with this fact, Oscar crumbles into inconsolable lamentations, in the second part of the song:

Fiz tudo para ver seu bem-estar	I did all I could for your well-being
até no cais do porto eu fui parar	I even went to the docks of the port
martirizando o meu corpo noite e dia	my body a martyr day and night
mas tudo em vão, ela é da orgia	all in vain, she wants to have fun

This woman and so many others who abandoned their husbands for revelry, relatively free from conventional bonds, were not at all compatible with the idealized image of the "proletariat housewife" as defined by the minister of labor, Marcondes Filho.[17] Much less was it in tune with the mixture of a real and ideal spouse conceived of by the legal scholar A. F. Cesarino Jr., in accord with the "traditional virtues of Brazilian matrons" (1942: 131). These "noisy" and "unruly" women were portrayed as making their husbands' lives miserable: they easily exchanged domestic obligations for parties, as in the samba "Madalena" by Bide and Marçal, recorded by the group Anjos do Inferno. This exchange also profoundly irritated the abandoned husbands, as can be seen in "Acabou a Sopa" (We ran out of soup) by Geraldo Pereira and Augusto Garcez.

In the recording of "Oh! Seu Oscar" the word *orgia* (orgy) is repeated nine times. The final verses of the first part ("Não posso mais / eu quero é viver na orgia") are reiterated seven times and assume, without a doubt, the key to the composition, acting as a conclusion to the recording. In the heat of Carnaval these verses were essential to exciting the crowds. At the same time, the man, in his despair, insists on affirming that he dedicated his body to labor in order to provide for his wife. Once again, in complete opposition to the ideology of work, labor is confronted and lived as martyrdom and as a difficult burden to carry (Salvadori 1990).

There were also other themes that interested popular composers between 1940 and 1945, notably the war and rationing (of water, flour, wheat, and gasoline). Indirect and good-humored criticisms sometimes acted as a way of expressing dissatisfaction with the turn things were taking. Throughout this era one finds the great creative energy of Geraldo Pereira who had deep associations with the malandro style with his syncopated samba, later rediscovered by João Gilberto in the golden years of bossa nova. During that period samba and *batucada* were brought into the same semantic field and marketed as "musical genres" that became conflated in countless recordings. Batucada gained strength formally, as an expressive genre, in the first half of the 1940s. There had never been as many recordings under that rubric as there were in that period, to the displeasure of some Estado Novo intellectuals, who defended the need to ceaselessly struggle for the "social rehabilitation of samba."[18]

This crusade, motivated by "educational" and "civilizing" goals, proposed to free samba from the lawlessness, sensuality, the drumming of the ghetto. Samba was, therefore, an enemy to be subjugated and drawn into the sphere of government influence. It is evident that the imagined paradise of certain elite defenders of the dictatorship was not as rosy as they intended. As the Estado Novo had just ended, the Carnaval of 1946 metaphorically came to terms with the ideology of work hitherto propagated in the four corners of Brazil. The song "Trabalhar, Eu Não" (Work, Not Me!) by Almeidinha was an astounding success in the song competition. This samba, taken up by strik-

Geraldo Pereira (FUNARTE).

ing dockworkers that same year in Santos, during a confrontation with the police, continued to protest against the brutal inequality of the profits generated by work in a capitalist society. Its verses offer an acute critique:

Eu trabalho como um louco	I work like crazy
Até fiz calo na mão	Calluses on my hands
O meu patrão ficou rico	My boss got rich
E eu pobre sem tostão	And I poor without a dime
Foi por isso que agora	Now that's why
Eu mudei de opinião	I changed my mind
Trabalhar, eu não, eu não	Work, not me, not me!
Trabalhar, eu não, eu não!	Work, not me, not me!
Trabalhar, eu não!	Work, not me!

DISCOGRAPHY

Almeidinha, with Joel de Almeida. "Trabalhar, Eu Não" (78 RPM). Odeo, 1946.

Alves, Ataulfo, and Wilson Batista, with Ciro Monteiro. "Oh! Seu Oscar" (78 RPM). Victor, 1939.

Barro, João de, Alberto Ribeiro, and Alcir Pires Vermelho, with Francisco Alves. "Onde o Céu Azul É Mais Azul" (78 RPM). Columbia, 1940.

Barro, João de, and Alberto Ribeiro, with Caetano Veloso. "Yes, Nós Temos Banana . . ." (single). Philips, 1968.

Barroso, Ary, with Francisco Alves, "Aquarela do Brasil" (78 RPM). Odeon, 1939.

Batista, Wilson, and Geraldo Pereira, with Moreira da Silva. "Acertei no Milhar" (78 RPM). Odeon, 1940.

Batista, Wilson, and Germano Augusto, with Dircinha Batista. "Inimigo do Batente" (78 RPM). Odeon, 1940.

Figueiredo, Sebastião, with Joel and Gaúcho. "O Amor Regenera o Malandro" (78 RPM). Columbia, 1940.

Machado, Orlando Luiz, with Noel Rosa and Ismael Silva. "Escola de Malandro" (78 RPM). Odeon, 1932.

Souza, Ciro de, and Augusto Garcez, with Aurora Miranda. "Não Admito" (78 RPM). Victor, 1940.

Souza, Ciro de, with Ciro Monteiro. 78 RPM. Victor, 1940.

Valente, Assis, with Carmen Miranda. "Recenseamento" 78 (RPM). Odeon, 1940.

1. The allusion to Greek tragedy as a metaphor of heroic discourse on politics is suggested by José Nun (1983: 104–5).

2. For a more specific critique of these notions, see Chaui 1978.

3. This is the argument made by Antonio Pedro (1980, chap. 2). A later work that also points towards the adhesion of popular composers to New State ideology, is that of Moby 1994: 105–27.

4. Hegemony, as Antonio Gramsci has shown, should not be confused with domination or absolute rule, much less with uniformity. Hence Thompson's warning that, "the very term 'culture,' with its cosy invocation of consensus, may serve to distract attention from social and cultural contradictions, from the fractures and oppositions within the whole" (1991: 13).

5. For a critique of this view, see Paranhos 1999a: 15–39.

6. At that time, certain proponents of musical nationalism viewed popular urban music suspiciously because it was "always threatened by foreign 'contamination'" (Barros 2001: 359). Not by chance Mário de Andrade pondered in 1939, while on praising the talent of Radamés Gnattali: "It's true that he 'jazzes' it up a little too much for my defensively nationalistic taste" (Andrade 1976: 286). Heitor Villa-Lobos was not far behind: he turned his nose at everything that sounded like "Americanized chords," in musical productions not in tune with the true "Brazilian Brazil" (quoted in Barros 2001: 360).

7. I am here thinking of arrangements such as those conceived decades later by Rogério Duprat, at the height of Tropicália.

8. For this reason, Paul Zumthor calls attention to the "expressive richness of the voice" and to the "values which its volume, its inflections, and its trajectories attribute to the language which it formalizes," and concludes: "the interpreter . . . signifies" (2001: 134, 228).

9. For a critique of the excessive attachment of historians to written sources as texts, with all of their methodological implications, see Carlo Ginzburg 1987: 17–18.

10. The sheet music to "O Amor Regenera o Malandro" was edited by the publishing house A Melodia, Rio de Janeiro. Even with an author attentive to the reception of the song, and the appreciation of its musical elements, this aspect was unnoticed to the point that its recording was grouped among those in the Estado Novo camp (Furtado Filho 2004: 239).

11. For these reasons and others, I disagree with the interpretation of the musicologist Ary Vasconcelos (1982: 2), who identifies in "Recenseamento" a patriotic manifestation of Assis Valente. I admit he was a self-proclaimed nationalist, but not in the Estado Novo style. Another researcher relates "Recenseamento" to the group of *sambas-exaltação* of the dictatorship (Barros 2001: 363–64, 383).

12. It is in this context that the statement by Maria Célia Paoli should be understood: "The ambiguity of rights promoted by the State—its success in promoting identifications and its relative failure in producing citizens based on an idea of social justice—demonstrates a political experience of social integration whose structure was derived from multiple practices that remain alive, even though the State spectacle was a unique act" (1989: 65).

13. See Naves 1998: 66–141. It could be added that simplicity was equally accompanied by the process of production and/or the use of various musical instruments: the bass drum, made from cow skin (known as *raspa*), the matchbox, or the straw hat, converted into artifacts of percussion.

14. For a detailed analysis of this song, see Matos, 1982: 114–18.

15. One year earlier, the presidential speech to the workers had hammered home this point: "The word of the day which we must obey is to produce, to produce, without fail, to produce ever more." See Getúlio Vargas, *Boletim do Ministério do Trabalho, Indústria e Comércio* 93 (1942).

16. On the concluding attack on the "corrupting slang of the national language," see Martins Castelo, "Rádio, VI," *Cultura Política* 6 (1941): 329–31. The polemicist later argued against the "degradation" promoted by "dirty language" in "Rádio, XI," *Cultura Política* 11 (1942): 299–301.

17. See the lecture on the proletarian housewife, delivered in 1942 on the national radio news program *Hora do Brasil* (Marcondes Filho 1943: 51–55).

18. For an empirical analysis of song lyrics from the 1940s, see Alcino Santos 1982. For an analysis of the musical section of the magazine *Cultura Política*, published with the blessings of the DIP between 1941 and 1945, see Eduardo Vicente 1996.

::: Orpheonic Chant and the Construction of
Childhood in Brazilian Elementary Education

Flávio Oliveira

Music and education in Brazil have historically been linked through
an ideology of civilization, as visible in the colonial catechization of Indians
in the sixteenth century and seventeenth, in the musical practices of blacks
and mulattoes in the eighteenth-century Catholic brotherhoods of Vila Rica
(present-day Ouro Preto) during the golden age of the Baroque period in
Minas Gerais, and especially in the ambiguous and erratic relations between music and nationalism from the late nineteenth century to the end
of Getúlio Vargas's first administration, in 1945. School education played a
major role in forming citizens adapted to the profound transformations in
society during that period. More than offering education of the mind, the
dominant educational thought intended to consolidate a sense of Brazilianness anchored in aesthetic, moral, civic, hygienic, and even eugenic principles. One of the most important pedagogical strategies to reach this goal
was the teaching of collective singing in elementary school. The influence
of racist ideas in early twentieth-century Brazilian intellectual circles contributed in a subtle but decisive way to eliminating musical manifestations
rooted in the *mestiço* culture of the population. Tangos, maxixes, and sambas
were systematically avoided and even condemned in school musical practices. Singing lessons in schools were connected to an aesthetic education
aimed at forming new habits and tastes in the population.

One of the main characteristics of the pedagogical renewal that took
place in late eighteenth-century Europe was the valorization of aesthetic
education, with emphasis on children's musical education during the first
years of schooling. Children's senses and moral education became the basis
for civility-oriented education with a view to lessening rudeness and vulgarity in the population. In addition, philosophers and pedagogues such as
Jean-Jacques Rousseau, Immanuel Kant, Johann Heinrich Pestalozzi, Fried-

rich Fröebel, and Friedrich von Schiller presented solid arguments in favor of education that promoted the integral formation of the human being, that is, the simultaneous enhancement of the intellect and the sensibility. Children's art exhibits were organized, and art education manuals for teachers and learners were published.

The integral formation of the human being found its best definition in the German concept of *Bildung*, established in the late eighteenth century and the early nineteenth. It referred to the aesthetic, moral, and intellectual betterment of humanity, leading to the ideal of fraternity among peoples expressed in the motto of the French Revolution. The concept of Bildung translated the Enlightenment ideal of civilization as well as many of the principles of Romantic pedagogy. Schiller, for instance, considered that an aesthetic education of the people would be the best way to face political problems of the time, as for him beauty was the privileged path to freedom. This set of ideals prepared the way for the emergence of the school as a central institution in modern societies and consequently for the role acquired by pedagogy as a civilizing instrument. The notion of Bildung decisively influenced the development of all of nineteenth-century pedagogical thought. Beginning in the first school years, the enhancement of children's senses became an essential component in the civilizing role of modern pedagogy. Singing exercises for children in elementary schools became more and more recommended as a fundamental part of the education of the senses.

The last decades of the nineteenth century also witnessed renewal in educational thought, along with the ruling elites' belief in the fundamental role of schooling in the nation's development and modernization. This renewal was anchored in late eighteenth-century Romantic pedagogy and was disseminated in Brazilian intellectual spheres during the implementation and consolidation of the republic. As was the case in Europe and the United States, this review of pedagogical methods was connected to the valorization of the education of children's senses. Aesthetic education came to the forefront of Brazilian pedagogical thought. Practices such as collective singing, dancing, and gymnastics were increasingly recommended. Songs were composed specifically to be taught in schools. Many of them were authored by composers and poets steeped in the erudite tradition. Most of these songs had a Romantic inspiration, displaying themes that evoked love for the country, nature, family, and, obviously, school.

In Brazil, the idea of education as a civilizing practice was clearly defined in Rui Barbosa's *Pareceres*,[1] written when he was the head of the Public Instruction Committee of the Congress between 1882 and 1886, during the reform proposed by the education secretary, Leôncio de Carvalho. These writings had a great influence on Brazilian pedagogy at the turn of the century. For Rui Barbosa, freedom was a basic condition for progress, and only a democratic regime would be able to provide it. In his view, since democracy rests on citizens' free choice, the formation of individuals with a higher degree of autonomy and discernment is the key to progress. His *Pareceres* is the expression of liberal-education thinking with a view to the building of new civility for the population though formal schooling. This notion of civility, based on the individual's power of autonomy and discernment, reached its most polished form in Barbosa's advocacy of the so-called intuitive method in Brazilian schools: "that which penetrates human intelligence through sensitive intuition"—wrote Rui Barbosa, quoting João Amós Comenius, the author of *Didáctica Magna* (1627–32)—*"imprints itself through the senses upon memory, always to be remembered" (1946: 203)*.

The intuitive method had its roots in seventeenth-century empiricist philosophy, especially in Francis Bacon and John Locke, who saw in the senses of perception the origin of human knowledge. Comenius may have been the first to notice the importance of the senses for education at the time. Rousseau, Kant, and especially Pestalozzi and Fröebel then developed a pedagogy that directly influenced the teaching of philosophy through sense intuition. They started by critiquing the emphasis on abstract knowledge and on memorization over comprehension. Barbosa exposed the failure in the Brazilian educational system and regretted the absence of education based on children's direct experience with the world of the senses. In Barbosa's view, only an education that favored the enhancement of the senses from early infancy could contribute to the formation of free, creative individuals fully able to exercise judgment. Barbosa's defense of the intuitive method stemmed from his belief that individuals who were educated according to these principles would be better prepared to perform active roles as citizens of a modern and progressive state.

Rui Barbosa's legacy played a major role in the advance of pedagogy in Brazil. His support for the reform of teaching methods and for the modernization of public instruction drew the attention of Brazilian educators to the relation between an aesthetic education of the people and the possibility of shaping a new Brazilian mentality more in tune with social, political, and economic changes brought by republican modernity. In his *Pareceres*, Rui Barbosa devoted extensive attention to the issue of aesthetic education, emphasizing the potential of artistic culture as a fundamental basis for popular education that supported the country's development.

Rui Barbosa recognized in artistic practice an outlet for creative manifestations of students' direct observations of the world. He took to defending the teaching of singing in schools for aesthetic and pragmatic reasons. For Barbosa, school singing should lend itself to educating children's musical taste, ears, and voices, making them softer and more in key. It should also promote children's physical, moral, and intellectual improvement. Art, especially school singing, became an important instrument of popular education; it gradually occupied a place at the core of educational practices. For educators, singing helped familiarize children with that which is "truly beautiful," making them able to experience aesthetic feelings and understand that human actions are not defined simply by their immediate meaning or purpose, but also by their form or sensible content.

In the early 1920s, educators such as Antonio de Sampaio Dória (1920), Anísio Teixeira (1925), and Francisco Campos (1927) promoted reforms in educational systems respectively of São Paulo, Bahia, and Minas Gerais (Marta Maria Chagas de Carvalho 2000). These reforms were some of the most significant results brought about by the notion of intuitive teaching in the Brazilian educational system. Elementary schools, in particular, saw a major increase in the use of dance and theater exercises, educational movies or radio broadcasts, drawing, modeling, needlepoint (for girls), and other practices that stimulated students' inventiveness and refined taste. Above all, there was an intensification of eurhythmics and singing exercises, particularly collective singing. Better than any other human activity, it was thought, art could contribute to soften the spirit of new generations by developing a solid feeling of sociability, responsibility, and cooperation. For taking on such a civilizing role, art lent itself to the unprecedented civilizing purposes that oriented the ideal of a massive spread of education in the country.

Much as Schiller had intended, the refining of popular taste through art also played an important role in the self-identification of emerging nations in their routes toward consolidation. In Brazilian society, this idea acquired a special connotation since in the transition to a republic the country struggled culturally and politically with formulating a national identity. In fact, the country emerged as a pioneering nation in territorial extension and diversification at the time. Starting in elementary school and conceived as part of the population's aesthetic, civic, and moral education, collective singing practices helped reinforce the feeling of "Brazilianness" necessary for the consolidation of the republican project. For Escola Nova, or New School, innovators, art and particularly collective singing should be incorporated into school curricula to open channels of communication between academic and popular cultures. More than a luxury, art was the spontaneous way through which people expressed their own understanding of life, as they turned hopes into songs, happiness into dances, most commonplace morals into proverb or popular sayings. Songs *are, for the people, documents of their disgrace and happiness"* (Azevedo 1958: 121). For him, even higher art was born out of people's souls and should return to them to replenish itself with beauty and emotion.

Aimed at forming critical and transformative subjects while disseminating universal and instrumental reason engendered by European culture, the ideal of enlightened pedagogy that followed Rui Barbosa was at the root of these renewals in Brazilian pedagogical thought. The civilization modeled after this culture could only lead a long and full existence if all social classes were reached by the civilizing ideals of modern Western culture: "it is from the will to colonize the space of the masses' subaltern culture that modern pedagogy extracts its force and necessity" (Moriconi 1996: 126). The aesthetic, civic, and moral education of the people promoted by the school system located itself at a strategic position in the modern civilizing process and, more specifically, in the modernization of Brazil in the first decades of the twentieth century.

::: Singing as a Curricular Subject for Children

In Brazil, the production of a repertoire of songs dedicated to children happened simultaneously with the proliferation of children's books and the massive spread of the toy. These phenomena did not happen casually, but were linked to the emergence of the Escola Nova pedagogical approach and to a new concept of childhood. School songs, often from musical plays, were published in children's literature anthologies, along with poems and fables. Lyrics were filled with teachings of good habits; good behavior; love for school, work, family, and particularly the nation. As for the musical content, school songs usually had simple melodies, composed in comfortable textures and regular rhythms, so that children could easily learn them. Songs, readings, and plays attempted to develop good habits, good manners, and noble feelings. In elementary schools of Minas Gerais, this intention is apparent in the first collection of school songs, published in 1925.

Educational legislation and pedagogical journals of the time help explain the purposes of musical education in Brazil in the early twentieth century. *Revista do Ensino*, the official publication of the Minas Gerais secretary of education of state, founded in 1925 with the goal of spreading the new pedagogical school among educators, was responsible for widely promoting collective singing in elementary as well as teacher preparatory schools. In one of the journal's first issues, of May 1925, the teacher and musician José Eutrópio stated that *"the importance of singing lessons in Brazilian schools is finally recognized, as the school itself is finally becoming what it is meant to be: a home for happiness and spirit, from which the processes of terror, once so prevalent, have been banished."*[2]

Eutrópio here referred to the gradual assimilation of New School ideas by the elite of Brazilian pedagogical thinking. He proposed, however, that there was still much to be done for the effective modernization of schools. Music, as a powerful influence on the human spirit, was to play a key role in that permanent transformation. The author also argued for maximizing art's educational potential. For him, no other form of art was as able to follow the evolution of the human soul as did music, since for each stage of intelligence there was an appropriate musical modality. The basic principle was to offer students the repertoire that best suited their developmental stage. It was necessary that music should always be within the reach of children's comprehension.

Eutrópio also lamented the lack of songs and hymns adequately chosen and prepared for school use, which he regarded as one the main obstacles facing musical education in Brazilian schools. In order to fill this gap, he insisted that teachers be able to take advantage of the meager extant song collection, but also enrich it by gathering from children songs learned from the oral tradition. The author also suggested that teachers be attentive to lyrics in order to pass on moral teaching to their students: "The singing lesson, in addition to being a happy moment for children, also becomes an extension of classes, a lesson that students learn as they laugh happily. School singing thus acquires its true role in educating sensibility and guiding one's sense of beauty."

Eutrópio's ideas were in perfect consonance with norms of a good school musical education defined by late nineteenth-century pedagogy. As we compare his arguments with entries on music and singing in E. M. Campagne's *Dicionário Universal de Educação e Ensino*, several points in common emerge, revealing that school singing practices were being adopted in several other countries at the time.[3] As for the choice of repertoire to be offered to the children, Campagne's dictionary made it clear that for educational purposes, music should be limited to vocal music, since singing was the only form of musical art *"general and simple enough to match the conditions of popular teaching"* (Campagne 1886: 2:900). Another point in common was the simplicity that should characterize school songs. The dictionary also recommended that in order for songs favorably to influence the people, it was essential that the feelings they expressed were *"general enough and collected from the depths of the human essence"* (ibid.). Finally, it was also necessary that means of expression were simple so as to ensure the possibility of full understanding. More than simply important for education in general, singing was one of its fundamental components.

Aesthetic education became a powerful way of promoting citizens' moral education, much as Friedrich Schiller had proposed in his *Aesthetic Education of Men* ([1793] 1954). A school that educated sensibility in addition to the intellect was seen as more capable of adequately contributing to the full development of children's intelligence. Morally and aesthetically educated children, in their turn, were better prepared to contribute to a more harmonious society. Seen from a curricular as well as a moral and intellectual viewpoint, music was recommended particularly in the first school years, as it would lead to love of school and the development of a taste for study. More easily understood than literary beauty, music was the best way to make children feel the emotion and happiness of contributing to the production of beauty. The deep feeling for art and taste provided by music was to operate and influence the development of children's intelligence. From a moral point of view, music was believed to be a way of keeping children away from mundane distractions, as long as the repertoire actually helped them develop a taste for so-called true musical beauty.

The message disseminated among teachers in Minas Gerais was that children should breathe respect and even worship for music from early infancy. As soon as they entered school, they would have their first music lessons. Evoking Fröebel's principles on the importance of music for children's integral education, the text reminded teachers that children as young as those in kindergarten should experience physical and musical games that favored the development of muscles and eurhythmics. It was desirable that such lessons gradually continued until the last year of schooling, so that students were able to express their aesthetic feelings by means of musical writing as adequately as their verbal language expressed their other ideas.

In another article in *Revista de Ensino* (October 1926), José Eutrópio stated that musical education was not only a means for promoting moral and aesthetic education of children. It was also the first seed of musical talents that are now hibernating and could blossom in the future:

> If there are any children with talent for music, this learning will contribute more efficiently to consolidate this calling and play a decisive role in their future. How many beautiful vocations die, disappear unsuspected for lack of incentive like this? School singing is not a musical class, but a powerful element of culture and progress that demands conscious and serious guidance from the teacher. (68)

The status of collective singing as an academic subject in Brazilian elementary school curricula dates back to the 1920s. It is noticeable that there was great control from the state over the choice of repertoire. This is understandable, as civic and patriotic hymns were a key element for an education that attempted to convey the feelings of nationality necessary for the consolidation of republican ideals sponsored by the country's elites.

In elementary school curricula, singing lessons were placed next to subjects such as drawing, reading and writing, grammar, practical arithmetic, general world knowledge, introduction to Brazilian history and geography, rudiments of civic and moral education, natural sciences, hygiene, and physical exercises. Singing was part of the curricula throughout elementary school, which reveals the great importance that education authorities attributed to it. In Minas Gerais, the singing program for elementary schools, established by a decree of 1925, attempted to instruct teachers about the best way of conducting classes.[4] Teachers should choose the best voices and appoint those students as the first choir and maintain the remaining students in silence for a few days, until they had learned words and melody to the hymns and songs chosen for exercise. Only then should teachers allow this last group of students to participate in collective singing. In the first lessons, teachers should not allow students to go beyond the range between C at the first ledger line below the G clef and C at the third space in the G clef. Teachers should adopt the diapason (tuning fork) to give the key and, if possible, use a piano, a harmonium, or another instrument, first for solfège and later for accompanying collective singing. Singing exercises should be held on a daily basis but should not exceed eight minutes. Selected songs should initially be simple and easy; popular songs ordinarily sung by students in their daily play sufficed. Only after voices were firmer and clearer should teachers use hymns and other stronger and more difficult songs. The major concerns should be to make students sing effortlessly and with good vocal projection. According to musical educators of the time, it was important that teachers remain vigilant in order to prevent children's voices from coming out of the throat or sounding nasal. Likewise, teachers should prevent children from screaming instead of singing, as this practice broke collective singing harmony in addition to physiologically damaging the voice. It was also essential that teachers take advantage of the lyrics to songs and hymns to convey moral and civic teachings.

In order better to understand the role of collective singing in elementary schools, one should observe the school time and the spaces assigned to it. Students, teachers, and at times family members would gather every other week in school auditoriums. These meetings did not exceed two hours and were used for musical auditions, collective singing practices, lectures on topics of interest, or social work. On national dates, such as Flag Day or Mother's Day, principals and teachers were asked to attend school celebrations. On these occasions, the principal or another appointed teacher was in charge of making a speech that corresponded to a civic education class. After that, students sang hymns and patriotic songs. This practice points again to the relation between school singing and children's moral and civic formation. Musical educators of the time reminded audiences of the emphasis placed in Plato's *Republic* on singing, whether or not accompanied by instruments, as a fundamental part of citizen formation from a very early age. Brazilian education laws of that time concurred.

The teaching of singing in elementary schools was not isolated from the other subjects. Lyrics to hymns were interpreted in Portuguese-language classes. Brazilian-history classes commented on the composition of the national anthem and cast its author, Francisco Manoel da Silva, as an outstanding Brazilian composer. There was also a focus on the composer Carlos Gomes and his major work, the opera *O Guarani*, inspired by José de Alencar's novel.[5] Fully based on musical rhythms and harmony, gymnastics also helped promote learners' aesthetic enhancement. In museums and school collections, there were hymnals, diapasons, and other musical instruments, as well as pictures of notable foreign composers, along with Brazilians such as Carlos Gomes.[6] This activity was all intended to promote a permanent connection between children and music.

::: Eugenics, Fatherland, and Songs

The content of school songs increasingly became a topic of debate during the 1930s. These discussions often brought up racist arguments, in accordance with Getúlio Vargas's governmental project of "cleansing and educating" Brazil. The eugenic component of discourses on hygiene became evident.[7] In association with other discourses of moral and civic nature, they proscribed from schools songs and dances genres widely disseminated at the time, such as tango, maxixe, and samba. Those rhythms were considered immoral and uncivilized products of an aesthetic contrary to the time's ideals of whitening. In 1933, Levindo Lambert stated in *Revista do Ensino*:

> Tangos and maxixes, sambas, burlesque musical fragments, whose lyrics— don't we all know?—are usually an assault to grammar and to morality are performed by children in various acts, in theatrical representations, and even in auditoriums. Not only are they a fiery repository of vulgarity and swear words, but they also become a dangerous distraction leading to the habit of bad prosody and bad grammar.[8]

In another article on music in schools, published in the same *Revista do Ensino* two years later, Georgina Machado da Cruz recast this argument in her discussion of "good music," organized as a denial of Afro-Brazilian popular culture. She began her article by stating that the main mission of the educator should be the promotion of the moral, intellectual, and physical formation of the individual, with the purpose of turning children into perfect—that is, strong, free, conscious, and responsible—adults. She defended music as one of the most efficient subjects in this tripartite enhancement of humanity. As an essentially divine art, music brought man closer to the path to good and virtue. However, as we can infer from her opinions, not all music had such a gift. According to her, school songs only had a positive effect on children if their lyrics had a fruitful nature and if they were always in accordance with students' age and school level. Only in this way would these songs incite interest, taste, goodwill, and discipline. By returning to Levindo Lambert's lesson, Machado da Cruz made clear the school's repudiation of a certain type of music, not by chance the one that revealed the popular mestiço traditions of Brazilian people:

> In tangos and maxixes, in sambas and burlesque musical fragments, there is a frequent concentration of curse words and vulgar language that weakens the irresistible readiness for perfection, beauty, and truth in children's souls. As they do not represent valuable assets or educational means, these pieces should be banned from schools that aim at the full triumph of education.[9]

She also prescribed the genres to be adopted. For her, it was not appropriate to teach songs related to the school universe only, as songs learned in school would forever be *"man's inseparable companions in the daily labor of his life of responsibility."* It was thus essential that from a very early age children learned songs that could stir in them the love of work and the permanent desire to contribute to the enrichment of the country: *"The march, whichever it is, always conveys the idea of the soldier, in whom children see the incarnation of their country."* Symbolically, the national anthem was the most representative song for those ideals. It is no wonder that patriotic hymns and marches were the most widely adopted styles in that period.

Another representative song was "A Escola," music by J. B. Julião and lyrics by Antônio Peixoto. As far as the relation between music and text is concerned, this is an excellent song to observe, due to the strong descriptive appeal of the melody,[10] and to its coherent "balance" between that melody and the literal part of the song (Tatit 2002). The composer was careful in the employment of each note. The result is not only a beautiful song, but also excellent pedagogical material, due to the song's ability to achieve the goals of an aesthetic, civic-patriotic, and moral education while advertising fundamental values of love for family, school, and the nation. The descriptive content of the musical part was in perfect synchronicity with the widely disseminated assumptions of the intuitive method. Evocative melodies were a valuable element to reinforce the ideological content of the verbal message. In this particular song, all literal and musical discourses revolve around the trio of family, school, and nation, central to the reaffirmation of the sense of Brazilianness that characterized the period. It is worth mentioning that the composer J. B. Julião received an invitation to collaborate with the conductor João Gomes Jr. in the preparation of school choirs for celebrations of the "Centenary of Independence" in 1922. "A Escola" had all the civic and musical elements to become part of those celebrations, as it exalted school as a vanguard institution in the building of a free, strong, and independent nation:

Essa escola é nosso ninho	This school is our nest
regaço feito de amor.	haven made of love.
Tem a graça de um carinho,	It has the grace of a caress,
a pureza de uma flor.	the purity of a flower
Da escola se apronta e parte	School prepares and sends off
a raça forte e gentil,	the strong and gentle race
que levará o estandarte	who will bear Brazil's
auri-verde do Brasil.	golden and green banner.

Although seemingly simple, "A Escola" provides interesting material for analysis, due its discreet sophistication. Composed in waltz tempo (3/4 time), this little musical piece is divided in two parts, A and B. In A, corresponding to the first stanza of the lyrics, the four lines are sung in C major, in two somewhat similar musical phrases, ensuring uniformity maintained in the verbal meter, composed in eight-syllable lines. The rhymes, easy and predictable in Portuguese (*ninho/carinho*; *amor/flor*) are quite appropriate for memorization and for children's taste. They also offer their contribution to the aesthetic balance of this first stanza. However, the song had not been made to reach exclusively children. Although it was to be performed by children, its audience would be composed mostly of adults. Written by and listened to by adults, the lyrics also conveyed part of the modern concept of childhood, emphasizing children's need for tenderness and protection in order to become self-confident civilized adults. These characteristics are well marked by the use of the words *forte* (strong) and *gentil* (gentle) in the second line of the second stanza.

The piece's discreet sophistication appears in the well-arranged weaving between melody and prosody, which subliminally and intelligently reiterates the text's message. Part A of the melodic structure, developed in C major, is composed in two musical phrases as follows:

G A/ B A /G E/ G/ G/ B A G/ F E D/ E
Essa escola é nosso ninho; regaço feito de amor.
G A/ B (flat) A G E/ A/ A/ E F G/ F E D/ C
Tem a graça de um carinho; a pureza de uma flor.

These two phrases, of eight bars each, are identical in everything, except that the second line wanders, for four bars, in D minor, while the harmony remains in the original key, C major; that is, it remains unmodulated. The subtlety of this small melodic alteration resides in the fact that it coincides exactly with the words "it has the grace of a caress." From aesthetic and musical points of view, this small alteration provides special color to the melody, musically emphasizing the verbal message. Technically speaking, the fast movement through the key of D minor takes place when the B flat appears in the musical phrase. Thus in the phrase "G–A–B," the latter is altered (flatted), which causes a subtle sensation of surprise and distinguishes this phrase from the first. Interestingly, the aforementioned B flat falls exactly on the word *grace*, thereby reinforcing its meaning. The grace of a caress, attributed to school, is expressed both in the melody, with the spring season suggested by the use of *nest* and *flower* and caress represented by the slightly altered sonority provided by the B flat, and in harmony, which almost shifts to the key of D minor.

The lyrics second stanza presents the refrain lines and corresponds to part B of the musical structure, which is no longer in C major, but has modulated to G major. This part is responsible for a small change in the mood of the musical piece, giving it a little more movement and reaching its major point of tension. The words in this stanza are notable for the abundant occurrence of alliterations with the letters *P*, *T*, or *D*. This figure of speech, besides offering a special sonority to the verses, evidences the thoughtfulness employed in the composition. In this stanza, there is an alternation between eight- and seven-syllable lines. It is introduced by the eight-syllable line "da escola se apronta e parte" (school prepares and sends off), which indicates a change in the movement of the song. Due to the efficient balance between text and melody, the image of a schooled generation rising to construct a magnificent nation also finds its correspondence in part B of the song's melodic structure. Thus, the first line is sung over an ascending melody that develops itself in four bars, musically describing an action that takes place from inside the school then moves beyond, into society. The following verse—"the strong and gentle race"—in turn, develops in three bars with no significant changes in melody. The composers made direct reference to the fact that the goals of schooling were associated with the formation of a strong and civilized race. The suspiciously eugenic content was visible: the words *forte* and *gentil*, conveying the quality of the "race" to be "prepared" by school, fall exactly on the same musical note, as if melodically to reinforce the value assigned to these "virtues" of the Brazilian "race." Furthermore, the note in question is an A, the reference note for the tuning of the whole orchestra. It is as if Brazilian people's character should be "tuned" by the diapason of school, a lesson that, as musical educators stated in the pages of the *Revista do Ensino*, children would learn as they played.

The two following verses and the musical phrase that corresponds to them set the piece off to its glorious conclusion. The first verse, again an eight-syllable one, "que levará o estandarte" (who will bear the banner), resorts to the ascending melody formula, which is able musically to evoke the image of the raising of the national flag. In this exaltation of the nation, the word banner strategically falls on the higher note in this scale. However, in this fragment, the national colors have not yet reached the top of the pole. The ascending musical movement continues in the next verse, "auri-verde do Brasil" (Brazil's golden and green), until the national colors can triumphantly reach tension with the melody's highest point, on D. The image now is the national flag triumphantly waving at the top of the mast, representing the most elevated task of school education: the formation of individuals morally and intellectually prepared to serve the fatherland's goals. Finally, in the descending phrase that follows, the melody starts its path toward rest, concluding the song's literal and melodic discourses with the sacred word not yet uttered. After having prepared the mood of patriotic fervor through aesthetic emotion, the song ends in the exaltation of the name—Brazil—prolonged by a full bar in the score, but presumably forever in the hearts and minds of children who would sing it after months of rehearsal in joyful and contagious school festivities.

::: The Orpheonic Experience

The year 1930 brought great transformations in the political, social, and educational realms. José Silvério Baía Horta (1994) notes that in Rio de Janeiro the Liberal Alliance announced its platform for Getúlio Vargas's candidacy to the presidency early that year. For Vargas education and sanitation were related problems that demanded a common solution. He intended to promote the moral and physical sanitization of the country through intensive hygiene education campaigns accompanied by the universalization of public schooling. In effect, Vargas intensified his concern with issues of education and health at the same rate as he deepened his government's authoritarian characteristics. From an early stage, education was put in service of authoritarian politics, echoing regimes such as Italian Fascism or German Nazism which, as Franco Cambi (1999) points out, had been promoting a centralization of state control over the educational system and an accentuation of religious teaching, civic education, and military culture in schools at all levels. It is noteworthy that all policies of the Ministry of Education, Health, and Public Instruction were directed to the formation of a "strong and civilized race." During Getúlio's time, civic discourse had as its corollary the concepts of nation and race, that legitimated the adoption of collective singing as a required subject in all schools after 1934.

In fact, during the 1930s and 1940s, singing as a school subject established ample penetration in schools all over the country, at all levels, with the support of the federal government. That influence was due to the adoption of a proposal for mass musical education, implemented by schools and formulated by Heitor Villa-Lobos, the Brazilian conductor and composer who was already internationally acclaimed.[11] From that moment on, collective singing as part of curricula became broadly known in Brazil as *canto orfeônico*, or orpheonic song.[12] This type of musical education received special attention from educational authorities, who tried to regulate orpheonic song and disseminate it throughout the country. Such attention was due, undoubtedly, to the subject's great civic appeal, which corresponded to the political interests of the regime established in 1930.

In 1931 Heitor Villa-Lobos arrived from Europe, where he had lived since 1923, and immediately received an invitation to direct civic and musical activities in São Paulo from João Alberto Lins de Barros, appointed by Vargas as governor, or *interventor federal*. Thus, already in 1931, the first great civic and artistic demonstration of orpheonic song was held under his supervision. The event gathered a group of approximately 12,000 voices of teachers, students, academics, soldiers, workers, and other sectors of society. In 1932, in order to enhance the musical movement in schools in Rio, then the capital of Brazil, Villa-Lobos created, with the support of Anísio Teixeira, director of the Rio de Janeiro Municipal Department of Education, the course in the pedagogy of orpheonic song directed to those employed in teacher preparatory schools. They were in charge of disseminating knowledge on musical theory and procedures of orpheonic song that should be adopted in municipal schools. In May of that year, the Teachers' Orpheon was founded in order to strengthen orpheonic movements in the schools of the Federal District.

School education became one of the major instruments for promoting

Heitor Villa-Lobos directs school children, Rio de Janeiro, 1940
(Museu Villa-Lobos / Academia Brasileira de Música).

government propaganda and Vargas's nationalist ideology. Learning patriotic hymns and folk songs in schools and the grandiose civic-musical spectacles of orpheonic singing promoted by Villa-Lobos adjusted perfectly to the propaganda interests of the Vargas administration, which in turn, offered the conductor the conditions fully to develop his ambitious project. These grand orpheonic singing spectacles, held at stadiums in São Paulo and Rio de Janeiro, gathered up to 40,000 students who sang patriotic and folk songs in two, three, and four voices. The orpheonic song program was "one of the most unusual and ingenious nationalistic projects ever devised—the deliberate and systematic use of music and a means of shaping national character" (Vassberg 1969: 55).

Some of Villa-Lobos's old comrades of the modernist movement of the 1920s, such as Mário de Andrade, criticized him at the time for his connection with Vargas's regime.[13] He was also the target of criticism by conservative musicians, who believed he would bring the modernist aesthetic of his first works to schools, which did not actually happen. Despite all this, Villa-Lobos's orpheonic song project was widely successful in the 1930s and '40s. In November 1942, the education secretary Gustavo Capanema created the

Heitor Villa-Lobos directs mass chorus, Rio de Janeiro, 1942
(Museu Villa-Lobos / Academia Brasileira de Música).

cnco (Conservatório Nacional de Canto Orfeônico; National Conservatory of Orpheonic Chant), directed since its opening by Villa-Lobos. The cnco was designed to offer guidelines for orpheonic song in schools all over the country and determine "which programs should be followed, which hymns and songs should be sung . . . , even which evaluation criteria should be used" (Horta 1994: 187). It is noteworthy that civic attitude and strict group discipline were among these criteria.

Modernity consolidated the notion of a child as a dependent, albeit teachable, individual. To some degree, this notion prevails to date. Beginning in the eighteenth century, the school, the institution in charge of promoting such education of children, played a fundamental role in politico-cultural transformations brought about by the so-called modern era. Schooling was gradually converted into a compulsory activity for children. Thus, attending school became their natural destiny, insofar as, in the opinions of most educators, school would be the institution that best prepared the individual wisely to face different situations in the course of life. At the core of this modern pedagogical thought, aesthetic education emerged as an ideal for constructing children's autonomy and for developing their ability to judge, make decisions for themselves, and become free, self-confident adults and civilized citizens.

In the late nineteenth century and early twentieth, those who defended music as an integral part of school curricula with its own space, time, and materiality found support for their arguments in debates outside the field of musical education. These arguments were corroborated by concepts then being developed in Europe and the United States—particularly the intuitive method in education, which prescribed that elementary schools should adopt strategies for educating the senses. Eugenic and hygienist ideas were being fully disseminated in the intellectual spheres of the country starting in the late nineteenth century. In accordance with these principles, music was adopted as a civilizing procedure, due to its intrinsically aesthetic nature, the moral and racial content that lyrics could convey, and the athletic value of breathing exercises. The educational potential of collective singing was justified by the fact that it enabled the strengthening of collective solidarity and harmonic instincts more than any other musical practice.

It was thus argued that music was an instrument capable of forming citizens in agreement with the Brazilian republican principles of the early twentieth century. As Schiller proposed in his letters on the aesthetic education of man, only through the enhancement of culture could humans fully develop their sensitive and moral capabilities. Perhaps the best example of the ambiguity between utilitarian and strictly artistic aspects of musical education offered in Brazilian schools beginning in the 1930s is the orpheonic song project initiated and implemented by Villa-Lobos. As Goldemberg noted, the prominent Brazilian conductor and composer was concerned with elevating Brazilians' artistic and musical taste (1995:103). He considered collective singing the most efficient way not only widely to promote musical education of the population, but also to strengthen its civic education, since orpheonic song arguably contributed to a disciplined feeling of love for the nation among the population. In the conductor's opinion, orpheonic song was the logical solution to the problem of musical education in Brazilian schools. In 1932, Anísio Teixeira created the SEMA (Superintendência da Educação Musical e Artística; Superintendence of Musical and Artistic Education), whose direction was offered to Villa-Lobos. The superintendence was designed to coordinate educational actions related to orpheonic song, which, thanks to Villa-Lobos's increasing institutional prestige, rapidly reached the national sphere.

In the 1930s, by the time the secretary of the department of education and health made the teaching of orpheonic song mandatory and disseminated its methodology throughout the country, elementary schools already had accumulated experience in collective singing. This does not necessarily indicate the qualitative nature of these experiences, but suggests that in one way or another the debate on school singing, as well as its practice, was already a reality in Brazilian schools. When orpheonic song methodology started to be disseminated in the country, it addressed regional goals, needs, and solutions related to musical education that were described in the pages of the *Revista do Ensino* in Minas Gerais. The journal's editorial stance was keen on an educational model that privileged the creative impulse of students over the educational practices of a stricter nature. In all of this experience, including the period of dissemination of orpheonic song, it is possible to detect fewer historical ruptures than continuities. In short, early twentieth-century musical education in Brazilian schools was permanently balanced between the civic and the aesthetic, the moral and the hygienic.

NOTES

My sincere thanks to Dr. Cynthia Greive Veiga and to my research assistant Juliana Ferreira de Melo.

1. Rui Barbosa was a lawyer, journalist, jurist, politician, diplomat, essayist, and speaker from Bahia. He was a founding member of the Brazilian Academy of Letters, "deputy and counselor of the empire" under Dom Pedro II. In the republican period, he was appointed to the Departments of Treasury and Justice.

2. All articles by José Eutrópio cited here can be found in the *Revista do Ensino: Orgam Official da Directoria da Instrucção* [Belo Horizonte] (May 1925–January 1928).

3. See E. M. Campagne, *Diccionário Universal de Educação e Ensino. Transladado a Portuguez e Ampliado nos Vários Assumptos Relativos a Portugal por Camillo Castello Branco. Nova Edição Portugueza Ilustrada* (Porto: Editora Porto, Livraria Internacional de Ernesto Chardron, Casa Editora, Lugan e Genelioux, Sucessores, 1886 [Typographia de A. J. da Silva Teixeira]), vols. 1–2.

4. See *Coleção das Leis e Decretos do Estado de Minas Gerais* (1925), decreto 6.758, Arquivo Público Mineiro, Belo Horizonte.

5. Composed between 1865 and 1868, the opera *O Guarani* opened in Milan's Scala Theater on 19 March 1870. The opera was performed in the major European cities and, due to its extraordinary success, the author was knighted by the Order of the Crown in Italy. Acclaimed in Europe, Carlos Gomes joined the ranks of the world's top lyrical composers.

6. The idea of creating pedagogical museums in Brazilian schools was inspired by

the dissemination of the intuitive method and first appeared in Leôncio de Carvalho's reform of 19 April 1879. It was also defended by Rui Barbosa.

7. The term *eugenics* was coined by Francis Galton in 1883 and referred to studies related to the "enhancement" of the human race, with strong racialist content (Pichot 1997). Those ideas were brought to Brazil by Arthur de Gobineau around 1865, during the rule of Dom Pedro II, and slowly gained influence among national intellectuals through speeches of doctors, engineers, and sanitation specialists.

8. See Levindo Lambert, "Cantos Escolares," *Revista do Ensino* 87–89 (1933): 29–34.

9. See Georgina Machado da Cruz, "O Canto nas Escolas," *Revista do Ensino* [Órgão Technico da Secretaria da Educação] 10.110 (1935): 8–9.

10. The Canadian composer, researcher, and educator Murray Schafer proposes, in *The Thinking Ear* (1986), that descriptive music is capable of evoking visual images simply by the combination of sounds.

11. Villa-Lobos was one of the greatest musical personalities of the twentieth century. His work portrays a monumental and varied collection of compositions played by orchestras and musicians from all over the world.

12. The term *canto orfeônico* comes from the French *orphéon*, meaning a society of members dedicated to singing. In Brazil, musical educators established a fundamental difference between orpheonic song and choir music. The latter refers to music by a vocal group of a strictly artistic nature featuring singers with refined vocal technique. In orpheonic song, the emphasis fell primarily on civic and pedagogical intent. For important studies on the origins and implementation of orpheonic singing as a subject in Brazil, see Jusamara Vieira Souza 1993, Júlio da Costa Feliz, 1998, and Maurício Barreto Alvarez Parada, 2003.

13. Paulo Renato Guérios (2003) quotes Mário de Andrade in which he virulently accuses the composer for his "will to serve" the regime. The critic and composer Oscar Guanabarino also published criticism of Villa-Lobos in an article in the *Jornal do Commercio* in February 1932. The criticism targeted the appointment of Villa-Lobos, considered by Guanabarino as a "second rate artist," as director of the teaching of collective singing in Federal District schools.

Carlos Sandroni

> Democracy faces a difficulty. We no longer really know what exactly "the
> people" is. The Romantic national people? The Marxist worker? The diverse
> and disparate sub-peoples that organize themselves in social movements in
> contemporary society?
> —L. C. Bresser Pereira, *Folha de S. Paulo, Mais!*, 9 December 2001

It was not without some effort that I wrote the title for this chapter.
Both as a musician and as a citizen I feel profoundly connected to the set
of aesthetic and ideological notions that echo in the acronym MPB (Música
Popular Brasileira). Three events, however, have contributed to challenge,
if not my love for it, then at least my faith in its powers of representation.
Before speaking of those events I should stress that this text starts from the
observation that the idea of "popular music" shares a common premise with
that of the republic, that is, naturally, the notion of "the people" (*o povo*).
Whoever thinks of Brazilian popular music has in mind some conception
of "the Brazilian people," as much as does someone who shares the ideals of
the republic. I will discuss the first event here and the other two later in the
chapter.

The first event took place upon my arrival in France for graduate studies
in the early 1990s. One of the many problems of linguistic adaptation that I
faced had to do with the research I intended to carry out. It happened many
times that as I employed the phrase *musique populaire* to refer to certain
genres of Brazilian music, my French colleagues would manifest vivid ob-
jection: "But that is not *musique populaire!*," they said. "This is written music,
composer's music, commercial music! Jobim n'est pas de la musique populaire, le *choro* n'est pas de la musique populaire, même pas les disques com-
merciaux de samba ne sont de la musique populaire!" (*Jobim is not popular
music, choro is not popular music, not even commercial samba records are popular
music!*)

This was one of the first practical lessons in ethnology that a research trip made possible to me. Indeed, I soon realized that the term *música popular*, which I had learned early to apply to a range of composers, vocalists, and practices, was not as universal as I naively supposed. Even in societies with significant cultural affinities such as Brazil and France, the ways of delimiting styles of music may have important variations. French *musique populaire* does not correspond to the Brazilian term *música popular*, but rather to what in Brazil we would call *música folclórica*. On the other hand, the French phrase *musique folklorique* is charged with derogatory connotations that, in the Brazilian case, are not present or at least not as strongly.

I was unable to find in Molière's language an exact equivalent to the Brazilian phrase *música popular*. In French one speaks, for example, of *musique de variétés*. This term, however, is also charged with a certain connotation of artistic inferiority. A highly valued author such as Georges Brassens does not usually get cataloged in the variétés, but in the *chanson française* category, which carries some nobility. In Brazil música popular is value neutral. It even tends to be positive, insofar as the musical practices to which the term applies are often considered to be among the main manifestations of national culture. These differences in nomenclature express ways in which the two countries have constructed forms of dealing with their respective musical diversities. Clear as it is that the musics we make and hear are cultural artifacts, it may not be as clear that the categories through which they are lived—the styles in which we delimit musical styles, so to speak—are cultural artifacts as well. How does one go about separating one thing from the other?

It can be seen that phrases such as *música popular* and *música folclórica* do not designate natural and unchanging realities but rather, as anthropologists would say, "native categories" that express how the ones who employ the terms slice up the world of particular musics. This awareness led me to formulate questions regarding the genesis of the category of MPB. The first noteworthy thing is that up to the 1940s the phrase *música popular* was commonly used in Brazil in a sense similar to the one now prevalent in France. The best example of this use is Oneyda Alvarenga's book *Música Popular Brasileira*, published in 1947, which devotes only 20 of its 374 pages to urban music. The association of the "popular" with the predominantly rural in art harks back to Brazil's first folklorists, such as Celso de Magalhães (with his pioneering articles on "Brazilian popular poetry") and Sílvio Romero (with his books on *Contos* [Tales] and *Cantos Populares do Brasil* [Brazilian popular songs]). This association reached Oneyda Alvarenga through her mentor, Mário de Andrade, who appreciated aspects of urban popular music.

Mário de Andrade may be the author of the first Brazilian essay devoted to music on records ("Sung Pronunciation and the Problem of the Brazilian Nasal through Records," written in 1937) in which he praised Moreira da Silva and the Bando da Lua (1991: 109), among others. But there can be no doubt of the predominance of the rural world in his characterization of the popular. Both the investigations he conducted (in his 1927–29 trips) as well as the ones he advised were devoted to traditional northeastern music. If in some cases his research took place in capital cities, it always dealt with cultural manifestations of rural origin. Although Mário also employed the term *folklore* to refer to his favorite subject—and did employ the modifier *popular* at least once to speak of urban music, in the article "Música Popular" about Rio samba (1976: 278–82) he most commonly employed the phrase *música popular* when the theme was rural ([1928] 1972: 153–88), and *popularesco* when it was urban ([1928] 1972: 167; 1976: 321–22, 331, among others). The latter phrase has a strong derogatory charge. Augusto Meyer, in his *Cancioneiro Gaúcho*, gave us a definition of it that does not hide this connotation: "that transition from popular poetry as such to the employment of caricature in its motifs and the clumsy imitation of its language" (1952: 29).

Beginning in the 1930s, however, urban musics disseminated through radio and records became an ever more relevant social fact. It is interesting to note that a new kind of intellectual production about music emerged at the time, carried out by people such as Alexandre Gonçalves Pinto and Francisco Guimarães (known as Vagalume)—authors of the first books devoted to samba and choro—as well as Almirante (singer, composer, radio announcer, researcher, and writer) and Ary Barroso (pianist, composer, radio announcer, and city councilman). They were the first intellectuals of urban popular music in Brazil who synthesized their opinions "organically," that is, without outside influences imposed on them. These are people who would not have called the musical world with which they were involved *popularesco*. On the contrary, they would have preferred to appropriate the modifier *popular* for their own use, thereby embodying, in the musical sphere, another conception of "the popular" as well as of "the Brazilian people." For this conception to materialize, it was not unimportant that the heirs of Sílvio Romero and Mário de Andrade—that is, the folkloric movement developed between 1940 and 1960—accepted the new definition (Vilhena 1995). In fact, at a folklore conference in the 1950s Oneyda Alvarenga proposed the adoption of a split between "folklore" and "popular," following the definition that prevailed in the second half of the twentieth century. Even though she considered "popular music" contaminated with commercialism and cosmopolitanism, and regarded "folkloric music" as the guardian of national character, she attributed to urban and radio music a "thread of conformity with the people's deepest tendencies" (quoted in Almeida 1958: 9–10), which is what finally explains the abandonment of the term *popularesco*. The distinction is thus no longer value laden and accedes to the plane of analytical categories: one of them is rural, anonymous, and nonmediated; the other, urban, authorial, and mediated. This way of conceiving the difference between them has been consecrated. It appears, for example, in the subtitle to the *Enciclopédia da Música Brasileira*, published in 1977: *Erudita, Folclórica, Popular* (the order in which the terms are listed seems to suggest a remnant of the value-laden system).

In the 1950s a journal devoted to music on radio and records was created in Rio de Janeiro named *Revista de Música Popular*. In 1966 José Ramos Tinhorão published a polemical book about the same field with the title *Música Popular: Um Tema em Debate*. In the following year José Eduardo (AKA Zuza) Homem de Mello began to conduct a series of interviews with composers and vocalists that were published in 1976 with the exact same title as Alvarenga's book, *Música Popular Brasileira*. In the thirty years that separate the two books, therefore, the term concluded its transition toward the current meaning. In 1976 it was already sharply opposed to folkloric music in the Brazilian cultural landscape. Just as everyone understood Alvarenga's title in 1946, they also understood Zuza Homem de Mello's in 1976. These two titles, however, referred to rather different things.

Indeed, throughout the 1960s the words Música Popular Brasileira always used together, as if hyphenated, began unequivocally to designate the urban musics disseminated through radio and records. In the framework of the intense ideological debates that characterized Brazilian culture in that period, they would soon serve to delimit a certain field within those musics. This field, though ample enough to contain the samba of a Nelson Cavaquinho (who might be considered close to folklore) and the bossa nova of a Tom Jobim (who might be considered close to erudite music), was sufficiently narrow to exclude recent arrivals such as the electrified music influenced by Anglo-American rock. The expression "Brazilian popular music" played, then, a role of "national defense." In that regard it occupied a position that had belonged to folklore in previous decades as is apparent in Mário de Andrade's influential *Ensaio sobre a Música Brasileira* ([1928] 1972). Toward the late 1960s it actually turned into an acronym, almost a password of cultural-political identification: MPB.

The idea of a "Brazilian popular music" ideologically marked and crystallized in the MPB acronym was a moment in the history of the republic in which the idea of "Brazilian people"—an increasingly urban people—came to the forefront of many debates. In those debates the role played by music was not, by any means, minor. It may be enough to recall the CPC (Centro Popular de Cultura; People's Centers for Culture) of the UNE (União Nacional dos Estudantes; National Student Union), the *Revista Civilização Brasileira*, and above all the *Show Opinião* (Opinion Show) in which Nara Leão, Zé Kéti, and João do Vale performed musically the student-peasant-worker alliance.

It was at that moment that being fond of and recognizing oneself in MPB amounted to believing in a certain conception of the "Brazilian people" and simultaneously, therefore, in a certain conception of republican ideals (much like in previous decades being fond of and recognizing oneself in folklore—even at the cost of the latter's transfiguration, as in Villa-Lobos's music or in Mário de Andrade's preaching—had meant believing in another version of what "the people" was). This link explains, for the most part, the hostile reaction that part of the audience had to Tropicalism at the time. Let us recall Caetano Valoso's sentence, directed at the audience of a 1968 festival while they booed him: "If you are in politics what you are in aesthetics, we are done for!" The distinction was then more artificial than ever. Tropicalism diverged from a certain politico-aesthetic orientation with which, through MPB, the audience identified (Napolitano 2001).

This political and aesthetic knot found in music a privileged means of expression throughout the 1970s, marked by censorship and democratic struggles. The figure of Chico Buarque de Hollanda is paradigmatic here. I stress that the link in question works not only for his political songs. To enjoy listening to Chico Buarque and to be fond of his aesthetic implied the election of a certain universe of values and references that embedded a number of republican conceptions crystallized in MPB, even in the instances where his lyrics were far from politics. I think the same applies to the others, including presumably depoliticized figures such as Tom Jobim or João Gilberto (of whom Veloso affirmed, in a piece written for the show

Totalmente Demais in 1986, that "his art transformed all culture and even the whole life of Brazilians").

But since then, and concomitantly with political opening in the country, the acronym MPB began to be adopted ever more broadly. It was used in circumstances as alien to the democratic struggle as naming a festival of songs sponsored by a multinational and broadcast by the Globo TV network ("MPB-Shell"). Its early, restrictive sense was diluted, allowing the representatives of Brazilian rock in the 1980s—when the genre gained great momentum—to be considered, without a problem, part of "Brazilian popular music." It was also in that decade that I heard from the singer-songwriter Joyce the expression "MPB-chato" (MPB-bore) to designate musicians too attached to nationalist aesthetic paradigms.

Here the second event alluded to at the beginning of this chapter as challenging my previous notions of MPB comes into play. Upon returning to Brazil in the late 1990s, I encountered a new way of regarding MPB, a new meaning attributed to the acronym. It began to be understood also as a market label. In record stores it was possible to find an MPB shelf next to the "brega," "samba," "country," or "axé" sections (Ulhôa 1997: 81). An irresistible parallel in the political field begs inclusion here, and I refer to the political party MDB (Brazilian Democratic Movement). Both the party and the musical acronyms shared an agglutinating character. After the party reform of 1979 the old front gave way to PMDB (Partido do Movimento Democrático Brasileiro; Party of the Brazilian Democratic Movement), which at first even attempted to maintain its character, but soon became one option among many others in a dispersed political market. The same happened to MPB, which since the 1980s has become a sort of PMPB, that is, a kind of post-popular Brazilian music. It is not by chance that toward the end of the twentieth century, the third edition of the *Encyclopedia of Brazilian Music* was dismembered into a series of small volumes, devoted to "samba and choro," "sertaneja music," and so forth.

I believe the strength of the notion of MPB from the 1960s to the 1980s was linked with the confluence of three factors discussed above: it was simultaneously an analytical category (by distinguishing itself from "erudite" and "folkloric" musics), an ideological option, and a profile of consumption. In that period, to the question "What kind of music do you like?" one would answer: "I like MPB," and it would be immediately clear that the person would have, in his/her collection, as was the case with mine, works by people from Tom Jobim to Nelson Cavaquinho, from Roberto Carlos to Gilberto Gil. The latter, in fact, is said to have stated: "There are several ways of doing MPB. I prefer all of them." This was not merely a phrase with an effect. It shows that the acronym was intended to be unifying, and it was indeed able to unify. It was really possible for people such as Gil and his audience to "prefer all of them" without incoherence or artificiality, and thereby create a range of taste that is both diverse and organic.

Beginning in the 1990s, on the contrary, the statement "I like MPB" began only to make sense if interpreted as an act of joining a certain segment of the musical market. For neither the old acronym nor any other term seemed able to unify or synthesize the multiple identities expressed in the Brazilian musics spread by the mass media since then. For example, who would have in their musical collection, except for scholarly or professional reasons, São Paulo rap, Rio *pagode*, Bahian axé, Pernambuco *mangue beat*, and works by Ná Ozzetti? I do not mean to suggest that this list is any more heterogeneous than the one mentioned above, from Nelson Cavaquinho to Roberto Carlos. Maybe it is not, and in any case perceptions of musical homogeneity or heterogeneity, if dependent upon the sounds themselves, depend more on the listener's ear. What I stress is the first group could be felt as the expression of a coherent musical taste, and could thus serve as support for an act of identification, as attested by Gilberto Gil's sentence quoted above. In the second set, however, the same does not apply. Its isolated components are the ones that are serving, and very well at that, social groups of diverse backgrounds to gather and make themselves heard (a good reflection on these new fragmented identities are to be found in Hermano Vianna 1998).

The third event influencing my view of MPB, to which I referred at the beginning, comes into play in this context. In addition to the fragmentation of popular musics, an important and undernoted feature of the Brazilian musical scene since the 1990s was the relativization of the difference between movement members and "folkloric music." This is due, in great part, to people involved in so-called folkloric manifestations taking positions not assigned to them in the traditional dichotomy. In Pernambuco, where this tendency seems to be particularly strong, the first case may have been that of Dona Selma do Coco, a woman who worked as a tapioca maker in Alto da Sé de Olinda, and in her free time sang *coco* songs—coco being a traditional musical-choreographic genre, found all around the northeastern states of Brazil, from Sergipe to Ceará—above all during the *festas juninas*, the June saints' festivals (Andrade 1984; Ayala and Ayala 2000). But in 1996 her remarkable voice was "discovered" by a Europe-based Brazilian musical producer who approached her with the idea of recording a CD. The disc included the coco "A Rolinha," which turned out to be Carnaval's big hit in the neighboring cities of Recife Olinda in 1998 (even as coco was not, in principle, a typical Carnaval genre). Dona Selma later had a disagreement with her producer, but has continued to make CDs and perform, including on international tours.

A similar case is that of Master Manuel Salustiano (1945–2008), Mestre Salu for short. Born in the northeastern Zona da Mata, a region of Pernambuco with recognized folkloric richness, he was raised among sugar-cane manual laborers and in the *maracatu* and *bumba-meu-boi* dramatic dances, and learned how to play the fiddle from him father. As a young man, however, he moved to the metropolitan area, setting up in a suburb of Olinda, where he created his own maracatu collective. Maybe it was the "rediscovery" of the fiddle by artists such as Antônio Nóbrega and "Siba" Veloso (from the band Mestre Ambrósio) that encouraged him also to create, around 1996, a group to perform professional musical shows, which he baptized *O Sonho da Rabeca* (The Fiddle's Dream). Mestre Salu toured nationally and internationally with his group, performing adaptations of traditional musical genres, and also recorded several CDs.

In other states, people whose life stories have a lot in common with those of Salustiano and Selma are obtaining relative success in the same kind of endeavor. This is the case of, for example, Dona Tetê do Cacuriá, in Maranhão; Bule-Bule and their *samba-de-roda* (ring samba), in Bahia; and the *jongo* group known as Serrinha, in Rio de Janeiro. But the most remarkable and certainly the most widely known example of the dissolution of boundaries between "folkloric" and "popular" manifestations is Boi de Parintins, whose *toadas* have been recorded in dozens of CDs and have sold thousands of copies. I would agree with the reader's possible remark that transgressions such as these have always happened in Brazilian music. After all, what is samba of Rio de Janeiro if not the most successful of them all? What about Luiz Gonzaga, even with all his respect for his father Januário's eight-bass accordion? Or Jackson do Pandeiro, with his *coco social* that passed unashamedly from "Carnaval to the ballroom," thereby anticipating today's Salus and Selmas by decades? The novelty in recent years may have been, however, precisely a possible change in the way in which the relation between "Carnaval" and "ballroom" is conceived, leading us to face the question of republican ideals again.

Indeed, the whole of MPB is, in great part, the result of a process of elaboration and assemblage of "folkloric" musical materials and practices (and by that I mean no criticism: on the contrary, much of the marvel here is how it managed to combine these processes with the culture industry's injunctions and resources, with academic musical knowledge, and with the creativity of its artifices). But this great movement of "cultural translation" repressed those materials and practices while simultaneously transforming them. The passage from the sugar-cane fields to the ballroom, at least on the level of dominant representations, erased the former as a sort of perennially agonizing relic, ever dependent on official patronage and devotion by folklorists. Going back to Luiz Gonzaga's example, if the song "Respeita Januário" (Respect Januário) expresses his admiration for his father—a "local" accordion player who never made his own records—it expresses, above all, in great irony, the victory of the son's shining *fole prateado* (silver bellows) over his progenitor's old *oito-baixo* (eight-bass accordion), the latter of which henceforth probably received well-deserved respects in some museum.

It is this set of representations of the relations between different musical contexts in Brazil—of which the idea of MPB cannot be dissociated—that has increasingly come under critical scrutiny by some historical actors who have adopted new practices. These no longer seem to be, if they ever were, very comfortable in the role of relics; in any case, they increasingly look like they wish to alter the rules that have presided over the conditions of mutual transit and visibility (or rather, audition) between Carnaval and ballroom. Listeners of CDs such as those of Selma and Salu come away with the impression that they are commercial CDs untouched by folklorists or anthropologists but with sonorities closer to what is actually heard in popular celebrations than any other commercial record of popular music produced in Brazil before the 1990s.

In sum, the distinction between popular music and folkloric music in Brazil was also linked with the idea that the former was alive while the latter was dead. The integration of folkloric aspects into the modern musical market is only one of the ways in which this conception has been put into question in recent years. The growing interest by anthropologists, musicians, and cultural institutions for these manifestations points in the same direction. As a conclusion, it becomes clear that a redefinition is taking place in the field of musical categories employed in Brazil. I do not venture to predict where this redefinition will take us. But I do note that if the parallels I have drawn here—their latent reductionism notwithstanding—make some sense, asking what is understood by "Brazilian popular music" from now on (or asking even if the phrase will make any sense in the future) also means asking what will be understood by "Brazilian people." This is a question that concerns not only music, but also our trampled ideals of the republic.

::: From Mr. Citizen to Defective Android

Tom Zé and Citizenship in Brazil

Christopher Dunn

The lived experience of "citizenship" and the corollary subject position of "citizen" are uneven and mutable, determined both spatially and temporally. Several chapters of this volume attest to the spatial dimension of citizenship with use of metaphors that connote distance such as "marginality" to describe the position of poor Brazilians living in both rural and urban spaces who are deprived of the rights of citizenship enjoyed by others. The idea of citizenship may also be understood in temporal terms with attention to the vicissitudes of political, social, and cultural contexts. As Teresa Caldeira and James Holston have observed, citizenship is not a fixed and stable set of rules and forms of conduct that proceed in linear fashion toward ideal civility. Instead, the historic process of citizenship is "always becoming and unbecoming, often confusing and unstable" (1999: 717). With this in mind, I would like to focus on one singer-songwriter, Tom Zé, who has been composing, performing, and recording music since the early 1960s. By examining his work diachronically, we gain insight into how ideas of citizenship in Brazil have changed since the period of authoritarian rule to the present.

Tom Zé has described his music as a form of *imprensa cantada* or *jornalismo cantado* (sung journalism) calling attention to its debt to the *cancionistas*, itinerant rural musicians who used the song form as a vehicle for commenting on current events while paying acute attention to changes in spatial and temporal contexts. Traditional cancionistas work with an established song repertoire, introducing variations in lyrics and arrangements depending on the context and immediate situation (Zé, 44). Likewise, many of Tom Zé's compositions are contingent and incomplete, available for topical alterations according to the context. Several of the songs discussed here were written decades ago, but have been revised and resignified to address present concerns. His work is also indebted to classical and avant-garde composition he learned at the University of Bahia in the 1960s before embarking on a career in popular music. In recent years, Tom Zé has theorized this aesthetics of contingency and imperfection by presenting his recordings as mere versions among multiple possibilities. His live shows involve abrupt interruptions to explain the lyrics, make tangential commentary, or address a technical problem with the sound. Much of his music is presented as a work-in-progress, as strategy that, despite its appearance of spontaneity, is conscious and often planned.

Tom Zé's approach to music composition and performance as imprensa cantada informed by avant-gardist experimentation and within the realm of pop music also entails specific ways of addressing politics, society, and artistic production in Brazil. It is possible to trace the contested idea of citizenship in his music, from the earliest days of military rule in the mid-1960s to the present context of Brazil's uneven or "disjunctive" democracy (Caldeira and Holston 1999: 716–17).

::: Consumers and Citizens in the Tropicalist City

The central theme of Tom Zé's first LP (1968) may be found on the back of the album cover in at the beginning of a manifesto-like statement: "We are an unhappy people, bombarded by happiness." Despite Brazil's international reputation for carnivalesque exuberance and its modern self-fashioning as a place of easygoing pleasure, Tom Zé's statement may be located squarely within a tradition of melancholic critique of national dilemmas (Scliar 2003: 170–71). With its direct, matter-of-fact diction, his statement echoes the famous opening line of *Retrato do Brasil* (1928), Paulo Prado's canonical treatise on national character: "In a radiant land lives a sad people." Prado's statement is about the melancholic disposition, regarded as both congenital and historically determined, of "three sad races" (the Portuguese, the Indian, and the African) that live in a sunny, tropical land. Tom Zé's opening salvo is about the false promises of media-driven consumption in a land of social inequality and frustrated desire: "Today, the smile is industrialized, sought after, photographed, expensive (sometimes), and marketable. It sells toothpaste, travel tickets, cold remedies, diapers, etc. And since reality has always been confused with gestures, television proves daily that nobody can be unhappy" ([1928] 1997: 1).

In the context of cultural politics during military rule in the 1960s, Tom Zé's position was shared by many other prominent left-wing artists of the time who were wary of mass culture (Ricardo 1991: 60–64; Ridenti 2000:

323–34). Yet Tom Zé was also a key figure in Tropicália, a movement that embraced the culture industry, pop music, and mass-mediated youth styles. The urban, industrial context of São Paulo—then supplanting Rio as the dominant center of mass entertainment, advertising, and cultural production—was decisive for the Tropicalist project. Tom Zé's first hit, "São São Paulo" received first prize at the 1968 Brazilian Song Festival of TV Record, providing him with national media exposure. The song was endearing to the middle-class *paulista* audience in the way that it satirized the city's hurried, work-obsessed environment from an outsider's perspective:

São oito milhões de habitantes	There are 8 million inhabitants
De todo canto e nação	From all places and nations
Que se agridem cortesmente	Who courteously trample each other
Correndo a todo vapor	Running at full steam

We have here a snapshot of São Paulo as a global city with inhabitants from "all places and nations" who experience citizenship or belonging in terms of a formalized civility that masks hostility related to competition in a large modern city.

Much of his music from that period was influenced by pop music driven by guitar and electric organ of the Jovem Guarda, the Brazilian version of post-Beatles rock, known as *iê-iê-iê*, which dominated the airwaves at that time. At the same time, Tom Zé was also informed by the musical avant-garde, having received training in experimental music at the School of Music at the University of Bahia under the direction of the Swiss composer Ernst Widmer between 1962 and 1967 before moving to São Paulo. In Salvador he had also worked with the Swiss composer and luthier, Walter Smetak, who was engaged in microtonal experiments with invented instruments made from local materials. After moving to São Paulo, he worked with several composer-arrangers connected to the avant-gardist Música Nova group of São Paulo, most notably Damiano Cozzella.[1] Unlike his Bahian colleagues— Caetano Veloso, Gilberto Gil, and Gal Costa—his music evidenced little affinity to bossa nova, the remarkable innovation within the samba tradition developed by singer-guitarist João Gilberto and the composer-pianist Antonio Carlos Jobim in the late 1950s. In fact, Tom Zé has described his particular musical approach as a compensatory solution to his inability to master bossa nova, which so influenced the generation of artists that came of age in the 1960s under the banner of MPB—Música Popular Brasileira (Pinto, 1990: 5). By 1968, when the Tropicália movement was in full swing, his music was a sui generis mixture, or juxtaposition, of Brazilian iê-iê-iê, northeastern satiric ballads, and contemporary avant-garde music. At the level of composition and arrangement, his music of this time was based on a dual tension between urban modernity and northeastern tradition and between pop appeal and formal experimentation.

Tom Zé was both fascinated and repelled by the hypercommercial, urban-industrial context of São Paulo when he relocated there in 1967 (Dunn 2001: 105–8). "Parque Industrial" (Industrial Park), a song from his first album, places advertisement, industry, and consumption at the heart of civic life under authoritarian rule:

"Retocai o céu de anil	Touch up the blue sky
bandeirolas no cordão	streamers on a string
grande festa em toda a nação	a great national festival
despertai com orações	rise and hear the orations
o avanço industrial	industrial progress
vem trazer nossa redenção.	has brought our redemption.

The imperative *vós* verbs, the reference to patriotic phrases, and the staging of collective celebration are set to the music of a military band, suggesting a ritual of civic nationalism. In "Parque Industrial" national development and citizenship are related directly to consumption, yet with ironic distance. A first-person voice narrates the process of media interpellation and its intended effect:

Tem garota-propaganda	There are publicity girls
aeromoça e ternura no cartaz	flight attendants and tenderness in the billboards
basta olhar na parede	merely by looking at the wall
minha alegria num instante se refaz	my happiness instantly returns.

The satire is implicit, bringing us back to his wry observation from the album cover that Brazilians are "bombarded by happiness" amidst a context of privation for the great majority. After all, how many Brazilians in 1968 could afford a ticket to fly on an airplane and be served tenderly by flight attendants?

Néstor García Canclini has argued that in complex urban societies, citizenship is frequently expressed through private consumption rather than explicit appeals to democratic values and practices (2001: 5). In cities with profound social inequalities, such as São Paulo, the inability to consume would therefore limit the exercise of full citizenship for large numbers of people. Tom Zé was acutely sensitive to the class implications of consumer society, since vast segments of the population were either excluded from it or able to participate in it partially or sporadically. In "Curso Intensivo de Boas Maneiras" (Intensive Course in Good Manners), his satire is more explicit and brutal as he invokes a popular radio program from late 1960s São Paulo about "good manners" that instructed its listeners how to behave and present themselves: "Primeira lição: deixar de ser pobre / Que é muito feio" (First lesson: stop being poor / because it's quite unseemly).

In the early 1970s Tom Zé's work developed in two, yet frequently interconnected directions as he attempted to maintain a presence in the market with radio-friendly pop songs, while also experimenting with new forms of musical and poetic expression. His second LP featured Tom Zé's first song to explicitly invoke the figure of the "citizen" in contemporary Brazilian society. In this song citizenship is related directly to notions of public presentation and satirized as an affect of bourgeois style, referring with obvious irony to a male citizen who would dare venture out into the street without a wearing a necktie:

Um cidadão sem a gravata	A citizen without a tie
é a pior degradação	is the worst disgrace
é uma coroa de lata	is a tin can crown
é um grande palavrão	is a big curse word
é uma dama sem pudor	is a lady with no shame
é stripitise moral	is moral striptease
é falta de documento	is a lack of personal I.D.
é como sopa sem sal	is like soup without salt

In this satire, not wearing a tie is equated with all manner of social transgression, from the verbal-performative (using vulgar language), to the sexual (a "shameless" woman), and even the legal (not carrying proper identification, a potentially serious transgression during the dictatorship). The necktie functions as a metonym for the proper, law-abiding citizen and as a metaphor for social and political repression, as suggested in the refrain: "The tie has bound me / the tie has strangled me / amen." The "citizen" in this song appears as a figure complicit with conservative tradition and authoritarian rule, a critique Tom Zé would further develop in subsequent recordings.

::: Senhor Cidadão: Satirizing the Citizen

Tom Zé's ironic depiction of the Brazilian "citizen" related more generally to a critique of citizenship by left-wing artists and intellectuals. Brazilian society maintained an ambivalent, if not contradictory, relationship with liberal conceptions of citizenship, typically defined in terms of three types of rights—civil (equality before the law; fundamental liberties pertaining to speech, thought, faith, property ownership), political (participation in the political process through voting, governing, or dissent), and finally social (economic welfare, access to education, health care, and so on).

For much of Brazilian history, citizenship rights were not universally applied, nor did they achieve any measure of consistency or durability over time. Limited social rights would later be introduced in the 1930s during the rule of the populist-authoritarian Getúlio Vargas, but basic political rights weren't established until 1945 and then were abruptly curtailed in 1964 when the military took power. Citizenship was either conceived as an exclusive privilege or a limited right used for purposes of social control to maintain order and stave off more profound transformations in society. Marilena Chaui has argued that Brazil is "a society that came to know citizenship through a new type: the *senhor-cidadão*, who reserves citizenship as a class privilege, making of it a regulated and periodic concession to other social classes and that can be taken away when the dominant class decides (as during dictatorships)" (1986: 54). Even during periods of formal democracy, voting rights were restricted at different times by requirements pertaining to gender, property ownership, and literacy. After 1964, political rights were severely curtailed, and after the establishment of the Fifth Institutional Act in 1968 the most basic civil rights, such as habeas corpus, were suspended. The regime's economic program of conservative modernization—which emphasized the rapid development of infrastructure, communications, and industry—depended on the suppression of political and civil rights. In this context, the "citizen" was associated with class privilege, bourgeois propriety, and social control.

Tom Zé recorded the song "Senhor Cidadão" in 1972, nearly fifteen years before Chaui would apply the term to the development of citizenship in Brazil. A somber anthem, the song is about the petty existence of a model citizen in a competitive capitalist society. The lyrics of Tom Zé's song are structured as an incisive inquiry directed at an anonymous male citizen engaged in a daily struggle to succeed and prosper in an urban capitalist environment, inevitably at the expense of others. In this struggle, the senhor cidadão may achieve wealth and power, but ultimately leads a "bitter life" exploiting others, while the accuser, evidently representing the narrative voice of Tom Zé himself, claims to live a contented life without the burden of vicious competition. The refrain introduces a curious abstraction that further emphasizes the burdensome weight of social forces motivating the citizen that can be reduced simply to fear:

Oh senhor cidadão,	Oh Mr. Citizen
eu quero saber, eu quero saber	I want to know, I want to know
com quantos quilos de medo,	with how many kilos of fear
com quantos quilos de medo	with how many kilos of fear
se faz uma tradição?	does one make a tradition?

The refrain "Com quantos kilos de medo se faz uma tradição?" was used as the name of a live musical event for the promotion of the album. A poster produced for the show featured Tom Zé's band huddled around a weight scale. One of the musicians is wearing a necktie (again, that symbol of the proper citizen) that rests on the weight scale as if to suggest the burden of keeping up appearances. The lyrics explicitly associate citizenship in Brazil with class privilege, exploitation, social alienation, and fear.

Tom Zé further radicalized his poetic and musical experiments on his 1973 recording *Todos os Olhos* (All of the Eyes), an album that gained retrospective fame some twenty year later when it was revealed that the album cover featured a close-up photo shot in soft focus of a green marble resting over a pink anus, producing an uncanny resemblance to a floating eyeball (Zé, 230). The visual gesture outwitted with humor and guile the government censors during the most repressive phase of military rule in Brazil while also alluding to the regime of surveillance that monitored the activity of political dissidents and left-wing artists. *Todos os Olhos* featured the song "Dodó e Zezé," his first experiment with a dialogic lyric structure invoking a conversation between two friends, one playing the role of the earnest neophyte and the other a wise, if somewhat inscrutable, critic of modern society. As in "A Gravata" and "Senhor Cidadão," the citizen invoked here is the integrated subject who is passively complicit with a conservative and repressive society. The term *marginal* typically refers to someone who lives "on the margins" or outside of the law, but with the rise of the counterculture in the late sixties and early seventies could also be used to describe middle-class dropouts and other people leading "alternative" lifestyles. As the Dodó suggests in his question, the *marginal* is imagined to be the opposite of the *cidadão*:

Por que é que a gente tem que ser marginal ou cidadão?	Why is it that we either have to be outcasts or citizens?
diga, Zezé.	tell me, Zezé.
É pra ter a ilusão de que pode pode escolher,	So that we have the illusion that we can choose,
viu, Dodó?	understand Dodó?

In a context in which the rule of law is arbitrary and compromised, the song also suggests that citizens are routinely mistaken for and treated like criminals. In all of these songs from the early 1970s, the figure of the "citizen" is integrated into the conservative order in contrast to those who are excluded or marginalized.

Within this same logic, it is possible to show the inverse by portraying the citizen as an integrated subject who is complicit with the social order, but suffers for it. Writing around the same time as Chaui, the anthropologist Roberto DaMatta argues that "citizenship" in Brazil meant subjection to the impersonal laws of the state and its repressive social and coercive forces. Although they assign different values to the concept of citizenship, both arguments are compatible in that both refer to a hierarchical society in which principles of equality before the law and access to resources are applied differently according to personal status. DaMatta's argument hinges on the notion that the citizen is essentially perceived and treated as an anonymous "individual" in the classic liberal sense of the term, which is a severe disadvantage in a "relational society" such as Brazil, which privileges the "person" with a name and a face who can successfully exploit ties of kinship and friendship. Abstract principles and laws that would in theory protect individuals (or citizens) in Brazil are often used to coerce, exclude, and otherwise disfavor them. DaMatta argues that "in the Brazilian case, the citizen is typically subjected to impersonal (and universal) laws, as well as to the brutal force of the police, which function to systematically and mercilessly differentiate and exploit him, making him a *debased equal* in a clear perversion of liberal political ideals" (1997: 79). In situations of routine interaction and negotiation in the public sphere, it is always preferable to be treated as a person rather than as an individual, which for DaMatta is synonymous with a citizen (87).

This is precisely the type of citizen portrayed in Tom Zé's ballad "Identificação" (Identification), which refers to the state-issued documents that define a subject's legal and professional identities. The bureaucratic logic of measurement and statistics extends further, taking account of the subject's biological functions, psychological symptoms, affective needs, and consumer-driven desires—"the state control of the biological" (Foucault 2003: 240). The totality of human existence is tallied up in numbers, for the purposes of bureaucratic control, consumer analysis, and actuarial prediction. "Identificação" presents a view of what Foucault called "bio-power"—that which "brought life and its mechanisms into the realm of explicit calculations and made knowledge-power an agent of transformation of human life" (Foucault 1990: 143). The song was written in the waning years of military rule and appeared on his 1984 album *Nave Maria*. It was then rearranged in the 1990s and featured on *Imprensa Cantada* from 2003. Much of the humor of the song derives from the positioning of Tom Zé himself as a downtrodden citizen identified and statistically analyzed in the song. Whereas in "Senhor Cidadão," the composer is positioned as the countercultural outsider and social critic, in "Identificação" he is cast in the role of the beleaguered yet conscientious middle-class citizen who is inexorably worn down to death.

The first part provides a bureaucratic montage of the individual (in DaMatta's sense) with the various numbers that identify him as a citizen, taxpayer, professional, and receiver of services provided by the state. It is worth remembering José Murilo de Carvalho's observation that in Brazil, social rights provided by the state (such as social security, health, benefits) have typically expanded during periods when civil and political rights were suppressed (2001: 192–93). The second part identifies him as a person with specific needs, desires, shortcomings, and pathologies, largely determined by the ubiquitous presence of mass culture that produces a kind of alienation from authentic emotions in everyday life. Finally, the citizen is described in terms of average life expectancy in Brazil at that time—six hundred thousand hours, or about 68.5 years:

Tempo de vida previsto para o cidadão	Life expectancy for the citizen
600 mil horas de vida, de vida, de vida	600 thousand hours of life, life, life
Abatimento pelo consumo de	Reduction due to the consumption of

alimentos envenenados	poisoned food
Refrigerantes, remédios e enlatados,	Soft drinks, medicines, and canned goods,
1125 horas	1125 hours
Abatimento pelo desgosto que se padece	Reduction due to the unpleasantness of waiting
Naquela fila do INPS, 1125 horas	In that line at INPS,[2] 1125 hours
Abatimento por ficar só no desejo	Reduction due to frustrated desire
Daquela mulher bonita que aparece na propaganda de cigarro, 1125 horas	For that pretty woman in the cigarette advertisement, 1125 hours
Pelo medo de doenças incuráveis	Due to fear of incurable disease
Como cólera, câncer e meningite, ê ê ê	Like cholera, cancer, and meningitis
1125 horas	1125 hours
Abate aqui, abate ali	Reduction here, reduction there
Abate isto, abate aquilo	Reduction for this, reduction for that
E jaz pela cidade	And he lies throughout the city
Um zumbi sem sepultura	A zombie without a grave
Classificado, numerado	Classified, enumerated
É o cidadão bem-comportado	The well-behaved citizen

The humor of the song lies in how the life expectancy of a Brazilian citizen, in this case Tom Zé himself, is reduced in increments of 1,125 hours by unhealthy consumer products, unattainable media-driven desires, and daily frustrations in an inefficient bureaucratic state. In "Identificação" the figure of the citizen is no longer associated with privilege and exclusionary right, but fated instead to anonymity and inevitable death, the only release from the biopolitical force field (Foucault 1990: 138; 2003: 248). He is not victimized by the repressive forces of the military regime, then in its last throws, but rather by the incessant exposure to the regulatory powers of a modern state apparatus and an industrialized consumer society. The "well-behaved citizen" is ultimately reduced to a "zombie without a grave" left to wander through the city.

::: The Garden of Politics

The late 1970s witnessed the reemergence of civil society revolving around oppositional political journalism, renewed labor militancy that led to the founding of the PT (Partido dos Trabalhadores; Workers' Party), and new social movements connected to black consciousness, feminism, gay pride, and community activism that demanded a greater role in the political process. In August 1979, political amnesty was granted to political exiles who began to return to Brazil within the context of a gradual and negotiated "opening" of the political and cultural realms. The new political conditions associated with the beginning of a redemocratization process allowed for more open forms of protest against military rule. At the same time, redemocratization created the context for debate and self-critique within the Left itself, as formerly silenced or marginalized groups asserted political and social rights. Under the leadership of Luiz Inácio Lula da Silva, the PT had begun to consolidate a position of power, especially among the working class of São Paulo. An incipient discourse of popular citizenship began to take form.

A relatively obscure live recording of one of Tom Zé's performances at the club Lira Paulistana reveals a shift toward a new discourse on citizenship. Recorded in 1985, it was only released in 1998 under the title *No Jardim da Política* (In the garden of politics), which alludes to a space for diverse flora and fauna, a metaphor for a flourishing civil society on the eve of formal redemocratization. The *abertura* (political opening) occasioned the revival of debates within the Left and, more broadly, among pro-democracy forces in general about the role of middle-class artists, intellectuals, and professionals in mobilizing society. Tom Zé examines the problems of representation in "Classe Operária" (Working Class), a ballad sung in duet with Charles Furlan. Constructed as a critique of the left, Tom Zé refers to himself in the third person as a political avant-gardist who is endowed with the right of representation for the mass of politically naive workers. With obvious hyperbole and ironic paternalism, it is metasong that narrates the actual performance of the "engagé singer Tom Zé," who enters the stage singing about the needs of the working class:

Sobe no palco o cantor engajado Tom Zé,	The engagé singer Tom Zé comes on stage
que vai defender a classe operária,	to defend the interests of the working class
salvar a classe operária e cantar	save the working class and sing
o que é bom para a classe operária	about what is good for the working class
Nenhum operário foi consultado	No workers were consulted
não há nenhum operário no palco	there are no workers on the stage
talvez nem mesmo na platéia,	perhaps not even in the audience,

| mas Tom Zé sabe o que é bom para os operários. | but Tom Zé knows what is right for the workers. |
| Os operários que se calem, que procurem seu lugar, com sua ignorância, porque Tom Zé e seus amigos estão falando do dia que virá e na felicidade dos operários. | The workers should just shut up, stay in their place in total ignorance, because Tom Zé and his friends are talking about the coming day and the happiness of the workers. |

In raising the critique of left-wing paternalism, he implies a parallel between those who exploit and suppress the workers and those who would defend and speak on their behalf. The audience, for example, would have likely understood the phrase "dia que virá" (the coming day) as a reference to redemptive protest songs from the 1960s.[3] Judging from the slightly uncomfortable laughs he elicits throughout the song, his wry observations about speaking for the working class seem to have hit their intended mark. As a song about citizenship and politics, "Classe Operária" functions negatively as ironic critique, but as satire it doesn't provide any possible response to the impasse of representation in class society.

In another song from *No Jardim da Política*, "Desafio do Bóia-Fria" (The Peasant's Challenge), Tom Zé proposes a dialogic model of critique in which a *bóia-fria*, or landless peasant, speaks back to an abusive landowner who opposes any change in the status quo. The dialogic model is proper to the actual song form he employs, the *desafio* (challenge), a Brazilian song tradition popular in northeastern Brazil that involves dueling guitarist-vocalists who compete to outwit the other while offering running commentary on society, politics, and everyday life. Challenge singing was brought to Brazil by Portuguese colonizers, but most likely originated in dueling song traditions of North and West Africa (Fryer 2000: 2–3). The dialogic song form itself offers a partial solution to the impasse of representation satirized in "Classe Operária" as the artist articulates the positions of the sugar-cane cutter and his landowner boss. The performance becomes less about speaking for the subaltern than about exploring the terms of social conflict in rural Brazil.

Tom Zé's "Desafio do Bóia-Fria" calls attention to a more insidious form of bio-power and its effect on notions of citizenship: the boss justifies his opposition to civil rights based on the racial indeterminacy and otherness of the peasant. In stating his opposition to worker's rights in racial terms, the

Tom Zé performs "Classe Operária" with megaphone, São Paulo, 2009 (Christopher Dunn). Christopher Dunn, "Tom Zé and the Performance of Citizenship in Brazil," *Popular Music* 28.2 (2009): 217–37. © Cambridge University Press. Reproduced with permission.

boss echoes a long discursive and ideological tradition that figures the rural poor as subhuman degenerates.

Patrão:	Boss:
Meus senhores, vou lhes apresentar	Gentlemen, I present to you
uma gente não sei de que lugar,	a people from who knows where
uma coisa que imita a raça humana:	a thing that imitates the human race
eis aqui o trabalhador da cana.	behold the sugar-cane worker
Pois agora eles só querem falar	Now they want to talk about
em direitos e leis a registrar,	rights and laws to pass,
imagine a confusão que dá!	imagine what a mess that will make!
Eu explico pra eles a tarde inteira	All day long I try to explain to them
esse tal de registro na carteira	that this employment registry
atrapalha, é burrice, é besteira.	gets in the way, it's hogwash.

In response the sugar-cane worker invokes the language of legal rights, introducing a discourse of social citizenship that would support the right to register officially as a laborer to receive protection and benefits. The boss wishes to preserve an informal economy of exchange based on clientelist relations in which the sugar-cane worker would depend on his goodwill and favor. The worker seeks to formalize a labor contract recognized by the state in order to guarantee labor rights before the law, proclaiming that his "true cause" will be to secure a state-issued card as a registered employee.

Bóia-Fria:	Peasant:
Mas o traquejo da lei e do direito	This business of laws and rights
não degrada quem dele se apetece	doesn't degrade those who use them
pois enquanto se nutre de respeito	when nourished with respect
é o trabalhador que se enobrece.	the worker is made noble
Além disso quem chega-se à virtude	Besides this, those who arrive at virtue
e da lei se aproxima e se convém	and get acquainted with the law
tá mostrando ao patrão solicitude	are showing the boss respect
por querer o que dele advém.	by desiring that which comes from him.
Desse modo o registro na carteira	In this way the labor registry
será nossa causa verdadeira.	will be our real cause to defend.

In contrast to "Identificação," which portrays the bureaucratic state as inefficient and alienating, "Desafio" suggests that the state may serve as a guarantor of civil rights (access to legal protection) in the face of traditional forms of exploitation. "Desafio do Bóia-Fria" is a song about the struggle for formal civil and social rights in a context in which informality, personalism, and authoritarianism define the relationship between capital and labor, or between the boss and his worker. "Identificação" and "Desafio do Bóia-Fria," which were both composed and recorded in the early 1980s, may be understood as companion pieces that suggest Tom Zé's ambivalence in relationship to the idea of citizenship in the waning years of military rule. If, on the one hand, the modern state functions to discipline and control its citizens, while often serving them poorly, it can on the other hand provide a formal structure for social and civil rights that even the most disenfranchised may use to their own advantage.

The struggle for formal social citizenship is dramatized more poignantly in "Menina Jesus," a ballad from his 1978 album *Correio da Estação do Brás*, which is largely dedicated to the experience of northeastern migrants in São Paulo. The song is narrated from the perspective of a young man from the rural northeast who dreams of finding a decent job in the city and acquiring modern accouterments (a portable radio, a wristwatch, and sunglasses) to show off when he returns to his hometown on vacation. In addition to consumer items, he seeks a place in the formal economy, which will accord him rights and responsibilities of citizenship, while providing for a more "civilized" life:

Botar filho no colégio	Send the kid to school
dar picolé na merenda,	provide popsicles for snacks,
viver bem civilizado,	have a civilized life,
pagar imposto de renda	pay income tax
ser eleitor registrado	be a registered voter
ter geladeira e TV	get a fridge and TV
carteira de ministério	get official ID
ter CIC, ter RG.	get CIC, get RG.[4]

The rhetorical power of the song lies in how it juxtaposes the desire for modern consumption with the formal requirements of citizenship, including aspects sometimes considered onerous, like paying taxes and acquiring work papers. All of this is contrasted to the miserable informal economy of the rural northeast, where his only work opportunity is to plant beans. Citizenship becomes an object of desire associated closely with the power to consume, but also contingent upon securing a place within the formal urban economy. The song ends, however, with an image of despair and broken dreams as the migrant finds himself among a sea of cars, presumably selling cheap goods to motorists stuck in traffic.

Eu fico aqui carregando	I'm still here carrying
o peso da minha cruz	the weight of my cross
no meio dos automóveis, mas	in the middle of cars, but
Vai, viaja, foge daqui	Go away, hit the road, flee from here
que a felicidade vai	happiness is going
atacar pela televisão	to attack on TV

Returning to the critique developed on his first album, he suggests that happiness for the excluded is an illusion promoted by mass media, but nearly impossible to attain. The ideal of becoming a "consumer citizen" is never fully realized, leading to urban marginality and frustration in the face of false promises of happiness.

::: Defective Androids, Biopolitics, and Citizenship

The two decades following the restoration of a formal democracy in 1985 witnessed a dramatic expansion of civil, social, and political rights in Brazil. The so-called Citizen's Constitution of 1988 is widely considered to be among the most progressive in the world, enshrining as law various mechanisms for ensuring universal suffrage, protecting racial and ethnic minorities, promoting gender equality, and alleviating poverty. A wide range of social movements and nongovernmental organizations, both national and international, maintain an active presence throughout rural and urban Brazil. Since 1985, Brazilians have gone to the polls multiple times for national presidential elections, which are nearly universally accepted as fair and legitimate. In 2002 and then again in 2006, Brazilians elected Lula, the former union leader and founder of the PT, which seemed to indicate a significant national commitment to progressive social change, albeit within a reformist, gradualist paradigm. Despite these positive developments in electoral democracy with attendant social advances, fundamental civil rights are regularly abused with impunity by the state.

Brazil remains one of the most unequal class societies in the world with high indices of rural and urban poverty. Class status is also closely related to other factors such as race, as the poorest Brazilians also tend to have darker skin. In urban areas, Brazilians of African descent are particularly disadvantaged with regard to educational opportunities, employment, income, health, and just about any other index for measuring quality of life. They are also more exposed to official and extraofficial violence associated primarily with the escalation of drug trafficking in the last two decades and the formation of large and well-armed criminal organizations that defy official authorities in major urban areas. Globally integrated and market-oriented economic policies have expanded opportunities for some, but have also exacerbated social inequalities and degraded living conditions for many.

Tom Zé experienced a period of creative and professional revival within this post-dictatorial context and following the international success of the compilation *The Best of Tom Zé* (1990) and a follow-up collection of new material *The Hips of Tradition* (1992), both released by the New York–based label Luaka Bop under the creative direction of David Byrne. The albums *Com Defeito de Fabricação* (1998) and *Jogos de Armar* (2000) were based on what the artist called the *estética do arrastão* (dragnet aesthetics). The organizing metaphor of the *arrastão*, traditionally used to refer to the dragnet used by fishermen, was resignified in the early 1990s after a series of coordinated disturbances that caused panic and confusion, providing the opportunity for petty thievery on the beaches of Rio de Janeiro. Tom Zé appropriated the arrastão metaphor to articulate a cultural strategy that involves what he called "plágio-combinations."

In his critique of global capitalism, Tom Zé proposes the figure of the android, an emblematic figure of a kind of dystopian bio-power in which global capital exercises total disciplinary and regulatory control over the citizens of a weak peripheral state. Third World androids exist only to supply cheap labor for developed economies of the First World: "The third world has a huge and rapidly increasing population. These people have been converted into a kind of 'android' almost always illiterate," he writes in the liner notes. In Tom Zé's formulation, these androids are born with *defeitos de fabricação* (factory defects) that allow for some measure of agency and resistance (Dunn 2001: 201; Rollefson 2007: 311). These defects including thinking, dreaming, and dancing, which makes them less pliant, even "dangerous," to transnational capital interests.

The key conceptual song of the album, "Esteticar," is described as an arrastão of the rural *baião*, a traditional accordion-based dance music from northeast Brazil that was popularized in Rio de Janeiro and São Paulo by poor, mixed-race migrants who make up a large percentage of the urban labor force—the "androids" of globalization.

Pensa que eu sou um andróide candango doido	You think I'm a mad android *candango*
Algum mamulengo molenga mongo	Some mongoloid mongrel monkey
Mero mameluco da cuca lelé	A mere *mameluco* with half wit
Trapo de tripa da tribo dos pele-e-osso	A tattered member of the skin and bones tribe
Fiapo de carne farrapo grosso	Strands of meat-thick rag
Da trupe da reles e rala ralé	One of the ragged, shabby mob
Penso dispenso a mula da sua ótica	I reject your mule-like optics
Ora vá me lamber tradução inter-semiótica	Come lick me inter-semiotic translation
Se segura milord aí que o mulato baião	Hold on milord 'cause the *mulato baião*
Smoka-se todo na estética do arrastão	Tuxedo-izes itself in the aesthetics of *arrastão*

Much in the same way that "Desafio do Bóia-Fria" enacts a dispute between a rural peasant and his authoritarian and racist boss, "Esteticar" is expressed from the point of view of a northeasterner responding to a middle-class *paulistano* who harbors prejudices against poor migrants. Instead of portraying them as passive victims of neoliberal globalization, Tom Zé represents the northeastern migrant as savvy in his defiant stance toward social and racial discrimination. With absurd humor and erudition, the refrain describes the basic operation of arrastão aesthetics as a moment of "inter-semiotic translation" between several cultural realms. It is the moment when the mulato baião dresses up in a tuxedo.

The album also addresses the meaning of citizenship from the perspective of the upper classes in São Paulo, who have increasingly retreated behind what Teresa Caldeira has called "city of walls" for fear of violent crime. Spatial segregation and social homogeneity provide some level of security for affluent people, but also cut them off from the rest of society. His song "Tangolomango," from *Com Defeito de Fabricação*, offers a perspective on the effect of fear on the wealthy:

Rico hoje, coitado,	Nowadays the rich man, poor soul
É preso, todo cercado	Is imprisoned, totally surrounded,

| Arrodeado de grades | All fenced in |
| Porteiro, guarda e alarme | Doormen, guards, and alarms |

This "new culture of fear" is not a response to political repression, but rather has emerged in the context of increasing urban violence and police brutality coupled with the privatization of security and justice (Caldeira and Holston 1999: 715).

Tom Zé's recording *Jogos de Armar* may be read as a companion to *Com Defeito de Fabricação* and the most complete musical expression of arrastão aesthetics. It is oriented toward social critique, protesting social inequality, political corruption, sexual exploitation of minors, and what he calls "globarbarization." The album was conceived as a provisional version, providing material for others to cite or "plagiarize." The original Brazilian recording on the Trama label came with an auxiliary CD containing the rhythmic, melodic, and harmonic "cells" of each song to facilitate new combinations and compositions. Some of these sounds were produced by a series of invented electro-acoustic instruments that Tom Zé had originally built in 1978 and rebuilt in the late 1990s for this recording. The project explicitly encourages musical citation and intertextuality, providing a model for more dialogic, participatory forms of cultural production, inspired by hip-hop sampling techniques. Tom Zé has expressed with increased frequency his admiration for hip-hop and funk cultures of the urban peripheries, which he regards as the vanguard of musical invention in Brazil today.

On *Jogos de Armar* Tom Zé performs multiple arrastões that resignify his own compositions, mostly overlooked songs of his repertoire from the 1970s and 1980s. The most remarkable instance of what we might call an *auto-arrastão* is his revision of "Desafio do Bóia-Fria." In the updated version, renamed "Desafio," the dispute is no longer between rural landowner and peasant, but rather between the *doutor*, or privileged "expert," and the *homem*, or "common man" with limited social and civil rights:

Doutor:	Expert:
Meus senhores, vou lhes apresentar	Gentlemen, let me introduce to you
A figura do homem popular,	An example of the common man
Esse tipo idiota e muquirana	This guy, idiotic, and base
É um bicho que imita a raça humana.	Is a beast that imitates the human race
O homem:	The common man:
O doutor exagera e desatina	The expert is crazy and mean

Tom Zé, Teatro FECAP, São Paulo, 2009 (Christopher Dunn).

Pois quando o pobre tem no seu repasto	When the poor child eats and grows
O direito a escola e proteína	With the right to school and protein
O seu cérebro cresce qual um astro	Their brains expand just like a star
E começa a nascer pra todo lado	And all around are born
Jesus Cristo e muito Fidel Castro	Jesus Christs and lots of Fidel Castros

In "Desafio," the common man appropriates the expert's discourse, but changes its terms: social inferiority has nothing to do with "race"; rather, it relates to the lack of education and poor nutrition.[5] Tom Zé focuses particularly on the access to protein as a key determinant of cerebral growth, creativity, and political action, suggesting a direct correlation between access to nutrition and education and the biopolitical expansion of revolutionary minds and bodies (Jesus Christs and Fidel Castros) that would transform the Brazilian hinterlands.

In rewriting "Desafio," Tom Zé also adds a refrain, clearly indebted to the verbal experimentations of concrete poetry that introduces an Afro-diasporic dimension to the song:

Africará mingüê e favelará	Africa waning slums arise
Mérica de verme que deusará	America infested will deify
Iocuné Tatuapé Irará	Iocuné Tatuapé Irará

The stanza introduces suggestive neologisms based on the transformation of substantives into verbs (e.g., "favelará") and makes references to several indigenous place names in Brazil including his hometown, Irará. The refrain refers to the forced relocation of Africans to the Americas, leading eventually to the expansion of poor, high-density urban communities, such as the favelas. The second line is particularly striking in its reference to the Americas as the site of misery, suggested by the presence of "vermin," but also of new forms of transcendence, implied in the neologism *deusará*. The neologism echoes the popular expression "deus dará" (God will provide), while negating its implicit fatalism.

In 2000, the same year he released *Jogos de Armar*, Tom Zé received the Citizen-Artist Award from the city of São Paulo for his musical, poetic, and performative work to promote an ethical critique and debate in Brazilian society. The award was a measure of his critical acclaim and to some extent popular success as an artist, but also of the shifting semantic terrain of citizenship in Brazilian society. By that time, various ideas of citizenship had meaning and import that were either suppressed or conceptually unavailable when he had begun his professional career in the mid-1960s. Through his creative work Tom Zé has reflected on what José Murilo de Carvalho has called the "long road of citizenship in Brazil," evident in his lyrics, but also in the formal aspects of his music, which convey an aesthetics of contingency and incompleteness. He has theorized citizenship in progressive and regressive (or conservative) dimensions in relation to national identity, community formation, consumption, mass culture, bourgeois privilege, state-sanctioned control, class consciousness, insurgent biopolitics, antiracist critique, and neoliberal globalization. Like an urban *cancionista*, his musical and poetic ideas take the form of *imprensa cantada*, in the familiar language of everyday life, with it the force of sudden and unsettling revelation.

DISCOGRAPHY

Tom Zé. *The Best of Tom Zé: Massive Hits.* Luaka Bop and Warner Bros. 26396, 1990.
———. *Fabrication Defect: Com Defeito de Fabricação.* Luaka Bop / Warner Bros. 946953, 1998.

———. *The Hips of Tradition.* Luaka Bop / Warner Bros. 945118, 1992.

———. *Imprensa Cantada.* Trama 894–2, 2003.

———. *Jogos de Armar.* Trama 111–2, 2000.

———. *Nave Maria.* RGE 3086062, 1984.

———. *No Jardim da Política.* TZ 1073, 1998.

———. *Se o Caso É Chorar* on *Tom Zé: Série Dois Momentos.* Vol. 14. Continental 857384242–2, [1972] 2000.

———. *Tom Zé.* Sony 495712, [1968] 2000.

———. *Tom Zé.* RGE 3476007, [1970] 1994.

———. *Todos os Olhos.* Continental 10121, 1973.

NOTES

This chapter is an abbreviated version of the article "Tom Zé and the Performance of Citizenship in Brazil," *Popular Music* 28.2 (summer 2009): 1–21. I wish to thank Cambridge University Press for permission to reprint a revised version of this article.

1. The most famous member of the Música Nova group, Rogério Duprat, composed the arrangements for most Tropicalist albums, including the collective concept album *Tropicália, ou Panis et Circensis.*

2. Created in 1967 by the military government, the INPS (Instituto Nacional de Previdência Social), is responsible for providing health care and other social services.

3. In an article written in the late 1960s, Walnice Nogueira Galvão singled out the expression "dia que virá" to describe the kind of redemptive protest music that refused or negated the quotidian experience of the here and now. See Galvão 1976: 95–96.

4. The RG, or *Registro Geral*, is a simple identity card for all Brazilian citizens. The CIC, or *Cartão de Identificação do Contribuinte*, was a federal document akin to a social security card in the U.S. that was replaced by the CPF, or *Cadastro de Pessoa Física*.

5. Here Tom Zé revisits an intellectual debate of the early twentieth century between racial pessimists, who believed in the biological inferiority of blacks and *mestiços*, and culturalist reformers, who argued that social inequalities were a function of poor nutrition and substandard education. See Skidmore, *Black into White* [1974] 1993: 182–84.

::: Rude Poetics of the 1980s

The Politics and Aesthetics of Os Titãs

Angélica Madeira

A gente não quer só comida.	We don't just want food.
A gente quer comida, diversão e arte.	We want food, entertainment and art.
A gente não quer só comida	We don't just want food.
A gente quer saída para qualquer parte.	We want a way out to anywhere.
—Os Titãs, "Comida," 1987	

For a brief time in the mid-1980s, Brazil experienced euphoria with the end of the dictatorship, the end of official censorship, and a return to democracy after twenty years of military rule (1964–85). An important segment of aesthetic production, particularly in the field of music, can be better understood by focusing on the historical context of the decade, marked by the expansion of digital technologies and by the internalization of consumption as social practice. A post-Tropicalist and post-punk phenomenon, known as "Rock Brasil" or "Brock," featuring the rock bands that emerged at the time, formed the poetics and musical tastes of a generation, bringing together thousands of young people as participants and fans. Distancing themselves from well-behaved arrangements, metaphoric or allegorical lyrics, and the melodic tradition of Brazilian popular music, rock bands of the decade created unique sounds, with guitar distortion, heavy percussion, a critique of all social institutions, and a poetics of disgust and abjection. This chapter will explore this particular moment in Brazilian cultural history through the music of one emblematic rock band from São Paulo, Os Titãs (The Titans), which forged the ethical and aesthetic parameters of action and entertainment for their generation through direct, brutal, and scatological lyrics.

::: Brazilian Rock and the End of Utopias

We might say that the decade of the 1980s actually began in August 1979 with an amnesty law that allowed for the return of political exiles, the end of official censorship, and the first moves toward the reestablishment of basic civil liberties. The first signs of a return to democracy were soon felt in politics, art, and society. There were discussions about elections for the president of the republic, the call for a Constituent Assembly, and the emergence of new social movements, independent unions, and NGOs oriented toward social, gender, racial, and environmental issues. A reinvigorated civil society appeared to be looking for new directions for the country. There was a hunger to appear in the public and in the media realm after two decades of silence. In all fields of art, young people emerged with vitality and a desire to participate in the democratic process. It was a time to question archaic political practices, disastrous economic plans, the exasperating violence of inequality, and entrenched corruption. As one observer has remembered the period:

> Heirs of silence, this new generation dreamed a lot about sound, sun, and rock'n'roll. A feeling of freedom, a longing to be happy, to paint the world with strong, vibrant colors, and a value associated with gesture and action permeated the arts. . . . This hedonist attitude, this urge for joy found its roots in the collective desire "to participate" in a democratic collective about which they dreamed. (Marcus de Lontra Costa 2004: 7)

Broad sectors of middle-class urban youth coming of age in the 1980s sought to go beyond nationalism, cultural or biological heritage, and sought to create a dialogue with the world, particularly with other young people from other countries who spoke the international language of rock. They were not unlike the youth of the 1960s, yet in many ways the conditions for enacting these cosmopolitan gestures were more evident by this time. This can be seen in the numerous cover songs from English and American bands, in the inclusion of sections in Spanish and English within mostly Portuguese songs, and in the desire for a wider audience. Cultural nationalism was regarded as outdated; new forms of economic and technological globalization mapped social relations and cultural circuits, permitting young people to strengthen their international connections through the language of rock. As in any big city in the world, it was possible to find a particular "tribe" or socio-cultural milieu. The decade closed with images of the "painted faces" in the media. These were the middle-class students who went to the streets in 1991 with their faces painted in the colors of the Brazilian flag to demand the impeachment of Fernando Collor de Mello, the first popularly elected president after the dictatorship, who was indicted for massive political corruption. On the world stage, the 1980s closed with the end of the cold war, the fall of the Berlin Wall, and the disintegration of the Soviet Bloc. It witnessed the strengthening of neoliberalism through the privatization policies promoted by Margaret Thatcher and Ronald Reagan. At the movies macho heroes made their own law through military force. Yuppies and fashion models, among other media identities, served as points of reference for young people.

We might say that the 1980s also witnessed the beginning of a new moment in defining the economic and strategic potential of art. All cultural practices, from the traditional to the most contemporary, became more exposed to instrumentalization by global capital and technology. All of these forces appeared to support hegemonic values, ever more unified under a powerful ideology that embraced any movement or action with the potential for profit. In any specific field affiliated with the many cultural industries, one could find an accentuated tendency to regard consumption as a value in and of itself, which was naturalized rather than becoming the object of reflection or estrangement. The values that constructed such a perception came into conflict with the values that had informed aesthetics, critique, and the history of art since the eighteenth century, namely, the concept of representation as mimesis and the Kantian concept of aesthetics, as the "practice of disinterested interest." Consumption also disrupted categories used to distinguish the erudite from the popular, as well as the hierarchical classification of culture through terms such as *kitsch*, *pop*, *highbrow*, *lowbrow*, and others, since everything was absorbed by the same logic of consumption. A new logic, which came to manage the cultural field, demanded of artists more attention to pragmatic questions. This discussion became particularly relevant in the field of popular culture, in which cultural goods and pop stars already emerged as merchandise, as is the case of most rock music. The privileged role of young people as producers and consumers propelled the emergence of this form of culture in which struggle and rebellion merely became part of an attitude and ethos shared by the majority of urban youth. Today the great quantity of globalized culture cannot be denied; it is a powerful catalyst of the imaginary and social practice of the youth, which multiply in an avalanche of brand names, sound systems, records, films, magazines, cars, motorcycles, and fashion items that vary according to the seasons (Ortiz 1996). The existence of pop culture highlights the centrality of money and culture understood as business, and its vulnerability—even in the most elite sectors of its production—to the demands of capital (Yúdice 2001).

Rock is a relatively recent cultural phenomenon capable of explaining the capacity of music and related consumer items to function as parameters for the identification of existential styles. The internationalization of rock culture allied with new technologies of electronic reproduction, made possible the emergence of different movements and a wide range of rock-pop genres in the world. Rock movements emerged throughout the non-Anglophone world, decentering the Anglo–North American tradition, which never lost, nonetheless, its hegemony over the others. In Brasília, where I conducted research about the taste and practices of youth entertainment, there were at least 300 rock bands in the mid-1980s.[1] This study clarified one of the most obvious paradoxes of consumer culture: the unifying international tendency of global aesthetics combined with the ability to multiply in plurality, incorporating various forms of traditional music.

New readings of traditions and methods of recycling ambient sound and images have emerged, demonstrating novel forms of mixture and the predominance of polysensory language (like the experience of a rock concert) in which art finds itself at the edge of other social fields (Chiarelli 1999; Moser et al. 1996). Rock has become more political, not in its representation or thematization of social issues, but rather in its demand for happiness and pleasure in the present. The music and the show, always so ritualized, act as strong antidotes to daily boredom, to the hypocritical values of decadent institutions, to the ruin of all utopias. With the waning of pop iconography, the 1980s witnessed the inauguration of new technologies of sound and image production such as the sampler—a machine that permits the manipulation, cutting, pasting, and blending of musical fragments—which played a central role in the soundscape of the period. The culture industries were ever more ready to profit from whatever appeared susceptible to market interest. The so-called high culture invested in the entertainment industry and new ways of perceiving and consuming traditional "treasures of humanity" emerged, often presenting a distracted and superficial perspective (Urry 1990). One of the major taboos of modernity was broken in a single gesture: "serious" culture could no longer be appropriated as such; thus the necessity of making it palatable and accessible for entertainment.

Of the values disseminated among young people (but empty to society as a whole), entertainment possessed the aggregating power for groups in search of identity. Entertainment became one of the symbolic goods most sought after, even to sell an infinite number of products: CDs, videos, all types of electronic appliances, and the like. As in the field of visual arts, these practices introduce new cultural mediators, such as producers and DJS, in a position of power and authority. They create fashions that are followed even in an ephemeral way. They compose visual, sound, and movement patterns that provoke replicas and simulations of identities. While rarely adding to the meaning of cultural goods, electronic media add value and are responsible for the model of culture of this postindustrial era. They are also responsible for important mutations that have occurred on the level of perception and subjectivity (Costa 2003). Most youth culture transmitted through the culture industry, from the 1980s until today, is intrinsically marked by various sounds the field of pop music comprises—rock, hip-hop, and all the technopop genres such as house, ambient, and lounge. Pop music has acted in a decisive way as a backdrop, set, and soundtrack for the most subjective experiences. The production of art for fashion and immediate communication helps us to understand one tendency of contemporary art oriented toward disturbing experiences, or the search for "a direct exposition without symbolic mediation of events which provoke chaos and repugnance in addition to aversion and horror" (Perniola 2002: 18).

What is the meaning of a disturbing poetics such as that developed by bands identified as punk rock or the nihilist rock of the 1980s? Is the choice of a distorted sound and a poetics that provoked feelings of abjection a mere counterfeit of English and American bands? Did it reveal disinterest in what was happening in Brazil or a disregard for the country's musical tradition?

Young middle-class Brazilians of the 1980s were taking stock of their childhood and adolescence, in a country emerging from a military dictatorship and in a world that appeared ever more labyrinthine and devoid of utopias. In the words of the Legião Urbana (Urban League), one of the rock bands from Brasília that attained the greatest popularity in the 1980s, they belonged to the "Coca-Cola Generation." This song became a hymn shared and sung in chorus during the shows and parties of the decade. The refrain suggests the ethical tone of the song:

| Somos os filhos da revolução | We are the children of the revolution |
| somos burgueses sem religião | we are bourgeois without religion |

| somos o futuro da nação | we are the future of the nation |
| Geração coca-cola | Coca-cola Generation |

Middle-class urban youth were raising questions about the political framework, consisting of repression and consumption, in which they grew up. As the vocalist and composer of Legião Urbana, Renato Russo, has remarked: "They say we have no character, that we grew up in the middle of the dictatorship, watching National Kid and the Three Stooges. How do they expect me to know what the Prestes Column was? I mean, you deny someone nutrition and then complain that the person is malnourished" (A. Macus Alves Souza 1995: 108).[2]

In the face of criticism by progressive intellectuals, Renato Russo points to the closure of the channels that were supposed to promote the intellectual formation of young people. Despite the redemocratization process, redemptive art was in crisis in the 1980s. The increasingly expanding international media circuits made available to young Brazilians the extravagances of punk rock, which contributed to the re-creation and dissemination of the anarchist ideas of this movement. Faced with disenchantment and the loss of utopias, Brazilian rock bands of the 1980s responded with expressions of romanticism and violence, accentuating the absolute primacy of the moment, the body, and sexuality.

::: The Rude Poetics of Os Titãs

In its so-called classic formation between 1984 and 1991, Os Titãs was a rock band composed of eight musicians: Arnaldo Antunes (vocals), Tony Belloto (guitarist), Branco Mello (vocalist), Nando Reis (bass and vocals), Charles Gavin (drums), Marcelo Fromer (guitar), Paulo Miklos (vocals, saxophone), and Sérgio Britto (keyboards, vocals). Since the early 1990s, the band has gone through a series of changes, beginning when one of the principal lyricists, Arnaldo Antunes, left the group, but it continues to record and perform. In the mid-1980s the band emerged as a sort of happening articulated in a single voice as a way to speak to the issues of the time.

Instead of pursuing obvious strategies, Os Titãs invented for themselves a new place on the cultural map, escaping from the paranoid-narcissist or schizorevolutionary "libidinal conflict" described by Deleuze (1972: 444). Their performances induced aesthetic, physical, and energetic pleasure, principally through the serial repetition of rhythms and words. Through

Arnaldo Antunes and Tony Belloto of Os Titãs perform at the Canecão Nightclub, Rio de Janeiro, 1987 (Luis Bittencourt, CPDOC JB).

the reiteration of shared truths, the band created the conditions to catalyze the sensibility and desire of their audiences. Uniqueness appeared to be the radical necessity of each of the band members. Playing with various modalities of aggression, from anger to good-humored satire, they subverted the somber and repressive organization of society; they attacked any constituted form of power represented by the father, the family, or the state. Up to a certain point, they managed to work collectively, liberated from the limits of individual egos.

The poetry of Os Titãs retained formal affinities with a range of earlier modernist and postmodernist experiments such as concrete poems, ephemeral poems, and joke poems as well as *poesia marginal* (underground poetry of the 1970s), which opted for the direct, colloquial use of words. While it generally remained aggressive, the poetics of Os Titãs seemed to have abandoned rebel ideologies, which had characterized the language of rock. Their album *Cabeça Dinossauro* (Dinosaur Head; 1986) radically engages these aesthetic questions in the search for a language, an ethos, and an attitude for the group. In the song "Estado-Violência" (State-Violence), all institutions—the church, the police, the family, school, the state, mass media—are held responsible for the moral emptiness of the subject who speaks in the lyrics:

Sinto no meu corpo	I feel my body
A dor que angustia	The pain of anguish
A lei ao meu redor	The law surrounding me
A lei que eu não queria	The law I didn't want
Estado-violência	State—violence
Estado hipocrisia	State of hypocrisy
A lei não é minha	The law is not mine
A lei que eu não queria	The law I didn't want

In this ethical and libidinal economy, everything that prevents loving, thinking, and feeling must be expelled. In the song "Homem Primata" (Primate Man), all is reduced to vegetative functions—"mammoth belly / pork spirit"—by the brutality of "savage capitalism." Only a reduced subjectivity remains, tired of "exotic and vulgar things," of "moralism and bacchanalia," "crazy from thinking so much, hoarse from screaming so much." The word, cell of poetry, is exposed to a variety of expressive situations, acts simultaneously in two directions, and is exploited to the limits of its ability to produce shock and beauty.

The poetry of Os Titãs moves beyond aggressive negation to the affirmation of a singular subject, who desires and not just needs. The final bastion of bourgeois morality, the word as a pure facade or video screen, is exploded into fragments when exposed to the rawness of Os Titãs. The preferential usage of the forbidden word—the vulgar or obscene—becomes important for revealing divisions that deaden the subject and its desire, divisions that become ingrained in the body through social values. Free from previous significations and then recycled, the "shit-bomb" word (to use Antonin Artaud's expression [1958]) becomes a neutral word in a variety of sonorous and emotional peaks. Os Titãs transform verbal garbage and reprocessed clichés into art. The use of the obscene word has as its primary function the articulation of heterogeneity, connecting the inside to the outside, the ingested to the expelled.

The song "AA-UU," also from Cabeça Dinossauro, announces one way of producing meaning that is most common in the poetics of Os Titãs—the exploration of dualities: thought/body, seeing/hearing, and eating/sleeping; lunching/dining, going to bed / getting up. The lyrics define a pattern of poetic production through exhaustive repetition and symmetrical distribution of words that designate bodily functions. The first stanza opens: "I eat, I sleep, I sleep, I eat," followed by "I don't eat, I don't sleep, I don't sleep, I don't eat." Meanwhile an impersonal voice continues to order: "It's time to wake up, it's time to go to bed / it's time to have lunch / it's time for dinner." In the transition from the first to the second stanza the subject becomes conscious of his or her desire, and this affirmation is coded as negative, while the negative sentences are coded as positive. The song "Comida" (Food) from their second album, *Jesus Não Tem Dentes no País dos Banguelas* (Jesus Has No Teeth in the Country of the Toothless; 1987), appears to synthesize this confrontation, while affirming the desire to move beyond basic necessities:

Bebida é água	Drink is water
Comida é pasto	Food is hay
Você tem fome de quê	You're hungry for what?
Você tem sede de quê	You're thirsty for what?
A gente não quer só dinheiro	We don't just want money
A gente quer dinheiro e felicidade.	We want money and happiness.
A gente não quer só dinheiro,	We don't just want money,
A gente quer inteiro e não pela metade.	We want it all and not just half.

From the same album, the song "Todo Mundo Quer Amor" summarizes centuries of poetic, lyrical, and satirical compositions that have expressed what Lacanian psychoanalysis designates as the lack (manqué). Backed up by an arrangement in counterpoint, vocals, drums and percussion, each verse is delivered from the hollow of the stomach:

Todo mundo quer amor	Everyone wants love
Todo mundo quer amor de verdade	Everyone wants true love
Quem tem medo quer amor	The one who is afraid wants love
Quem tem fome quer amor,	The one who is hungry wants love,
Quem tem frio quer amor	The one who is cold wants love
Quem tem pinto saco boca bunda	The one with a dick balls mouth ass
ou buceta quer amor	or pussy wants love

The album *Tudo ao Mesmo Tempo Agora* (Everything at the Same Time Now; 1991)—which was composed, arranged, and produced by the band—reveals a mature phase of the group's collective work. The compositions are no longer individually signed; the arrangements are dirty and distorted, practically eliminating melodic conventions. Each song becomes a kind of hidden recitation of free-floating words—strong, direct, scatological—pronounced with all the sounds, screamed in a range of emotional states. It is not an accident that the cover of the album portrays a montage of photographs and drawings: the lyrical face of a young man emerging from a pile of exploded organs, skeletons, broken bones, blood and tripe, from images taken from the *Encyclopedia Britannica*. Several songs from the album, notably "Isso para Mim É Perfume" (For Me This Is Perfume), employ the theme of abject, rejected elements. Taboo themes—menstruation, feces, cum—are pronounced—without the slightest hint of fear, guilt or disgust—in this most explicit and absurd love poem. The word, now freed from prejudices, is newly pronounced, simply and directly.

The song "Clitóris," from this same album, radically accentuates this mode of use of the obscene. A melodic riff on the electric guitar, which culminates in a distortion lasting several seconds, precedes the entrance of the drums. The arrangement of the vocals, the modulations of intensity and duration, the clarity or opacity used in the vocal expression gesture toward a new frontier for the word. So often repeated, it is hammered into pure sound. The aesthetic exploration at the level of sound—phonetic and rhythmic accentuation of the word—becomes a source of pleasure, entertainment, and art.

"Clitóris" is almost entirely constructed in free verses, with only two of the thirteen verses making explicit syntactic connections. The word-title forms the base of the two first stanzas with eight occurrences. It is pronounced in different intensities and modulations, distributed among the vocalists according to a pattern that opposes the two exclamations: "AH! OH!," marvel and horror. This is also the pattern of the second word of the third stanza: "Genuflectory, AH! Genuflectory / Genuflectory, OH! Genuflectory." We sense the associative play on words, the pleasure of articulating occlusive and liquid consonants (which have the effect of blocking the flow of air and sound that lead from the lungs to the tongue), the feeling of the timbre in the body, and the rhythm of a word of difficult accentuation. The fourth stanza is composed of four verses. Two of them, coming back to the pattern "AH! OH!," play on the contradictory opposition "dirty virgin" and around the phonetic opposition "suja/surja" (dirty/surge). The other two verses, containing syntactically connected words (decasyllables split entirely according to the same rhythmic pattern), employ images, internal and external rhythms, and alliterations. The final screams—"Papa Nicolau, Papa Nicolau" (Santa Claus, Santa Claus)—act as a coda, and return to the desacralizing and ambivalent character of the profane.

Is the association between clitoris and genuflection a reference to some common theme? Or is it that at this level of rawness, the song brings some solemnity to sex? While both are technical words, one from the medical-gynecological vocabulary, and the other from the religious domain, what other links exist between them? Only the suspension of guilt makes possible the flooding of the other body—the woman's body (dirty virgin), metaphorically represented by the cradle and the hole—of "slimy sperm" and "thick cum." The extreme condensation of the first verses, where only disconnected words and word-refrains are utilized, continue to reverberate throughout the rest of the song. The speeding up and slowing down of the duration, the rhythm in which the rotation moves, and other sound techniques exploited by the vocals contribute to this process of the transformation of the word.

In the 1980s, during the first years of return to democratic rule, Os Titãs created a rude poetics, sketching the distance between body and language, making the word the surface—sonorously and rhythmically—for new conjunctions and juxtapositions. Heterogeneous and parallel actions—to think and scream; talk and eat; spit and swallow; expel and shock—were connected through the functional use of the obscene word, attacking society by targeting familiar tropes of good taste and decorum. Going beyond the voluntary demolition of values, Os Titãs invented another place, where the word gained aggregative functions. The obscene word, in their poetics, is neither erotic nor pornographic, neither sadistic, nor masochistic. In becoming neutral, bathed in saliva and sweat, the poetic word rejects the discourse of statements and arguments. Os Titãs would not attempt to scale Olympus, since they believed that perfection doesn't exist and ideas must be on the ground. In the polymorphic play of words they discovered the power of semantic pollution and the brilliance of nonsense.

Os Titãs succeeded in forging for their generation a singular understanding of music and poetry, an artistic practice that mixed ethics and aesthetics, political and existential questions. The decision to attack society through language is not new—it was one of the objectives of the historical avant-garde. Language persists as the terrain of struggle, the most radical means of casting light on conflicts and wounds. Language is a zone so sensitive that touching its laws or its taboos is to touch the core of prohibitions and obligations, which codify and deaden the subject (Kristeva 1982). Although it is impossible to think of the lyrics of Os Titãs as isolated from the songs and arrangements, they demonstrated the most direct path for understanding the strategic use of words: the "shit-bomb" words crafted like homemade explosives. Seen from close up, an obscene word makes a connection between heterogeneous meanings, helps to diminish the distance between language and the body, and exorcises the social codes responsible for moral damage and disease. Os Titãs showed that the "shit-bomb" word could be used for radical poetic explorations and societal critique.

Os Titãs moved beyond the common positions found in artistic circles, above all among rock bands—the charismatic narcissism of the star or the effacement of subjectivity in order to embrace an ideology. They articulated their message from another place, fleeing from the rules that make human beings brutal and values stupid. In "Eu Não Sei Fazer Música" (I Don't Know How to Make Music; 1991) they affirm,

> I don't know what to say
> but I speak
> No one knows anything
> No one knows anything.

From the position of radical skepticism, it's best is to continue with the open question articulated in their song "Desordem" (Disorder; 1987): "Who wants to maintain order? / Who wants to create disorder?" The refrain from "Desordem" connects images captured from television, offering a chronicle of disparate events from the 1980s: prisoners fleeing from prison, a fight amongst soccer fans, an angry population setting fire to a police car, vigilante violence, and so on. The song proposes a question:

> I don't know if everything will burn
> like some flammable liquid
> what else can happen
> in a poor and miserable country?

All urban social movements stemming from music have a very tenuous link to politics, in traditional terms. Their aim, they insist, is to speak in their own name, with their own voice, instead of representing a group or an ideology. The 1980s was a decade of huge contradictions, with the hopeful political opening taking place in the context of economic crisis, increasing urban violence, and magnified social problems. In this context rock culture was an important catalyst of youth energy, spontaneous vitalism, sexuality, and humor. Os Titãs knew better than any of their contemporaries how to release those repressed forces. They represented a collective endeavor to re-compose unraveled memory and distorted information, while embarking on a search for pleasure. They made music and poetry even without knowing how, without any certainty, without any clarity about the paths to follow, either their own or those of the country.

DISCOGRAPHY

Os Titãs. *Cabeça Dinossauro*. WEA, 1986.
———. *Go Back*. WEA, 1988.
———. *Jesus Não Tem Dentes no País dos Banguelas*. WEA, 1987.
———. *O Blesq Blom*. WEA, 1990.
———. *Televisão*. WEA, 1985.
———. *Tudo ao Mesmo Tempo Agora*. WEA, 1991.

NOTES

1. This research project titled "Music and Society: The Youth Music Movements of Brasília," was developed between 1985 and 1989 in its first phase and between 1991 and 1994 in its second.

2. *National Kid* was a Japanese superhero TV program that was broadcast in Brazil in the late 1960s and early 1970s. The Prestes Column was a legion of rebels led by Communist leader Luiz Carlos Prestes in the 1920s.

Audiotopias of Postdictatorship Brazil

Frederick Moehn

"With how many Brazils do you make a Brazil?"
—Lenine and Lula Queiroga, "Sob o Mesmo Céu," 2005

A 2004 concert review in the *New York Times* by Larry Rohter bears the headline "The Two Brazils Combine for a Night at Carnegie Hall." It describes how the classical pianist Marcelo Bratke, from a prominent family in São Paulo, and young musicians from the percussion ensemble Charanga came together to perform pieces by the composers Darius Milhaud, Heitor Villa-Lobos, and Ernesto Nazareth. The professional musician Marcelo Alves formed Charanga with five youths he had met at the Despertar Community Center in Jardim Vilas Boas, of the city of São Paulo, which Rohter identifies as "one of the toughest sections of this metropolis of 20 million people." In a society as stratified as Brazil, he writes, "there is no reason for people from such markedly different backgrounds ever to meet, much less perform together." They did, however, meet to make musical sound, in Carnegie Hall no less. This chapter explores how discourses about music as well as musical practices themselves narrate the figurative space between the proverbial two Brazils (*space* here should be understood as a conceptualized location, while I use the term *place* to refer to specific physical and cultural geographies). Shared and sometimes contested beliefs about music, national identity, the historical trajectory of development in Brazil, and the country's role on the global stage are powerfully intertwined, with the result that music has a prominent role in current reimaginings of Brazilian citizenship.

Because music is so closely associated with national identity in Brazil, it enjoys special currency as a mediator between different social classes and spaces on the one hand, and between the state and civil society on the other. I see discourses about music and practices associated with making, consuming, and even legislating music as framing a "third Brazil" between the two Brazils. This "space in between" (Santiago 2001) bears comparison with what Josh Kun calls *audiotopias*, or the "spaces that music helps us to imagine" and in which one can take "refuge" (2005: 14). The psychologist Maria Rita Kehl, for example, writes of having "dual citizenship": one in the Brazil, "of widespread injustices and futile struggles"; the other in the country of popular song, "where all Brazilians have the right to exile when real life becomes too insipid" (2002: 60). Arthur Nestrovski, similarly, maintains that Brazilians "live daily in two countries: a few minutes with intensity, imagination, and carelessness in Brazilian popular music; the rest of the time, in the other one" (2002: 12). Kehl and Nestrovski seem ambivalent about their national political citizenship, but popular music constitutes an alternative "country" to which one has the "right" to exile for a few transcendent minutes.

For Kun, audiotopias are "sonic spaces of effective utopian longings where several sites normally deemed incompatible are brought together" (2005: 23). They are "identificatory 'contact zones,' in that they are both sonic and social spaces where disparate identity-formations, cultures, *and* geographies historically kept and mapped separately are allowed to interact with each other" (23). Kun's desire to engage problems of nation, identity, and citizenship in the United States through audiotopic spaces where difference is not erased but is instead listened to resonates with my analysis here. But while Kun is primarily concerned with how music is intertwined with problems of race and identity in an America that has often struggled with its own multiculturalism, where musical homes of "dual belonging, dual culture, dual identity" coexist in audiotopic *tierras* that supposedly destabilize dominant discourses of assimilation (221), in Brazil the prevailing narratives of nationhood have tended to emphasize heterogeneity and the juxtaposition of contrasts, the capacity to choose not to choose between oppositions but rather to combine them (the "virtue" of the middle ground, in Roberto DaMatta's phrase, [1978] 1995). It is a discourse not of assimilation into a supposedly already existing American identity, but of continual mixture and transculturation into ever new formulations.

Yet discourses of mixture and heterogeneity may obfuscate certain persistent structures of inequality and opposition in Brazil, potentially signaling the danger in placing too much store in audiotopias. Recent policies for affirmative action in government hiring and university admissions in Brazil challenge narratives of relatively harmonious race relations. I am concerned to emphasize the instability of audiotopias, and the competing interests in and different uses of them by individuals and groups variously situated in the fabric of civil society. Where Kun harnesses popular music to remap the present in service of a more just world—not an impossible future utopia but rather an "effectively enacted" heterotopia (from Michel Foucault) that helps us cope with this world (2005: 23)—my elaboration here reveals an eminently fragile, ambiguous musical space of hope where culture meets class, history, violence, and the state. Some may seek refuge in this space in order to cope; others may mobilize this space as part of an agenda seeking change in a society of extreme social stratification. I focus here on musical examples from urban contexts, from both working-class and middle-class artists.

::: Citizenship, Social Class, and Audiotopic Rhythms

Most writing on citizenship begins with the typology famously outlined by Thomas H. Marshall in his essay "Citizenship and Social Class," originally presented as a lecture in 1949. Focusing on the English case, Marshall argued that there are three components to citizenship: the civil, the political, and the social, historically emerging roughly in that order. A citizen possesses a set of rights and duties associated with each of these components as defined, protected, and enforced by the legal-political apparatus of the nation-state. The civil component pertains to legal inclusion in the definition of citizenship and the political primarily to suffrage, while the social is generally understood as pertaining to those rights and duties associated with the modern welfare state. In Marshall's analysis, there is a progressive historical expansion of these components to citizenship. Increasing levels of democratic representation would seem to go hand in hand with the extension of citizenship rights and duties to greater portions of the population. However, as Teresa Caldeira and James Holston have argued, in Brazil there is a disjunction between the expansion of democratic representation since the end of the military dictatorship in 1985 (the political component of citizenship), and the extension of civil and social components—in particular, egalitarian legal protection of citizens and the right to decent living conditions, which have become even less accessible for many citizens (1999). José Murilo de Carvalho argues that Marshall's typology is in fact inverted in Brazil as many civil rights—which formed the foundation of Marshall's sequence—remain inaccessible to the majority of the population (2001: 219–20).

I find it worthwhile to retain Marshall's emphasis on social class in relation to citizenship, for what most obviously separates the two Brazils is
a highly polarized class structure. A standard index of income inequality
used by economists for the purposes of comparatively gauging development
is the Gini coefficient; the closer the coefficient is to 1, the greater the inequality. At about .57 in 2005, Brazil's Gini coefficient remains among the
worst in the world (while the U.S., at about .47, is significantly more unequal
than most of the more "developed" nations). The lowest 20 percent of income earners live below the poverty line and account for just over 2 percent
of total income in Brazil, while the highest 20 percent earn 64 percent of
the total income in the country (and the top 10 percent of earners account
for 45 percent of income).[1] Yet class should be understood in relation to various other determinants such as race—with the poorest Brazilians tending
to be darker complexioned; or to violence, which is visited with greater frequency upon poorer (and younger) Brazilians than on the middle and upper
classes. Class status bears directly on level of education (including formal
musical training), access to the media and political leadership, and the degree of integration into consumer and information society. Finally, class is
also intertwined with place, as in, for example, the contrasts between the
wealthier "seaside" neighborhoods and the "hillside" favelas of Rio mentioned in Nega Gizza's rap "Filme de Terror," or between the downtown
upper middle-class neighborhoods and the "periphery" of São Paulo alluded
to in Max Gonzaga's song "Classe Média," both of which I examine below.

Traversing the space in between these Brazils is a symbolic economy
of Brazilian popular music making with roots in the period of Brazilian
modernism (1920s and '30s) when, for example, the influential intellectual and musicologist Mário de Andrade envisioned an aesthetic nationalism that navigated the received contradictions between popular and erudite,
local and cosmopolitan culture. Importantly, as Mariza Veloso and Angélica
Madeira observe, Andrade conceptualized Brazilian culture as a "synthesis that was not a mere sum of the parts, but a process of social relations in
transformation" (2000: 127). This emphasis on the *process* of constructing
Brazilian national culture; on the aesthetic and symbolic negotiation of social, structural, and cultural differences; and on this confidence that art can
do the identity work of nation building and citizen building are also present
in the cases I explore below. Andrade granted rhythm the ability to do much
of this "identity work" (a term I borrow from Isin and Wood 1999). In his

Ensaio sobre a Música Brasileira (1928), for example, Andrade wrote: "We are in a stage of rhythmic predominance," and he suggested that "in accommodating and adapting foreign elements to his own tendencies the Brazilian acquired an imaginative way of 'rhythmicking' [*jeito de ritmar*]" ([1928] 1962: 21). The connection between syncopated (and racialized) rhythms and national identity would help propel urban samba to the status of Brazil's national music in the 1930s and '40s.

Today, rhythm and drumming also participate in what might be termed the symbolic economies of nongovernmental organizations (NGOs) and citizens' action groups, some of which enjoy funding from international sources, such as the Grupo Cultural AfroReggae in Rio de Janeiro, which has received Ford Foundation support. AfroReggae even terms its identity work *batidania*, combining *batida* (beat) with *cidadania* (citizenship). The group, based in the Vigário Geral favela of Rio de Janeiro, initiated a remarkable series of residencies in 2005, joining the military police in the city of Belo Horizonte with favela residents. Lieutenant Colonel Josué Soares of the Thirty-fourth Battalion asserted, "Not long ago, a lot of officers believed we had to use force to stop criminality. Our mentality has changed in the way we approach *favelados* [favela residents]" (Reardon 2005). The sound of drumming here replaces the sound of guns—at least on a small scale—literally taking over both the space and the *place* dividing the police and the favela residents.

In the northeastern state of Bahia, which has the highest concentration of African Brazilians in the country, the Olodum cultural group has centered its community activities and commercial enterprise around drumming since the late 1970s, taking an active role in redefining the civic landscape of Salvador, the capital of that state. Also focused on Bahia is the "Rhythmic Uprising" project coordinated by a team of media professionals from Brazil and the U.S. who aim to "tell the world the inspiring tale of how a powerful grass-roots movement based in the arts is overcoming social and economic depression." Another organization with international ties and working in Bahia is called "Rhythm of Hope," an "informal network association" that aims to "strengthen social programs in the Bahia community, to better the quality of life of its marginalized populations, and to foster awareness, tolerance, and understanding on the part of non-Brazilians."[2]

In the song "Sob o Mesmo Céu" (Under the Same Sky), the MPB (Música Popular Brasileira) singer, songwriter, and guitarist Lenine—along with

Lenine, Ministereo Recording Studio, Rio de Janeiro, 2007 (Fred Moehn).

his songwriting partner Lula Queiroga—describe rhythm as mediating between—and bringing together—the various Brazils: "My heart has no frontiers nor clock, nor flag, just the rhythm of a greater song," Lenine sings.

> We come from the drum of the Indian
> We come from Portugal; from the black drumming . . .
> We come from samba, from *forró*
> We come from the future to learn about our past
> We come from rap and from the favela . . .
> from the center and from the periphery . . .
> We bring a desire for happiness and peace.

These lyrics describe a temporally ambiguous space emanating from a simultaneously individual and national body whose heart beats out a rhythm that
transcends difference, and whose mind dreams up a Brazil that in its inclusive diversity is also universal.

A performance of this song can be seen on YouTube ("Lenine e Varias
Cantoras Sob o Mesmo Céu [Premio Multishow]"), with Lenine joined on
stage by a small band of electric bass and guitar, drum kit, *pandeiro* (a tambourine used in a wide range of Brazilian popular musics), and several
female Brazilian MPB singers who are from various parts of the country

(and who are also racially diverse): Fafá de Belém, Margareth Menezes, Elba Ramalho, Sandy, Ana Carolina, Fernanda Abreu. The mood evoked is nationalistic and celebratory. It comes across as something like a pop anthem of the "country" of popular song to which Maria Rita Kehl says Brazilians have the right to exile. In fact, the song was composed for a French celebration of Brazilian culture (the "Year of Brazil in France," 2005), cosponsored by the Brazilian Ministry of Culture. The opening question in these lyrics hints that work remains to be done before a single country called Brazil realizes its "audiotopic potential" as a fully inclusive space. In many ways, the modernist musical vision of the Brazilian nation is evident in this song, but other musical spheres may interpret this space and its symbols differently, as the examples of Nega Gizza of CUFA will show.

::: The Central Única das Favelas (CUFA;
United Favela Federation) and Nega Gizza

According to the 2004 UNESCO Brazil report, *Map of Violence: The Youths of Brazil*, 92 percent of homicide victims are males between 18 and 24 years old and of these 74 percent are black. Furthermore, between 1993 and 2002, there was an increase of 88.6 percent of homicides among the total population in the age range of 15 to 24 (Waiselfisz et al. 2004). For Júlio Tavares of the Fluminense Federal University in Niterói, Rio de Janeiro, this violence amounts to a genocide of black and predominantly male bodies. Tavares sees hip-hop as a corporeal and narrative response to this genocide, collaborating "in the construction of a new social landscape for Brazil," and accelerating the "fight for civil rights and citizen-consciousness." Hip-hop, he argues, is a "third way," negotiating between institutionalized, formal capitalism and the informal parallel economy of the drug trade, both of which he views as complicit in this genocide.[3]

In Rio de Janeiro CUFA describes itself as an organization that unites residents of over 100 favelas as well as artists, producers, and people connected to residents associations. The mission statement of CUFA describes the federation as "a national organization that emerged in meetings of youths—generally black—from various favelas in Rio de Janeiro who were looking for a space in the city to express their attitudes, problems, or just their desire to live." Most of these youths were participants in or were oriented by the hip-hop movement; they organized around the ideal of transforming "the favelas, their talents, and their potentials in the face of a society in which prejudice based on color, class, and origin had not yet been transcended." Rap music can be useful in this effort, the mission statement argues, because it helps raise the consciousness of those who are on the periphery of their citizenship, and because it is gaining recognition in the media. There is, the statement adds, an affinity between the militancy of hip-hop and the work of CUFA: they both seek "to stimulate the residents of favela communities to take action; to promote a popular revolution in Brazilian culture."[4]

In June 2004 I attended some events CUFA and its partner group Hutúz organized at the Bank of Brazil Cultural Center in the center of the city. These events featured hip-hop bands from various countries of Latin America and took place in a theater during the middle of the day, rather than at night in areas of the suburbs. Such linkages between potentially trans-formative movements and corporate institutions are part of what George Yúdice has called the "privatization of culture" in Latin America, a trend which risks co-optation or the adoption of "expedient" culture-based pro-grams at the expense of real changes to the structural causes of inequality (2003). Despite such risks, these music-based movements can potentially draw increased attention to the problem of the two Brazils among the gen-eral population, and they provide a grass-roots community-centered space of solidarity for favela residents to debate problems of citizenship and repre-sentation, or to organize actions that seek to remedy such problems. For ex-ample, in 2005 CUFA received $60,000 in Ford Foundation funds to support a series of workshops on race, gender, human rights, and film with youths from the hip-hop movement in Rio as part of the organization's Citizenship and Audiovisual Project.

One of the founding members and current treasurer of CUFA is the rap artist Nega Gizza (Gisele Gomes de Souza). She was born in the favela of Parque Esperança in Rio de Janeiro. She and her brother, the rapper MV Bill (Alex Pereira Barbosa), contributed to the soundtrack for the film *Cidade de Deus* (City of God; 2002), based on Paulo Lins's 1997 novel by the same name, which portrayed the lives of two youths growing up amidst brutal vio-lence in that neighborhood. Also in 2002 Nega Gizza released her album *Na Humildade* (In Humility), which presents a black woman favela resident's perspective on rap, race, class, and Brazilian citizenship. It is a subject posi-tion she regards as alienated by the discourse of miscegenation, and de-prived of the full complement of rights associated with modern citizenship in the West. The album begins with a sparse, simple, minor key ostinato, a beat that stutters before settling into a groove, and periodic chordal inter-

Nega Gizza (CUFA).

jections on violins that evoke the suspense-inducing music of a horror film soundtrack, for from Nega Gizza's perspective, that is precisely what Brazil looks like. Evoking predominant stereotypes, she refers to the "country of racial democracy, of the *mulata* for export" in her rap "Filme de Terror" (Horror Film). It is a "happy," tropical nation that condemns blacks "to live like irrational animals," subdues them "by the ropes of the hangman," or transforms them into "doormats." Whites live in privileged neighborhoods by the seaside, or lock themselves behind the gates of their "castles," while blacks live on hillside favelas "without culture, without pride," and persecuted by the police. Declaring that she "won't die for Brazil," she calls on African Brazilians to follow in her footsteps to the sound of rap.

The general framework in these lyrics remains that of two Brazils—the elite and the poor or, alternatively, the whites and the blacks. Race mixture is mentioned but with deep irony. The temporal dimension is racialized: poor black Brazilians are people without a future, and this is due, Nega Gizza argues, to the normalization of social and racial stratification and violence within a conformist social order. "Let's pretend that it will pass, that it is natural." The poor live like starving, diseased animals (not citizens) whose teeth are falling out, hunted by the police. In this view the problem that Brazilian identity has with both the future and the past is race. More specifically, it is the naturalized correlation between race and class in Brazil that impairs the teleology of modernization and development. Rather than coming from the future to learn about the past, as in the Lenine/Queiroga song, the present reality makes the future almost beside the point for many.

Nega Gizza's "Filme de Terror" and Lenine's and Queiroga's "Sob o Mesmo Céu" both evoke a different Brazil through musical rhythm (the "rhythm of a greater song" in the Lenine/Queiroga piece). "Uncross your arms, follow in my footsteps," Nega Gizza sings. "The sound is rap, this is the beat." Lenine, however, uses the first person plural: "*We* come from the center and the periphery; *we* come from rap and from the favela." Lenine proposes to speak for the national "we." Nega Gizza, by contrast, claims to speak for the black and economically marginalized "we," while her musical beat has little direct connection to grooves traditionally associated with blacks and *mulatos* in Brazil, such as samba. Rather, the musical connection is more Black Atlantic; it is transnational and diasporic. Her track "Larga o Bicho" (Release the Animal) further elaborates on her subject position qua citizen: "I'm not a *mulata*; I'm not a she-mule [*mula*]," she declares. Instead, she's "a cannon," a "black woman with the warring spirit," and an African descendant whose "dialect is rap." Her co-rapper on the song, Yeda Hills, adds, "I'm black in skin and mind; this makes me courageous, because I know that I'm a descendant of the fighting Zumbi," referring to the legendary African Brazilian who, in the seventeenth century, led the Palmares escaped slave colony (*quilombo*) in battle against the colonial forces. With her microphone as her weapon, Yeda raps, she lives "one day after another" in accordance with her *ritmologia* ("rhythmology"). It's "the sound of black," she asserts.

Rap production in Brazil is broad and highly varied, and Nega Gizza cannot be taken as representative of the full breadth of this output. Most rap artists, however, tend not to celebrate miscegenation and the harmonious juxtaposing of differences, as MPB musicians such as Lenine often do. The hip-hop "sound of black" provides a more "militant" and politicized rhythm for conjuring this audiotopic space than would, for example, traditional samba (although Brazilian hip-hop does sometimes mix in samba rhythms).

::: "The New Music of Brazil"? An MPB Festival,
    the Middle Classes, and a Cyberdebate

If the musical output of Nega Gizza in association with CUFA interrogates problems of citizenship and class as they pertain to social welfare, violence, and civil rights, what of those social sectors that enjoy relatively higher economic security, specifically, populations considered middle class? It is a demographic group that "although with relatively little property," "is characterized by high and intermediary positions both in the social-occupational structure and in the distribution of income and wealth." As such, the middle class is understood as "possessing recognized social status and authority and a superior level of consumption" (Pochmann et al. 2005: 16). Middle-class music makers often serve a mediating role, such as, for example, Dudu Marote, who was one of the producers of Nega Gizza's recording *Na Humildade*. Such mediations can have important aesthetic consequences. One reviewer of Nega Gizza's album writes that her sound has a greater musical richness than that of her brother, MV Bill, "not exactly from her style of rapping . . . but from knowing how to put herself in the hands of the right producers. . . . They managed to create a rarity: a disc of Brazilian hip-hop which balances the strength of the verses with the musical part; electronic interventions in the exactly perfect measure mixed with acoustic instruments, scratches, and changes in the musical ambiance on each track" (Barbosa n.d.). "The right producers," in this case, are taste brokers who make sure the CD meets certain aesthetic standards that appeal to middle-class listeners.

The role of mediator may include using publicity clout to support causes that agitate for social reform, such as when the MPB star Caetano Veloso offers his support to the Grupo Cultural AfroReggae, or when the pop musician Fernanda Abreu crosses from the so-called south zone of Rio (where many of the city's white middle-class and upper-class residents live) to the north zone (where many of Rio's favela-based hip-hop communities are located) to appear at events with artists such as Nega Gizza, AfroReggae, and MV Bill, as she often does. There exists also a network of intellectuals, professionals, and government officials who may act in a role that mediates between the haves and have-nots, or between the state and civil society, such as certain NGO staff, or the minister of culture Gilberto Gil. Yet there is also a heightened sense of ambivalence amongst the middle classes, as suggested by the statements from Kehl and Nestrovski about "dual citizenship," cited above. The economist Waldir José de Quadros at the University of Campinas (Unicamp) fears that the Brazilian middle class is angry. "It just hasn't exploded yet," he says, "because it is also confused" (quoted in Sugimoto 2004: 8). According to economist Márcio Pochmann, the median income of middle-class workers fell 19.4 percent between 1995 and 2005, while in the same period taxes increased 20 percent (cited in Caçado e Neves, 2005: 76). Carlos Antonio Ribeiro Costa, a specialist on social mobility at the State University of Rio de Janeiro, says, "The fight to stay in the middle class is tougher" (quoted in Caçado e Neves, 2005: 75).

The MPB artist Max Gonzaga, from São Paulo, captured the anxieties of this social sector in his song "Classe Média" (Middle Class), which he presented in a televised song festival in 2005. "The Festival Cultura—A Nova Música do Brasil" took place in the SESC (Serviço Social do Comércio; Social Service of Commerce Center) Pinheiros Theater in São Paulo city from 31 August to 14 September 2005. The event was a song contest recorded in front of a live audience in the tradition of the legendary festivals of the '60s that launched the careers of Chico Buarque, Caetano Veloso, and Gilberto Gil, among many other household names of MPB, and that also became the main forum for so-called *canção engajada* (engaged song), that is, the Brazilian protest music that paralleled the *nueva canción* movement in the rest of Latin America. The contest, broadcast on the public television station TV Cultura, commemorated forty years since the first such festival. The project was to be "open to all the musical tendencies and rhythms of the country" and it sought to "present, without restrictions, the best of what exists of a Brazil of living and vibrant colors and rhythms."[5]

"Classe Média" made it to the semifinals, and it seemed to strike a chord among many viewers, listeners, and bloggers in Brazil despite the fact that it was eliminated in that round. Musically, the song is firmly in the MPB mold: Gonzaga's low tenor voice is smooth and practiced, and the song features a rangy, well-constructed, pop melody. The altered chords the songwriter fingerpicks on his nylon-stringed classical guitar evoke jazzy bossa nova harmonies with moderate syncopations, as does the discrete accompaniment played on synthesizer. An "MTV Acoustic" sound predominates, with bongos and other light percussion completing a sophisticated pop texture, and judicial amounts of reverberation added to the *pop acústico* (acoustic pop) mix. One of the organizers of the event said of the stage sound, "We have opted for subtlety, to show acoustic music, music that is a little more elaborated in terms of instrumentation."[6] "Subtlety," "acoustic," "elaborated instrumentation"—these are terms describing a fairly constrained and nostalgic aesthetic, recalling the preferences of the original song festivals of the 1960s, where electric guitars, for example, were at first notoriously rejected by a public composed largely of middle-class college students.

Max Gonzaga's song lyrics frankly capture the interrelationships between consumption, violence, and the media from a perspective that Gonzaga suggests is shared by a significant portion of the Brazilian middle classes today. Singing in the first person and assuming an imagined middle-class subjectivity, Gonzaga describes an individual who avoids public transportation, pays too much in taxes, bounces checks, charges clothes and gas on a credit card, and drives a car bought with a loan. This Brazilian is unconcerned about drug traffickers controlling the favelas, or about people dying from a flood in the low-income neighborhood of Itaquera. "I wish the entire periphery would explode," Gonzaga sings, in reference to the vast spaces of poverty outside of the upper middle-class areas of São Paulo. But the typical middle-class Brazilian, he suggests, is "indignant with the state" when "inconvenienced" by starving beggars or soapy windshield washers at intersections. Then, switching to the second person and heightening the ironic tone of his voice, Gonzaga notes that if there is a robbery, murder, or rape in the exclusive Moema or Jardins neighborhoods of the city, the media are there. "You begin to think about the death penalty again, or lowering the age of majority," Gonzaga cynically sings, while quietly slipping back into first person: "And I who am well-informed agree and join a demonstration." It is easier, the singer-narrator concludes, "to condemn someone already condemned to death." Here the middle-class subject is placed in direct opposition to Nega Gizza's refusal to "die for Brazil."

The contrast between the "smooth jazz" acoustic sound of this song and its primarily middle-class live performance setting on the one hand, and the biting irony of its lyrics on the other, disrupt the space in between that Kehl describes as an "other" Brazil to which everyone has the right to exile. This Brazil in the middle is troubled by the two Brazils on either side of it: it is the coexistence of the grossly overprivileged and the embarrassingly impoverished that inhibit the full realization of a modern middle-class cosmo-consumer consciousness and way of life. "Classe Média" also subtly interrogates the premises of the festival itself: whereas the latter celebrated the great MPB artists of the '60s—whom the military dictatorship censored or even forced into exile—Gonzaga sings about joining a demonstration in favor of the death penalty.

An MPEG video recording of Gonzaga's performance of the song circulated through cyberspace and generated mixed reactions (and it is now on YouTube). Several bloggers felt that Gonzaga captured an uncomfortable truth: "This song really says it all!" comments one. "A really good song," writes another. "The lyrics speak for themselves."[7] One blogger observes that "the average middle class type . . . can be summarized with the phrase 'for the masses, charity or the police.'"[8] In contrast, a reporter writes that this kind of pop music and criticism is simply out of step with the sound of today, which is better represented by rap music's "electronic, accelerated, and rhythmic" (*ritmado*) urban beat, and its "concrete poetry of a reality marked by inequality."[9] Yet another blogger appreciates Gonzaga's talent but is incensed by the lyrics and provides a perspective on the Brazilian middle-class that merits quotation:

> The middle class in this country is being squeezed year after year and its ability to generate income and consumption has been reduced to an extent never before seen here. Taxes, interest rates, impunity in the government, the lack of an efficient health-care system, excessive embezzlements, the manipulations of the media, the absurd protectionism of the worker's statutes [*leis trabalhistas*], and so forth, only managed to destroy the vitality of those who still held out any hope for this country (namely, the middle class). . . . Please, Mr. Gonzaga, be more attentive to the possibility that you might offend one who . . . works, sometimes 12 to 14 hrs a day to pay for decent schooling for his children (as if he had not already paid for this in taxes), to stay employed despite being over 40, etc. Have more respect for those who have lost someone (middle class or not) to the violence so in vogue these days (what happened to the security that we pay for with our taxes?).[10]

Clearly this blogger is unable to distance himself from the topic enough to appreciate Gonzaga's irony, perhaps understandably. His concerns give a broader picture of the contexts of inequality into which music, violence, social movements, and public policy are thrust in Brazil. Music makers I have researched in Rio de Janeiro have expressed similar grievances (see Moehn 2009).

Max Gonzaga's song "Classe Média" is significant to this analysis, therefore, not because it is harnessed to a social movement or an NGO seeking greater equality and basic citizens' rights, but because it speaks to a fundamental problem blocking the transformation of civil society in Brazil: on the one hand, many in the middle classes see themselves as living in a different country from "the periphery"—which some hope would just "explode"; on the other, social programs seeking to elevate the poor into the middle sectors are not supported by a sufficient amount of economic growth, while high taxation threatens the middle-class consumer-citizen lifestyle. This musical example is also significant for the aesthetic and media context in which it was presented. Neither peripheral nor marginal, MPB and the Festival Cultura are mainstream. Yet contemporary middle-class singer-songwriters such as Gonzaga (or Lenine and Lula Queiroga), who have been influenced by the great festival musicians of the '60s and '70s, no longer have a dictatorship to criticize, or a countercultural leftist student audience. Instead, they may feel stuck between violence and the rising cost of a secure, stable middle-class lifestyle, between consumption and taxation. Chico Buarque himself ruffled a few feathers in an interview for the newspaper *Folha de São Paulo*, when he made the following observations: "The fear of violence in the middle class turns into a rejection not only of the so-called marginal individual, but of the poor in general, of the guy who has an old car, of the *mulato*, the one who is poorly dressed. To be reactionary became the popular tone to take."[11] Max Gonzaga's "Classe Média" is unusual in its destabilizing of the audiotopic "refuge" of MPB described by Kehl as a country to which one has the right to exile, and given sonic form in Lenine's and Queiroga's "Sob o Mesmo Céu."

::: MinC: The State "Massaging" the National Cultural Body

"Either Brazil does away with violence, or violence will do away with Brazil," declared the minister of culture, Gilberto Gil, at his inaugural speech (Brasília, 2 January 2003). "We must complete the construction of this nation, include the excluded groups, reduce the inequalities that torment us," he continued. "The role of culture in this process . . . is not merely tactical or strategic—it is central: to objectively contribute to overcoming social inequalities, all the while focusing on the full realization of human potentials" (Gil 2003a: 42). As might be expected of the state, questions of violence, inequality, difference, and cultural expression are of critical importance in the management of national identity, development, and Brazil's image in the global community. The ministry (MinC) states that its activities are based on three interwoven dimensions: "culture as a symbol factory, culture as a right and as citizenship, and culture as part of the economy" (Gil 2003b: 8). It is noteworthy that Gil spoke of *completing* the construction of the nation, consistent both with development discourse and with Brazilian identity discourse wherein, as mentioned above, the process of cultural mixture is understood as central and also incomplete.

Gilberto Gil's remarkable career took off with his participation in the Tropicália movement during the above-mentioned song festivals of the late 1960s. Years later, in his role as minister, Gil traveled widely to publicize his "Living Culture: National Culture, Education and Citizenship" program. This sophisticated and ambitious cultural policy emphasizes working with already-existing social actors, organizations, and mechanisms, following the critical geographer Milton Santos, who has argued that "utopia should be founded on possibilities, on what already exists as an embryo, which thus holds the potential of being realized" (as paraphrased in Ferreira 2003: 11). The program is consistent with an administration that has a social agenda but that is also responsive to the market and to the global economic and political landscape. In the words of Juca Ferreira, formerly the executive secretary of MinC and now minister of culture (since Gil's resignation from Lula's cabinet in 2008), the Living Culture program is intended to encourage and enable "a large scale convergence of low-income groups with that other portion of society that has kept its distance due to a lack of security . . . and that today enjoys greater access to the university, services, and cultural goods" (2003: 11). The program seeks to draw together "the various Brazils" through the circulation of merchandise, values, symbolic production and dialogue, and by "bolstering the transit of popular culture through mass markets and stimulating a creative dialogue between local and foreign cultures" (11).

Here I will only make brief mention of the *pontos de cultura* (culture points) part of this program. These are spaces that should stimulate dialogue between civil society and the state following, in part, Jürgen Habermas's conception of the public sphere (Gil 2003a: 42; Habermas [1962] 1989). Gil described the culture points as "anthropological do-ins" that massage "vital points that have been momentarily left aside or dormant in the country's cultural body" (2003a: 42). Financial support; computer and other digital equipment; free open-source software to aid in producing music, video, and so on are among the items provided through the program to help develop existing grass-roots and other cultural agents and organizations. The culture points should also be connected with each other, especially via the Internet. One community-based and music-centered organization that is participating in the program is the MHHOB (Movimento Hip Hop Organizado Brasileiro; Organized Brazilian Hip Hop Movement) that, according

The Brazilian minister of culture (2003–8) and the musician Gilberto Gil at
Columbia University, 2004 (Fred Moehn). First published in "Music, Citizenship,
and Violence in Postdictatorship Brazil," by Frederick Moehn, in *Latin American
Music Review* 28.2 (2007): 181–219. Copyright © 2007 by the University of Texas
Press. All rights reserved.

to Lamartine Silva—one of the movement's coordinators—has a presence in sixteen different states. "The public programs of digital inclusion," reports Silva, referencing a part of the ministry's plan," "give peripheral youths access to other technologies besides weapons."[12]

The Piauí Hip Hop Association (Associação Piauiense de Hip Hop), also associated with the MHHOB, is another example of a culture point established where a grass-roots organization had already shown initiative. The center began to take shape in an old building belonging to the secretary of education of the state government but abandoned for ten years. Youths from the hip-hop movement occupied the building until they could get official permission to stay there. Rap and other music groups use the rehearsal space and recording studio at the center, and there are classrooms used on the weekends. Also supporting the site are the United States–based Kellogg Foundation, the nongovernmental organization FASE (Federação de Órgãos para Assistência Social e Educacional; Federation of Social and Educational Assistance Organizations, which is itself supported by the Rio de Janeiro musical group O Rappa), and the students of a local school who are associated with the international group SIFE (Students in Free Enterprise). The Ministry of Labor, which is working jointly with the MinC on the culture points project, has provided eighty-five work stipends for youths that the organization helps. The French NGO Acajuyê also provides materials and has sponsored exchange programs, bringing youths to France.[13]

This list of positive dialogues traversing various sectors of civil society is, I would note, reported on the Ministry of Culture's own website. As of this writing, little public critique has emerged of the culture points program. Some musicians I spoke with were skeptical, but I also visited two culture points in Rio de Janeiro that have benefited from the program: the Ação Comunitária NGO and the Jongo da Serrinha cultural organization, both of which were in existence for many years before receiving MinC support (see Moehn 2007). One complaint I encountered pertained to delays of several months in the transfer of the promised stipends to certain MHHOB culture points, but this seems to have been a bureaucratic delay stemming from the fact that the stipends actually come from the Ministry of Labor.[14] Others complain that the initiative is *pra inglês ver*, or "just for show."[15] The jury is still out, then, on how well the culture points massage the public sphere, and what kind of effect the program will have on citizenship in Brazil.

::: Conclusions: The Identity Work
  of Cosmopolitical Citizenship

Some of the recent literature on "cultural citizenship" understands rights associated with cultural practices and identity as an important fourth component not envisioned by T. H. Marshall. This literature tends to focus on the recognition of alternative or oppressed social identities within a polity, and in many ways it parallels the rise of theories of multiculturalism. It has emerged in a context in which scholars argue that the complexity of postindustrial society rendered class divisions less important than identity politics. The new social movements that organize around issues such as the environment, gay rights, or democratization are also interpreted as displacing class-based mobilization. In the cases explored here, however, questions of collective identity and cultural expression are very much about "citizenship and social class," to evoke Marshall. These examples suggest that it is not so much a question of whether class *or* identity (as we explored it through music) is more important in new social movements; rather, we see new ways in which class is tied to other aspects of the group experience of citizenship such as race, place, gender, violence, aesthetic preferences, and development.

Max Gonzaga's song "Middle Class" shows an alternative class perspective on some of the same problems that preoccupy Nega Gizza of CUFA. However, that perspective does not represent a social movement identity—at least not yet. It has the potential, perhaps, to become a "postcitizenship movement" in which participants who already enjoy most or all of the normal rights of citizens have established channels for mobilizing and putting pressure on political decision-makers (Jasper 1997). Some, such as the economist Waldir Quadros, fear that the right wing could exploit such potential. It seems vitally important, therefore, to play close attention to how relationships between culture, identity, and citizenship change inflections across class lines, rather than seeing these as distinct realms of experience and practice. Few studies take the cultural expressions and preoccupations of the Latin American middle class—that "rather gelatinous and opaque sector," as Altamiro Borges refers to it, as their object, and perhaps this should change.[16]

The MinC's culture points initiative demonstrates, on the other hand, that state policies may traffic in some of the same discursive currency permeating the identity politics of social movements, pop music, or even a disillusioned middle-class. Francesca Polletta and James M. Jasper observe that new social movement scholars have inadvertently turned collective identity into "a kind of residual category" that describes what happens "outside structures, outside the state, outside rational action" (2001: 285). Research on identity and social movements, they argue, should allow "for a number of different relationships between cultural and discursive practices on the one hand, and legal, political, economic, and social structures on the other" (285). The collection of examples I briefly explore here support Polletta's and Jasper's argument that the analytical challenge is to "identify the circumstances in which different relations between interest and identity, strategy and identity, and politics and identity operate, circumstances that include cultural processes as well as structural ones" (285).

I began this chapter with the two Brazils in Carnegie Hall, and I have employed throughout Josh Kun's concept of audiotopias, a neologism he coined in reference to music and the politics of difference in the United States. To close I want to bring back into the discussion the United States as a country where social stratification has been on the rise, and which has its own dynamics of violence. In his inaugural address as minister of culture, back in January 2003, Gil asked what message Brazil can send to the world in a time when "fierce discourses and banners of war are being raised across the globe" (2003a: 43). This was nearly eight months before the Brazilian diplomat Sergio Vieira de Mello, the UN special representative in Iraq, was killed there in a hotel bombing on 19 August. Can Brazil, a country also struggling with problems of violence and inequality, set a global example of "opposites living side by side," in Gil's words, of the tolerance of differences? That is obviously not a question I can answer, but posing it is important to the urgent task of bringing this discussion into a larger frame of reference where musical audiotopias intersect with global dynamics of difference, identity, class, violence, and civil society.

NOTES

A longer version of this chapter was published as "Music, Citizenship, and Violence in Postdictatorship Brazil" in the *Latin American Music Review* 8.1 (2007). In that version, I also considered musical examples associated with the MST (Movimento dos Trabalhadores Sem Terra; Landless Workers' Movement), which has been studied by Malcolm McNee (this volume). Since I wrote this chapter some of the cultural, economic, and government manifestations I examine in it have undergone changes.

For example, Brazil's economy grew impressively, Lula's approval rating soared in his second term, and there may be less middle-class anxiety than when I wrote this. At the same time the historic economic crisis of 2007–9, which is still not over, will have a lasting impact. The framework of my analysis, however, remains pertinent. All translations from Portuguese sources, including song lyrics, are my own.

1. Sources: IPEA (Instituto de Pesquisa Econômica Aplicada; Institute for Applied Economic Research); IBGE (Instituto Brasileiro de Geografia e Estatística; Brazilian Institute for Geography and Statistics); the World Bank; and U.S. Census Bureau (2005 Gini coefficient for the United States is estimated). There is substantial lag time on published Gini coefficient data; estimates suggest that Brazil has reduced its Gini since Luiz Inácio Lula da Silva became president.

2. The Rhythmic Uprising documentary project is coordinated by the American Benjamin Watkins. It highlights four performing arts groups, of which one is a female drum troupe, one is a capoeira group, another is a children's circus, and the last is a youth theater group. The project website is http://www.rhythmicuprising .org. Rhythm of Hope (http://www.rhythmofhope.org) was founded by the American Phillip Wagner, a former IT professional who is also associated with Watkins's Rhythmic Uprising project.

3. Júlio César Tavares, "Uma Proposta para os Candidatos à Prefeitura da Cidade do Rio de Janeiro," n.d. Web pages of the Central Única das Favelas, www.cufa.com .br, visited 28 October 2004, printouts on file with author.

4. Web pages of CUFA (Central Única das Favelas; United Favela Federation), www.cufa.com.br, visited 15 October 2005, printouts on file with author.

5. Festival announcement, "A Nova Música do Brasil—TV Cultura," web pages of TV Cultura, www.brasilcultura.com.br, visited 16 June 2006, printouts on file with author.

6. Revista e no. 101, "Música," web pages of Serviço Social do Comércio, www .sescsp.org.br, visited 17 June 2006, printouts on file with author.

7. Bloggers "StRaNgE," 14 November 2005, and "alltrillian," 17 November 2005, respectively, web pages of RadarPOP, www.radarpop.com.br, visited 9 February 2006, printouts on file with author.

8. Ricardo Antônio Lucas Camargo, 16 January 2006, blog pages of private citizen titled "Túlio Viana: Direito penal—Direito Informático—Direito Humano" (Túlio Viana: Criminal Law—Communications Law—Human Rights Law), tuliovianna .org, visited 9 February 2006, printouts on file with author.

9. Ludmila Ribeiro, "Nem Verso, Nem Prosa: Críticas Rasas e Pouca Poesia na 3ª Eliminatória do Festival Cultura," *Jornalismo Cultural*, 17 August 2005. Web pages of www.jornalismocultural.com.br/, visited 2007, printouts on file with author.

10. Blogger "Abrão," 18 January 2006, web pages of RadarPOP, www.radarpop .com.br, visited 9 February 2006, printouts on file with author.

11. Fernando de Barros e Silva, "Chico diz que vota em Lula de novo," *Folha Online*, 6 May 2006, http://www1.folha.uol.com.br/folha/ilustrada/ult90u60177.shtml, visited 18 April 2010, printouts on file with author.

12. Quoted by Spensy Pimentel in "Cultura Digital É Aliada no Combate à Violência, Avaliam Jovens do Hip Hop," 28 July, 2005. Web pages of the Ministério da Cultura do Brasil, www.cultura.gov.br, visited 2007, printouts on file with author.

13. Spensy Pimentel, "Associação Piauiense de Hip Hop É um dos Mais de 200 Pontos de Cultura," 29 July, 2005. Web pages of the Ministério da Cultura do Brasil, www.cultura.gov.br, visited 2007, printouts on file with author.

14. "A Cultura Vive do Que Tece," *Revista ARede*, 15 May 2006.

15. Blogger ricardo.ruiz, "Esses Pontos de Cultura São Fracos," 26 June 2006, web pages of Conversê: Uma Rede de Pontos, Uma Rede de Conversas, converse.org.br, visited 26 June 2006, printouts on file with author.

16. See Altamiro Borges, "As Oscilações da Classe Média," 2006. Web pages of *Adital: Notícias da América Latina e Caribe*, www.adital.com.br/site, visited 23 June 2006, printouts on file with author.

::: Soundtracking Landlessness

Music and Rurality in the Movimento
dos Trabalhadores Rurais Sem Terra

Malcolm K. McNee

Traced to mass occupations of large estates in Rio Grande do Sul in the late 1970s, the history of the MST (Movimento dos Trabalhadores Rurais Sem Terra; Landless Rural Workers' Movement) is an integral part of the larger history of the loosening of the military dictatorship's hold on power and processes of political reorganization over the following decades. The MST's efforts to define agrarian reform as a fundamental dimension of democratization and to articulate new mechanisms for the rural poor to contest meanings of development and citizenship are among the most dramatically recognizable examples of dissident activism in Brazil.

The MST's mobilization strategies have been studied from multiple disciplinary approaches.[1] Less understood is the significance of the MST as a cultural phenomenon, in terms of production and mediation of cultural artifacts as well as critical engagement with Brazilian cultural discourse at large. While attention has duly focused on the MST's politics of redistribution—with Landlessness defined literally by lack of access to land as the means of production and social reproduction in the countryside—the movement also articulates a politics of recognition, with Landlessness proposed as an affirmative cultural identity recovering and defending what leaders identify as traditional, Brazilian peasant culture. That is, Landlessness is articulated as a political subjectivity and cultural identity, both as a means to a more universal freedom from want and a freedom to be different, to remain or re-become, in a particular sense, rural (McNee, 2003, 2005).

I have chosen to capitalize Landless and Landlessness throughout so as to emphasize the identitarian dimensions to the movement, beyond the material want that the terms literally designate. This diverges from common usage but is not without precedent, even in Portuguese, which does not typically capitalize proper nouns and adjectives designating a people (by race, ethnicity, nationality, religion, etc.). Imagining a successful end to the struggle for land, Zé Pinto writes in the poem "Assim Vou Continuar" (Thus I Will Continue):

E se tu me perguntar	And if you ask me
Agora não será mais sem terra?	Now you're no longer landless?
Respondo: claro que sim	I'll respond: of course I am
Pois uma coisa é ser sem-terra	Because while it's one thing to be landless
Outra coisa é ser Sem Terra	It's another thing to be Landless.
(Vieira 2003)[2]	

This chapter proposes a reflection on the intersections between these dual idioms of Landlessness and the field of popular music. This reflection involves an overview of musical production and performance in the MST, readings of genre and lyrics in songs produced and circulated by the movement, and analysis of cultural criticism and identity politics articulated by activists working with the movement's Culture Sector. Throughout, I will consider aesthetic and thematic affiliations with genres of Brazilian popular music, including that which most powerfully informs the contemporary Brazilian imaginary of rurality, *música sertaneja*, itself a remarkably understudied phenomenon.[3] While earlier examples of music in the MST are characterized by generic eclecticism and lyrical expression of the movement's politics of redistribution, more recent recordings, festivals, and criticism mediated by the Culture Sector attempt to demarcate a generic authenticity to correspond with the movement's articulation of an identity politics for the Landless. Specifically, the MST has become a politicized site for the resurgence and reinvention of *música caipira* or *música sertaneja de raiz*, with its counterpoint as the commercially dominant *música sertaneja*, an opposition roughly parallel to that between bluegrass and country and western music in the U.S. and the distinct visions of rural authenticity they evoke. This trend in the MST's mediation of music reveals an urge to "relocalize" or "re-ruralize" sertaneja music, to reauthenticate it and purify it of urban or global influences. Ultimately, I hypothesize ways in which the redemptive urge and assertions of rural authenticity—certainly red flags to scholars trained in the critique of bounded, essentialist notions of culture—are expedient to the MST's broader struggle for redistributive justice and expanded citizenship rights in countryside.[4]

Musicians of the Movimento Sem Terra performing at the Semana Nacional da Cultura e da Reforma Agrária in Rio de Janeiro, 2002 (Malcolm McNee).

Though music certainly has accompanied the Landless since the genesis of the MST, the first published collection of songs dates to 1996. *Sem-Terra: As Músicas do MST*, organized by Ires Silene Escobar de Campos, includes lyrics to fifty-eight songs. Though some songs are not attributed to an individual songwriter, in most cases the composer is identified, with the majority by Ademar Bogo or Zé Pinto, the former a prominent poet and ideologue of the movement and the latter the best-known MST musician. Both Bogo and Pinto are founding activists of the movement's Culture Sector.

Examples of a nostalgic, pastoral register, a recollection of a rural idyll of harmonious integration of human and natural landscapes, are present but sporadic in this collection of songs. Ribamar Nava's "O Ser da Floresta" (The Forest Being) (the sixty-ninth song), clearly evokes an idealized, peasant existence:

Moro muito longe na floresta	I live far away in the forest
aonde tristeza não tem lugar	where sadness has no place
pois, eu vivo cantando	thus I'm always singing
tirando versos ao luar	snatching verses from the moonlight
Só quero que me deixem lá ficar	I only want them to let me remain there
não tentem mais roubar o meu lugar	that they don't try to steal my place
pois, eu lá tenho tudo	because there I have everything
só preciso cultivar.	I only need to plant.

And Zé Pinto's "Devoção à Amazônia" (Devotion to the Amazon) personifies an unspoiled, tropical nature and naturalizes forest-based communities (indigenous Brazilians and rubber tappers). In these songs, the protagonism of the Landless, in their nominal absence, is implicitly that of solidarity and identification but with recognition of distance and difference. More fragmentary expressions of a pastoral register in this collection are articulated through environmentalism and a general identification of the Landless with a sublime enchantment with nature, only obliquely invoking a traditional peasantry or past rural utopia. Examples include personification of nature—"Mother-Earth, work and love / it is the cry of nature / the troubadour's guitar"—or affective identification with the cultivation of crops—"The rice budded and the beans blossomed / corn in the husk, heart full of love."

What predominates in this collection's articulation of Landlessness is less a sense of longing for lost peasant traditionalism than a poetics of denunciation and class-based resistance, with a postcapitalist utopia located on a future horizon. Two songs reference a peasant and worker alliance: in Ademar Bogo's "Hino do Movimento Sem-Terra" (Hymn of the Landless Movement) the phrase "pátria livre operária camponesa" (peasant-worker free homeland) and in Zé Pinto's "Sem Medo de Ser Mulher" (Not Afraid to Be a Woman) the phrase "na aliança operária-camponesa" (in the worker-peasant alliance). However, the affirmative subjectivity most frequently evoked is the worker, with variations specifically marked as rural: "tomorrow belongs to us, workers," "workers with callused hands," "if he's a farm-hand he weeds the fields / if a mason he builds the house / . . . / with sacrifice they do everything closed-mouthed"; "He's not a farmhand nor a factory-worker / . . . / He's a tool for any job, he laughs to keep from crying."[5]

The common narrative here is of labor against capital, mapped onto the countryside and urban peripheries, with landless rural *workers* denouncing the labor regimes, material want, and dislocations imposed by clearly iden-tified adversaries, specifically the *latifúndio*, *latifundiário*, and *grileiro* (forger of land titles), but also more generally the *capitalista*, the *burguesia rural*, and *patrões* (bosses), and the most frequently referenced negative symbol of Landlessness: the fence. Ademar Bogo's "Prisão da Terra" (The Prison of the Land; song 56) is among the many variations of Marxist-inspired critique:

Terra não é capital	Land is not capital
É fator de produção . . .	It's a means of production . . .
Pois a terra é de todos	The land belongs to everyone
Ela é livre sem patrão	It is free, without a boss
Pelas correntes da lei	But by the chains of law
A terra foi segurada	The land was held captive
Tornou-se escrava dos grandes	It became the slave of the powerful
Sendo medida e cercada	Measured and fenced

The songs in this collection are thus primarily an articulation of a poli-tics of redistribution and of Landlessness as an emergent political con-sciousness and subjectivity. There are few clues in this publication as to whether in formal, musical terms they maintain as a referent a notion of traditional, rural cultural expression. However, seventeen of these songs, plus two others by Zé Pinto and a poem by Ademar Bogo, were recorded for the MST's first CD, *Arte em Movimento* (1997). The CD, capturing a particular moment of performance and mediation intended for circulation within and beyond the movement, provides some insights into generic parameters of Landless music.

This effort to produce a soundtrack for the MST is characterized by a diverse range of genres. Genres traditionally identified with rurality are most present, specifically *forró* and sertaneja. However, also represented are samba, *axé* (the pop genre that originated in Bahia fusing different Afro-Caribbean rhythms) or samba-reggae, romantic ballad, and classical anthem. Featured instruments including accordion, *cavaquinho* (the small Portuguese four-string guitar), acoustic guitar, and percussion instruments such as the triangle—often key markers of generic affiliation—vary across songs. However, with the exception of one exclusively vocal track, "O Hino do Movimento Sem Terra," performed by the University of São Paulo Choir, there is consistent backup instrumentation featuring keyboards and electric bass-guitar. This often recalls stylistic features of *brega* music, including *brega sertaneja*, a genre that leaders of the Culture Sector have since identified as a counterpoint to the authentically peasant rurality they defend.

The MST's nationally coordinated music project, as captured by this CD, is less an expression of a redemptive search for rural authenticity than a reaffirmation of the movement's political platform, emphasizing redistributive justice. Graciano Lorenzi—active in the Musician's Collective, which later expanded to become the Culture Sector by the late 1990s—describes the CD as marking a recognition of music as an important channel of communication with society. He writes, "The CD should not be aggressive. It should, above all else, conquer the sympathy and the support of the people" (liner notes to CD *Arte em Movimento*). An interest in music as a channel of dialogue with broad sectors of society may explain the diversity of genres and standardized instrumentation. It also likely explains another aspect of the CD: the collaboration—as featured vocalists—of nationally prominent musicians, including Leci Brandão, Chico César, Cida Moreira, and Beth Carvalho. Music is thus expedient in expanding and publicly demonstrating networks of solidarity with the Landless.

In this sense, it is worth noting Chico Buarque de Hollanda's CD *Terra*, released in 1997 to accompany Sebastião Salgado's homonymous book of photographs. Buarque's CD includes two new recordings of older classics from his repertoire, "Brejo da Cruz" (Bottomlands of the Cross) (1984) and "Fantasia" (1978), as well as two songs composed for this CD, "Assentamento" (Settlement) and "Levantados do Chão" (Raised from the Ground)—the latter written and performed with Milton Nascimento and evoking the novel by José Saramago (who, in turn, authored the preface to Salgado's book). The songs are stylistically located within the jazz- and samba-inflected MPB (Música Popular Brasileira) tradition, with some subtle rural and regional references, including a forró-inspired, clip-clop percussive detail in "Assentamento" and a variation on a melody from Luiz Gonzaga's seminal "Baião" in the flute solo in "Brejo da Cruz." Lyrically, the songs present portraits of rural communities in states of disintegration and dislocation—"What now? Uprooted from the land? / . . . / With the ground beneath our feet / Like water running between our fingers"—and dispersed toward the anonymity of urban life—

Mas há milhões desses seres	But there are millions of these people
Que se disfarçam tão bem	That disguise themselves so well
Que ninguém pergunta	That nobody asks
De onde essa gente vem	Where they came from.

When the CD begins, however, with a vision of rural redemption in "Assentamento," the narrator calls upon his displaced community to abandon the city and return to the natural cycles of the interior:

A cicade não mora mais em mim	The city no longer lives in me
Francisco, Serafim	Francisco, Serafim
Vamos embora	Let's go
Ver o capim	Let's go see the high grass
Ver o baobá	Let's go see the baobob
Vamos ver a campina quando flora	Let's go see the field in bloom.

Buarque's song, though, is not simply about a return to lost rurality. Its narrative depth includes a sense of tragic danger that pervades the struggle for land as well as the idea, central to arguments for agrarian reform as an attainable development initiative, that there are vast tracts of uncultivated lands in Brazil's interior:

Quando eu morrer	When I die
Cansado de guerra	Tired of war
Morro de bem	I'll die happy
Com a minha terra	With my land
. . .	
Onde só vento se semeava outrora	Where only wind used to sow
Amplidão, nação, sertão sem fim.	Vastness, nation, endless backlands.

The MST's second CD, *Canções Que Abraçam os Sonhos* (Songs That Embrace Dreams), brings together new voices and songs composed specifically for the Primeiro Festival Nacional da Reforma Agrária, held in 1999 in Palmeira das Missões, Rio Grande do Sul. Like the first CD, the festival emphasized the expediency of music in terms of building networks of solidarity. The centerpiece of the festival was a series of performances by professional musicians featured on the first CD—Chico César, Leci Brandão, Zé Geraldo, and Antônio Gringo—and a song contest including twelve entries from MST musicians and twenty-four entries from musicians in solidarity with the movement, with eighteen songs to be selected for the CD. A jury awarded prizes for the best song, interpretation, performance, lyrics, and arrangement, and the audience voted for the most popular song.

The resulting CD, like *Arte em Movimento*, is characterized by remarkable diversity in terms of musical styles and genres. This diversity is reinforced by the absence of the relatively standardized instrumentation that characterizes the first CD. *Canções Que Abraçam os Sonhos*, again, includes songs clearly drawing from forró, sertaneja and brega-romântica, samba-reggae, and rock- and jazz-influenced MPB. It also features examples of hip-hop, tango, *canção de protesto*, and more regional genres such as *maracatu* and variations of música sertaneja de raiz, revealing influences of Paraguayan *guarânia* and Mexican mariachi. The songs recognized with awards include an acoustic-guitar-accompanied protest song "Procissão dos Retirantes" (Procession of the Drought-Migrants) by Pedro Munhóz (first place), a percussively rich, saxophone-accompanied maracatu, "Cordão do Povo em Busca da Terra" (Dance of the People in Search of Land) by Gilvan Santos (second place), the *forró eletrônico*–inspired "A Bandeira Conduz o Povo" (The Flag Carries Forth the People) by Neya Medeiros and Nery Neto (third place), and an axé/samba-reggae song, "Vamos pra Luta" (Let's Fight) by Marquinhos Monteiro (most popular song).

Lyrically, the collection expands upon the poetics of denunciation, resistance, and redistributive politics introduced in the published collection of songs and the movement's first CD. There are, again, protests against poverty, hunger, dislocations, and violence suffered by the Landless and calls to address historic injustices. Pedro Munhóz, for example, in "Procissão dos Retirantes," writes:

Lavradores nas estradas	Farmworkers on the Roads
Vendo a terra abandonada	Seeing the land abandoned

sem ninguém para plantar	With nobody to plant it
Entre cercas e alambrados	Fenced and barbed-wired
vão milhões de condenados	Millions roam condemned
a morrer ou mendigar	To die or beg.

A notable difference in this CD is the relative absence of the vocabulary of class struggle and socialist utopia that punctuates, in particular, a number of the earlier songs authored by Ademar Bogo and Zé Pinto, who dominate the songbook and the first CD.[6] In fact, visions of transformation outlined across these songs are for the most part more precisely contained within the realm of the countryside, whether expressed as ambitious rural development projects including production cooperatives and schools — or, more simply and frequently — as if to emphasize with the diminutive the humbleness of their desires, individual access to a small plot of land: "Oh, plot of land / I carry so many marks / And the dream in my hands"; "Land / I just wand a little piece / To plant"; "I'm just another nameless Indian / Searching for a bit of land."[7]

The first-person singular voices articulating this shared desire for land call attention to another difference between these two CDs. While the first-person plural predominates in *Arte em Movimento*, collectively asserting grievances and demands, *Canções que Abraçam os Sonhos* includes intimately developed portraits of Landless individuals. In "Por Honra e Amor" (For Honor and Love)[8], a tango-inspired composition by Talo Pereira and José César Matesich Pinto, we meet not only "landless Ana," struggling to survive in a squatter's camp, but also a man — it is not clear if he is a landlord or a "hired gun" — who has come to love her yet is tragically compelled to evict her and her fellow Landless. Another strongly individualized portrait is presented in "Um Naco de Chão" (A Piece of Floor). Musically the song is inspired by modern sertaneja and, with its strong storytelling register and notable elements of regional popular speech, it also recalls more traditional *moda de viola*. It tells of the arrival of a stranger who, invited to share the fire and tea of his hosts, tells his tale of hardship and displacement and then hopeful news of the organized camps of Landless:

Deu 'Oh de casa' na estáncia	He shouted a greeting toward the ranch
Trazia o pó das distâncias	He carried the dust of faraway places
. . . .	. . . .
Falou, sem sobra ou mistério:	He spoke without excess or mystery:
. . . .	. . . .

Me vim rastrear as verdades	I come carrying truths
de uma paixão redomona	of an untamed passion
que vive em ranchos de lona	that lives among the tarp-covered shacks
E ostenta rubras bandeiras;	And hoists red flags;
São almas livres, parceiros	They're free souls, my friends

Though these characters are quite perceivably archetypal, the simultaneously expressive singularity in their narratives humanizes the Landless and presents a new dimension to the place of music in the MST. In addition to articulating collective grievances and demands, building through an affective medium an ideological consensus, and making visible networks of solidarity, music is here a way to express individual life-stories of the Landless and the meaningful points of divergence and contact between them. As a further example, it is worth noting the winner for best lyrics, "Tralhas de um Acampado" (A Squatter's Possessions), by Clodoveu Ferraz dos Campos. A mariachi-inflected example of sertaneja de raiz, this song, after a self-introduction of the singer, lists the objects that accompanied him to MST camps:

Nestes versos simples eu quero relatar	In these simple verses I want to recount
Detalhes das tralhas de um acampado	Details of a squatter's possessions
Já desgastadas de tanto se lesar	Already well worn out from so much use
Porém para mim muito representaram	But to me they mean so much
Porque me ajudaram terra conquistar.	Because they helped me conquer land.
Um machado bueno e um três listras que	A good axe and machete
não entrego	I'll never give up
Um maço de prego, um martelo e umas	A pack of nails, a hammer and some
lona preta	black tarps
Uma caneta e um caderninho para	A pen and a little notebook
escrevinhar.	to scribble in.

A final contrastive observation about this CD regards the cumulative sense of Landlessness not only as the shared experience of being trapped on the margins of society, without means to autonomous productivity nor the sense of belonging to a place, but also as the experience of dangers, hopes, and hardships that resistance demands. If the predominant symbol of Landlessness in the first CD is the fence, in the second the tarp-covered tent takes its place. And it is less a clearly negative symbol than a richly ambivalent one, simultaneously evoking a precarious, bare existence, under constant threat of violent dislocation, but also a rebellious sense of hope:

Debaixo de uma lona preta	Under a black tarp
Existe um ser angustiado	Exists an anguished being
Com fome de vencer	With a hunger to succeed
Com sede frio	Suffering thirst and cold
. . . . . .	. . . .
Lonas pretas, que bordam beiras de estrada,	Black tarps, that border the edge of the highway
São marcos de uma busca e de consciência	Are signs of a quest and conscience
A desafiar os que oprimem à mão armada	Defying those that oppress with their guns.[9]

Beyond these differences, however, these CDs together present coherent parameters of musical production for the MST, and a model that has been reproduced, at the state level, for at least two additional CDs: *Um Canto pela Paz* (A Song for Peace), organized by the Pará State Directorate in 2001, and *Regar a Terra* (Watering the Land) produced by the Maranhão State Directorate in 2006.[10] Embracing generic eclecticism, the participation of regionally prominent professional musicians, and the articulation of Landlessness as a common experience of bare existence and dreams of redistributive justice, there is among these CDs little emphasis on rural cultural authenticity as a fundamental dimension of music in the MST.

José de Souza Martins (2003), reflecting on the contemporary "agrarian question" in Brazil and its sociohistorical underpinnings and permutations, argues:

> The rich social and political potentials of the *struggle for the land* have been reduced, in the struggle for *agrarian reform*, to simply a question of land-tenure. The social inventiveness of the land-poor in situations of crisis and change has been, in a sense, channeled towards social and political objectives that don't necessarily coincide with what it is that the poor want or are able to accomplish. (223–24)

The distinction between the "struggle for land" and the "struggle for agrarian reform" is central to Martins's argument. By the former he refers to struggles by poor rural communities—diverse regionally and in terms of their relationship to cash-crop, export-oriented economies and the labor or property regimes they have wrought—to secure access to land. By the latter term, he refers to the ideological agglutination of those localized struggles by mediating agents, including the MST. This struggle for agrarian reform, he proposes, is a reduction that displaces the locally situated originality and creativity of peasants and rural workers with the vicarious doctrinal consciousness of mediating agencies dominated by the middle class.

Others, including Miguel Carter (2006), contest assertions that the MST is rigidly hierarchical and tutelary, pointing to evidence of its decentralization and effective processes of grass-roots democratization. Rather than a result of co-optation by ideologues, for Carter the expansion of the grass-roots base of the movement and the relative homogenization of tactics and demands represent an example of effective mobilization of ideals and interests and the "development of *citizenship rights* in Brazil—in all three contemporary dimensions . . . : civil, political and social rights" (20).

I invoke this critical debate, which pivots on tensions between negation and negotiation in articulating a subalternist politics,[11] for the questions it brings to a consideration of expediencies in the soundtracking of Landlessness. Martins's reminder of the localized structural contingencies of historical and actual struggles for land, as well as his pointed assertion of a doctrinal divide between MST leadership and its grass roots,[12] must be considered in terms of the dynamics of cultural production and mediation in the movement. Based on examples analyzed thus far, we can hypothesize this expediency of music in terms of its articulation of an ideological consensus and a unified Landless subjectivity intended to transcend discontinuities underlying land or labor regimes across time and space. Whether or not taken as evidence of a tutelary hierarchy in the MST, as Martins perceives it, or as under the sign of democratization and "grounded on practical considerations rather than any dogmatic ideology," as Carter sees it (2006: 1), these parameters of expediency may not fully account, however, for another dimension to the production and mediation of music in the movement, that which emphasizes a redemptive ruralism.[13] Here we find a demarcation and assertion of rural cultural authenticity, an articulation of Landlessness through a politics of recognition and defense of rural cultural difference against its erosion by forces of urban-centered modernization.

Though this emphasis on music as a means of exploring and expressing rural cultural roots is largely absent, both lyrically and generically, in the CD projects described above, it has become increasingly recognizable in other projects and texts mediated by the MST's Culture Sector.[14] As a first example, Zé Pinto's CD, *Uma Prosa sobre Nós* ("A Chat about Us"), recorded in 2000, is a remarkable departure from his songs included in the MST's songbook and first two CDs, in which he was among the most strident and even prosaic in lyrics of class struggle and an impending socialist transformation of society at large. In *Uma Prosa sobre Nós*, Pinto's politics of redistributive justice are more subtly intertwined with an exploration of personal history and the memory and ruins of the local culture of the rural Minas Gerais of his youth. In the CD's liner notes, he writes: "They are folk songs inspired by the stories of my father and my mother, the singalongs, the work parties in the coffee fields, the festivals. Stories that rescue from oblivion the saga of a family that, like so many others, planted and harvested for years and years on someone else's land." The songs are an evocation of a singular cultural heritage, a lamentation of its loss, and an expression of hope for its reinvention through remaining fragments. This shift in register from explicit denunciation to celebratory expression of place, identity, and memory is announced in "No Cheiro do Pó de Arroz" (With the Scent of Rice-Flour):

Quem causou tanta miséria eu sei	I know who has caused so much misery
Mas o jeito tem de se alegrar	But the solution has to become joyous
Pois o vale é como um rio	Because the valley is like a river
Transbordando de cultura popular	Overflowing with folk-culture
Os poetas, cantadores violeiros	The poets, troubadour guitarists
Se arreunem sobre os olhos do luar.	Gather under the gaze of the moon.

Alongside numerous references to flora and fauna, Pinto's songs emphasize the quotidian and cyclical festivity of this agrarian community. In "Brilhantina e Água de Cheiro" (Pomade and Perfume), Pinto sings of the anticipation of June festivals:

Quando a fulô de São João	When the St. John flower
Se abrir lá no alto da serra	blooms there at the top of the ridge
Vou colher uma com zelo	I'm pick one with zeal
Pra por nos cabelos de Ana	To put in Ana's hair
. . . .	. . . .
Noite inteira é festa na capela.	All night long there's a party in the chapel.

In "Costumes do Lugar" (Local Customs), festive culture is connected to cycles of agricultural work: "Tune your *viola* young man / 'Cause the party's going to start / All the hoeing is done." In "Ser Tão Meu" (So Much Mine), Pinto draws intimate connections between nature, music, and labor:

A viola apaixonada de um peão roceiro	The passionate *viola* of a farmhand
Quando um pássaro cantando alegra seu viver . . .	When a singing bird cheers him up . . .
Sabiá na capoeira dá o seu sinal	Song thrush in the bush gives its signal
Vai passando a homarada, enxada no ombro	The gang passing by hoes on shoulders
Vão ouvindo o som do rouxinol.	They walk listening to the nightingale's song.

Longing for this rural idyll and singular, articulate cultural universe is connected in Pinto's CD to two dislocations. The first is explicitly autobiographical and tells of his family's move to the agricultural frontiers of Amazônia. In "Lamentos e Sonhos" (Regrets and Dreams) he sings, "Mommy lamenting left behind / Maria's month, the prayer of the rosary / The coronation, the festival, the auction." In "Nesses Trilhos de Saudade" (On These Trails of Longing), without revealing if what he found upon his return was what he left behind, Pinto recalls his journey back:

Regresso à terra natal,	I return to the land of my birth
Ao sul de Minas Gerais,	To the south of Minas Gerais
. . . .	. . . .
A vontade de encontrar,	A desire to find
Os antigos seresteiros,	The old singers
Que um dia deixei por lá.	That one day I left behind.

The second dislocation is toward the city. In "Um Caipira no Metrô de São Paulo" (A Hick on the São Paulo Subway) and "Cantiga de Retornar" (Song of Return) — and in a more archetypal than autobiographical register — Pinto affirms the persistence of rural identity in migrants to the city, a sense of being out of place and desire to return to the place of origins. In the tumult of the São Paulo subway, Pinto's caipira declares:

Vou voltar pra trás, pra Minas Gerais,	I'm goin' back to Minas Gerais
Lugar bom da gente viver,	Where the living is good,

| Porque lá tem lua, roda de viola | Because there they've got the moon, *viola* circles |
| E lá ficou meu bem querer. | And there remained my true love. |

And addressing his boss and the city of São Paulo, perhaps one and the same, the narrator declares, "I'm leavin,' boss, and I ain't comin' back / . . . / Forgive me São Paulo / But I wanna go back."

The most explicitly political song of the album, "Pra Onde Vou?" (Where Will I Go?), presents a peasant dispossessed by the encroachment of a cattle ranch. When he asks himself who he is now and where he'll end up, a stark choice with two outcomes is presented: either acceptance—

Tô conformado, conformado, conformado,	I'm resigned, resigned, resigned
Porque foi Deus quem quis assim	Because it was God that wanted it this way
Alienado, alienado, alienado	Alienated, alienated, alienated
Uma favela será meu fim	A slum will be my end

—or engagement in a collective, utopian struggle that might in the end bring him back home:

Vou nesse trem que traz o novo amanhecer	I'm getting on this train that will lead to a new dawn
. . . . .	. . . . .
Quem sabe esse trem, que tanto convém	Maybe this train, so long in coming
Me leve de volta, pra Minas Gerais.	Will take me back to Minas Gerais.

The redemptive ruralism of Pinto's lyrics is matched by the generic parameters of the CD. Featuring acoustic guitar and *viola caipira*,[15] often backed up by solo flute or saxophone and single-instrument percussion, Pinto's repertoire here is more firmly located within *cantador* or *violeiro* (troubadour) and *música caipira* traditions, ample enough to include a diversity of rhythms and vocal styling, including *toadas, cantiga, polca, baião, moda*, and *guarânia*. Though not consistent throughout the CD, Pinto's use of a distinctly caipira accent and terminology (*vortá* for *voltar, fulô* for *flor*, etc.) is another evocative marker of rurality.

A shift toward more clearly rural musical parameters is also notable in a 2001 CD produced by the MST with support from the University of São Paulo School of Communications. The CD, *Movimento no Ar* (Movement on the Air), is a live studio recording, from the MST's Rádio Camponesa in Itapeva, São Paulo, of performances by musicians from the region's land-reform settlements and occupations. The privileged form here is the classic moda de viola or moda caipira, accompanied by acoustic guitar. Though primarily a showcase for a younger, male duo, Toninho e Zezinho, the intention is also to bring together different generations of Landless musicians, and the CD includes single songs by three older *cantadores*—Serraninho, Barboza, and Nelson Souza—a duo of teenage sisters, As Irmãs Mendes; and Márcio and Paulinho, another young duo. Lyrics tend toward a storytelling register common to the moda form and are inspired by landscapes and elements of the natural world ("Chuva Gostosa" [Lovely Rain], "Lá no Sertão" [There in the Backlands], and "Seca" [Drought]), farm life ("Má Colheita" [Bad Harvest] and "Roceiro" [Farmhand]), love ("Semente de Amor" [Love's Seed], "Desejos Desejos" [Desires Desires]), and comical or heroic episodes ("Prá que Rir Da-quele Moço" [Why Make Fun of That Kid], "João Sem Medo e o Gigantão" [Fearless John and the Giant], and "Os Véio Tem Que Se Cuidá" [The Old-Timers Have to Take Care of Themselves]). Just one song directly names the Landless, simply declaring a certainty that someday they will have land to live and work.

These two CDs present a different, more oblique dynamic of representation of Landlessness than that of the projects directly mediated and circulated by MST national or state-level leadership. They should be considered, though, among a constellation of projects mediated by the MST's Culture Sector as well as pronouncements and writings by Culture Sector activists that advocate the recovery of peasant culture as among the pillars of a cultural politics for the movement.[16] In "O Papel da Cultura no MST" (The Role of Culture in the MST), a 1998 essay that is among the foundational texts of the Culture Sector, Ademar Bogo proposes a return to what he romantically describes as traditional, peasant culture, including "pacific coexistence, visiting neighbors, work-parties, lending and borrowing, folkloric festivals, popular wisdom and the *true sertaneja music*" (4, my emphasis).

This call to demarcate rural cultural authenticity echoes in a number of events subsequently organized by the Culture Sector, including conferences held in Rio de Janeiro in 2002 and Recife in 2004. The gatherings, titled the National Week of Culture and Agrarian Reform, featured debates on the cultural policy, media, and typologies of culture, including an opposition between "quality popular culture" and "commercial culture." It also involved concerts and workshops on songwriting, instrument building, and various types of musical performance. Though the promotion of "peasant art" was highlighted, also proposed was dialogue with urban popular culture, and the two conferences featured events involving youth activists from the favelas of Rio and Recife alongside Landless from MST settlements and occupations. The second conference included appearances by the then minister of culture, Gilberto Gil, and the secretary of cultural identity and diversity, Sérgio Mamberti, inaugurating a federal project in partnership with rural social movements—the Projeto Rede Cultural da Terra (Cultural Network of the Land)—with the mission of supporting Brazil's "popular and peasant" culture. In partnership with the MST, the project proposed cooperation with settlements and occupations to train 200 "cultural agents" to coordinate events in their respective regions.[17]

Returning more specifically to music, Bogo's allusion to generic authenticity through the notion of *real* sertaneja music is reaffirmed in a 2002 MST publication, *Gerações* (Generations), an anthology of poems including song lyrics. Bogo dedicates the book to prominent, mostly mid-twentieth-century figures from the sertaneja genre—João Pacífico, Zé Fortuna, Tonico, Xavantinho, João do Vale, Tião Carreiro, and Cascatinha e Inhana—whom he describes as "the great poets of our country that taught us to dream from the beauties of our land" (Bogo 2002: 3). Here the MST is participating in a long-running critique of stylistic and thematic transformations of sertaneja music since the 1970s and a revaluation of "traditional" parameters of the genre, now frequently designated as música caipira or música sertaneja de raiz.[18] Though the formation of the genre over the course of the twentieth century was originally hybrid and connected to the development of Brazil's urban-based recording and radio industries, this contemporary critique of mainstream música sertaneja represents a resistance to hybridity, the formal and epistemological synthesis and destabilization of antinomian spatial and temporal cultural referents: urban versus rural, traditional versus modern, national versus global, popular versus elite, and so on.

Mineirinho, among the Culture Sector's prominent activists, elaborates on this distinction between sertaneja and sertaneja de raiz through emphasis on the viola caipira, an instrument he describes as "mystic, sacred, one of the oldest in Brazil."[19] For Mineirinho, the viola is a symbol of authentic rural diversity in opposition to a globalized culture industry:

> This instrument is found throughout the countryside, but in each place it is tuned and played differently. The entertainment industry is not interested in

this diversity. They only want to find culture they can reduce to a simple formula to sell more CDs. In rural Brazil, they've pushed U.S.–influenced country music, along with Wrangler jeans and Texas-style cowboy hats, effacing local peasant cultures.[20]

The viola caipira has become a focal point for further solidarity networking and public events. These include the "National Gathering of *Viola* Players and Corn Harvest Festival in Honor of St. Joseph the Worker" organized in Ribeirão Preto, São Paulo, in 2003 and in 2004.[21] An essay by Lucília Maria Sousa Romão introducing the event is worth quoting at length:

> The banalization of lyrics and melodies seems to have taken hold in an irreversible way. Radio and television stations insist on bellowing either English-language songs or caricaturist *sertanejas*. . . . The traditional beliefs, practices, and knowledges historically accumulated by the people must be heard again. To open up space for roots music . . . is more than celebration. To invite folk-dance groups . . . is more than celebration. . . . To cook on a wood stove old farm recipes with fresh corn is more than celebration. It's a political act, a utopian and emancipatory act. . . . It's to be certain that the land needs to be distributed so that the rhythm of thousands of dormant artists can be heard.[22]

Simultaneously celebrating music, material culture, and popular religiosity (under the shade of a 400-year-old fig tree, as highlighted in press releases), the event attempted to delineate a timeless, articulate cultural universe as an untimely memory, resistant to the hegemonic cultural present.

The overall shift in music production and mediation in the MST toward a politics of recognition centered in rural authenticity and difference reveals multiple dimensions of expediency regarding the movement's overall struggle to advance its demands across diverse sectors of society. Outwardly, the call to preservation and defense of "peasant," or *caipira*, cultures functions with the movement's calls for agrarian reform in a sort of tautology of expediency. On the one hand, the configuration of rural authenticity presents the Landless as a minority culture and as bearers of multicultural diversity worthy of redistributive justice and protection from continued dislocations. On the other hand, the MST's proposal for agrarian reform is reframed as expedient precisely to meet that goal of preserving a cultural diversity understood as an essential source of Brazilian national singularity. In this sense, where socioeconomic justice and development arguments for agrarian reform may fall short in terms of their persuasive power, culturalist ones may compensate.

One is reminded here, for example, of the culturalist arguments made on be-half of state support and protections for small farms in a number of European Union countries, for example, farm subsidies to sustain a distinctly French rural cultural heritage. More broadly, the MST's proposed delineation of peas-ant cultural authenticity fits within the sort of dynamic between demands for cultural rights and material claims described by Bruce Robbins and Elsa Stamatopoulou (2004): "Just as 'we' discover that culture is constructed, fluid, and ever inventive, 'they' begin to articulate demands for rights in terms of a cultural identity asserted to be primordial and fixed" (419). Momentarily set-ting aside discomfort with the essentialization embedded in claims for cul-tural authenticity, Robbins and Stamatopoulou suggest that the turn to cul-ture is a means of making material claims that "seems more likely to win international assent than some of the other tactics currently in play" (423).

Inwardly, there is also an important pedagogical dimension. It is aimed at facilitating—through common cultural referents and performative prac-tices, in addition to ideological referents—the integration of Landless, whose "rurality" is understood as interrupted, tenuous, or even, perhaps, false. Mineirinho states the fundamental importance of addressing "that human being that has lost his identity, that's in the urban periphery and that returns to the land. That man needs to rediscover himself through peasant culture"[23] Also cited is the need to make Landless settlements culturally vibrant places in order to sustain them across generations, to compete with the cultural pull factors that draw rural youth to migrate to cities. In both these senses, MST participation in the delimitation of música sertaneja de raiz from música sertaneja—along with their respective caipira and coun-try/cowboy/rodeo iconographies—coincides with a presumption of the im-plicit expediency embedded within the latter. Reflecting on some of the sty-listic transformations of música sertaneja over the 1970s and '80s, Martha Ulhôa (1993) proposes that this genre was "used by migrants as a means of facilitating the absorption of new cultural values. It mediates that adaptation of rural-originated people to urban society" (75). Writing on the prolifera-tion of rodeo and U.S.-inspired *cultura country* in Brazil, João Marcos Alem (2004–05) argues that it corresponds with a reinvention of an agrarian elite capitalized anew by agribusiness multinationals and seeking popular legiti-mation. The symbolic construction of *this* new rurality

> seeks to preserve part of the social memory of *caipira* and *sertaneja* culture and evoke traditions rooted in our old agrarian society, but it also evokes modernity,

when it draws on the influences of U.S. *country* culture. In this way, it undoes the old dichotomous opposition between traditional and modern identities. (95–96)

Música sertaneja de raiz, in its resistance to this hybridity, seems an apt choice to soundtrack the MST's vision of a newly authentic Brazilian rurality, as an alternative to continued urbanization and the agribusiness expansion of monocultures that sustain and can only be sustained by highly concentrated land-tenure systems and corresponding socioeconomic and political inequalities.

By way of conclusion, we should emphasize questions that call for more thorough ethnomusicological mappings of Landlessness. In terms of lack of consensus on the representative nature of the MST's leadership, including of the Culture Sector, and the centralized or decentralized nature of its organizational structures, we are left to wonder if this shift toward identity politics is a recognition on the part of the leadership of the organic presence and resonance of "peasant" cultural forms among the grass roots, or, instead, a top-down pedagogy of distinction.[24] It might better be framed as a question of the leadership providing one of a number of normative models of rurality negotiated through the sorts of performative processes described by George Yúdice (2003): "processes by which identities and the entities of social reality are constituted by repeated approximations of models . . . as well as by those 'remainders' ('constitutive exclusions') that fall short" (31).

More specifically regarding the privileging of sertaneja de raiz and caipira culture, we might consider ways in which this act reveals a tension between diversity and singularity in the MST's identity politics. Will the caipira, a regional identity centered in the interior southeast and central-west of the country, come to stand in for the cultural difference of a broad spectrum of rural localities and regional ethnic or cultural matrices across Brazilian territory? José de Souza Martins (2003) reminds us of the challenges the MST faces in articulating Landlessness as a redemptive, Brazilian peasantry, whether as culture, mode of production, or both:

> Different from . . . other Latin American countries, whose peasantry has an ethnic and historical profile reasonably defined by its indigenous origin, in Brazil it is difficult to even speak of a peasantry. That's because many of these groups do not come from truly peasant historical and cultural traditions, and they don't have an organic structure defined by a shared identity. The understanding of the current situation of this peasantry, its struggles, its impasses,

its difficulties, its contradictions, its victories, its defeats, its transformations, depends on the reconstitution of the diversity of these histories. (198)

As the MST continues to confront this challenge, music will certainly continue to be a privileged channel for articulating Landless identity and for negotiating tensions between the expediency of expressing a singular notion of authentic rurality and of reconstituting the diversity of rural Brazil.

DISCOGRAPHY

Buarque de Hollanda, Chico. *Terra*. Sonopress, 1997.

Pinto, Zé. *Uma Prosa sobre Nós*. Sonar Music, 2000.

Various artists. *Arte em Movimento*. MST / Discografia Gravações, n.d.

————. *Movimento no Ar: Gravado ao Vivo na Rádio Camponesa com os Músicos de Itapeva — SP*. MST, FURB, ECA, USP, 2001.

————. *1° Festival Nacional da Reforma Agrária: Canções Que Abraçam Sonhos*. Studio Master, 1999.

————. *Regar a Terra*. MST-Maranhão, 2006.

————. *Um Canto Pela Paz*. MST-Pará, n.d.

NOTES

1. Carter (2003) reviews a multidisciplinary range of studies of the MST, while a more recent article (2006) outlines the debate on the MST's relationship with democratic processes and institutions. See Miguel Carter, 2003. "Conference Report: The Landless Rural Workers' Movement (MST) and Agrarian Reform in Brazil," 17 October, 2003, web pages of Brazilian Studies Program, www.brazil.ox.ac.uk; and "The Landless Rural Workers' Movement (MST) and Democracy in Brazil," Centre for Brazilian Studies, University of Oxford, Working Paper 60 (n.d.), web pages of Brazilian Studies Program, www.brazil.ox.ac.uk, visited 9 June 2006, printouts on file with author. For more general histories in English of the MST, see Sue Branford and Jan Rocha 2002; and Wendy Wolford and Angus Wright 2003. Wolford (2004) also considers differing genesis narratives of the MST in two settlements. Among publications in Portuguese, Bernardo Mançano Fernandes (2000) presents a state-by-state history and analysis of the MST's mobilization strategies. For studies of the demographics and socioeconomic outcomes of land-reform settlements, see Benício Veiro Schmidt, Danilo Nolasco C. Marinho, and Sueli L. Couto Rosa 1998; and Sérgio Leite and Leonilde Servolo de Medeiros 2004. Martins offers theoretically engaged reflections on the movement's grass roots, leadership, and ideology (2000, 2003, 2004–5). Also see Maria da Glória Gohn (1997, 2000) for an analysis of the MST's relationship with other sectors of civil society, namely, the media and NGOs.

2. Else Vieira, 2003. "The Sights and Voices of Dispossession: The Fight for the Land and the Emerging Culture of the MST (The Movement of the Landless Rural Workers of Brazil)," University of Nottingham, web pages of the Landless Voices Web Archive, www.landless-voices.org/, visited 2007, printouts on file with author.

3. Suzel Ana Reily (1992) notes that sertaneja was outselling all other Brazilian styles by the 1980s, and she cites José Ramos Tinhorão as indicating that the genre already dominated 40 percent of the market by the mid-1940s. Dent (2005, 2009) writes that revenues from sertaneja concerts outpace those from soccer matches and that album sales range from 11 percent to 16 percent of the market.

4. My use of the notion of expediency follows that proposed by George Yúdice (2003). That is, expediency does not merely point out an inherently negative in-strumentalization of culture, but instead draws attention to the unavoidable play of interests in the invocation of culture. Citing Yúdice: "Expediency [generally] refers to what is . . . 'merely politic (esp. with regard to self-interest) to the neglect of what is just or right.' . . . This understanding of expediency . . . implies that there is a notion of right that exists outside of the play of interests. A performative understanding of expediency of culture, in contrast, focuses on the strategies implied in any invocation of culture, any invention of tradition, in relation to some purpose or goal" (38).

5. From, respectively: Ademar Bogo's "Hino do Movimento Sem Terra," Zé Pinto's "Não Somos Covardes" (We Are Not Cowards), and the anonymously composed "Novo Amanhecer" (New Dawn) and "Bóia-Fria" (Migrant Laborer).

6. Of the first CD's nineteen songs, nine are by Zé Pinto. Ademar Bogo wrote lyrics for six songs plus a poem. The songbook includes seventeen songs attributed to Pinto and sixteen to Bogo. The second CD includes no songs by Bogo and only one, "A Luta Faz Valer" (The Struggle Makes it Happen), by Pinto, in which he again ar-ticulates a general critique of capitalism and reaffirms a peasant and worker alliance across rural and urban space.

7. From, respectively: "Pedacinho de Chão," by Ribamar Nava; "Mãe Terra," by Erlon Pericles; and "Um Naco de Dhão," lyrics by Carlos Gomes.

8. For a close reading of this song and its intertextuality with the tango genre and Érico Veríssimo's literary character, Ana Terra, see Else Vieira, "Sem terra / des-terrados: The Music of Dissent of the MST in Dialogue with the Tango Culture." *Image [&] Narrative: Online Magazine of the Visual Narrative* 10 (2005), web pages of www.imageandnarrative.be, visited 2007, printouts on file with author.

9. In, respectively, Alex Della Méa's and Antônio Gringo's "Chão e Terra" and Ed-uardo Amaro's "Tributo ao Trabalhador sem Terra."

10. A press release states:

The CD brings together diverse musical styles such as rap, *baião, cantoria rural*, and reggae, with the objective of reaching a varied public that might thus understand and discuss through the songs the social work of the MST and the reality of families in the countryside. According to the state coordinator of the movement, Jonas Borges, the challenge was to reunite compositions from consecrated names in the history of *maranhense* music and contemporary artists.

See Marina Mendes, "MST no Maranhão Comemora 20 Anos de Luta e Lança CD Musical," 20 January, 2006; web pages of the Agência Notícias do Planalto, www .noticiasdoplanalto.net, visited 9 June 2006, printouts on file with author. To avoid repetition of arguments above I'll forgo comments here on the Pará CD *Um Canto pela Paz*, except to note that many songs denounce the 1996 Eldorado dos Carajás massacre, in which nineteen Landless were killed by military police.

11. For a useful outline of this larger theoretical debate, see Yúdice's introduction to Néstor García Canclini's *Consumers and Citizens* (2001).

12. He notes the postsettlement tensions that have emerged due to the leadership's privileging of cooperative production models and to desires of many Landless to individually manage their plots.

13. My use of this term draws inspiration from Jack Alden Draper (2005). Draper uses "redemptive regionalism" to describe contemporary forró music that though largely centered today in the cities of São Paulo and Rio de Janeiro, still strongly expresses a regional ethos through a refusal to cognitively map the city.

14. This is not to say that it is necessarily new in the cultural production of the Landless. Assessing its currency would require more extensive field-research across different Landless communities. However, among Culture Sector activists, who mediate projects and articulate a cultural politics with national circulation, the idea of Landlessness as a redemption of rural cultural difference has become more prominent.

15. A smaller version of a guitar said to have been disseminated throughout Brazil by Jesuit missionaries during the early colonial period. Commonly associated with "classic" sertaneja music, the instrument is currently undergoing a relative renaissance and rediscovery. See Rafaela Müller 2002.

16. For broader consideration of the MST's cultural politics, see McNee 2003.

17. See Rodrigo Valente 2005 for a journalistic account of this second conference.

18. For analysis of transformations of the genre, see Samuel Araújo 1988; Reily 1992; Martha Ulhôa 1993; and Waldenyr Caldas 2004–5. Commonly noted transformations include the incorporation of electric instruments and elaborate orchestration, singing in standardized Brazilian Portuguese rather than rural dialects, fashion and iconography drawing from urban youth and U.S. country-western cultures, and lyrics emphasizing romantic love rather than anecdotes of rural life. Some changes parallel the brega transformation of other popular genres and are seen as the urbanization of a rural music accompanying the urbanization of the population. For a history of the genre, also see Rosa Nepomuceno 1999.

19. See Eliane Amaral, "Rico Não Gosta Que Pobre Pense," interview with Minei-

rinho (Felinto Procópio dos Santos), 2005, web pages of Núcleo Piratininga de Comunicação, www.piratininga.org.br, visited 9 June 2006, printouts on file with author.

20. From an interview conducted by the author in Teodoro Sampaio, São Paulo, 7 June 2001. Also cited in Malcolm K. McNee, "Stage-Might: Brazil's Landless Find Strength in Art," May 2002, web pages of the Resource Center of the Americas, www.americas.org, visited 2007, printouts on file with author.

21. This event drew 10,000 participants, and many prominent artists of música caipira, and led to the founding of the Associação Nacional dos Violeiros do Brasil. Sharing affinities, if not official affiliation with the MST, the association clearly articulates one dimension of the expediency of this shift in MST cultural politics toward a demarcation of rural authenticity. As Pereira da Viola, the association's president, explains the objectives of the organization: "We want to be included in public policies . . . , in order to counter the prejudicial vision of the *caipira* as backwards" (quoted in João Bernardo Caldeira 2004).

22. Lucília Maria Sousa Romão, "Violão Ensolarado" (n.d.). Web pages of Movimento dos Trabalhadores Rurais Sem Terra, www.mst.org.br/violeiros, visited 10 June 2006, printouts on file with author.

23. Quoted by Sofia Prestes, "Cultura em debate: Somos sem-terra, mas não temos que gostar de lixo cultural, diz dirigente do MST," *Radioagência NP*, 2 February 2006, web pages of www.radioagencianp.com.br/node/95, visited 9 June 2006, printouts on file with author.

24. Tensions between the performative and the pedagogical in the cultural politics of the MST's Culture Sector recall those debated among the "engaged" artists and intellectuals of the CPCs (Centros Populares de Cultura; Popular Centers for Culture) in the 1960s. In addition to mediating engagement between professional artists and intellectuals and "the people," the Culture Sector is rearticulating the typology of culture—including the notion of revolutionary popular culture—once proposed by CPC leaders such as Carlos Estevam and Ferreira Gullar. There are, of course, significant differences between the movements and moments. The CPCs emerged within intellectual and student circles at a moment of revolutionary optimism, whereas the Culture Sector has developed within a grass-roots movement at a particularly postutopian moment. While CPC theorists advocated appropriating popular cultural forms as vehicles for ideologically appropriate content, the MST's Culture Sector also is increasingly focused on rescuing from oblivion "authentic" cultural forms that themselves are perceived as forms of resistance. For a history of the CPCs, see Marcelo Ridenti 2000. For an influential critique of Estevam's manifesto, see Heloísa Buarque de Hollanda 1980.

::: Zhen Brasil's Japanese Brazilian Groove

Shanna Lorenz

Japonês da pátria filhos	Japanese sons of the fatherland
Ver contente o sol nascente[1]	See the rising sun content
Somos pardos e patrícios	We are mulattos and brothers
Amarelos descendentes	Yellow descendants
"Los Hermanos" de Colombo	The "Brothers" of Columbus
Oriundos do Oriente	We come from the Orient
Kurosawas e Kurombos	Kurosawas and *Kurombos*[2]
Kamikazes dos quilombos	Kamikazes from the *quilombos*[3]
Siamo tutti buona gente	*Siamo tutti buona gente*[4]
Já nem sei mais o que sou	I no longer know what I am
Do atabaque e do taikô	From the *atabaque* and the *taiko*[5]
Já nem sei mais o que sei	I am no longer what I know
Se nissei, sambei, dancei	Fourth-generation, I samba(ed), I danced
No Japão sou brasileiro	In Japan, I am Brazilian
E no Brasil, sou japonês	In Brazil, I am Japanese
De shogum a "Padim Ciço"	From shogun to "Padim Ciço"[6]
Templos, taipas e tapuias	Temples, mud huts, and *tapuias*[7]
Queimo incenso no feitiço	I burn incense at the ritual
Chá e cauim na mesma cuia	Tea and manioc alcohol[8] in the same gourd
Sou BANZAI e alleluia	I am BONZAI[9] and hallelujah
Samurai do "deixa disso"	Samurai of "let it be."
Sou bonsai das seringueiras	I am the bonsai of the rubber tappers[10]
Pau-brasil das cerejeiras	A brazilwood cherry tree
Cabra-ninja, sou mestiço.	Cabraninga,[11] I am *mestiço*.

—Adolfo Mizuta, "Tupy-Nikkeys," 2008

Zhen Brasil walks onto the stage of *Sem Limites para Sonhar* (No Limits to Dream), a talk show hosted by singer Fábio Jr. To their audience the group is both familiar and uncanny. Their costumes cite the most familiar and toxic tropes of Japaneseness. Dressed as a rice farmer with a broad straw hat, one of the lead singers, Yuiti Shiraishi, squints and bows repeatedly. The kimono- and sunglass-wearing Samurai, Fábio Fukuda, who serves as the band's *pandeiro* player,[12] and as the other lead singer, holds himself with steely erectness, grasping the sword at his waist. Hugo Koike, a percussionist and back-up singer, is a geisha demurely batting his eyelashes from behind a hand-held fan. His milky white face paint sets off the rich colors of his kimono. The *cavaquinho* player,[13] and back-up singer, Andre Fujiwara's outdated suit and suspenders mark him as a newly arrived postwar Japanese immigrant. However, the band cites these reified stereotypes of Japanese otherness with a difference as they take up their instruments and begin to undulate to the grooves of samba. Waves of sound flow through rigid bodies, turning these exquisite statues into living challenges to all notions of what is considered to be "natural" to Japanese Brazilian bodies.[14]

Part of what is so compelling to me about the Zhen Brasil phenomenon is that during the five years the band was together (1998–2003) their quirky samba piqued the interest of a huge fan base from all corners of Brazil, as attested to by the thousands of e-mails sent to the band. Moreover, as they toured and appeared on the most popular syndicated talk shows, for a time, they were among the most well-known Japanese Brazilian musicians in São Paulo. The band was able to touch so many fans precisely because their sonic interventions shaped and amplified the sounds of change vibrating through the Japanese Brazilian community, sounds that have transformed the ways that Japanese Brazilians see themselves and are seen by other Brazilian ethnic groups.

When Zhen Brasil burst onto the musical scene, they wanted to change the ways that Japanese Brazilians are perceived both within and without the Japanese Brazilian community. While intolerance toward Japanese Brazilians has become less vehement in recent decades, the concept of Japanese Brazilians as inassimilable continues to circulate. Japanese Brazilians are generally seen in a positive light by other Japanese ethnic groups, yet they continue to be seen as cut off from the mainstream of Brazilian culture, and unable, due to their racial heritage, to master basic tenants of Brazilian sociability. It is for this reason that representations of Japanese Brazilian inclusion, like those offered by Zhen Brasil, continue to be relevant in post-dictatorial Brazil. The group's often contested sonic misbehaving provides a fertile site to explore the ways that Japanese Brazilians are striving to transform the cultural and social landscapes they inhabit. By shaking the foundations of Brazilian racialization, Zhen Brasil called into question an entire system of cultural and racial categorization that continues to enforce limits on Brazilian citizenship, as it supports the financial and political supremacy of white Brazilian elites. In the five years they toured, they found creative ways to explode commonly held myths about Japanese racial and cultural heritage, Japanese Brazilians, Brazilian national identity, and the relationship between the three.

In his song "Tupy-Nikkeys," Adolfo Mizuta gives voice to the disorientation that ensues when culture categories begin to lose the ability to define self and other, insider and outsider. In his song he recalls the dilemma that has confronted Japanese Brazilians in recent years: "In Japan I am Brazilian, In Brazil I am Japanese." Founded by Mizuta in 1998, Zhen Brasil emerged at a moment when old constructs of "Japanese" and "Brazilian" had become too rigid and oppositional to explain the complex transnational consciousness of Brazil's 1.4 million Nikkei, who, during the period of redemocratization, initiated a movement of large-scale circular migration between Japan and Brazil. Following the economic crash of the 1980s, more than a quarter million Japanese Brazilians, referred to as *dekasegui* (guest workers) went to Japan, where they found jobs in the labor-hungry industrial sector. A large number of these immigrants later returned to Brazil, shuttled back and forth between the two countries, or did both, a pattern of cyclical migration that has had a profound impact on the Brazilian Nikkei community (Linger 2003; Roth 2002; Tsuda 2003). Indeed, investment by return migrants has fueled economic growth in several communities, particularly in São Paulo State, and established Japanese Brazilians as an important consumer constituency.

While economic motivations were important for these immigrants, many also went to Japan with a desire to know the country that had been idealized by parents and grandparents. Taeco Toma Carignato (2002: 63) describes this idealization of a Japanese homeland, which had a nostalgic pull even for Japanese Brazilians who had rejected much of their cultural heritage: "Brazilian dekasegui tried to reconnect with the culture they had idealized. They tried to recover the traditions, which, in the process of integrating into Brazilian society, they had often ignored or avoided accepting." In the years before the "return" migration boom, many Japanese Brazilians saw Japanese culture as the embodiment of ideals such as community cohesion, dedication to work, and respect for elders, which were understood to be lacking in the mainstream of Brazilian culture. However, faced with an unruly Japan that could not be contained by frozen idealizations of distant sojourners, the dekasegui were forced to radically rethink their relationship to their Japanese heritage. While many expected to be embraced as countrymen after lifetimes of being referred to as "Japanese" in the Brazilian context, dekasegui workers instead encountered a Japanese populace who often regarded them as suspicious foreigners. While dekasegui found different paths through this unknown territory, for many, idealizations of Japanese difference were shattered in the face of dangerous working conditions, xenophobia, and the shock of encountering an unfamiliar "social-scape" so different from the memories of parents and grandparents who had emigrated to Brazil (Linger 2003). For many Brazil-based Nikkei, the dekasegui phenomena has contributed to a sense of belonging and allegiance to a Brazilian homeland, regardless of whether they themselves have made the transatlantic trip.

Adolfo Mizuta, a talented musician in several Brazilian musical idioms and the founder of Zhen Brasil, never went to Japan. Like most Nikkei Brazilians, he has friends and relatives who have gone in recent years. Stories of these circular migrants have changed his understanding of Japan, which he now sees as a place where he would not be welcome. And while they differ in their competencies and commitments to Japanese culture and social worlds, the musicians who collaborated with Mizuta on the Zhen Brasil have a common understanding of how deeply they have been imprinted by their Brazilian upbringings. For some, this understanding has inspired feelings of belonging to the Brazilian nation-state. However, this identification with Brazil involves a critical reevaluation of the exclusionary tendencies of the Brazilian racial formation, accompanied by a deep suspicion of cultural categories that have excluded Nikkei Brazilians from full belonging in both the Japanese and Brazilian contexts.

According to the band member Yuiti Shiraishi, Brazilians see Japanese Brazilians through a narrow set of categories that ultimately exclude them:

> Japanese either have to be reserved and proper, or funny. They play the role of the comedian so people can make fun of them . . . If you turn on the television you will just see satires of Japanese who are dry cleaners or pastry chefs . . . What

we [Zhen Brasil] did was to call attention to the Japanese. Japanese are not just that proper thing; we are also Brazilian. We are [Japanese] descendants but we are also the Brazilian people.[15]

Yuiti Shiraishi resists mainstream representations of Japanese Brazilians, which, at their best, present them as hardworking, honest, traditional, and hopelessly square, and at their worst, as bucktoothed immigrants, who inspire ridicule with their excessive smiling, bowing, and broken Portuguese. Japanese Brazilians are seen as model minorities, who symbolize progress and technological know-how. However, this model minority status also casts a shadow, as Japanese Brazilians are constructed as perpetual outsiders, and continue to be objects of ridicule both in the media and in everyday encounters with their non-Nikkei compatriots (Daniela De Carvalho 2003: 65). Stereotyped in Japan as "Brazilian" others, and Brazil as "Japanese" others, many Japanese Brazilians struggle to find space between the hyphens as living, breathing transnational subjects, shrugging off the fixity of the cultural stereotypes both in Japan and Brazil. However, to abandon the cultural categories through which one has understood self and other is not a simple matter; rather, it is a path of disorientation and doubt that has contributed to the alarmingly high rates of depression and other mental illness among dekasegui who return to Brazil (Debieux Rosa 2002).

Mizuta's song "Tupy-Nikkeys," hints at this disorientation, which leaves the narrator in doubt about his own identity and about being able to adequately describe an emergent self that exists in excess of that which can be known ("I don't know who I am any more / I am no longer what I know"). Here Mizuta uses aporia, or the expression of doubt about his identity, to begin the work of destabilizing stereotypical constructs of Japanese in Brazil. Negotiating social constructs that interpellate Nikkei as Japanese and un-Brazilian, the song binds together elements of Japanese and Brazilian culture that are commonly seen as contradictory. For example, the song's Japanese Brazilian subject is a mellow samurai ("samurai do 'deixa disso'"). As such, he combines stereotypically Japanese and Brazilian cultural prerogatives. This gesture of grafting together cultural elements that have been cast as binary opposites is symbolized by the image of the (Japanese) cherry tree made of brazilwood. In binding together these contradictions, Mizuta threatens the integrity of exclusionary understandings of Nikkei Brazilian selves and, in the process, shatters social models that have become too antiquated and brittle to explain the living material they are meant to describe.

In "Tupy-Nikkeys," and in the performances of Zhen Brasil, there are many examples of the binding together and mixing of cultural icons, a strategy that I will refer to as cultural *mestiçagem* (hybridity). This strategy is informed by majority strategies of nation building, as well as by ethnic challenges to elite models of nation. Turning now to a closer analysis of Zhen Brasil, I will tease out some of the overlapping moments of humorous mestiçagem in the band's musical performance, which complicate monolithic understandings of mestiçagem as a cultural strategy. Indeed, I will suggest that the mestiçagem employed by Zhen Brasil pulls in radically different directions, sometimes reasserting the possibility of adequately knowing and representing Japanese Brazilian selves, at other times calling into question the very processes of signification that seek to establish and reify minoritarian subjects and to constitute the limits of community belonging. We might think of this diverse use of mestiçagem as a shuffling back and forth between modern and postmodern strategies of identity formation, a complex dance that answers the contradictory interpellations that call Nikkei Brazilians into existence. What I will refer to as "restorative" strategies involve the restoration of a knowable self out of the shards of previous social models. In contrast, I will use the phrase "postmodern" strategies to refer to artistic responses that are underwritten by a deep suspicion of the ability of social models to adequately describe Japanese Brazilian subjects. While the band makes use of both of these strategies, I will argue that ultimately the postmodern mestiçagem of Zhen Brasil tends to amplify rather then foreclose aporia.

Zhen Brasil appeared twice on Fábio Jr.'s talk show as part of "Japanese" theme days, where they performed alongside other guests with some link to Japan or Japanese culture (including an Afro-Brazilian samba group that had toured Japan, Japanese Brazilian hip-hop and belly-dancing ensembles, and a Japanese Brazilian soccer player). In the footage, one can see the guests are all treated as oddities who must demonstrate their strange skills to a titillated public. "Did you know that Japanese dance samba?" Fábio Jr. asks his audience, his quizzical expression making it clear that he is himself skeptical at best. "Japanese samba? I don't understand a thing," he declares. Like many of his compatriots Fábio Jr. refers to his Japanese Brazilian guests as Japanese or simply *japas* ("Japs"). Even third- and fourth-generation Japanese Brazilians are regularly called *japas* by non-Nikkei Brazilians. This ahistorical conflation of Japanese and Japanese descendants in Brazil sustains the continuing outsider status of Nikkei Brazilians.

Zhen Brasil arrives dressed in "Japanese" attire, ready to take up the challenge. Before the band has played a note, Fábio Junior wants to know, "Can you dance with just the *pandeiro*?" as he calls his kimono- and sunglass-garbed namesake (Fábio Fukuda) onto the stage to demonstrate his skills as a samba dancer. "Hold my sword," demands the uv-protected samurai, a phallic offering that a knowing Fábio Jr. refuses with a hearty chuckle. Accompanied by just the rhythm section, Fukuda proceeds to shake out a respectable if excessive samba, replete with spins and flirty leg flashes that he achieves by pulling back his kimono. His intention, he later explained to me, was to parody the ornate dance styles of black Brazilian pagode performers.[16]

This performance fragment offers a glimpse into the embedded cultural stereotypes with which Japanese Brazilians must contend on a daily basis. By questioning the group's ability to samba, Fábio Jr. reinforces a widely held view that Japanese racial difference is mutually exclusive with qualities that are understood as essential to *brasilidade*. When Mizuta formed Zhen Brasil, he wanted to show the world that Japanese Brazilians were as Brazilian as any other ethnic group in Brazil: "The deeper message of Zhen Brasil is that people with slanted eyes of the yellow race can play typical Brazilian instruments." On the surface Zhen Brasil's social critique is straightforward. Encountering a racial formation that constructs them as fundamentally un-Brazilian, they set out to prove that Japanese Brazilians can take part in the most Brazilian of music making. While the original aim of the band was to perform many types of regional Brazilian music, it soon became clear that audiences were most impressed when the Japanese Brazilian band played samba. Repeatedly, it was the ability of these musicians to interpret samba grooves that surprised and amazed Brazilian audiences, who had long internalized a notion of Japanese Brazilian culture as diametrically opposed to African-influenced Brazilian culture forms. According to Mizuta, "They thought it was bizarre. Could it be that Japanese people are playing samba? They were always doubting; they had to see in order to believe."

A central facet of Brazilian racial discourse is the idea that Japanese bodies lack the "groove," or *ginga*, that is a part of the definition of the Brazilian national character. Repeatedly the band members told me that Japanese are seen as lacking ginga. The concept of ginga is a skill associated with Afro-Brazilians that is, among other things, a marker of physical grace and dexterity on and off the dance floor, and a mode of personal comportment that involves being quick on one's feet and able to respond effectively to the uncertainties of life (Lewis 1992: 97–98). Likewise, this ability to move gracefully is intimately tied to Brazilian concepts of physical beauty, and it should therefore be no surprise that Japanese Brazilians (particularly men) challenge Brazilian aesthetic ideals. For the band member Fábio Fukuda, part of what was so important about the Zhen Brasil project was that for the first time, Japanese Brazilians were being shown as graceful and sexy as they demonstrated the ginga that is so important to Brazilian ideals of beauty. Fábio Fukuda himself became the object of the rapt attention of audience members, particularly the screaming girls who swooned as he came near.

Why should it be so unbelievable that Japanese Brazilians could be capable of playing samba? Since the 1930s, when samba was elevated to the status of national icon, it has been intimately tied up with constructions of Brazilian nationhood (Rocha 2002: 55). However, samba has historically been a highly contested artistic medium, used by dissenters to circulate alternative public discourses, even as the Brazilian elites harnessed it as a vector toward the consolidation of centralized state power. Indeed, samba still carries some of the burden of representing the Brazilian nation both internally and abroad. For this reason, it is particularly loaded for Japanese Brazilians to claim samba culture as their own. Insofar as samba and Brazilian national identity are irrevocably intertwined, to do so goes against deeply ingrained ideas of national belonging and exclusion. In the act of playing music, then, Zhen Brasil pushes toward a general inclusion of Japanese Brazilians within the cultural frame of what is understood as essentially Brazilian, that is, samba culture.

The original premise of the band was to insert Japanese Brazilians into the mainstream social milieu by accentuating the Japanese racial heritage of band members who would seamlessly perform samba music and dance. Moreover, a closer look at the contents and contexts of this samba performance reveals that the band also attempts to rework majoritarian constructs of a homogeneous Brazil built upon the cultural and genetic mixing of three races. Excavating multiple strategies to confront a national myth that excludes them, Mizuta and Zhen Brasil offer alternative versions of mestiçagem. If the majoritarian version of mestiçagem involves the mixing of three races to form a unified Brazilian race, Zhen Brasil offers a series of restorative mestiçagens in an attempt to rewrite Japanese descendants into the Brazilian patrimony. These strategies, which I will examine in turn, involve

(1) redefining mestiçagem as a mosaic in which ethnic minorities coexist in a state of differentiated multiculturalism and (2) hybridizing Japanese and Brazilian cultural icons based upon constructions of cultural affinity.

In "Tem Purê no Tempurá" (There's Mashed Potatoes in the Tempura; Mizuta and Campos), from the CD *Zhen Brasil: Os Japinhas do Pagode* (2001), we see examples of strategies that we might think of as "mosaic" and "affinity" approaches to mestiçagem, respectively:

Ele preparou sakê, missó e sashimi prá ela	He makes her sake, miso, and sashimi[17]
E ela pôs azeite de dendê na came de panela	And she uses *dende* oil in the saucepan
Eles misturaram cama, mesa, banho e frigideira	They mix bed, table, bath and frying pan
Ele é japonês e ela é brasileira	He is Japanese and she is Brazilian

A mosaic approach shows Japanese and Brazilian culture existing in tandem but retaining their original attributes, while the affinity approach proposes similarities between the two cultures. A medium-paced samba, the song comically tells the story of a mixed-race couple each bringing their own cultural capital to the marriage. Indeed, the song writes Japanese Brazilians into the "foundational fiction" of Brazil, substituting a Japanese Brazilian coupling for the coupling between Europeans and native Brazilians that was so idealized by the Brazilian Romantics. The marriage works as a symbol for a form of cultural parallelism in which two cultures occupy the same space while remaining differentiated. In this symbolic house/nation, Japanese foods such as miso and sake are consumed along icons of brasilidade such as feijoada. According to Andre Fujiwara (personal interview, 2003), who sees "Tem Purê no Tempurá" as a "felicitous" union of Japanese and Brazilian culture, the song works against common-sense ideas of Japanese and Brazilian culture as mutually exclusive: "[Tem Purê no Tempurá] took the stereotypes of both Brazilians and Japanese and showed them living side by side . . . Some people think it has to be one thing or another."

In addition to creating a space in which Japanese and Brazilian cultures can coexist in an easy interdependence, the song's text constructs affinities between the two cultures as points of intersection are accentuated. For example, while the Japanese husband removes his shoes upon entering the house, his Brazilian wife dances barefoot with her feet on the floor. Later, musical and semantic plays likewise aim at uncovering cultural affinities. Specifically, the chorus incorporates a "triple play," detailed below, that articulates linguistic and cultural affinities between Japan and Brazil. Here I refer to the moment of erotic climax, when the wife cries out the Japanese word a*ikido* while his "*sushi* plays *sumo*." Aikido is a Japanese martial art that uses the energy of an oncoming attack in order to control or throw an opponent. In "Tem Purê no Tempurá," both the squeaky timbre with which the word is sung, and a downward melodic leap of an octave between the syllables *ai* and *ki*, evoke the sounds of the cuíca drum, which commonly accompanies samba performance. The *cuíca* is a friction drum with a stick attached to the skin which, when rubbed up and down with a damp cloth, creates a grunting or squeaking sound that is evocative of sexual penetration. The first part of this word and sound play, therefore, involves sexualizing and Brazilianizing the word *aikido* by linking it to the sound of cuíca.

In the next line of the melody, this play is extended. A shift into a more open-throated timber and the addition of *eu* converts *aikido* into, "Oi que eu dou" (I give). Here, in the second part of the play, "to give" refers to the sexual role that in North American parlance is commonly constructed as the passive role. The chorus therefore links the sounds of Japanese and Brazilian utterances both to each other, and to the musical sounds of the cuíca. However, this wordplay (the third part of the triple play) also explores a cultural affinity involving constructions of "passivity" or receptivity as an active and powerful stance: both the aikido practitioner and the sexual giver find their power in guiding the momentum of corporeal energies that engage them. By exploring affinities between Japanese and Brazilian culture, the song suggests that Japanese and Brazilian cultural elements can coexist as separate yet intertwined entities, and that commonalities between the two cultures make this coexistence all the more felicitous. Moreover, by constructing this mosaic version of mestiçagem that allows for Japanese Brazilian inclusion in Brazilian national identity, Zhen Brasil excavates a strategy that Jeffrey Lesser (1999: 5) has referred to as a hyphenated Brazilian identity, "a joining (rather than mixing) of different identities."

"Tem Purê na Tempurá" therefore challenges majoritarian ideas of homogeneous brasilidade by showing Japanese Brazilian culture existing in tandem with Brazilian culture, and by reworking the sexual imagery that has been so foundational to Brazilian nationalism. Taking their inspiration from modernist models of nation building, what these two strategies of restorative representation (which I have called mosaic mestiçagem, and cultural affinity) share is a faith in the fidelity of representation, and in the ability of musical performance to offer alternatives to majoritarian constructions of Nikkei Brazilians. But what Zhen Brasil soon discovered through their musical experimentation was the power of reception to mark Japanese Brazilian bodies as other. As Yuiti Shiraishi explained to me, when the band first formed, they tried to offer a more-or-less "straight" performance, without much of the parody that they later introduced. For example, they originally performed in brightly colored button-up shirts, imitating other popular pagode bands. However, their performances were repeatedly met with laughter as they found themselves unwittingly read in terms of comic stereotypes of Japanese Brazilians. Indeed, Japanese Brazilian bodies are so intractably marked as nonnormative that at the moment of reception, they are read through familiar tropes of otherness. Karen Shimakawa traces the fraught path of counterrepresentation in her discussion of Asian American theater when she argues: "To directly challenge current abject/stereotypical constructions of Asian Americanness by presenting a wholly contradictory construction would be to suppose that one could somehow stand outside that process, at an objective distance, in order to critique it and then *choose* a different cultural identity" (2002: 101).

Encountering a social formation that marked them as other, Zhen Brasil entered into a series of polemic discussions. One faction argued that the band should continue to strike a "serious" tone in their performance as they performed counterconstructions of Japanese Brazilians, while other members sought more subtle ways to take on the toxic stereotypes that interpellated them. According to band members, discussion centered on the ironic use of "Japanese" costumes and the parodic humor of Japanese and other ethnic stereotypes. Ultimately the more traditional faction became disillusioned and left the band, while the remaining musicians began to explore what I have referred to as postmodern strategies of mestiçagem.

The musicians who stayed with Zhen Brasil until the band broke up in 2003 shared a style of parodic humor that irreverently reflected back distorted and exaggerated versions of the Japanese types that circulate in mainstream media. It was during this period that the band began to abandon their conventional pagode attire, first experimenting with karatelike outfits and later settling on the four hyper-Japanese costumes that I have described above. As Andre Fujiwara, the group's cavaquinho player, explained, the costumes of geisha, samurai, rice planter, and immigrant were chosen because those are the "main [Japanese] characters that are known to Occidentals." When I asked Andre if their intent was to "break" the stereotype of Japanese Brazilians, he responded, "I don't think we wanted to break it exactly. When someone has a big nose and starts to make fun of the nose, it ends up being smaller. You exaggerate so much that it ends up being a small thing." While dismissing the possibility of completely dismantling these stereotypes, Fujiwara argues for a more limited but affective agency in exaggeration. Encountering the limits of mestiçagem strategies that seek to answer the question "What is Japanese Brazilian?," Zhen Brasil reached toward a mimesis that works against discursive logic in which Japanese Brazilian is always defined as a lack or the negative of brasilidade. This strategy is something like the mimesis explored by Luce Irigaray (1991: 126), who argues that the only way for women to self-represent within the logic of discourse that seeks to erase them is to find excessive ways to inhabit the role of the feminine (Shimakawa 2002: 103).

While the counterimages of Japanese Brazilians that I discussed above work on a principle of offense, attempting to forcefully displace "false" stereotypes, critical mimesis is a defensive strategy, working to channel and displace the social energies that reify Japanese Brazilian subjects. Indeed, the sexually infused image of aikido from the song "Tem Purê no Tempurá" hints at the power of such defensive strategies, a corporeal metaphor that models a defense against the disciplining of racialized bodies. The power *of* aikido lies precisely in using the force of the attacker in order to undermine the power of the attack. It is precisely the transformation of conventional conceptions that Zhen Brasil reaches toward as they irreverently mime the worst stereotypes of Japanese Brazilians.

This strategy of mimesis is particularly visible in the band's rendition of their most requested song: "Kapotaro Nomato." Also from the CD *Zhen Brasil*, "Kapotaro Nomato" reworks a joke that according to Mizuta was popular two decades ago, although it still circulates today and is commonly cited on web-based humor publications. The joke pivots upon the double meaning of the word *derrame*, which literally means "to spill out" but is commonly used to refer to a stroke, evoking the image of blood overflowing from a burst vessel. In the original joke, a Japanese Brazilian immigrant recites—in heavily accented Japanese—the improbable list of family members who have died "derrame." His interlocutor is confused about how an entire family could die of stroke until he is informed by the punch line that, in fact, the family died when an airplane headed for Japan turned over and they "spilled out." In the Zhen Brasil version of the joke, the family dies when the truck carrying them home from the fields turns over upon hitting a pothole:

Nóis vinha do roça e não sabe dize	We were coming back from the county
Coçando o saco e tomando sakê	Taking it easy and drinking sake
No curva tinha buraco fundo	There was a deep hole in the curve
Capotô caminhão e derramô todo mundo	The truck rolled and everyone spilled

The title "Kapotaro Nomato" is therefore a Japanized version of the phrase *capotaro no campo* (crash in the country). The joke demonstrates the ease with which violence to Japanese Brazil bodies becomes fodder for humor in popular discourse. A perpetual immigrant, he is often portrayed as lacking the basic linguistic and cultural skills to fully integrate into Brazilian society.

In a video recording of their performance of this song on "Sem Limites para Sonhar," the camera jumps repeatedly between Shiraishi, who takes the lead voice, and the band members. The camera returns often to the image of the *ton ton*–wielding geisha, Hugo Koike. Her hefty drum is stamped with the band's logo, a Japanese flag painted with the colors of Brazil. When Yuiti Shiraishi sings the verse which describes his happy, hardworking family returning from the country, he squints his eyes, keeps his upper torso still and bent over in a slight bow, and takes small timid steps through the space. He sings in a heavy Japanese accent, pronouncing his *l*s as *r*s, and using a nasal timbre. Similarly, with downcast eyes, the geisha takes gentle and precise steps from side to side, coyly imitating traditional Japanese dances learned from grandparents. The first verse tells of the family returning from the country, hardworking and happy laborers. The slow measured rhythm of the bolero that accompanies the verse seems to sonically mimic the slow, steady ways of these simple country folks. While the text is generally congruous with the stereotypical image of the heavily accented, hardworking Japanese laborer, the band members embody Japaneseness with such exaggerated gusto that the stereotype is rendered completely ridiculous. Their over-the-top costumes combined with exaggerated gestures and speech render the band members cartoonlike in their mimetic engagement with toxic conceptions of Japanese Brazilians. Here the attack of toxic interpellation is parried with a defensive excess deflates the stereotype.

An even more radical rupture of Japanese stereotypes takes place at the transition into the chorus, when the rhythm switches from a slow bolero into a boisterous samba. The geisha is transformed, her coyness completely gone as she assertively beats out samba rhythms, her head now erect. Gone are the "feminine" guiles of the geisha, replaced by a "manly" affect that is incongruent with Koike's hyperfeminine attire. Likewise, the affect conveyed by the "farmer," Yuiti Shiraishi, changes completely as he begins to move more expansively around the space executing basic samba steps. Fluid undulations pass through his hips and torso, breaking the rigidity of his previous stance. Meanwhile, he sings the dark lyrics of the chorus, which recount the list of family members and pets who have died derrame, as it were. Here again, exaggeration is at play. Transforming the original joke by adding a dog and chicken to the list of departed family members, the band members fall to the floor and act out the dying pains of these beloved pets. Meanwhile, a smile has replaced the scowl of Shiraishi's earlier persona as he abandons his nasal timbre for a more robust singing voice. Suddenly relaxed and cheerful, he demonstrates his ability to embody the most Brazilian of qualities. Likewise, his back-up band undulates to the rhythms of samba, which they beat out, and they strum their instruments with seeming ease. Here Brazilian cultural imperatives are performed by kimono-wearing bodies that flaunt the markers of Japaneseness. This rhythmic rupture has begun to transform the prevalent societal image of the Japanese family. In the second verse, when the bolero rhythm returns, the hardworking family (esforçado) that we first met is now "coçando o saco" (scratching one's balls, i.e., hanging out) and drinking sake. Here we have a coming together of two cultures—the Brazilian appreciation of leisure is enhanced with the most Japanese of cultural icons, sake.

In the final moments of their performance, Zhen Brasil adds yet another layer of parody as they jump into a rap interlude. Imitating the hand gestures and wide-legged stance of Brazilian hip-hop artists and singing in a deep chest voice, Shiraishi transforms the hit song "Um Tapinha Não Dói" (A Little Slap Doesn't Hurt), made popular by As Meninas. In the Zhen Brasil version, the title line is transformed into "Um Japinha Não Dói" (A Little Japanese Doesn't Hurt), a line delivered as the band members measure out an imaginary (small) phallus between their thumbs and index fingers. Working against a cultural logic that feminizes Japanese Brazilian masculinity through a mythology of deficient sexuality, the band inverts the stereotype of the small Japanese penis. Like the tapinha, or little slap, that is lauded in the original song, the Japanese penis is transformed into a source of violent pleasure. Problematic insofar as it reasserts a heterosexual gender norm that links violence, sexuality, and masculinity, this performative gesture offers a concrete image of heterosexual masculinity in the interest of destabilizing race-based prejudice.

However, at other moments, the band's gender play seems to work in the opposite direction, as the geisha's drag performance denaturalizes heterosexual gender roles. Judith Butler (1993: 231) explains the potential of drag performance to "serve a subversive function to the extent that it reflects the mundane impersonations by which heterosexually ideal genders are performed and naturalized and undermines their power by virtue of effecting that exposure." In the case of Zhen Brasil, the switching of the geisha's gender code parallels a racial subversion that calls into question the "mundane impersonations" through which Japanese Brazilianness is performed and understood. Like the gender transformations of the geisha, the rapid code switching between "Japanese" and "Brazilian" expressive conventions works toward the deessentialization of racially marked bodies. Encountering a social formation that depicts them as stiff and formal, they perform in other ways to inhabit Japanese bodies. As the musicians move between musical genres, their body language and emotional affect change to mimic the conventions of the subcultures they parody. The point of this postmodern mestiçagem is not to join together different cultural strains in a felicitous union, but to create a shocking rupture at the moments of rapid-fire code switching. And by using excessive parody to juxtapose stereotyped cultural norms, they call attention to the constructed nature of these norms of expression, while disavowing any necessary link between "Japaneseness" and any particular form of cultural or corporeal expression. Rather than aiming at an assertion of an ontological truth about Japanese Brazilians, the play throws us into an aporia of misrecognition as we are asked to ponder these processes of normalization.

Zhen Brasil's postmodern mestiçagem was highly controversial within the Japanese Brazilian community. While some, particularly younger, spectators felt that the band's iconoclastic message worked in positive ways toward countering prevailing public discourse, others could see no difference between the band's parodic citation of toxic stereotypes and the original versions that circulate in pubic discourse. Phillip Auslander (1992: 27) speaks to this problem of postmodern representational strategies, arguing that they can "turn into their own opposites by reifying the very representations they supposedly deconstruct." I spoke with the band members about this resistance. Several encountered resistance from older family members who argued that the band was disrespecting their Japanese cultural heritage and perpetuating humiliating stereotypes of Japanese Brazilians.

Repeatedly, when I asked the band what they wanted to accomplish, they would talk of the sonic interventions of Os Demônios da Garoa. Performing the Italo-Brazilian samba of Adoniran Barbosa, this *paulista* band gave voice to the experience of the poor and to immigrants in the city of São Paulo. Like Os Demônios da Garoa, Zhen Brasil questioned the relationship between laboring bodies and progress. Japanese Brazilians are often constructed as icons of technological progress that can model for Brazil a path toward Brazilian economic success in the global arena. Returning for a moment to the song "Mestiço," Mizuta's answer to aporia—"Já nem sou mais o que sei" (I am no longer what I know)—is to assert the ontological presence of the body, which provides an alternative form of knowledge. His lovely assertion "Yonsei, sambei, dancei" translates literally as "Fourth generation, I samba(ed), I danced." However, in Portuguese, the final syllables ring out "sei" (I know), as though knowledge infuses the body of this fourth-generation Japanese Brazilian alight in dance. The most dramatic intervention is to demonstrate that Japanese Brazilian bodies are not, as they are so often seen, efficient and technologically advanced working machines dutifully answering the imperatives of progress, but rather, somatic beings that move to the rhythms of their own needs and pleasure. Often cast as efficient if uncreative technocrats, their sexually infused improvisations in dance and wit demand that Japanese Brazilians be recognized as desiring beings who refuse to stand as reified signs of technological progress.

NOTES

1. The first two lines rework the Brazilian "Hymn of Independence," by Evaristo da Veiga.

2. A reference to the Japanese filmmaker Akira Kurosawa (1910–98). According to the author, black Brazilians are referred to as *kurombos* by Japanese Brazilians, perhaps a derivation of the Japanese word *kuromero* (black) or the Brazilian word *quilombo*.

3. *Quilombos* were communities built by escaped slaves in the Brazilian backlands and have become an important symbol of Afro-Brazilian identity.

4. "We are all good people" in Italian.

5. An atabaque is an Afro-Brazilian hand drum. Taiko refers to a Japanese drum.

6. Father Cícero Romão Batista (1844–1934).

7. Native Brazilians.

8. Manioc-based alcoholic beverage made by Native Brazilians.

9. Japanese for "May you live for ten-thousand years!"

10. The Japanese art of cultivating dwarf trees.

11. *Cabraninja* combines the words *cabramacho* (goat man), a colloquial word from the backlands of Brazil that means a tough guy, with *ninja* (a traditional Japanese fighter-for-hire), thereby combining two models of Brazilian and Japanese masculinity, respectively.

12. A tambourine of between eight and sixteen inches, commonly used in samba.

13. A four-stringed plucked lute.

14. Following the suggestion of Daniel Linger (2003: 212), I cautiously use the terms Japanese Brazilian and Nikkei Brazilian to "refer to those who recognize in some way both 'Japanese' and 'Brazilian' components within themselves." As Linger notes, the term tends to reify a diverse group of people for whom ethnic self-definition may or may not have importance relative to other components of identity. However, I think it is a useful term in the present study as I examine music that foregrounds questions of ethnic identity. The informants with whom I spoke self-referred in many ways, depending on the context of conversation, including Brazilian, Japanese, Nikkei, Nissei, and descendant.

15. Interviews with Adolfo Mizuta and the Zhen Brasil band members were conducted in Jundiaí and São Paulo between April and October of 2003.

16. *Pagode* refers to a backyard samba movement that became commercialized in the 1990s by a wave of bands known for their light, romantic lyrics; pared-down rhythms; and use of electric guitar and keyboard. See Philip Galinsky (1996) for a discussion of the pagode movement.

17. The food terms refer to fermented rice drink, fermented soybean paste, and thinly sliced raw fish, respectively.

::: Embodying the Favela

Representation, Mediation, and Citizenship

in the Music of Bezerra da Silva

Aaron Lorenz

To Brazilian and international audiences, *sambandido*, or "gangsta samba," is perhaps a humorous notion. While samba lyrics have been reporting the life of urban Brazilians since the early decades of the twentieth century, it was only with the emergence of a repertoire closely tied to José Bezerra da Silva—a musician and samba interpreter who achieved success in 1979 with "Pega Eu" (Get Me)—that samba began to look exclusively at the themes of drug consumption and trafficking. Known as the inventor of sambandido, Bezerra da Silva is an interesting anomaly in the Brazilian music scene of the 1980s, where the samba renaissance known as *pagode* was pushing saccharine samba crooners who sang love songs. Despite having signed with a major record label, Bezerra's controversial songs were rarely heard on the radio. He innovated new strategies of reaching working-class audiences, playing in local auditoriums and in gang-controlled favelas, in music halls, prisons, and other suburban venues (Letícia Vianna 1999: 32, 69).

Bezerra da Silva attained prominence as an ambassador of the favelas in the 1980s through his politically provocative satires phrased in traditional *partido alto* style. His work touches on a number of thematic crossroads in Brazilian literary and musical criticism. First among these issues is the relationship between the artist and the people, and the ways in which the people come to be represented in the mass media. Secondly, his interpretation of songs dealing with polemical subjects such as drug use, traffic, corruption, immunity, and discrimination transformed old-school samba into cutting-edge critique. Finally, Bezerra consciously fashions himself as the epitome of the "good *malandro*" (Letícia Vianna 1999: 116). This figure has been at the center of Brazilian discourses on nation in popular music and citizenship since the 1930s, when the term became popularized by samba. The malandro represents a kind of trickster in Bezerra's use of the word, an individual who knows how things are and what he wants, who has money and can't be compared to a dupe: "A *malandro* is really a cool guy, who isn't tied to a single woman" (Sandroni 2001: 156–68). While it is principally a term that describes a macho aesthetic of independence and respect, it also carries political connotations in relationship to solidarity, to opposition to repression, and to one who speaks truth to power.

The image of the sprawling urban shantytowns, or favelas, which mark Brazil's cityscapes have been a consistent source of inspiration for artists, musicians, and writers of the twentieth century. In Brazil, the term *favela* refers to a variety of different geographic, political, economic, and social configurations, which range from extreme poverty in urban squatter settlements to historical working-class neighborhoods. In Janice Perlman's *The Myth of Marginality* (1976), an analysis of Rio de Janeiro's favelas conducted in the late 1960s and early 1970s, she underlines the conflation of myths associated with the favela. Marginality is central to these myths and is deployed strategically as a means of signifying the favela along numerous levels. First of all, the *favela* is defined spatially as peripheral to the city, even in the cases of neighborhoods such as Mangueira that are older and more centralized geographically than much of the fancy south zone of the city. Secondly, the social stigma of the favela as an area of criminality makes favela residents second-class citizens, particularly when looking for work. Politically these areas also suffer from underrepresentation, and its residents are among the lowest-paid sector of the economy. Finally, the wave of migration from the northeast in the 1940s and 1950s altered the perception of favelas to include recent immigrants to the city, or in other words, outsiders.

Despite convincing arguments by Perlman and others as to the heterogeneity of favela residents, the image of the favela has continued to move closer to stereotypical associations with social problems of violence, drug trafficking, and poverty. To add an even more surreal note to this complex portrait, the excoriation of the favela as a social evil simultaneously coexists with a pride and celebration of it as the cradle of samba, both in samba lyrics and national discourse. On the level of popular discourse, Bezerra's repertoire points to some of the contradictions inherent in the stereotypes of the favela as the fortress of marginal criminals and compares them to stories and anecdotes of a "poor and marginalized" people. His lyrics distinguish between poor thieves who steal out of necessity, and corrupt politicians and corporations. Extremely self-conscious of his role as social critic, Bezerra projects in his lyrics and discourse a vision of autonomous and independent favela voices. As Bezerra says in "Eu Sou Favela" (I Am the Favela), "the favela is a social problem," as opposed to a criminal one.

The music of Bezerra da Silva is a testament to this double identity of the favela. His songs tell the daily survival stories of favela residents and their struggles against discrimination. He affirms and celebrates a positive masculine identity of street smarts, or *malandragem*. This chapter offers as interpretation of a few selections of Bezerra's vast repertoire within a social context centered on discourses of citizenship. I view his songs as a kind of testimonial literature, a performative testifying to the realities of favela life. Because of this connection to basic rights of citizenship, Bezerra cannot be solely contextualized within discourses elaborated by samba historians, though the works of Nei Lopes, Muniz Sodré, Hermano Vianna, and Carlos Sandroni, among others, are useful in looking at his music. Rather, I suggest that from the dictatorship to the present day, questions inspired by Rio de Janeiro's favelas, such as marginality and second-class citizenship, have permeated intellectual and artistic, cinematic, and literary discourses in Brazil.

Genres like samba, which include pagode and partido alto, cannot simply be seen as "traditional," despite the genre's longevity in the field of Brazilian cultural production. The question is, rather, how do *sambistas* innovate in music and performance? In the case of Bezerra da Silva, his performance of daily life struggles, slang-filled anecdotes and proverbs, and political satires evade easy classification from the strict perspective of samba history. Bezerra positions himself as a metonym of the favela when he says, "I am the favela." Like Nei Lopes, he is a representative of the community, a public intellectual who testifies about its realities. As in testimonial literature, Bezerra's songs witness injustice, speak truth to power, and denounce the endemic problems of favela life.

Bezerra da Silva's repertoire also self-reflexively questions notions of individual authorship through his collaborative approach. He is obviously connected to a whole apparatus of the recording industry, which involves a series of steps resulting in the marketing and sale of his records and CDs. Many of his interviews acerbically critique the musical production apparatus, which he intimately experienced as a professional percussionist on the radio and television as well as an interpreter of other composers' songs. He

Bezerra da Silva at a bar in Cidade de Deus, a neighborhood on the periphery of Rio de Janeiro, 1980 (Aguinaldo Ramos, CPDOC JB).

also proposed a collective approach to recording new songs by performing the work of over a hundred composers. This is an exceptionally high number of composers and strengthens his position as community representative in conflict with the recording industry, police repression, and political corruption.

::: "Eu Sou Favela"

The late Bezerra da Silva, who died on 17 January 2005, was best known for his scandalous songs that resonated with messages, hidden in plain sight, of drug use, trafficking, and political corruption. His repertoire was a portrait of the lives of millions of Brazil's favela residents. Known as the "ambassador of the favela" and the "product of the hillside," he interpreted the songs of little-known composers of stigmatized working-class neighborhoods. His first popular hit, "Pega Eu" (Arrest Me)—from his 1979 release, *Partido Alto Nota 10*, vol. 2—cemented his role as a performer of a certain type of musical *crônica*, or commentary, about day-to-day issues of survival in the favelas. The corpus of his recording career encompasses over twenty albums, and he has sold over ten million copies over the course of his career (Letícia Vianna 1999: 70). Initially relegated to the "freezer" by his recording company in favor of more pop samba recordings with a romantic edge, he pioneered a uniquely community-based marketing campaign that complemented his favela savvy.

In part to challenge this exclusion from the airways, he performed at shows sponsored by drug traffickers, bookies, and local communities in favelas, in (as mentioned earlier in this chapter) prisons, and in concert halls around the country in working-class suburbs. The lyrics of his songs are quoted in prison rebellions; in letters to the editor in nationally syndicated newspapers such as the *Folha de São Paulo*; and in conversations about corruption, drugs, and malandragem such as Magalhães, Da Silva Júnior, and Esmeralda Ortiz. Bezerra da Silva has also inspired a younger generation of artists who reached artistic maturity in the 1990s. In fact, he has created a unique community of listeners that far exceeds the frontiers of the favela. Letícia Vianna has noted that Bezerra da Silva's listening public is not restricted to the favela, but includes the middle classes in a kind of politically savvy form of "slumming." Noting his appeal to younger audiences and his partnership with rock, hip-hop, and reggae bands, Letícia Vianna links his diversified listening audience to the "stigma of marginality which weighs on Bezerra's image . . . his work is refashioned with a kind of glamour . . . (and) is worn by middle and upper classes stigmatized by the use of drugs, and/or leftist ideology, and/or fans of black culture" (1999: 154). Over the years, his audience expanded from its origins in the working-class audiences of Rio de Janeiro to include many different "tribes." Despite his exclusive use of samba and partido alto genres since the 1970s, his hit song, "Malandragem Dá um Tempo" (Street Smarts, Give me a Break), which deals with the finer points of smoking marijuana and staying safe, was covered by Brazilian rock giant, Barão Vermelho. Hip-hop, rap, rock, and mangue beat have also adopted him, and he has been cited as a role model by such musicians as Chico Science, Marcelo D2, Seu Jorge, Racionais MCs, Planet Hemp, and O Rappa. His track "Eu Sou Favela" is the first song of the internationally released *Favela Chic Postonove 1* produced in France. Nevertheless, as late as 2000, his music was still experiencing radio censorship, despite the desire of his label to provide the traditional payola to DJs as an incentive to play his music. Before the development of Brazilian hip-hop and Rio de Janeiro's funk scene, Bezerra's repertoire was one of the earliest musical forums for the airing of contemporary issues affecting the Brazilian favelas.

In fact, Bezerra was one of the first musicians to address drug trafficking, an influx of new weapons, and the subsequent rise in violence in the favelas and political corruption.

Despite the unique character of his politics, Bezerra is part of a samba genealogy—black and white, middle and working class—which has dealt with politics through samba. His career is no doubt indebted to the rebirth of interest in samba in the 1970s that gave new strength to the careers of Nelson Cavaquinho and Cartola, as well as to an entire new wave of samba musicians under the banner of pagode. These artists were experimenting with more intimate and local forms of samba. In contrast to the bright lights and showiness of the samba school aesthetic, these pagode and partido alto musicians promoted a *fundo de quintal* (backyard) samba. Formed in a circle around the musicians—with the audience singing the chorus (and lead sometimes) and clapping their hands to the beat—these events were seen as a return to samba's origins, despite the introduction of new instruments such as the *repique de mão*, and *tantã*, small lead and base drums played with the hands, and the banjo. From the perspective of the dictatorship, ironically, this was safe music, and because of this, many sambas with political references escaped censorship. Even so, this wave of samba music exploited a "low frequency politics,"[1] that dealt primarily with local issues, reflecting a general tendency in the 1970s toward local political activism. Along with the relaxation of the dictatorship in the 1980s, Bezerra's interpretations openly addressed political corruption and drug dealing.

A review of the themes of intellectual copyright in Brazilian samba and the financial rights of composers shows that the 1930s witnessed the crystallization of musical professionalism in samba through a musical division of labor. Group endeavors gave way to individual compositions, which were polished by professionals. Typically, one composer came up with the chorus; another added the first verse; then, finally, a professional composer finished the piece and gave it a second verse. Frequently, the songs were performed by a singer with some fame, and were either sold to or partnered with the singer. This process of increasing specialization created a class of professional musicians that did not necessarily benefit unknown black composers like the one represented by the actor Grande Otelo in the film *Rio Zona Norte*, by Nelson Pereira dos Santos (1957).

Working in this system for over fifty years as a composer, musician, and interpreter, Bezerra lightly subverted the rules of production by performing the works of unknown composers from local neighborhoods and favelas around Rio de Janeiro. He saw himself as the "ambassador of the favela" and worked with a team of composers. His albums and CDs sometimes had as many as thirty composers involved in the arrangement and writing of new songs. For this reason, his work maintains a tight relationship between the consumers and producers of his music. As Léticia Vianna notes, Bezerra da Silva

> doesn't purchase song rights or share in them, but trades song rights for his promotion of the music. He is adamant about abstaining from a share in song rights, since his strategy is to appear as an interpreter—not merely an interpreter, but *the* interpreter, or representative, of *favela* residents. His uniqueness as an artist, such as he constructs it, is directly related to collective identity. (1999: 55)

Some of the names of his more frequent partners are Edson Show, Adelzonilto, and Jorge F. Silva, but he worked with more than a hundred composers throughout his career. Obviously it is difficult to cut a first record, and composing for Bezerra represented a first step along the trajectory of musical recognition for working-class artists. The most paradigmatic of these collaborations was with Dicró, an unknown composer who, through his work with Bezerra, established himself in his own right as a performer. Bezerra partnered with Dicró in his parody of the early 1990s "Three Tenors" phenomenon on the recording *Os 3 Malandros in Concert*. This arrangement of crediting his composers acted like a helping hand for them as well as a cementing of Bezerra's name to a community-based aesthetic.

Bezerra da Silva's first hit, "Pega Eu," from 1979, tells the story of a thief who while in the process of robbing a favela resident in his shack realizes that his poor victim is in fact more miserable than he is. The song questions the role of the common thief in relationship to poverty while promoting an ethic of solidarity within the favela. It begins with a warning, "rob a poor man's house and see what happens":

O ladrão foi lá em casa	The thief went to my house
E quase morreu de coração	And almost had a heart attack
Já pensou só se o gato tem um enfarto,	Can you imagine if the cat had a heart attack,
Malandro, E morre no meu barracão?	*Malandro*, And died in my shack?
Eu não tenho nada de luxo	I've got no luxuries that
que possa agradar ao ladrão	could please a thief

É só uma cadeira quebrada	Just a broken chair,
e o jornal aqui no colchão	and a newspaper on the mattress
Eu tenho uma panela de barro	I've got a clay pot
e os tijolos como portão	and bricks for a gate
O ladrão ficou maluco de ver	The thief went crazy seeing
tanta miséria encima de um cristão	so much misery piled on top of a
	Christian
E saiu gritando pela rua, pega eu que	And fled screaming, arrest me,
eu sou ladrão	I'm a thief
Pega eu pega eu que sou ladrão	Get me, get me, I'm a thief
Não assalto mais um pobre	I won't rob a poor man anymore
nem arrobo um barracão	or break into a shack

The interlocutor to whom Bezerra refers in the third line of his solo is the malandro listening to the story. In this song, as well as in many other songs of Bezerra's, the malandro is not the thief, but rather a streetwise companion, someone who would never stoop to rob a poor man. Contrary to historical definitions of the malandro—which represented a nuanced criminality characterized by con men, pimps, street fighters, sambistas, and bohemians—Bezerra recontextualizes this figure popularized by samba from the 1930s as a street-smart working man who refuses to be victimized by either local thugs or the police and employs a kind of survival tactic for the favela. As he noted in an interview, in contrast to criminals, informants, or dupes (otários) "in a figurative sense, the word means, 'intelligent.' Then they started to change the meaning to claim that the malandro was the guy who steals, who doesn't work."[2] The chorus of the song pleads, "Come get me, I'm a thief," thereby placing the listening public in the role of the poor thief who had the misfortune of trying to rob a favela resident. It plays with the social position of favela residents living in poverty as second-class citizens vulnerable to acts of violence by both thieves and the police. As Bezerra recounts in his biography, he was taken to the police station to verify his identity over twenty times, simply because he happened to live in the favela and was of the right age and color (Letícia Vianna 1999: 23). At the same time, he re-creates an ethic of solidarity in the favela, where even thieves must respect the grim reality of poverty.

The malandro aesthetic operates in a liminal area of activity between legality and illegality, social acceptance and rejection, morality and immorality (DaMatta 1991). As the ambassador of the favela, Bezerra's performance goes far beyond his interpretation of politically charged sambas, and into the performance of daily life. In many respects, his life embodies the malandro aesthetic. For this reason, and because of the positive and negative charges associated with the term, Bezerra was quite guarded about what he revealed to journalists. Despite the fact that he never denied interviews, he frequently avoided questions that focused on his relationship to crime, drug trafficking, and drug use. In one interview together with Zeca Pagodinho, the journalist attempts to reveal a relationship between Bezerra's music and drug dealing:

> Bezerra: I'm considered a singer of outlaws. That doesn't affect me, I'm conscious of what I'm doing.
>
> Folha de São Paulo: But you provoke . . .
>
> Bezerra: No I'm realistic.
>
> Folha de São Paulo: . . . with verses full of double meanings.
>
> Bezerra: In the 1970s we went to sing for free in the prisons, in Ilha Grande, to help inmates reintegrate into society. Suddenly, they're claiming that I made a song for Escadinha.[3]

He distinguishes in the interview between singing the "reality" of the favela and approving of criminal activities. However, like any good malandro, he acts in the area between intention and accident. His "Cocada Boa," plays on the homophony between *cocada boa* (good coconut candy) and *coca da boa* (good cocaine), "A Semente" (The Seed) relates the story of a poor marijuana grower victimized by the police, while "Malandragem Dá um Tempo" (The Malandro Waits) suggests that there is a time and place for both rolling and smoking joints. Yet his repertoire neither advocates drug use nor ignores its presence in the lives of many favela (and nonfavela) residents. The highly publicized trial and conviction of the pagode star, Belo, for connection to drug and arms traffickers points toward the real consequences for singers who get on the wrong side of the law, and helps explain the ambiguity of his position toward drug use and trafficking.

If Bezerra's early hits of the late 1970s and early 1980s make references to favela life, problems with the police, and tales of the daily life of the poor, by the late 1980s, with political redemocratization, his lyrics radicalize and articulate a broader critique of state and society. The song "Vítimas da Sociedade" (Victims of Society), composed by Jorge F. Silva and Bezerra da Silva, refers to a double consciousness of favela life, to cite an expression of W. E. B. Du Bois, taken up by Paul Gilroy (1993: 112–13). The favela is often perceived from the outside as a haven for criminals and, as such, creates concrete problems for favela residents such as wrongful arrest, house invasions, job discrimination, and lack of services and basic sanitation. The complement to the marginal world of the favela is the world of white-collar workers, often referred to in Bezerra's songs as *o asfalto* (the asphalt), in contrast to the irregular dirt paths of many favelas. The world of economic privilege is generally perceived as the inside, and reflects a middle-class perspective represented by large media outlets such as TV Globo. Unlike the favela, it is the world that needs protecting from crime, not the world from which crime originates. The lyrics accomplish an inversion of this dichotomy on two levels. First, the song positions the listener inside the favela and redefines the favela as a working-class neighborhood that is stigmatized from without. Second, it draws attention to unearned wealth, by pointing out that no one in the favela owns a summer house, has a Swiss bank account, or other luxuries associated with the Brazilian elite. This carnivalesque inversion of the two worlds reveals the favela as a scapegoat for political and economic corruption.

E se vocês estão a fim de prender um ladrão	And if you want to catch a thief
Podem voltar pelo mesmo caminho	You can go back the way you came
O ladrão esta escondido lá embaixo	The thief is hidden down there
Atrás da gravata e do colarinho	Behind a tie and little (white) collar
Só porque eu moro no morro	Just because I live on the hillside
A minha miséria vocês despertou	You only notice my misery
A verdade é que vivo com fome	The truth is that I live with hunger
Nunca roubei ninguém, sou um trabalhador	I never robbed anyone, I'm a worker
Se há um assalto à banco	If there is a bank robbery
Como não podem prender o poderoso chefão	Since they can't catch the powerful boss
Aí os jornais vêm logo dizendo	Then the newspapers soon say
Que aqui no morro só mora ladrão	That here on the hillside only live thieves.

Reflecting the opening political discourse of the 1980s, Bezerra's music of this period radically questions the links between the social chaos of the favela and issues of citizenship and political representation. Political corruption is a common theme in his work and acts as a frame for understanding drug trafficking, theft, state violence, and poverty. In his study on class and taste, Pierre Bourdieu has suggested that social divisions are naturalized in such a way that their borders become invisible (1984: 471). Similarly, in the day-to-day relationship between Rio de Janeiro's social classes, subtle naturalized divisions organize the rich and the poor, the favela and the asphalt. The song's strategy lies in the denaturalization of stereotypic associations.

The song "Candidato Caô Caô" (The Watch-Out Candidate) from the 1988 album *Violência Gera Violência* (Violence Begets Violence), describes an encounter between Bezerra and a corrupt politician during an electoral campaign. The song satirizes forms of populist politics during election time. Of the numerous and ridiculous encounters with the politician in the favela, Bezerra relates a dinner in his shack featuring guava paste tins as plates, marijuana smoking, and a session in a temple of *umbanda*, the syncretic Brazilian religion that blends the Yoruba-derived candomblé with the Spiritist current of Catholicism led by Allan Kardec. Unfortunately for the politician, Bezerra goes into a trance and reveals to everyone the true intentions of the candidate: he will send the police to arrest them if he wins.

E na colonia penal	And in the penal colony
Assim que você chegou	As soon as you arrived
Deu de cara com os bichos que você	You ran into the animals you
caguetou	turned in
Aí, você foi obrigado a usar fio dental	There you were made to wear a thong
e andar rebolando	and walk swinging your hips
Eis a diferença, canalha	That's the difference, son-of-a-bitch,
do otário do malandro	between a dupe and a malandro

From the perspective of this song, there is no possibility of collaborating with the police, even in the face of torture—the song even mentions the infamous *pau de arara* (parrot's perch), a torture instrument made famous from accounts of political prisoners of the 1970s. The informant in this case is made to suffer a kind of sexual abjection, whereby his punishment is to become a sexual object of the prison. Queerness here represents a punishment inflicted on informants, a kind of a physical doubling of their openness to reveal information—their bodies are made open for the pleasure of the manly men, the malandros. In this respect, manliness represents being closed: closed mouth, closed body while informants and losers have open mouths and bodies open to penetration. The particular scorn directed at informants operates on another level than his satires of corruption, politi-

Album cover of *Violência Gera Violência*, 1988 (Sony-BMG).

cal hypocrisy, and police brutality; it reenacts, rather, a kind of just violence on transgressors of favela law: informants, dupes, queers, and manly women. From this perspective, there is really nothing progressive or subversive about this collection of Bezerra's music; rather, it replicates the repression directed at favelas from the outside, now according to a logic of male solidarity.

::: Representation and Citizenship

It is perhaps useful to look a little bit more closely at the concept of cultural mediation as elaborated by Gilberto Velho and Hermano Vianna. While the concept originates in Gilberto Velho's study of domestics in Rio de Janeiro and their status as cultural travelers between the working class and the middle class, the term frequently emerges as a way of talking about a Brazilian brand of hybridity going back to Gilberto Freyres's Casa-Grande e Senzala (*Masters and the Slaves*), on the one hand, and Oswald de Andrade's concept of anthropophagy, on the other. In a recent article, Velho defines mediation as the

> possibility of coping with various codes and living various social roles, in a process of metamorphosis, [which] gives to specific individuals the condition of mediators when these practices are implemented in a systematic way. The greatest or least of success of their undertakings will provide the limits of their action as mediators. It is fitting to emphasize that it is not always possible to establish bridges and channels of communication or that often, they are fragile or ephemeral. The increasing violence of Brazilian society, primarily in large urban centers, can be a barrier between social categories, creating difficulties in the circulation and transit between social spheres and moral regions. (2001: 25)[4]

The mediator is a heroic figure of cultural fusion, of class and racial border crossing. In the field of Brazilian music, it is Hermano Vianna who popularized this notion through his insightful books dealing with artists, musicians, and academics that transit between different cultural spheres. Perhaps *The Mystery of Samba* ([1995]1999) is the most paradigmatic of his works dealing with cultural mediation. The book recounts the encounter between Gilberto Freyre, Sergio Buarque de Hollanda, and Heitor Villa-Lobos (all members of the white Brazilian academic and erudite musical worlds) with Pixinguinha and Donga (two black founders of samba as a genre) as an allegory for the birth of samba. While recognizing that samba experienced repression and marginalization starting with its foundation in 1917, Hermano Vianna reconfigures the ascension of samba to the status of national music within the inclusive discourses of citizenship solidifying in the 1920s and 1930s. Vianna's discourse runs counter to a number of other texts such as Vagalume's *Na Roda do Samba* (1978), which suggested that an original samba had become corrupted through its assimilation and co-optation by the white elite. On the contrary, for Vianna, samba has always been multiracial, integrating a number of different classes. Despite recognition of the simultaneity of racism and cultural mixing by authors such as Michael Hanchard, there is a seductive tendency among authors who write about mediation to frame it only in the positive sense, as a means of breaking down class and race barriers, and as a tool of national integration.

Léticia Vianna's attention to the ways in which Bezerra represents himself also implicates as positive her interpretation of Bezerra's work and the role of the critic in relationship to music as an authority of interpretation and the creation of academic meaning. According to her, it is "left to the social scientist to raise, mark, and interpret the meanings that a popular category can assume in the native universes which we investigate" (1999: 165). She concludes that Bezerra is a "catalyzer of creative energy, a broker, or mediator, according to Gilberto Velho, between the various instances of the productive process" (166). While Vianna recognizes the instability of authenticity as a category, she also appears to support an interpretation of Bezerra as a heroic world-shaker, world-creator figure. If it is indeed true that Bezerra is a kind of cultural mediator between the worlds of the asphalt and the street, what kind of mediator is he? And what is the role of music in this case? Does it acts as a forum for grievances, a testimonial of injustice, and a surrogate for citizenship?

As Bourdieu suggests, there is no disinterested position but rather only interested disinterest, a point that highlights the importance of representation and writing as a performance (1993:29–73). In the case of Letícia Vianna's book, *Bezerra da Silva: Produto do Morro. Trajetória e Obra de um Sambista Que Não É Santo* (1999), there is also the question of the discovery of Bezerra da Silva's music as a kind of heroic rescue of cultural forms, which have been stigmatized for political or aesthetic reasons. Bezerra has constructed a complex image of himself, which he projects through his music, his newspaper interviews, and his depositions. These varied sources reveal a slippage of personas between a malandro figure and the "ambassador of the favela." Létícia Vianna's attention to the creation of his image reflects some of the transformations which anthropology has undergone since the publication of Clifford's *Writing Culture* (1986) and her recognition that representations are fluid, negotiated, and contested. Like many artists or informants, Bezerra self-consciously fashions his image of himself and his relationship to the favela as an interpreter of the voice of the humblest of the "people."

Even having moved out of the favela and into a middle-class neighborhood, he has maintained a discourse of favela imagery. When asked whether he lives in the favela, he replies, "No, I live in Botafogo, but I'll always be favela" (Paulo Vieira 1998). Letícia Vianna questions this notion of authenticity as a given of partido alto, or of Bezerra's political critique, and suggests that it is rather an "invented value in the formulation of identities—it is invented, constructed, attributed, reclaimed, and deconstructed in different ways and with different purposes, in an interactive continuum between persons and groups which create and multiply identities" (1999: 150).

Vianna's insight into questions of authenticity here raise important questions as to the ways in which popular singers such as Bezerra da Silva act as witnesses and representatives for subaltern realities. Gayatri Chakravorty Spivak is right to argue that there is a constitutive impossibility of unmediated speech from the subaltern perspective, precisely because it is constructed as a place of silence (1988: 307). Rather, Bezerra's mediation of subaltern worlds through his music acts as a musical testimonial, much like *I, Rigoberta Menchú* worked in the field of literature. John Beverley has suggested that testimonials work as "an allegorical figure for, and a concrete means of the union of a radicalized (Marxist) intelligentsia and the subaltern" (1991: 5). Obviously the difference in the use of music rather than literature is a key distinction between Rigoberta Menchú's and Bezerra da Silva's representation of subaltern interests and one which fundamentally permits an amplification of Bezerra's public to include the very subaltern populations he represents. Part of the excitement Bezerra generated lies in his status as an organic intellectual in the Gramscian sense, speaking in a popular discourse, in a language that bridges class and race distinctions.

Part of this dilemma involves the relationship between subversive performance and citizenship, between speaking and belonging. While it can be argued that some of Bezerra's music acts as a kind of consciousness-raising process, we must be cautious in equating this performance with citizenship itself. One example of this discomfort can be seen in relation to Bezerra's approach to gender and heterosexuality, which is uncomfortably reactionary, violent, and repressive. The gender roles he advocates are static, and while his satires can be quite ferocious with regards to the hypocrisy inherent in a democracy where the majority of the population lives below the poverty line, his music is rather an aesthetic and political doubling of citizenship, a ghost of citizenship, which implies the consciousness of a lack. His musical parodies reveal an absence of citizenship when applied to the favela; yet, in writing on his work, we are confronted with a desire to elevate this list of grievances to a status of citizenship itself. Isn't citizenship the act of speaking out itself and the recognition that we are all one, regardless of class and race differences? Or is it rather the benefits and privileges associated with the dominant class, the recognition that everything is determined according to these precepts? There is thus a danger in overevaluating these types of interventions as acts of a kind of citizenship, as surrogates for a universal citizenship of humanity, while history and civil war tirelessly erode civil rights. Rather, Bezerra da Silva's best music is bent on tirelessly pointing to the lack, the difference, but not in the terms described by the dominant class, while at his worst, he reproduces a Manichean mentality of circular masculine violence.

DISCOGRAPHY

Barão Vermelho. *Barão MTV ao Vivo*. Warner Disco 2, 2006.

Bezerra da Silva. *Alô Malandragem, Maloca o Flagrante*. RCA Vik, 1986.

———. *Favela Chic Postonove 1*. BMG Intl., 2001.

———. *Justiça Social*. RCA Victor, 1987.

———. *Malandro É Malandro e Mané É Mané*. Atração, 2000.

———. *Malandro Rife*. RCA Viktor, 1985.

———. *Partido Alto Nota 10*. Vol. 2: *Bezerra da Silva e Seus Convidados*. CID, 1979.

———. *Presidente Caô Caô*. BMG Ariola, 1992.

———. *Produto do Morro*. RCA Vik, 1983.

———. *Violência Gera Violência*. CD/Vinil, 1988.

Bezerra da Silva and Marcelo D2. *Meu Bom Juiz*. CID, 2003.

Bezerra da Silva and Moreira da Silva Dicró. *Os 3 Malandros in Concert*. CID, 1995.

O Rappa. *O Rappa*. Warner Music, 1994.

NOTES

1. Paul Gilroy uses this term to refer to a "politics of transfiguration." He suggests that "this politics exists on a lower frequency where it is played, danced and acted, as well as sung about because words, even words stretched by melisma and supplemented by the slave sublime, will never be enough to communicate its unsayable claims to truth. The willfully damaged signs which betray the resolutely utopian politics of transfiguration therefore partially transcend modernity, constructing both an imaginary anti-modern past and a postmodern yet-to-come" (1993: 37).

2. See Adilson Pereira, "A Lição do Malandro," *Jornal do Brasil*, 27 June 2000.

3. Escadinha (José Carlos dos Reis Encina) was a famous drug trafficker from the Morro do Juramento, who became famous in 1985 for escaping from the Ilha Grande Prison by helicopter. He was murdered while working as a taxi driver in 2004. See Marcelo Rubens Paiva, "Especial para a Folha de São Paulo," *Folha de São Paulo*, 8 December 2000, E13.

4. See Velho 1994: 81 for a definition of cultural mediation.

::: Hip-Hop in São Paulo

Identity, Community Formation, and Social Action

Wivian Weller and Marco Aurélio Paz Tella

The Brazilian hip-hop movement emerged in São Paulo in the 1980s at a time when international black music had already attracted a large number of followers in the city. Instead of samba, people listened to *soul music* or *funk* at these events. According to José Jorge Carvalho (1994), a new black identity was manifested not only in the adaptation of international black music, but also through the identification with its political and ideological stances. This represented, on the one hand, a critical position of protest against social inequalities and racism, as shown in song lyrics beginning at the end of the 1970s. On the other hand, the embrace of international black music also suggested a new ethnic consciousness. Many political demands of the MNU (Movimento Negro Unificado; Unified Black Movement) were incorporated and articulated by these musical groups and their fans. Initially, hip-hop began in downtown São Paulo among young men who, on their lunch breaks and on weekends, would gather on 24 de Maio Street or in the entrance to the São Bento Metro Station to break dance. Subsequently, some break dancers went on to join rap groups, which adopted a form of organization based on the North American "posse" model. Posse refers not only to a group that is formed based on shared interests (such as rap); it also implies common experiences having to do with loyalty, origin, and identity will be shared (Back 1996: 212). In São Paulo, aside from the artistic work, posses tend to develop community and educational activities (Andrade 1996; José Carlos G. da Silva 1998).

The first Brazilian posse, Sindicato Negro (Black Syndicate), gathered at Praça Roosevelt (Andrade 1996; Guimarães 1998; José Carlos G. da Silva 1998). As time passed, the youth went on to organize new break-dance and rap groups in their residential neighborhoods and to establish new posses, thus taking hip-hop to their communities. One participant, Antonio, explains how the group Estilo Negro began:

It was the only movement for young people living in the periphery, we wanted to be the pioneers . . . The name Estilo Negro hadn't even appeared yet. We needed a name, something that, you know, that people would identify with us, right? What is it about? Ah! It's style, everyone's style. And then, let's put a color, so, the majority was black, right? The majority of Estilo Negro was black.

According to Antonio, people became involved with hip-hop for different reasons. His connection was through break dancing. His involvement with break dance represents the prereflexive phase in his hip-hop trajectory. With the movement of hip-hop to the periphery and the creation of new posses that went beyond the central elements (graffiti, break dance, and rap), a new dimension of the movement, described as "community work," took shape. Rap corresponds to the musical and recreational part of the movement, while hip-hop as a whole, is associated not only with art, but also with political and social activities developed by these young people. In this way, *paulistano* rappers began to articulate everyday problems in the neighborhood through music and to develop concrete parallel activities with the aim to transform their communities.

The following is a brief overview of the different phases of paulistano rap. Based on the themes explored in LPS from the 1980s and 1990s, José Carlos Silva (1998) distinguishes among three phases of paulistano rap: In the first phase, from 1985 to 1990, the personal daily experiences of adolescents in the metropolis constituted the principal themes of the songs. The second phase, from 1990 to 1994, was marked by "black consciousness," in which themes such as racism and discrimination against blacks were the main focus. The incorporation of these issues into the lyrics resulted from a process of rediscovering the collective history of blacks in Brazil, or, as Stuart Hall (1990) would say, as the result of a "symbolic trip" to Africa. This process of self-realization or "symbolic trip" took place, on one hand, through the virtual encounter with North American groups via the media, and on the other, through contact with the MNU. The principal theme of the music during this second phase was closely associated with the political demands of the MNU. In conjunction with NGOS, the rappers participated not only in certain educational programs; they were also invited to work as mediators and cultural agents through municipal government programs and through NGOS associated with the MNU.

In the third phase of paulistano rap, the ethnoracial discourse and racial protest were supplanted by a critique of the social problems in the periphery such as urban violence, segregation, and stigmatization of the residents. In this period, the hip-hop movement acquired more independence in relation to the organizations associated with the black movement, assuming its own identity (see João Batista de Jesus Felix 2000).

Based on research conducted on the genesis, structure, and function of the cultural styles of youth and adolescents that live in peripheral communities, we analyze the political and musical praxis of hip-hop among young paulistanos and its role in the development of strategies that oppose exclusion and discrimination and promote new forms of collectivity.

::: Biographic Dislocations and Discontinuities

The pitiful quality of life among residents of the poorest and most degraded neighborhoods in São Paulo is related to the precarious condition of public services and facilities, which limit the access of residents to high-quality resources and to citizen rights. São Paulo is one of the most striking examples of socioeconomic segregation of urban space, which places poor whites and a large majority of blacks side by side in outlying districts. A large part of the black population lives in the city's poorest areas, equaling and sometimes even surpassing whites in absolute numbers in the most marginalized districts of São Paulo, such as Brasilândia, Capão Redondo, Jardim Ângela, Lajeado, and Cidade Tiradentes. São Paulo reproduces the segregationist model that isolates its "stigmatized, shameful areas, spatially marginalizes its poor communities, and even avoids making roads that lead in their direction" (Véras 2003: 26). The state housing policy reproduces a model of appropriation, segregation, and control over territories that separate poor communities not only from those that have economic and political power, but also from wealthier regions of São Paulo, making it impossible for them to fully exercise their rights as citizens. Inequality in the distribution of public services and facilities and spatial segregation characterize the basic conditions of citizens.

The housing projects came about as an attempt to create basic infrastructure in those regions after part of the population closest to downtown was expelled from informal settlements. However, even today, those residential zones are in an extremely precarious situation in terms of housing, health, education, transportation, and leisure. Moving to a neighborhood of vertical apartment buildings and the loss of ties to kin and former social relations represented profound disruption, especially for the youth.

Dislocation to an unknown neighborhood far from the city center meant rupture with friends and family, the loss of quality of life, and the end to a relatively stable socioeconomic situation. Contact with forms of violence and criminality became a part of the quotidian life of youth who came to inhabit these residential zones along with their families. The construction of residential projects in the periphery geographically separated the rich from the poor as well as blacks from whites in São Paulo. For the black population segregated during this process, the experience was not exclusively negative, as indicated in our interviews with young rappers from the COHAB (Companhia Metropolitana de Habitação; Metropolitan Company of Residence) Fernandes housing project. In relation to their previous situation—in which they were excluded from social activities such as games, parties, and amorous relationships—residents see COHAB Fernandes as a place in which one is "at home," that is, as a space that is not hostile toward someone who is different and one that does not exclude social and leisure activities.

Once they moved into a neighborhood in which they made up the majority, residents found that belonging to a stigmatized ethnic group was seen as a mobilizing agent for individual and collective action. The migratory experiences, the segregation, and the discrimination experienced by the young blacks of COHAB Fernandes inspired the search for new forms of collectivity. Forming a posse brought together new rap groups that emerged with the recent arrival of so many young people to the neighborhood. Ralf Bohnsack and Bodo Wild describe this type of identity search:

> Collective milieus are not found only in traditional settings and in intact social contexts. Much to the contrary, it is those collective experiences of discontinuity and disintegration that serve as a base for new milieus and generation-specific life experiences as well as the new models of confronting (those experiences of discontinuity and disintegration). (1997: 162)

Belonging to the majority group, along with the construction of new collective forms of living with a basis in reciprocity and "brotherhood," made possible a positive association between social and territorial space in COHAB Fernandes. Open and sincere friendships, as well as a sense of freedom and well-being ("You are more at ease here"), supplanted the discrimination and isolation previously felt in other neighborhoods in the city, according to a statement by a young rapper, Carlos:

> I wouldn't trade COHAB Fernandes to live in a neighborhood like the one I lived in before. Because here I have very strong friendships—there is that brother-

hood thing, you know—we are always at one another's house talking. Where I used to live, even at my own house, it was really cool, but I would never be able to get a group of people together like this, just to talk. The guys wouldn't come to my house—"Ah, go to a black guy's house?" You could hear people saying that to your face, you know? So it was really hard. Not here. Here, you feel more at ease. In that sense, it's really cool here, in that sense.

::: Political-Musical Praxis and Worldview in a
    Context of Exclusion and Discrimination

According to Karl Mannheim, the worldview of a group is situated between social and spiritual realms:

> A world-view (of an era, a group, etc.) is a structurally linked set of experiential contexts which makes up the common footing upon which a multiplicity of individuals together learn from life and enter into it. A world-view is then neither the totality of spiritual formations present in an age nor the sum of individuals then present, but the totality of the structurally interconnected experiential sets which can be derived from either side, from the spiritual creations or from the social group formations. (1982: 91)

Worldviews are not articulated as readily perceivable forms, but they can be understood when analyzed in relation to a specific problem, thus becoming a theoretical object (Mannheim 1982: 91–94). They are constituted through practical action and belong to the realm of knowledge that Mannheim defined as atheoretical (1952). According to Mannheim, gaining access to the implicit understanding of the group being researched, making it explicit, and defining it theoretically are the role of the researcher. In this sense, the focus of analysis on the musical and artistic praxis of hip-hop does not entail the interpretation of music and its expressive meaning; rather, it entails the understanding of worldviews constituted through the articulations of young people engaged in the movement. The understanding and theoretical explanation of the social context or the *social spaces of shared experiences* are fundamental (Mannheim 1982). In the case of young blacks from São Paulo's periphery, collective praxis in the hip-hop movement and common experiences with discrimination and exclusion constitute these social spaces.

When comparing groups interviewed in São Paulo, we find that their worldviews are not exactly linked to local or cultural contexts. They transcend ethnocultural and geographic boundaries. Within the same neighborhood, we find two types of groups with different views on political-musical praxis within the hip-hop movement. The modus operandi that orient artistic practices as well as political and social activities are not the same. We find groups of youth with generation-specific orientations, who associate their practices and discourses with their own age group. We also find youth oriented toward class struggle, who see rap as a way of articulating social and political aspirations. In the sections that follow we present a brief discussion of the different types of worldviews or forms of collective representation among groups.

::: Groups Oriented toward Generation

A central characteristic of groups oriented toward generation is an identification with youth. These groups regard hip-hop as a youth cultural revolution, or a specific response from the generation to which it belongs, and not as a social or political revolution. In this way, hip-hop comes to be seen as a cultural revolution led by young people who have in common the same "kind of experiences," as Mannheim would say (1952: 297). Another characteristic is the sharing of common experiences, especially those relating to family life. Individual stories and traumatic experiences lived within the family are worked textually in rap lyrics to achieve communication with the members of the group and with the audience (Weller 2003: 43–48). By generalizing those experiences, the feeling of belonging to a group in which one's personal experiences are shared by other members of the same social circle also increases. This feeling generates the satisfaction of singing for an audience. In this sense, rap lyrics are not simply one individual's story, but the story of many other young people who are listening and singing along with the group. According to Antônio of the group Skateboard:

> It's like our song that to date has had the most success, "Pai Decepção" [Father deception], which is constantly playing on the radio. Every time we perform it, people stop to listen because they identify with what we are saying and with how we act on stage. We never come with an attitude of superiority . . . So people approach us without fear, and singing for them in this way is cool because they are our people.

Public presentations generate recognition of the performance ("how we act on stage") and of the band's musical elements, creating a moment of habitual and collective communion (Bohnsack et al. 1995) between the group and its listeners based on shared experiences. This type of shared experience is explicit in the song "Pai Decepção" and in the audience's reaction when it is sung. When young people sing this song, they establish a feeling of collectivity that is created by the critical analysis of the father figure in the family context.

The rap duo Thaíde e DJ Hum, a key point of reference for paulistano hip-hop of the 1980s, is another generationally oriented group. One of their main characteristics is they rap by offering advice to fans. In the song "Falsidade" (Fallacy), from their first recording— *Pergunte a Quem Conhece* (Ask Those Who Know; 1989)—they proclaim, "I'm not about preaching, but pay attention to my ranting in this song." On "Consciência" (Consciousness), from the album *Hip Hop na Veia* (Hip-Hop in the Veins; 1991), they rap, "Look my friend, do me a favor / I want you to think hard about what your friend told you." In "Não Seja Tolo" (Don't Be Stupid)—from the recording *Humildade e Coragem São Nossas Armas para Lutar* (Humility and Courage Are Our Weapons to Fight With; 1992)—they advise: "Pay attention, this is good for you / You need to listen good so you can understand."

In some of the duo's raps the theme of ethnoracial belonging may seem to stand out, such as in the rap "Afro-Brasileiro" from the recording *Preste Atenção* (Pay Attention, 1996). However, generation-specific orientation predominates in the majority of their lyrics, most of which are about specific problems and important choices for youth who live in peripheral neighborhoods. In the rap "Mensagens Pessoais" (Personal Messages), from the recording *Brava Gente* (Brave People, 1994), for example, the narrator wants to provide positive messages for the youth of the periphery by relating his personal experiences. The rap starts with Thaíde saying that his life had many obstacles, but upon listening to and reflecting on his mother's advice, the rapper came to a conclusion: "I couldn't be just another person in the world, a poor bum." Believing in his ability and knowledge, he fought for his goals, yet always kept his friends in mind: "Well-known people . . . made to adapt to poverty." The chief message is that Thaíde believes in change; he wants to hear the phrase "that brother overcame." Believing in yourself, following paths that don't lead to crime, and "discovering the importance of work" are victories. The narrator hints at what is needed to be a real man: "patience, intelligence / understanding and humility." Thus, Thaíde promotes values that are important for youth such as work, school, and family.

In many rap groups, it is common for MCs or rappers to present themselves as role models for other young people. Thaíde promotes himself as an example—"Do as I did, always behave"—making the point that if he doesn't behave, he won't be well regarded by other people. He tells his friend to avoid drinking and smoking, while doing everything to make his parents and friends proud of him. At the end of the rap, Thaíde asks his friend, whose mind is weak from using drugs, to listen to his advice. That experience made the narrator reflect on his future. If he hadn't changed paths, he "wouldn't have real friends, who are important to me / my family, my wife, my daughter." The narrator addresses his listener about options for people who live in the periphery. Choosing crime will lead young people away from their friends and family, and toward death. The rapper's personal story—a common story in the periphery—becomes a "myth," a point of reference for young, black kids also in the periphery, as suggested in this excerpt from "Mó Treta":

Passado algum tempo, os manos foram pro saco	After a while, the brothers got whacked
Fecharam eles de um jeito que não deu pra acreditar	They killed them in a way you wouldn't believe
Então parei pra pensar, que rumo tomar	So I stopped to think, what path do I take
Ou ficava nessa, ou tentava mudar	Either I stayed with them, or I tried to change
Se não tivesse mudado . . . também seria finado . . .	If I hadn't changed . . . I would be dead too . . .
E os amigos sinceros, que são importantes para mim	And the sincere friends, that are important to me
Minha família, minha esposa e filha	My family, my wife, and daughter
Enfim, tudo aquilo que até hoje eu consegui	All that that I've been able to get
Se tivesse insistido na parada	If I'd kept up the game
com certeza não estaria aqui	I wouldn't be here today for sure

The song shows the rap duo's concern with young people who are tempted by a life of crime. The story has relevance because it narrates a lived experience, presents alternatives to crime, and shows how rap was fundamental in changing Thaíde's life. Many of his lyrics try to give advice or examples of people who resisted a life of crime and drugs.

The lyrics of generation-oriented groups give special attention to the youth who have been through similar situations and are coping with the loss of loved ones, daily experiences in the periphery, and family life. Information and knowledge are fundamental in this process. In this way, rap serves as a foundation for youth of the periphery by providing information and provoking reflection, which can change the behavior and lifestyle of many people. Even though the lyrics are inspired by personal stories and experiences, this style of rap is geared toward larger social issues. By exposing his own problems, the rapper seeks the social integration of youth who live in the most precarious areas of the city.

::: Groups Oriented toward Class Struggle

In our examination of generation-oriented groups, we saw that ethnic consciousness, the acknowledgment of African cultural inheritance, and the affirmation of a black identity are not central concerns, even though they may appear in some lyrics and in some of the interviewee's responses. In contrast, issues relating to black identity and the African diaspora are predominant in the discourse of groups oriented toward class struggle. The relationship between hip-hop and ethnic consciousness results from a process of self-awareness and recuperation of "self-esteem," initially inspired by the music and history of African Americans in the United States. Through rap produced by North American groups, young black paulistanos were able to learn about the struggle against racism and to find similar experiences in the history of resistance among Afro-Brazilians. The hip-hop movement was also important in recuperating the history and culture of Afro-Brazilians, especially since school curricula, according to those interviewed, only include teaching of black history in relation to slavery, thus ignoring the black history and culture of the Americas before and after this period. Hip-hop emerges here as a way to recuperate and reinterpret the history of the black diaspora, while calling into question the official history taught in school (Weller 2003: 62–75). In the process of rereading history, young people come to know their "own heroes" and to begin to identify with them. By "seeing themselves" in history and in heroes of the past, they construct a bridge between the past and the present, constituting a relationship between official and lived history. In this act of rediscovering (Hall 1996b) and of comparing the past with the present, young people learn "everything they really wanted to learn," and develop an "identification with race" and a "notion of blackness," as noted by Darcy of Grupo Atitude:

In my opinion it's like this: I can say that hip-hop changed my way of thinking, you know? Especially because everything that I think I really wanted to learn in life was about identification, about identifying with my race. Those were things they didn't teach at school, things I didn't learn at school. Through hip-hop I started to have a stronger notion of blackness, you know?

He regards hip-hop as "a kind of magnet" that provokes new ways of thinking and modes of identification, which are related to lived experiences. Raising consciousness or changing the "way of thinking" brings the recognition and valorization of African roots (of the "race"), as well as the strong identification with "blackness." "Blackness" or *being* black is not essentially associated with phenotype, but rather with a process of *becoming* black. *Black* is thus synonymous with shared experiences of marginalization and struggle against racism, as well as the color of political resistance (Back 1996: 142–47). Becoming black implies a process of recognizing one's belonging to a group. In this sense, young people construct a notion of blackness by identifying with common elements in the history of the African diaspora and with shared experiences of discrimination and segregation. The process of relating past history to the current reality contributes to the formation of a black identity with a basis in collective memory and lived history (Halbwachs 1992). Black identity and ethnic consciousness emerge from that process of *becoming* and from the notion of *belonging* to a social space of shared experiences. The search for identity can be seen also as synonymous with the reinterpretation of official history and the construction of a narrative of the Black Atlantic marked by the process of colonization and hybridization (Gilroy 1993). However, black identity cannot be seen as a finished product. It needs a "foundation" on which to construct and renew itself continuously. The posse Estilo Negro, to which the young people interviewed belong, is important in the process of constructing a black identity and of ensuring "self-esteem." Carlos, of the Grupo Atitude, affirms:

Hip-hop was fundamental in this sense, because it increased our self-esteem, you know? Because we are considered a people without our own identity, because of the process of colonization and miscegenation, right? So starting from that point, we began to create our own identity, that has to have a base, right? I think that Estilo Negro was that foundation.

The reclaiming of "self-esteem" and the reconstruction of identity and collective memory generated creative energy among the young people of the group that was characterized by the search for new collective forms of living through community work. Community work also represented solidarity constituted by notions of "brotherhood" and "Africanness" among blacks. In spite of the solidarity that existed in the "old African society," it no longer seems like a model of orientation among Afro-descendants in the diaspora, especially among the youth. For this reason, groups oriented toward *class struggle* see the necessity of reclaiming and transmitting these values to new generations in order to combat "individualism" which is ever more present, as Carlos notes:

> Brotherhood works like this: for example, one hand washes the other, you know? So we really think about community. And it's that way of thinking that we have to instill in the youth of today, because there is too much individualism. People aren't interested in helping other people. And I think that's not the way to go because ever since the beginning of our community, of African society, we have always had a sense of community work, right? . . . Kids today don't have that vision, that connection to Africanness. So it is up to us—we are trying to make that happen—so that they can also start incorporating that spirit.

"Brotherhood" and "Africanness" are metaphors that symbolize a cultural and spiritual relationship with the continent of origin and the importance of solidarity among friends and neighbors. The expression Africanness is associated with a genetic inheritance ("of the same blood") that allows residents of the periphery to help each other, consciously or "unconsciously," by presenting models of solidarity similar to those of the "old African society." Symbolically, "blood" represents a relationship between reconstructed history and history lived today. In confronting experiences of personal disruption and the loss of social ties and kinship, blood becomes a myth that generates processes of identity formation. Through the symbolization of solidarity implicit in the idea of Africanness, the group reconstructs forgotten relationships and associations. In that symbolic trip (Hall 1990), re-learned values and life models are not simply implemented; they are made relevant to the present situation and adapted to the specific social context of "the kids of today." This symbolic trip to the African continent establishes an imaginary relationship to the various roots and traditions of the "old African society." By belonging to an "imagined community," as defined by Benedict Anderson (1993), the group attempts to build a relationship of unity and reciprocity, with the goal of making new milieus and forms of collectivity. Africanness represents a new concept of ethnicity that in addition to recognizing history, traditions, and differences, becomes an agent of renovation and transformation.

Class struggle orientation is also present in the lyrics of other important groups of paulistano hip-hop in the 1990s. Among them are DMN, whose first record, *Cada Vez Mais Preto* (Increasingly Blacker), was released in 1993 on the Zimbabwe label. The title suggests the outlook of the record, which reinforces racial discourse. In a tone of protest, the introduction of the record features excerpts from televised news programs in which various reporters narrate incidents of discrimination against the black population in Brazil and abroad. The track also narrates news of abuse and massacres in jails, such as that of the Carandiru Detention Center in 1992, in which 111 prisoners were assassinated and the police absolved of all responsibility. The lyrics of DMN invert stigmas and values attributed to the young blacks of the periphery who are searching for self-worth, pride, and confidence. By combating stigmatized identities, DMN directly critiques the basis of racist ideology, as in this excerpt from the rap "Lei da Rua" (Law of the Street) from *Cada Vez Mais Preto*:

Fui vítima como muitos	I was a victim like many others
Paga pau da lavagem cerebral de certos grupos	Blind follower of the brain-washing of certain groups
Quem olha bem, até hoje eu não sei	Who sees straight, even today I can't tell
Não me valorizei, me auto-violei . . .	I didn't value myself, I violated myself . . .
Certamente tinha em mente a definição	I must have had in mind the notion
De que tudo que era branco era lindo e bom	That all that was white was beautiful and good
Ilusão, natural	Illusion, naturally
E todo preto ignorante	And every black ignorant
E que cai, fazer transparecer	And in falling it became apparent
A todo instante a sua imagem de integrado	At every instant, this illusion of integration
Mais um irmão, mais então, mais um otário	One more brother, even more, one more fool

When the author says he was a "victim like many others," he is speaking of his personal experiences. He has realized that many of the things that happened to him were the result of prejudices and stereotypes that exist in the social imaginary. These experiences are very important for the worldview of many young people. Another positive reference in this rap is Africa, as the place of origin of the black population. Opposing the idea of a "people without self-worth," "without meaning, without definition," the song refers to a history of black people "constituted through glorious deeds" that "few remember." And, some verses later, the song quotes important artists and groups that represent black pride in Brazil ("Benedita da Silva, Racionais, Leci Brandão, Ilê Aiyê") with the hopes of rebuilding feelings of self-confidence and hope.

The group DMN seeks to transform young black kids without racial and social consciousness, without information, who lack self-esteem. Their song "4P" offers as a role model a young black person who is conscious of the history and culture of his people:

É quatro P, Poder Para o Povo Preto	It's 4 Ps: Power for the Black People
Para o Povo Preto . . .	For the black people . . .
Axé se soubesse o valor que sua raça tem	*Axé* if you only knew your race's value,
tingia a palma da mão pra ser escura também . . . Talvez não perceberam ainda	you'd dye the palm of your hand so it would be dark too . . . perhaps you haven't realized
que a nossa história é tão rica, mais que ouro,	that our history is so rich, more than gold,
é um tesouro em ideal e coragem,	it's a treasure in ideals and courage,
não é sonho, nem miragem . . .	it's not a dream, nor a mirage . . .
Não devemos esquecer o passado,	We shouldn't forget the past,
determinação e autovalorização.	determination and self-value
Cada vez mais a verdadeira história, Axé	More and more of the real story, Axé

The rap song "4P" cites examples of famous Afro-descendants throughout the Americas, including sports figures Mike Tyson and Pelé, musicians Michael Jackson and Jimi Hendrix, the filmmaker Spike Lee, and the historical Afro-Brazilian leader Zumbi dos Palmares. Not all of these figures are known for their involvement with black struggles. The soccer star Pelé, for example, was always criticized for not denouncing racism in Brazil. In this song DMN is not seeking to highlight models or heroes, but simply to cite people of African descent who have achieved success. The song also cites internationally recognized icons who struggled against oppression and prejudice in the United States, Jamaica, and South Africa: Marcus Garvey, Malcolm X, Nelson Mandela, and Martin Luther King Jr. The end of the rap returns to the original issues: memory, self-esteem, and racial identity.

The Racionais MCs is another group that is oriented toward class struggle and has had a tremendous impact on paulistano rap. Formed at the end of the 1980s, the Racionais MCs are the most successful hip-hop group of Brazil, having sold the most CDs and reached an audience outside of peripheral neighborhoods. Their songs are not characterized by racial discourse and black identity; instead they contain the critical analysis of social and economic inequalities in São Paulo. The group has developed a discourse that addresses social and political problems, denouncing the gap between the population that lives near the center of the city and those who live on the periphery. In the rap "Fim-de-Semana no Parque" (Weekend in the Park) from the CD *Raio X Brasil* (1993), Mano Brown, the leader of the Racionais MCs, exposes the difference between the lifestyles of middle-class and upper-class "playboys" and those of the youth on the periphery:

Feliz e agitada toda a playboyzada	Happy and agitated, all the playboys
As garagens abertas eles lavam os carros,	With their garages open, they wash their cars,
desperdiçam a água, eles fazem a festa	They waste water and are having a party
Vários estilos, vagabundas, motocicletas	Various styles, loose women, motorcycles
Coroa rico, boca aberta, a isca predileta.	A rich guy, mouth open, favorite bait.

He refers to the private areas not accessible to youth from the periphery, such as clubs, pools, courts, and cinemas and to the consumer items that they can't afford:

Me dê 4 bons motivos pra não ser	Give me 4 good reasons to not be
olha o meu povo nas favelas e vai perceber	Look at my people in the favelas and you'll see
Daqui eu vejo uma caranga do ano	From here I can see a brand new car
toda equipada e um tiozinho guiando	Fully equipped with a little guy driving
Com seus filhos ao lado, estão indo ao parque	With his kids by his side, going to the park
Eufóricos, brinquedos eletrônicos	Euphoric, electronic toys

Automaticamente eu imagino a molecada lá	I automatically imagine how the kids from
da área como é que tá . . .	the neighborhood are . . .
Eles não tem vídeo game,	They don't have video games,
às vezes nem televisão	sometimes not even a television

Brown suggests ways that the state could make improvements, securing space and funds for leisure and recreation, which don't exist in São Paulo's periphery. The rapper can no longer stand the degraded environment of the periphery and incites everyone to become conscious of its problems:

Milhares de casas amontoadas, ruas de terra,	Thousands of houses piled on top of each other, dirt streets,
esse é o morro, a minha área de espera . . .	that is the hillside, my waiting place . . .
Aqui não vejo nenhum clube esportivo,	I don't see any sports club here,
pra molecada freqüentar, nenhum incentivo.	for the kids to go to, no incentive here.
O investimento no lazer é muito escasso . . .	The investment in leisure is too scarce . . .
Mas aí, se você quiser se destruir	But if you wanted to destroy yourself
está no lugar certo,	you're in the right place,
tem bebida e cocaína sempre por perto . . .	there's booze and cocaine always nearby . . .
Mãe angustiada, filho problemático,	An anguished mother, a problem kid,
famílias destruídas, fim-de-semanas trágicos,	destroyed families, tragic weekends,
o sistema quer isso, a molecada tem que	the system wants this, the kids have
aprender, fim-de-semana no Parque Ipê.	to learn, weekend at Ipê Park.

In another part of the rap, Brown expresses displeasure again with where he lives, but also affirms that he is among "friends" and "equals," expressing a feeling of belonging to an imagined community. This rap can be the story of any young Afro-Brazilian from the periphery. It refers to the wishes and desires that cannot be fulfilled. Even at the beginning of the song, Brown draws attention to the *maldade* (malice) of young people with consumer desires. Although he recalls his admiration for the thieves and *malandros* (hustlers) who had expensive clothes and new cars, he also notes that they are all dead or in jail and arrives at the conclusion that crime is the worst option: "It took a while, but now I understand / that real *malandragem* is just staying alive." In this contradictory and violent context so common in the Brazilian periphery, every young person needs to find his or her own way by "learning to live" and taking advantage of information, knowledge, self-esteem, and black pride to make daily life easier.

::: Final Considerations

The international connections among cultural styles have generated diverse social formations among the young that share much in common. Understanding the transcultural character of youth practices in our societies requires an analysis of the contexts in which these styles are being appropriated, created, or re-created. We live in an increasingly globalized, or transnational, world and must understand the implications of ongoing transformations for new generations. While the generation-oriented groups look for ways to deal with personal disruptions, broken families, and other social problems, groups oriented toward class struggle see rap as a way of achieving their political and social aspirations. Hip-hop has a key role in developing practical action against prejudice and hostility toward the "other." Common goals and the recognition that "they are not alone" strengthen the spirit of collectivity, increases self-esteem, and inspires the search for new ways to combat problems faced on a daily basis.

Regardless of the specific orientation of any given rap group, hip-hop inspired new forms of collectivity that substituted for former ties and solidarities that were lost with the dislocation of poor families. Creating social spaces for shared experiences via aesthetic and political activities allows for the development of new strategies to confront discrimination. Group members inherit an ensemble of common narratives that generates the creative potential of rap groups oriented both toward generation and class struggle.

Although young people are seeking their own strategies to overcome discrimination, public policies geared toward strengthening these strategies are still necessary. Social inclusion through cultural policies (i.e., sponsoring workshops to teach rap, break dance, and graffiti) have been showing positive results in increasing creativity and "self-esteem," as well as in combating idleness, violence, and criminality. In addition to cultural programs, professional and vocational programs must also be supported. Reestablishing an intergenerational dialogue and reconstituting lost links should accompany these programs.

In this way, the construction of solidarity networks based on "brotherhood" and "Africanness"—as discussed by some of the people interviewed— calls for an effort to transform the negative image many young people have of older generations. This would include not just their parents and grandparents, but also teachers, politicians, and other social actors who have often neglected the problems faced by young blacks and second- or third-generation children of migrants who live in the peripheries of large cities.

DISCOGRAPHY

DMN. *Cada Vez Mais Preto*. Zimbabwe, 1993.
Racionais MC's. *Raio X Brasil*. Zimbabwe, 1993.
Thaíde e DJ Hum. *Brava Gente*. Hip Hop Brasil / Brava Gente, Independente, 1994.
———. *Hip Hop na Veia*. Eldorado, 1991.
———. *Humildade e Coragem São Nossas Armas para Lutar*. TNT Records, 1992.
———. *Pergunte a Quem Conhece*. Eldorado, 1989.
———. *Preste Atenção*. Brava Gente/Eldorado, 1996.

::: "Conquistando Espaço"

Hip-Hop Occupations of São Paulo

Derek Pardue

Yeah, we're professors. We teach citizenship. Hip-hop is about an attitude
of self and community. But, you know, beyond that, hip-hop is about taking
over a space.
—DJ Bris, Interview, São Paulo, 2002.

Recent efforts by local hip-hoppers in São Paulo in the field of popular or "alternative" education have gained attention from journalists, educators, politicians, academics, and, of course, from the hip-hop community
throughout Brazil (Andrade 1996, 1999; Pardue, 2004b).[1] Understandably,
criticism and praise of hip-hop educational projects have focused on important issues such as content and access within the larger discussion of
parameters and practice of contemporary citizenship in Brazil. In my experience with hip-hoppers over the past twelve years, I have been struck
by the value given to "occupation"—or as DJ Bris describes it in the above
quote—"taking over space" (*conquistando espaço*). The notion of hip-hop
"conquests" is an insight worth developing, for it illuminates the spatial
aspect of citizenship empirically through the practice of popular culture. In
this chapter I will move between two levels of discussion. Following a brief
discussion of the main operative term, *occupation*, I will theorize the concept of citizenship as it relates to the state and popular culture within modern Brazilian history. Next, I will focus my analysis on a very localized case
of citizenship-occupation articulation carried out by local hip-hoppers on
the extreme east side of São Paulo in the Cidade Tiradentes neighborhood.
Ultimately, I argue that the negotiation and opening of a community library
by the hip-hop posse Força Ativa (Active Force) stands as one (but not the
only) model of how hip-hoppers can utilize the present national and global
discourses of "citizenship" (*cidadania*) and education as domains of hip-hop

and part of what it means to be part of good, positive hip-hop (*hip hop do bom*).[2]

::: Hip-Hop Occupations

In her rendition of São Paulo as a metropolitan city, Teresa Caldeira (2000) highlights a transformation that has resulted in greater spatial proximity of elite and working-class social groups but has eliminated common spaces. Over the past twenty years there has been a proliferation of *condomínios* (gated communities). More and more São Paulo residents are hiring privatized security agencies, which strictly guard boundaries and monitor entry passages. Since these communities lie for the most part in areas once occupied by working-class residents of the *periferia*, the surrounding lots become neighborhood remnants to be reworked by remaining residents. As Caldeira notes, the environment outside the elite "fortified enclaves" is unstructured, makeshift, and leftover (Caldeira 2000, see in particular chap. 8).

While the growth of condomínios has occurred across the metropolitan area as a whole, its greatest concentration has been on the west and north sides of town. Coincidentally, my contacts have been mostly from the east and south sides of São Paulo along with the industrial satellite cities of Santo André, São Bernardo do Campo, and Diadema located in the southeast section of the overall metropolitan area.

Public spaces here are full of people. Participants engage these spaces as a platform for many different kinds of activities in a manner quite different from the leftover spaces of isolation Caldeira describes. Neighborhood streets and small public parks are the main stage for weekend hip-hop performances. Hip-hoppers work to organize these spaces into recognized places of hip-hop culture and community-building. Not always working for *união* (unity), hip-hoppers do succeed in organizing important public occupations. Such labor affords one the opportunity to engage the community park or the public library as an example of what the late Brazilian geographer Milton Santos described as *território usado* (territory in use), which he regarded as "an analytical category" (2006: 14).[3]

In conversations with teenagers at a local east-side posse meeting of União da Periferia in November of 2001, I realized the importance of weekend hip-hop shows in the park. The following transcription of our conversation illustrates Santos's idea of "territory in use" and the potential force of hip-hop on the local community as it relates to space and identity.

DP: How long have you been involved with hip-hop?

AA: This is my first time here.

BB: Until a few days ago, I really didn't know what hip-hop was about.

CC: Yeah, we heard something, and went to the park, right up the street, there, and checked out what people were doing.

AA: I mean, some people say there's nothing good that comes from these parks. You know, they're ugly and dirty and a shame for all of us to see everyday as we walk by. But, I mean, now we have a different outlook on the park. It can be a good thing. I feel better about walking by and thinking about hip-hop, and maybe one day I'll get up there and do something. You never know.

There is nothing attractive about these parks in and of themselves. They are either barren dirt patches or areas of weathered cement slabs partially covered by overgrown green brush. However, during hip-hop events the park becomes a strong, positive reference. Emcees often announce the location and thank God and the event organizer(s) for their efforts in the realization of the event. The park periodically becomes a symbol of the neighborhood as a whole, standing in metonymically for the gathered crowd in a shout out to the east side or to São Paulo in its entirety. During hip-hop events the park is a relatively friendly space, as audience etiquette requires applause for performers regardless of talent or experience level. Applause shows recognition of the performer's *attitude* (confidence) of being on stage in the first place.

Part of my overall intention in this chapter is to illustrate the *brasilidade*, or "Brazilianness," in local hip-hop. As I have argued elsewhere (2007), what is "Brazilian" about Brazilian hip-hop—just as is the case with any other cultural formation—must be understood in terms of practice and not simply a set of sounds, images, and gestures.[4] Part of hip-hop practice involves organizational and employment strategies. Beyond an evaluation of Brazilian hip-hoppers' engagement with the state as "educators," the evidence and analysis presented in this chapter suggest that Brazilian hip-hoppers see "globalized" discourses of hip-hop identity (e.g., the hip-hop posse, Afrika Bambaataa and the Universal Zulu Nation) and nationalist discourses of citizenship (e.g., a new meaning of *cidadania*) as potential assets for their agenda of representation and change. Thus, in this manner, this chapter contributes to the growing literature over the past decade regarding the continuing relevance of the state within postmodern, transnational, and translocal cultural practices (Dagnino 1998; Sujatha Fernandes 2003).

::: "Cidadão! O que você está fazendo?":
Citizenship and the State

As a modern concept, citizenship has produced a variety of discursive connotations, including legal codes, constitutional articles, and, as the phrase above exemplifies, quotidian forms of address. The social category of *cidadão* (citizen) depends greatly on the relation of the state to civil society. In part, such articulations reveal to what extent a particular state is coercive or hegemonic. The above phrase—"Hey citizen, what are you doing?"—was a common utterance popularized by police officers toward everyday Brazilians, especially those with notable markers of working classes, during the last military dictatorship (1964–85) and survived into the Brazilian political periods of the *abertura* and "transition" to representational democracy. During this time cidadão congealed as a forceful term of address loaded with a sense of obligation and relations of power. Not unlike the ubiquitous term *doutor* (doctor)—denoting class, educational, or general status—cidadão served Brazilians well, especially those representing the state and secondarily those in positions of corporate capital, in the everyday negotiations of influence and persuasion (if not coercion). Over the past two decades, as Brazil has changed from a more coercive to hegemonic state, many Brazilians have contributed to a different idea of cidadania and the cidadão. Namely, the citizen can be a concept of subjectivity and agency rather than a target of state attention and civic duties. As they have matured ideologically and politically, hip-hoppers have become a significant group to observe for those interested in the real efficacy of this latter understanding and practice of citizenship.

My analysis of hip-hop and (or as) Brazilian citizenship is based on the assertion that the state in Brazil presently is best characterized, following Gramscian scholars, as an "ethical state." The function of the ethical state is "to form citizens and to gain consent, the two distinct projects being in fact the same: the subject is to be formed as one who consents to hegemony . . . the work of formation is continuous, taking place not only through pedagogy but through the work of intellectuals in all the spheres of civil society" (Lloyd and Thomas 1998: 21). Culture, then, does not manifest itself only as artifacts of aesthetic production or "objects of knowledge," but rather as a process of "forming an ethical disposition" (7), which articulates to the representational structures of the modern state (17). In essence, the combination of citizenship and hegemony theoretically resolves the historical problem of political democracy and social inclusion within a system of hierarchy (Hagopian 2007: 21–22). Yet, the situation is more complex, because citizenship is not only an individual practice but also one of association. The associative factor is important, because it highlights participatory citizenship and potentially the weakening of government authority and thus complicates state hegemony (Walzer 1995). Within such a frame of theory and practice, hip-hop as an integral part of contemporary socialization in urban (or suburban) Brazil becomes potentially part of producing "normal" states through everyday fields of popular activity and imagination (Hansen and Stepputat 2001). Does hip-hop, as part of a more general phenomenon of "popular education" and "popular citizenship," contribute to a hegemonic formation with regard to citizenship, or do state-employed or state-dependent hip-hoppers transform or expand conventional notions of citizenship in their activities and projects? Referring to the title of this section, have hip-hoppers contributed to an understanding of "citizen" as a label of obligations or as a category of pride and entitlement?

In addition to the philosophy of the state and citizen formation there are particular factors related to Brazil and Latin America worth review with regard to macro-level structural developments. Throughout Latin America during the late 1970s and early 1980s, the idea of citizenship shifted from one of strict obligations to a growing sense of individual and collective rights. Following the paradigmatic analysis of T. H. Marshall (1950), "rights" include a range of practices and liberties on social, civil, and political levels. In the late twentieth century, "social rights" would encompass "human rights" and "cultural rights." Not surprisingly, much of this change was the result of regime changes (structure) and concurrent collective organizations (agency) as part of the so-called democratization of Latin America. As the military dictatorships and other forms of authoritarian rule ceded to more participatory political systems, people—especially those from the poor, working classes—discovered and "occupied" more space to articulate their concerns and enact changes in everyday life in their neighborhoods and workplaces. However, some of these new or adapted institutions of democratic citizenship were co-opted by suspicious state agencies or they reproduced long-standing corrupt practices of clientelism, also frequently implicating the state (Arias 2006; O'Donnell 1996). In addition, as many Latin American scholars have demonstrated, the triad of social, civil, and political rights rarely existed in an equal fashion from the very beginning of democratic transition. For example, systematic state violence, both physical and symbolic, targeting indigenous groups in Guatemala, Bolivia, and Peru—as well as the intensified privatization of security in places such as Brazil—have complicated the practical meanings of citizenship in these and other Latin American democracies.[5] Some scholars have argued that the problems of effective citizenship in contemporary Latin America are related not to democracy or capitalism per se. Rather, they are, in part, due to a particular "consumption" of democratic theory by local intellectuals and governmental administrations (Hagopian 2007). Specific to Brazil, this interpretation resonates upon consideration of the prevailing theory of how Brazilians historically have understood or "consumed" and consequently implemented discourses of "modernity" (Roberto Schwarz 1992) and "race" (Lílian Schwarcz 1993).

In sum, there is a common theme in the citizenship literature related to Latin America. Namely, as increasingly more heterogeneous groups "conquer" public space and exercise their rights under new and seemingly autonomous purviews of "citizenship rights," the democratic state's job of hegemony and, by extension, control of identity formation becomes strained (Dahl 1998; Jelin 2003). In Brazil, hip-hoppers' practices, as they relate to culture, education, identity politics, and community, reflect a multileveled approach. Some hip-hoppers articulate identity and citizenship to the extreme locality of the *quebrada* (any particular neighborhood) and have made alliances, both discursive and infrastructural, with local crime syndicates and thus challenge the essential authority and legitimacy of the state and NGOs. Others try to circumvent the state through transnational alliances with distant hip-hop organizations such as Universal Zulu Nation or B-boy/B-girl street dance collectives based in Europe. While, still others, insist that hip-hop must be in dialogue with the state in an effort to force the state to dedicate resources to public projects. My analysis of the group Força Ativa is an attempt to address this final hip-hop approach to citizenship. Before focusing on Força Ativa, I contextualize hip-hop in Brazil with regard to public culture and the Brazilian state.

::: Brazilian Hip-Hop: A Complex Manifestation
    of Public and State Culture

In Brazil, hip-hop emerged in the mid-1980s as an extension of two areas of cultural activity: B-boy (street dance) crews' public performances and rapper nightclub entertainment contests. The history of hip-hop's connection with state government agencies can be traced through the B-boy crews, while the trajectory of rap commercialization is historically tied to nightclub contests.

This divide of "state" and "entertainment" is a significant factor in the production of hip-hop in various locales. For example, in France during the mid-1990s and the rise of the brand of nationalism of the FN (Front National; National Front) leader Jean-Marie Le Pen, the state clamped down and exercised more control over the radio airwaves. According to Paul Silverstein (2002: 45–67), the adherence to an elevated percentage of "French" music actually benefited struggling rappers such as NTF and helped "space out" (Forman 2002) hip-hop. In the case of Cuba, the difference between "underground" and "commercial" reflects another articulation of hip-hop and the state. Sujatha Fernandes notes that hip-hoppers who consider themselves part of the "underground generally seek to negotiate with the state, demanding that it fulfill socialist ideals of racial egalitarianism, while rappers who identify as commercial predominantly evoke alternative means of survival such as hustling and consumerism" (2003: 577).

While the political and economic structures of France, Brazil, and Cuba differ, the idea of the state—especially among poor, marginalized, urban Brazilian youth—holds elements in common with the "underground" Cuban perspective. As Moisés from Força Ativa rationalized in response to claims that the group should become a NGO: "We have no interest [in doing that], because that would take pressure off of the state. They have obligations, and they need to know that. That's part of our job as an organized citizen group" (group conversation, São Paulo 2001).[6]

In Brazil, B-boy crews drew attention because of their occupations of public spaces and strong sense of group organization. Throughout the 1980s and 1990s, thousands of teenagers—the overwhelming majority of whom were male, periferia residents of African descent with little formal education—organized themselves into groups called posses. By 1990, leading members of posses, such as Kall of the south-side posse Conceitos de Rua (Street Concepts), had recognized that Brazil was a "disjunctive democracy" (Caldeira and Holston 1999) in the sense that although the political system had become organized as a representative democracy, the level of social inequalities, daily violence, and abuse of human rights had intensified. Through the experience of participating in posses, such as Street Concepts and Posse Hausa in the São Paulo industrial satellite city São Bernardo do Campo, hip-hoppers exploited the new political openings and learned, among other things, how to negotiate with state representatives so that they could organize events, hold collective meetings in public buildings, and occasionally work in state-sponsored social work projects. In short, these youth learned how to engage in a type of what Sonia Alvarez, Evelina Dagnino, and Arturo Escobar (1998) have defined as "cultural politics"—the use of public spaces and "social movement networks or webs" to articulate experiences of social inequality as legitimate fields of artistic expression and political change. In contemporary Brazil, "hip-hop," personified in the "hip-hopper," has become a "position" (Franco 1989), from which practitioners and nonparticipants (politicians, academics, journalists, community leaders) alike seek to destabilize conventional notions of knowledge, experience, and personhood.

The emergence of posses was not an unprecedented act of working-class agency articulating popular culture to state bureaucracy. In fact, hip-hoppers drew on either prior experience or advice from older kin on how to procure resources from state departments of culture and social services (i.e., urbanization initiatives) and maintain neighborhood organizations. Periferia organizers have successfully lobbied for resources (infrastructure for events, meeting places, a percentage of culture budgets) so that expressive art from the various musicocultural genres of samba to soul to funk to hip-hop's "elements" (rap, DJ, graffiti, street dance) can become integral to what defines "popular culture."

The relationship between popular culture and the state has an extensive history in Brazil. In order to contextualize Força Ativa's achievement of opening a public library in the name of "hip-hop and Cidade Tiradentes" neighborhood, it is important to understand the bureaucratic nature of culture in Brazil. The Brazilian state apparatus has traditionally organized and promoted "popular culture" as a series of nonlabor forums so that the majority of the population can build community and feel that they are practicing their citizenship.

Perhaps the most important shift with regard to the present meaning of subaltern citizenship occurred during the first administrative era of Getúlio Vargas (1930–45), in which popular citizenship became less an issue to be directly policed and more of a domain of state privilege and sponsorship. In short, Vargas legitimized in a cultural sense the category—"the people" (o povo). As William Rowe and Vivian Schelling summarize,

> Popular cultural forms became important sites where, on the one hand, traditional, ethnic and local identities were articulated by the state within a project of

national integration and development, and, on the other, they became a means through which the subaltern groups struggled to participate in the formation of the new urban social order, using popular cultural forms to represent their new identity, to make their presence as citizens felt. (1991: 44, see also Joseph and Nugent 1994)

The legacy of dictator Getúlio Vargas's paternal nationalism of the 1930s and 1940s remains in the institutional form of departments of culture, education, and social assistance (Baierle 1998; Boito 1982). Despite the fact that neoliberalism has dominated domestic policies for the past twenty years, a Vargas-esque idea of the state and citizenship pervades much of the Brazilian imaginary.

It is this residue of Vargas's populism that hip-hoppers have explored in order to make hip-hop work. Within the current political party system in Brazil, the PT (Partido dos Trabalhadores; Workers' Party) has interpreted with the greatest consistency the bureaucratic legacy of Vargas's populism to mean that departmental structure should include public participation in the formation of operational budgets. For example, popular forms of culture and education in the São Paulo metropolitan area benefited from the mayoral elections of 1989, won by the PT. Mayor Luiza Erundina named the famous pedagogue Paulo Freire as secretary of education, and he immediately launched a campaign called "education for citizenship" based on grass-roots, literacy programs (Stromquist 1997). It is during this period of 1989 to 1993 when hip-hoppers were most effective in organizing neighborhood posses and establishing employment channels through proposals to the Department of Education (Andrade 1996; Silva 1998: 162–65). Hip-hop proposals such as "ABC Rap," "Movimento Hip Hop Organizado (MH2O)," "Projeto Rappers," and the publication of the magazine *Pode Crê* argued that education should be articulated to include social organization and a more participatory sense of citizenship.[7]

However, Vargas also left a legacy of paternalism and what Brazilian political scientists have termed *clientelismo*. Since the 1930s popular culture and citizenship have been important fields of co-optation and what Abers described as a "politics of demobilization" (Abers 2000), in which popular discourses of inclusion are espoused but little to no concrete action is ever initiated and thus grass-roots organizing is stifled. This has been true in Brazil during macrostructural changes in political-economic systems moving from a populist dictatorship with large state bureaucracies to a military dictatorship to a neoliberal Christian democratic regime to a "progressive" PT regime. For example, there is no doubt that "citizenship" or cidadania, in Brazil and elsewhere, is part of contemporary corporate marketing strategies aimed at connecting consumption with a sense of agency or what in the United States one might call "freedom." Certainly, this is the operative logic for the recent sponsorship of Banco do Brasil and Red Bull as related to hip-hop events, where "citizenship" is central to the advertising campaign and has become a link on corporate websites.

The contribution of hip-hoppers to this long trajectory of working-class state negotiation is that for the first time, the "popular" and "citizenship" have become an ideology of social change and education. Sérgio Gregório Baierle (1998), Maria Celia Paoli and Vera da Silva Telles (1998), Rebecca Neaera Abers (2000), and others have noted that the relative success of the PT and such sociopolitical initiatives as the *orçamento participativo* (participatory budget) at the municipal level during the late 1980s and early '90s was significant in the development of "citizenship from below" (Dagnino 1998: 51). Furthermore, as Evelina Dagnino has demonstrated in her work on social movements in São Paulo and Campinas, the "new citizenship" in Brazil focuses on change, but this does not mean "a refusal of political institutions and the state but rather a radical claim for their transformation" (1998: 47). For their part, hip-hoppers' negotiation with the state has moved from event-based moments of party pleasure to contract-based programs of sustained and remunerated work. This trajectory is the most common for Brazilians, who stay with hip-hop and make it their profession.[8]

I have shown that the meaning of hip-hop in Brazil emerges, in part, from its public nature and its pragmatic and theoretical connections to the Brazilian state through agencies of education and culture. Furthermore, Brazilian hip-hop is not an aberrant cultural practice, but one within a certain historical trajectory of popular culture and structural change in politics. In the next section I return to the concept of hip-hop as a public culture to demonstrate the links local hip-hoppers and periphery (*periferia*) residents make between hip-hop, public space, the state, and citizenship.

::: *Correria* and Hip-Hop Spatialization

Hip-hop events are formations involving temporal and spatial development. The prelude and denouement of an event encompass trajectories of movement as participants and observers travel, in the case of hip-hop, across the city. Events are highlights, but as a social phenomenon they are better thought of as processes. Different notions of São Paulo emerge from activities within different circuits (Magnini 1985, 1996; Milton Santos 1979). The constitution of hip-hop spaces involves a particular intersection of location, sociality, and political negotiation.

In the case of the library opening by Força Ativa, a veteran hip-hop organization based on the east side of São Paulo, success was achieved through the operative term—*correria* (hectic rushing around). The linguistic essence of *correr* (to run) provides some insight as to how hip-hoppers see the process of organization, performance, and thus identity formation. It is not simply multitasking skills that hip-hoppers need to be successful; they also must travel long distances to meet with representatives of the Culture and Education Departments at the municipal level. Perhaps more importantly, hip-hoppers strategically utilize other weekend events to make alliances with hip-hop posses and other groups (local politicians, community leaders, activists, business owners, and employees) in distant neighborhoods within São Paulo or in the surrounding thirty-nine municipalities. To become *aliados* (allies), a key term frequently emphasized by rappers in their introductory remarks on a CD or during a performance, means not only becoming friends but also becoming *parceiros* (partners), another term of hip-hop salutation. As is evident in the field conversation excerpt that follows, hip-hoppers use their aliados for information to get the inside track on, for example, how certain governmental agencies proceed with budget and resource allocation. Such aliados can be become potential parceiros over a longer period and lead to a sense of empowerment for hip-hoppers.

DP: How did you start this process of working with COHAB [Companhia Metropolitana de Habitação, Metropolitan Company of Residence] related to the library?

Moisés: Well, you know, it took a long time. Some of the guys here and I went to several hip-hop events in other neighborhoods. We heard about them from people who make hip-hop 'zines, fliers, and pamphlets. We went to only the events that we thought had all four elements. You know, not just rappers, all of hip-hop. We researched who the sponsors were.

DP: Why is that important?

M: It's a guess, and so many things can go wrong. You have to be careful to not get involved with shady sponsors. Although we like to think that all hip-hoppers will help each other out, a lot of them are "snakes" [*cobras*] and they want to set you up to fail. Basically, the idea is to make allies. If you like the event, you want to meet the organizers and be genuine. You have to come with an "exchange of ideas" [*trocar uma idéia*]. This is how we got the name of Gilson within COHAB, and in the end this was helpful for the library project.

DP: What do you mean by "exchange"?

M: I mean there has to be some incentive; there has to be some give-and-take, especially with people you don't know very well. So, this kind of thing takes a long time to create. That's why we spent time and money going to a lot of different places. We went to events in Brasilândia and Perús (extreme north and northwest sides of São Paulo) and Jardim Ângela (extreme south side). It was hard and exhausting, but, you know, we met some serious people, and they have continued to be our allies until today. We help each other out, and we have respect for each other.

Place identity is "constructed out of movement, communication, social relations which always stretch beyond it" (Massey and Denton 1992: 14). The links between travel, knowledge, and recognition are not lost on São Paulo hip-hoppers. It is extremely important for hip-hop performers to know the various confines of the immense São Paulo periferia. Through live performances, all hip-hoppers—especially rappers—cover a great deal of territory going from one event to another. Beyond their own performances, rappers make cameo appearances in events across the metropolitan area starting in the afternoon and going into the morning hours of the following day.

The hip-hop performer and fan alike are weekend travelers covering up to a hundred miles without ever leaving the São Paulo metropolitan area. Weekend events in periferia clubs, radio stations, cultural centers, public parks, and the birthday party of a friend (*camarada*) outline significant spatial networks of culture, ones that engender alliances and promote what is optimistically termed *união* (unity).

::: Força Ativa and Projects of Occupation

And Polo said: "the inferno of the living is not something that will be; if there is one, it is what is already here, the inferno where we live every day, that we form by being together. There are two ways to escape suffering it. The first is easy for many: accept the inferno and become such a part of it that you can no longer see it. The second is risky and demands constant vigilance and

apprehension: seek and learn to recognize who and what, in the midst of
the inferno, are not inferno, then make them endure, give them space."
—Calvino, *Invisible Cities*, 1974

There are certainly many ways one might interpret Italo Calvino's provocative essay *Invisible Cities*. The passage above, poetic yet quite general,
captures the sentiment of hip-hoppers such as Moisés from Força Ativa
in their struggle against what they call *o sistema* (the system) or what Calvino through the character of Marco Polo calls "the inferno." In an academic
sense, the inferno or sistema is a type of hegemony, a common sense defined by lack of reflection to the point that "you can no longer see it." As
shown above in the conversation with Moisés, some hip-hoppers actively
seek out "who and what, in the midst of the inferno (or "system"), are not
[part of the] inferno and make them," in the case of hip-hop, "allies." The
case of Força Ativa helps illustrate the importance of hip-hop in the overall
struggle for spatial (and semiotic) control of and in the periferia vis-à-vis the
overall society or "system." The following ethnographic piece represents the
process of Força Ativa's involvement in the establishment of a community
library in December of 2001.

During my first stay in São Paulo, from 1995 to 1998, I heard many references to Força Ativa as one of the few remaining posses from hip-hop's
so-called second wave in the late 1980s. In a phone conversation I had with
Moisés, he characterized Força Ativa as an *organização juvenil* (youth organization) and said that it had "evolved" from a posse into a *núcleo cultural*
(cultural organization) in 1995. He explained that the motivation was to take
on a wider range of social issues than what hip-hop (especially rap music)
was capable of. Moisés summarized that hip-hop, which focuses on performance, was not succeeding in raising the level of consciousness of neighborhood people about such social issues as gender, racism, sexuality, and
politics. The members of Força Ativa felt that a profile and structure of a
"community cultural center" would improve the situation. Moisés explained
to me the organizational structure of the group. There are five "commissions"—Press, Hip-Hop, Culture, Public Speech (Palestra), and General.

Space and place have been important in the history of posses and hip-
hop organization in general. In São Paulo the first posses, established in
1986–87, were based downtown near the first public spaces of hip-hop performance, such as São Bento Subway Station and Roosevelt Plaza. Shortly

thereafter, hip-hoppers began to organize groups in the neighborhoods of the suburban periphery. This shift from the downtown to the neighborhood, in retrospect, established a stronger sense of periferia locality and resulted in garnering more support from long-standing community organizations. For many, this period transformed hip-hop in São Paulo into a "movement" as part of a trajectory of working-class social activism.

Força Ativa was founded in 1988 in the neighborhood cluster of Cidade Tiradentes. The district name, that it contains the word for *city*, is revealing in and of itself. When traveling to Cidade Tiradentes it seems as though one has left São Paulo. By way of avenues named after industries, one traverses long stretches of roads lined with occasional residential shacks and substantial forests, part of the remaining grassy areas in the metropolitan area.

Over a hill or two covered with tall, wetland brush and a thin line of improvised and dangerously precarious housing, one passes Negreiros, a supermarket chain located solely in the extreme regions of the east side. After taking a right, one suddenly faces an immense network of housing projects. The name *negreiros* refers to the Portuguese slave ships and, indeed, the store's logo contains a longboat icon. Emerging from the hilly "nowhere" just prior, I was taken aback when I first saw this corporate sign. I felt woozy in this surreal moment, a bizarre reminder of seventeenth-century high seas adventures coupled with coterminous, inland trekking à la the infamous Bandeirantes out to cultivate the indigenous populations of the São Paulo State countryside. Actually, in contemporary usage, *negreiros* is an occasional, pejorative nickname for the buses that travel out to the extreme neighborhoods of the periferia. Conflating racism and class prejudice, these uses of *negreiros* are one more example of how Brazilians frequently invoke colonial metaphors of segregation and difference as part of contemporary imaginations. However, the above association is not the official one. "O Navio Negreiro" is also the title of one of the most famous poems by Antônio de Castro Alves, an abolitionist of the nineteenth century. Further investigation confirms this logic, as one of the neighborhoods of Cidade Tiradentes is named after the abolitionist poet.

City construction under the agency of COHAB began in the late '70s, and in 1980 Cidade Tiradentes had 10,000 residents. Two decades later, the population stands at over 500,000 (Ponciano 2001: 70–71). In this sense the district of Cidade Tiradentes is a city, a separate community boasting over 200 four-story residential buildings. The center plaza features a statue of Tiradentes, the historical martyr of Brazilian Independence.

The opening of the community library as part of a larger project called "Vamos Ler um Livro: Centro de Documentação Jovem Agentes de Direitos Humanos" (Let's Read a Book: Center of Documentation and Youth Group for Human Rights), was the result of over six years of negotiation between Força Ativa and COHAB. According to Edilane, the closest public library to Cidade Tiradentes was in the Penha District, which is located at least forty-five minutes away by bus. Because the district area was almost entirely a project of COHAB, the company officially controls the commercial and leisure space. More recently, private church organizations representing a variety of Pentecostal denominations have developed impressive structures and networks in Cidade Tiradentes as well as in most of the periferia.

Cidade Tiradentes represents for most city-planning officials a governmental success. According to Teresa Caldeira (2000) and Céline Sachs (1999), among others, most financial aid for housing during the various twentieth-century state and federal administrations never reached the working classes. Cidade Tiradentes is one of the few large-scale and relatively completed housing projects in the São Paulo metro area. While this history distinguishes the COHAB project from most of the periferia, Cidade Tiradentes shares an important sociospatial characteristic with the other periferia locales. There is little to no social, health, or educational infrastructure. Edilane, a community activist who has worked for fifteen years in various districts within the São Paulo public school system, related a story to me, which demonstrates a critique of the district's cultural layout. Prior to the inauguration, community residents knew only by word of mouth that the library was open. One Sunday afternoon, during a torrential downpour in the middle of all the traditional weekend television variety shows, a woman faced dangerous mudslides to check out a book. Edilane recited the woman's words as inspirational and a positive sign for the library's future. The woman said to Edilane: "Thank you so much for not opening a bar [*boteco*] or a church."

Various organizations and individuals donated books to the library. The collection includes literature sections on Cuba, citizenship and human rights, and didactic subjects such as Portuguese grammar and world geography. In one of the inaugural speeches, Aldimir, a longtime neighborhood activist and honorary member of Força Ativa, stated: "You can't change the world without understanding it. To read is a principal way of understanding."

While the local hip-hoppers sometimes kid the fifty-something year-old

Aldimir for being so ideological in his activism, all the members of Força Ativa support him and ask him for Marxist bibliographic references as well as personal stories. After the speech, hip-hoppers repeated the phrase "ler é o jeito de entender" (to read is the way to understand) as a performative introduction. In the subsequent performance, Força Ativa rappers defined hip-hop as an important medium through which Cidade Tiradentes youth can articulate their knowledge (from reading) to social change. The record needle dropped, and Força Ativa rapped local stories as they passed around the microphone.

It is significant to note that many of the principal members of Força Ativa make a living with hip-hop culture and human rights issues through a wide range of either governmental organization or community education programs. Edilane gave the example of the Projeto Férias, which takes place during July, the winter break period for schools. Marcos Mendonça, of the São Miguel Paulista school system, organized this program for alternative education and sought out representatives of hip-hop. It was a success, and Djalmão, a Força Ativa member, at the time of this writing was living off of a modest salary from these activities. Ice-Ice, a twenty-eight-year-old widower I had met at a hip-hop organizational meeting of CEDECA (Centro de Defesa da Criança e do Adolescente; Center for the Defense of Children and Adolescents) back in 1997, received funding in 2002 to participate in an international exchange of groups from Italy, Belgium, Brazil, and Colombia. The meetings were organized around themes of human rights, and hip-hop was a significant sector of the participants and activities.

::: Conclusion

Hip-hop scholars in the United States, such as Murray Forman (2002) and Rose (1994), have argued that the very creation (discourse and performance) and cultivation (markets and dissemination) of hip-hop are spatial in nature. In Brazil, this is also true but in the case of São Paulo hip-hop, participants go further. Many practitioners, especially those with past or present experience in posses, articulate space in relation to knowledge and citizenship looking beyond hip-hop culture itself. This is sometimes referred to as the "fifth element" of hip-hop, which comes from Afrika Bambaataa's own warning to hip-hoppers in the United States to form social workshops that can give a more permanent structure for youth in the practices of "citizenship consciousness." Afrika Bambaataa founded the Zulu Nation Brasil organization in 1974 in the South Bronx. The fifth element perspective was fundamental in the establishment and administration of the Zulu Nation Brazil in 2002.

Borrowing from state discourses of popular culture and education, some hip-hop activists have used hip-hop as a conduit for more general debate. As I have discussed elsewhere (Pardue 2004a, 2008), "education" is a discursive category that includes citizenship. Hip-hoppers have been relatively successful in making the argument that the periferia as a social space needs not only investment in infrastructure but also resources and funding for programs that motivate residents to engage the *poder público*, or "civil society," and exercise their rights (not just obligations) as Brazilian citizens. The struggle has come in convincing state representatives that citizenship and popular culture, a long-standing pairing within Brazilian populist politics, is more than occasional public events and performances. Rather, it requires a program or what hip-hoppers term an "alternative system" that provides a more regulated and consistent option for youth in the periferia. This helps explain why so many activists have expanded posses into NGOS and "cultural agencies" (e.g., Força Ativa, Zulu Nation Brasil, Posse Haussa) in order to gain funding as an organization with wider agendas.

The case study of Força Ativa and their careful organization of the community library opening in late 2001 demonstrates that hip-hop is more complex than globalization models of style and rhetoric, frequently glossed as "the hip-hop nation." Local hip-hoppers use terms and categories such as "posse," "Zulu," and the "5th element" as tactics, along with national symbols such as "citizenship" and "popular education," to discuss "reality," work for change, and express themselves. Furthermore, upon consideration of the routine practices and keyword slang vocabulary employed by hip-hoppers, I have shown that hip-hop citizenship in São Paulo also is a spatial project and thus inspires reflection. Citizenship has spatial dimensions; it is a series of negotiated occupations. For their part, Brazilian hip-hoppers foreground this in their ubiquitous goal to *conquistar um espaço*.

NOTES

1. São Paulo hip-hop has also been covered in the popular press. See, for example, Pimentel (1998), Brito (2006), and Rohter (2007).

2. *Posse* is a term borrowed from United States hip-hoppers, who borrowed it from Jamaican dance hall and dub traditions (a mixture of reggae traditions and rap

vocal style). According to Dick Hebdige (1987), Jamaicans appropriated this term from American western movies (see also Cooper 1994).

3. See also Pedro Miguel da Cruz Calado's discussion of hip-hop in Portugal as an active and variable expression of territoriality (2007).

4. Even within the field of hip-hop material, there is cultural difference. For example, the use of gothic type by so-called marginal rappers in Brazil indexes a particular locality of São Paulo periphery "realities," which is by no means universal in its meaning. See Pardue 2005 for more detail. Sebastian Alexander Dent (2005) makes a similar argument with regard to the musical practice of "covers" in Brazil's *música sertaneja* scene.

5. The literature on these areas is quite extensive, but as an outline, for accounts in Guatemala, see Victoria Sanford 2004; for Bolivia, see Lesley Gill 2004, and Bret Gustafson 2006; for Peru, see Maria Elena Garcia 2004; and for Brazil, see Teresa Caldeira and James Holston 1999. For more on the link between privatization of security and politics and the weakening of the state's hold on citizenship, see Philip Oxhorn 2007.

6. George Yúdice found similar sentiments among AfroReggae group members. "[NGOS] run the risk of facilitating the State's retreat from social programs . . . The ideal is to establish an interface between civil society and the government" (excerpts from *Afro Reggae* [1997] in Yúdice 2001: 61).

7. Rap ABC was a project proposed by the former city council representative Neuza Borges in São Bernardo do Campo. Posse Hausa as an idea and organization emerged from this initiative. Projeto Rappers, MH20, and Pode Crê were created by members of Géledes Instituto da Mulher Negra, a*n* NGO that uses both international funding and state support to conduct studies primarily on Afro-Brazilian women and education.

8. See Pardue 2004a and 2008 for more on hip-hoppers' negotiation with state agencies for employment as "professors" in programs of "alternative education" located in places such as youth prisons. See also Olivia Maria Gomes da Cunha's analysis of GCAR (Grupo Cultural AfroReggae) as successful in articulating political projects, not to "missions but rather to possibilities of professionalization" (1998: 239).

::: Funk Music Made in Brazil

Media and Moral Panic

João Freire Filho and Micael Herschmann

British sociology of the 1970s used the concept of moral panic in studies of behavioral deviance and juvenile criminology (Cohen 1971, 1980; Cohen and Young 1973; Young 1971). The goal of those works was, in broad terms, to describe and analyze the process by which a certain condition, episode, individual, or group begins to be faced as a threat to the underlying values and pillars of a society. At times the object of panic is something fairly recent; in other cases it is something that has existed for a while but suddenly has received media spotlight and become the focus of public concerns by law enforcement officials, religious figures, intellectuals, and politicians, among other social actors with recognized credibility and morality. At times, panic withers away and is soon forgotten by all, except folklore and collective memory; on other occasions, it reverberates in more serious and lasting fashion, thereby conditioning changes in the spheres of law and social policy or, even, in the way in which society conceives of itself.

The so-called sociology of moral panic developed out of the then-familiar labeling theory, an analytical perspective that considers deviance a social construction and not an intrinsic quality of specific social acts or actors. This approach is especially associated with the work of the United States sociologist Howard Becker (1963), who emphasized the role of agents of social control—the "moral entrepreneurs"—in the production of deviant behavior.

The mass media are the great source for spreading and legitimating labels, thereby collaborating decisively toward disseminating moral panic. The interrelation between forces of social control, the mass media, and certain forms of deviant activity are studied by Stanley Cohen in his seminal *Folk Devils and Moral Panics* (1980). The book soon became a fundamental reference for sociological and cultural studies regarding spectacular youth subcultures and their demonization in the media.

Cohen focuses especially on the sensationalist coverage of the run-ins between mods and rockers in resorts in southern England in the 1960s. Conflicts were magnified by the media way beyond their real range and meaning, thereby generating a feeling of great unrest in the public vis-à-vis the cultural practices of both youth subcultures (composed by members of the working class). The English sociologist's interest lies in the symbolic dimension of panic waves—moral conflicts and threatened lifestyles. The creation of moral panic, according to the author, provides a precious opportunity for the defenders of a moral symbolic universe to forge an antagonistic moral universe, then attack it, and then redefine the borders between what is morally desirable and undesirable.

Among the most influential of Cohen's theses is the idea that each moral panic has its scapegoat, a "folk devil" upon whom the public projects their fears and fantasies. This is not to say that the folk devil is created by moral panic. The author makes it a point to stress that in spite of the fact that he uses terms such as *panic* and analogies with the study of hysteria and mass illusions, he does not mean to suggest that mods and rockers would not have existed were it not for the moral panic, or even that they would have disappeared if they had just been ignored. His intention, rather, is to suggest that the demonization of these movements is an inadequate solution for the "youth question." Most importantly, the activities of mods and rockers constituted only a temporary and superficial aspect of the "problem"; the underlying causes for moral panic are, in fact, the cultural ambiguities and tensions occasioned by social change. In short, the object of moral panic was the mods and rockers, and the postwar affluence and sexual freedom that they represented. These youth movements were therefore forgotten within a few years, and new embodiments of "Evil" would emerge to replace them.

The exaggerated reaction by guardians of morality was not only shortsighted, but also counterproductive, serving only to heighten social polarization. This may have been, in the end, precisely the desired political effect, as demonstrated later by Stuart Hall et al. (1978) in their attempt to insert the Gramscian concept of hegemony in the analysis of the forces through which moral panics create social conditions of consent necessary for a law-and-order-centered society, less inclined toward the "liberalism" and "permissiveness" proper to the 1960s. The most important facet of that work was the recognition that ideology is not a social process based only on the distortion of truth, but rather a force that continually operates by means of "the common sense."

Erich Goode and Nachman Ben-Yehuda (1994a, 19994b) present the most systematic historical and theoretical account of moral panic. Crusades and moral panic can reflect, according to them, a collective search for identity in spheres as diverse as politics, religion, science, or culture and even become a fairly disseminated phenomenon, mainly in heterogeneous and pluralist societies, whose structures allow morality itself to become a topic for continuous debate and negotiation.

Based on an examination of opinion pieces and written coverage published in major Rio de Janeiro and São Paulo media between 1992 and 2002, we have sought to explore the pertinence of the analytical model of *moral panic* to understand media treatment of the Rio funk movement, often associated with gangs or criminal organizations, imputations of anonymous sexual intercourse in parties, alienation, bad taste, and sexist dances, slang, and lyrics. In the early 1990s, the funk movement was also associated in the popular press with the *arrastões*, coordinated disturbances in a public space, especially beaches, that allowed for petty thievery.

We argue that no matter how useful moral panic theory may have been in crafting a vocabulary for understanding mediatic power, this theory needs to be theoretically revised and refined, so as to adjust to relevant social, economic, and culture trends of today. This kind of approach gets it right whenever it goes beyond sociological research focused on patterns of property and control as signs of complicity between government and the media. It gets it wrong, however, whenever it treats the production and consumption of media in a monolithic and monological way. It is imperative to be more attentive to the culture industry's multicapillarity, which is in no way subject to homogeneous commercial and ideological interests, and in some cases facilitates the expression of dissenting voices by means of technological innovations and myriad new distribution channels. Moreover, it is necessary to observe the complexity of the audience's interaction with the mass media. The whole campaign in newspapers and TVs to stigmatize Rio funk and create a new wave of moral panic ended up, in a way, contributing to the popularization of young *funkeiros'* lifestyle and cultural production among social groups situated way beyond the hills and domain of Rio de Janeiro. It is precisely to this ambiguous and interesting process of media glamorization of Rio funk music that we now turn.

::: Funk before the *Arrastões*

The origins of Rio funk hark back to the early 1970s, with the Bailes da Pe-sada (Heavy Dances) briefly promoted by Big Boy and Ademir Lemos at Canecão, one of the main venues for pop music in Rio de Janeiro. Those DJs played rock, pop, and especially soul music by artists such as James Brown, Wilson Pickett, and Kool & the Gang in their Sunday dances attended by some 5,000 young people from all over town. When the Canecão adminis-tration began to privilege MPB (Música Popular Brasileira; Brazilian popular music consumed by a predominately middle-class audience), the Bailes da Pesada were taken to the north side of town, where they took place in differ-ent clubs in the region. In order to continue holding dances of sizable pro-portions (some of them gathering up to 10,000 youth), the followers of this trend opened up Big Boy and Lemos and had to invest in equipment, mostly imported from abroad.

They inaugurated the new phase of funky rhythms in Rio de Janeiro, labeled by the press as "Black Rio." Explanations for the change from the ini-tial eclecticism of the Bailes da Pesada to soul music are not very dense or rich in details; in general, those who articulated these new dances say that it was an option for more danceable music (Hermano Vianna 1988). How-ever, in a reduced number of dances, it was a matter of attempting to de-velop a didactic and militant format. Dances sponsored by Soul Grand Prix, for example, frequently used a combination of media elements (slide shows, films, photographs, posters, etc.) that intended to "awaken" attendees to the "black is beautiful" style of the time. Before major media tired of the "black" novelty, recording companies unsuccessfully tried to consolidate national soul music in the market. With the exceptions of Tim Maia and Tony Tor-nado, the majority of these musicians and dancers have fallen into obliv-ion. Military repression during the dictatorship and the fashionable boom of disco music—enjoyed both in the south and in the north sides of town— buried once and for all the attempts to develop an ethnic movement at that time.

Following the disco fad, the south-side residents turned their attention to the emerging national rock scene, the so-called BRock of the 1980s in its most diverse styles, while the north side remained faithful to black Ameri-can music, with a beat far more similar to what is known today as *charme*.

Throughout the 1980s, several elements from American hip-hop and new funky rhythms were introduced in the dances. These dances were, by and large, changing slowly over time. Radio stations and even dances reserved less and less time for charme. Teams such as Furacão 2000, which successfully followed up on the founding teams, already sponsored balls in the outskirts of town in the second half of the 1980s, when dances were more group oriented and garments no longer recalled the soul, Afrocentric, or even B-boy hip-hop styles. Even though American hip-hop influenced the dynamic of Rio funk culture, and some of the songs played frequently in these dances held in the outskirts of town, few people associated it with any reference to the term *hip-hop*. Instead, words such as *funk* and *swing* (*suingue*) became the most widely popular labels. In fact, when we examine more carefully the songs played in Brazil, we conclude that they basically take as their main references the Miami bass and the freestyle rhythms, both from the United States.

It cannot be affirmed that the Rio funk music world was somehow part of hip-hop culture. It is certain that increasingly "the local reinterpreted the global" and an intense process of appropriation of hip-hop culture on the part of Rio consumers was under way. It gave rise to similarities but mainly differences between "national funk" and hip-hop in general, such as it has been recoded all over the world. While funk music consolidated itself in Rio urban culture throughout the 1980s, hip-hop found the most fertile ground for its development in the São Paulo night scene (Herschmann 1997, 2000). In fact, as funk became a national phenomenon, it also grew somewhat distanced from the hip-hop references. However, part of the most politicized black youth in Rio remained faithful to funk. While in Rio the content and rhythm were translated into a more danceable and not necessarily political music and atmosphere, in some São Paulo circles hip-hop affirmed itself as an important political discourse that has revitalized part of the demands of the black movement. Overall, the organs and "possessions" devoted to feeding this movement have found support in a vast practice of musical production labeled "afro"—reggae, hip-hop, charme, and even funk—as a strategy for mobilizing black youth.

Throughout the 1990s, as funk and hip-hop became "nationalized" and popular (one in Rio and the other in São Paulo), funkeiros and B-boys distanced themselves from each other: a dichotomy emerged between the "alienated" and the "engagé." This is not to say that the dichotomy really corresponds to what was happening. The mere fact that funk produces joyful, romantic, and good-humored music does not imply an apolitical posture. At any rate, the B-boys of hip-hop and other groups aligned with the

Youth dance at a *baile funk* in the neighborhood of Vigário Geral, Rio de Janeiro, October 1993 (André Arruda, CPDOC JB).

black movement (such as the *charmeiros*) accused funk of producing unconcerned music that only promoted entertainment. In a way, funkeiros were no longer welcomed at other dances.

In fact, this movement toward hip-hop had little visibility in Rio de Janeiro. Funk dances gradually became one of the main forms of leisure for poor youth in the city. One of the people responsible for the current phase of funk and the process of "nationalization" of the genre (i.e., for the appearance of music sung in Portuguese) was DJ Marlboro, who organized and produced the record *Funk Brasil no. 1* in 1989. The success achieved by this compilation redrew the national phonographic market, opening the way for several young artists to "acquire voices," come out of anonymity, and project this cultural expression of the periphery of the city. After that, the popularization of funk intensified and some nightclubs visited by the middle class began to play it and go as far as to devote special nights to the genre. With this acceptance some remixing of songs appeared, and funk house was created; sound equipment teams multiplied, and DJ Marlboro himself released new records with lyrics in Portuguese. Meanwhile, Brazil baptized the romantic version of funk as *melody*, a style that had a lot of success throughout the 1990s with singers such as Stevie B, Tony Garcia, and Latino. During that period a major innovation took place in the world of funk, with sound equipment teams promoting festivals in the slum community dances and then releasing discs with recordings made at the occasion. Some radio stations, such as RPC, were in large measure responsible for the expansion and popularization of the rhythm, by helping advertise these recordings and by promoting the careers of several MCs duos, such as Cidinho & Doca and Claudinho & Bochecha.

As demonstrated in the paragraphs above, the funk music movement did not start with the famous *arrastões* of the early 1990s; however, these events accelerated the process of its popularization, throwing those youth into the center of media stages and making them occupy not only the political sections of the news in major mass media, but also their cultural section.

::: Criminalization of Funk in the 1990s

In an article written in 1996 and devoted to discussing the criminalization of funk in Rio de Janeiro, Hermano Vianna recalls that on the occasion of the defense of his pioneering dissertation and later book on the theme (1998), neither intellectuals nor major media considered this cultural manifestation as a threat to the public order. In truth, funk was then defined as yet another form of leisure for youths in the periphery and slums in the city: "For a considerable portion of the Rio youth, funk is way more than that— it is a magic word under which is sheltered a ritual. These youth . . . are a community with their own codes of behavior, speech, dressing, and dating" (*Veja*, 11 May 1998, 31).

Keeping sight of the countless accusations made against funkeiros in the past few years, it makes sense to ask what, when, and why their public image changed. Who has changed: the media, society, or funkeiros themselves? The fact is that among many hypothesis and suggestions, a key moment can be identified in the projection and criminalization of funk music: the 1992 arrastões on the beaches in the south side of the city. According to Vianna, "the dance, after the arrastão, began to be seen as a violent phenomenon above everything else. Violence, not fun, became its trademark" (1996: 180–81). These arrastões became a point of "foundation" in the collective imaginary of the history of funk music and social life in Rio (increasingly identified with urban conflict). After that moment funk music—the cultural expression of slums and outskirts of big cities, and almost unknown to the middle class—gained a unique highlight in the media.

The incidents on the beach received ample coverage in national and inter-

Police arrest two young men at the Arpoador Beach in Rio de Janeiro following an *arrastão*, October 1993 (Michel Filho, CPDOC JB).

national papers and TV news shows, as though they were disturbances of great proportions putting in check the "urban order." Indeed, the quick TV images showing teenagers and children fighting in gangs, desperately running around the beach, and clinging to windows of overcrowded buses introduced this cultural manifestation to the middle class, but they also generated a strong fear on the part of the state and of this social segment. The fact is that the images disseminated by TV and newspapers were ingrained in the Rio urban memory; their broadcasting abroad contributed decisively, according to executives in the tourism industry, to emptying the city that summer. The local section of most major papers in Rio and around the country (*O Globo, Folha de São Paulo, Jornal do Brasil, O Dia*) began to devote meaningful space (at times filling up the entire section) to depicting funk; coverage pieces then proliferated with suggestive titles such as "Arrastões Terrorize South Side," "Hordes on the Beach," "Funk Gangs Create Panic on Beaches," "Panic in Paradise," and "Funk Movement Leads to Despair," thereby heightening the atmosphere of terror.

> What happened on Sunday on the south-side beaches was not simply disturbance of the order, and it would be risky to consider it an isolated episode. The hordes that were unleashed in a hallucinatory run along the sand did not steal

only bags and watches; they mainly wrested the precious good of Sunday peace away from the Rio citizen and city's guests. To go to the beach is an inalienable and historic right of the dweller of Rio de Janeiro . . . All of this has been trampled upon in Sunday's outrageous events . . . Will we now passively accept that the pleasure of going to the beach will be replaced by the fear of going to the beach? Will families be forced to stay locked in on sunny mornings because the beach now has new owners? Will tourists be scared away again, this time for good? The scenes shown by TV do not allow any doubts as to the organized character of the arrastões. Only groups with a command structure and well-drawn plans are capable of such concentration, infiltration, simultaneous action, and dispersion—all of this was seen on the beaches on Sunday. (*O Globo*, 20 October 20, 1992)

The *Jornal do Brasil* announces the event in the following way:

Yesterday the South Side of Rio turned into a war zone, with arrastões organized by teenage gangs from neighborhoods in the outskirts and in Baixada Fluminense, and armed with pieces of wood. The police, with 110 men armed with revolvers, shotguns, and rifles, had difficulty repressing the violence of the several assault groups. Even a parallel police, composed by the Guardian Angels— a volunteer group designed to defend the population—came into action. . . . Beachgoers and residents in panic had to search for refuge in bars, bakeries, and under street vendors' tents. The muggers' actions started around noon, at Arpoador Square, where several bus lines from the outskirts have their final stop. As they got off the buses, gangs would start the arrastões, which covered Copacabana, Ipanema, and Leblon. In outrage, residents demanded the death penalty and the presence of the Army in the streets. (*Jornal do Brasil*, 19 October 1992)

As we can see from the journalistic narrative presented, it did not take long until the principle suspects were identified as funkeiros who promote violence very similar to that of organized hooligans in soccer stadiums. They are identified as "urban gangs" or even as maladjusted youth who inhabited the slums and the west and north sides of the city and on weekends attend the funk dances:

The tribes that terrorize the beaches of Rio de Janeiro can be compared to the English hooligans or to the Mancha Verde, the Palmeiras soccer fan club. These are groups of youth that gather to walk around in bands and promote disorder wherever an opportunity turns up. The denomination *galera* was born in the funk music dances in the Rio outskirts, where gangs from neighborhoods, hills, and slums . . . The aficionados of disorder call themselves funkeiros and pay tribute to frequent confrontations as a leisure activity. (*Veja*, 28 October 1992)

However, the most serious accusation being made against funk music was already drafted in these first pieces published in the media—their association with narcotrafficking and, in general, with criminal organizations: "As the majority of the two million funkeiros live in the slums, they stay in conformity with the criminal leadership. By an exclusively philosophical influence, funkeiros get their share from the rivalry between the Red Command and the Third Command" (*Jornal do Brasil*, 25 October 1992). The media frame through which funk music reached "notoriety" was related to a polarization over proposals of public security for the country. The growth of marginalization and exclusion; the social commotion produced by massacres such as those of Carandiru, Candelária, and Vigário Geral—as well as the challenging presence of narcotraffickers in the "pockets of misery"—and the ever more spectacular crimes (especially kidnappings) shown by the media were some of the elements that make up the scenario where the question of public security has been seen in a rather "immediatist" and often radical way.

In this context, two tendencies were dominant in the major media. The first one, represented by NGOs and by human rights commissions, believed that the way to resolve the question of criminality was to address "social injustices." The second, represented by part of the business class and the more conservative sectors of society, considered public offices of security and justice to be incapable of resolving serious "social problems" and demanded reforms with "great impact" with a view to increasing the police contingent (with collaboration from the army) and reequipping these institutions. These measures would allow, according to their defenders, a "more efficient and efficacious crackdown on crime" and a better mediation of social life.

It could also be affirmed that the stigmatization of funk was not directed exactly against the dances (even though they were at the center of the debate among state, society, and security offices), but rather against the social sector that has assumed it as a strong identity marker. All of a sudden, funk music was seen as a pillar of an "ideology / worldview" that fed the growth of urban violence (Herschmann 1997). In the media's treatment of Rio funk at the moment of its "discovery" by the middle class of the south side of the city, one notes that labels such as "vandals" or "horde" began to be increasingly accompanied by photographs and images that not only lent more credibility to the journalistic text but also spectacularized the events. It became very common to use charts and graphs with crime statistics that confirmed the "criminal vocation" of these youth as well as opinion polls that "grounded" the fear among the population (Sneed 2007).

In the years following that event, the articles presented in the mainstream Brazilian papers, even in the culture section (and not only in the "local" or "police" sections), constantly used layout as a resource, bringing information in boxes that invariably reminded readers of the social origin of funk and often the supposedly "criminal" origins of its members. These "profiles of the funkeiro" and his world had very little in common with the rock crowd from the south side of town or with the *cara-pintadas*—middle-class students who had taken to the streets in face paint to protest the government of Fernando Collor, who was impeached for corruption in 1992.

::: Demonization and Glamorization of Funk

The trajectory of funk music is not only marked by stigma. If, on the one hand, media campaigns defended prohibition of young funkeiros' activities (sociocultural manifestations marked as an excuse for urban disorder; the exploitation of minors for eroticism, narcotrafficking wars, and organized gangs), on the other hand, the same media offered it visibility for the genre to become popular and find its niche in the market. Media stigmatization has not precluded that lifestyle and cultural production from exerting enormous fascination upon a large number of youth of different social classes, who seem to have found in that musical universe a fundamental form of expression and communication. The debate generated by this social diversification and broadening of the public gravitated, invariably, toward the following question: To what extent have youth been "corrupted" and "led astray" by funk music?

The state, supported by conservative sectors, has been involved since the mid-1990s in attempting to close down the so-called community dances that used to be held in sports arenas in the slums and outskirts. These dances gathered as many as 5,000 youths of all social segments who had their fun there, almost always in a peaceful way. In fact, the community's hospitality and concern for the well-being of those who attended the dance were notable. In a time of intense fear of urban violence, the warm welcoming of organizers and their attention to the security issue made this kind of dance a great attraction during consecutive summers.

Those who defended the closing down of dances (and of all kinds of balls) oscillate between the argument that funk music, in addition to disturbing the neighborhood with noise, is a threat to the youth from "good families" (read middle class) who attend, since these parties generate clashes between gangs and a mixing with "natives" connected with the world of narcotrafficking. The rivalry between groups is, however, merely one ingredient of the dance, of which joy, humor, and eroticism are also part. Most business figures and dance organizers try creatively to channel this rivalry by promoting *galera* festivals, in which competitions between groups take place. In addition, the relation of funk to criminal organizations, which has been part of everyday life in Rio's poorest communities way before funk emerged as a local form of cultural expression, is virtually nonexistent or is highly overstated. What concretely exists is a relative identification of these youth with the acts of virility and rebellion that criminal life allows, and this is expressed in songs that narrate daily life in the community (Herschmann 2000).

To the dismay of conservative segments of the middle class, the antifunk hysteria related to the mythic arrastões of the early 1990s did not prevent the musical genre from consolidating itself in the late 1990s as an important force in the local and national industries of entertainment and fashion. "It is one of the strongest fashion subcultures ever seen in the country. The *popozudas* have left the slums and the north side and, to the sound of funk music, have influenced even an opposed niche, those of the *patricinhas*," affirms journalist Erika Palomino, in an edition of the fashion section of *Folha de São Paulo* devoted to the São Paulo fashion week of 2001. In contemporary Brazilian youth parlance, popozudas are young women usually from poor neighborhoods known for their competence as dancers and sexualized performance style. Patricinhas (e.g., "little Patricias") refer typically to light-skinned young women of the middle and upper classes. On the cover, the very white and blond model and TV announcer Fernanda Lima in the *popozuda-chic* style illustrates the main piece: "Popozuda culture—get to know the style of girls who are dominating the summer in Rio." Palomina summarizes for the neophyte the desired style of the funk music girls: "The look is sexy, of course. Tight jeans, tops that expose the bellybutton, and hair extensions" (*Folha de São Paulo*, 30 January 2001).

The journalist adds that there are no lack of popozuda hits in the hyped-up parties of Rio or São Paulo. The first crossover, according to her, happened in the "glamorous" party for the release of Forum perfume at Copacabana Palace in December 2000, when forty seconds of the popozuda anthem by DeFalla left guests worn out. A short time later, socialites, *dondocas* (older ladies), and women of presumably refined taste had a feast at Rio's Canecão to the beat of funk music; glamorous and unashamed, they barked, jumped, train-danced, and did much more. At the end of the ball, although very happy, many of them reported pain in their joints and muscles (Freire Filho 2006).

But not everyone was having fun with the territorial and social expansion of Rio funk. The speeches of government authorities and intellectuals against the genre began to focus in the late 1990s on the question of sexuality: most emphatically condemned was the supposedly exaggerated eroticism of the dances and the derogatory treatment of women in some songs (see, e.g., Luciano Trigo, "Um Tapinha Não Dói" [A little slap doesn't hurt], *O Globo*, 13 March 2001). The shocking titles leave no doubt as to the general atmosphere of panic created by coverage and op-ed pieces published at that time: "O Funk Picante da Periferia" (Spicy Funk from the Periphery) (*Época*, 22 January 2001); "Bonde a Toda Velocidade" (Train at Full Speed) (*Jornal do Brasil*, 18 February 2001); "A Explosão do Funk" (The Funk Explosion) (*IstoÉ*, 28 February 2001); "'Engravidei no Trenzinho'" (I Got Pregnant in the Train Dance) (*Veja*, 28 March 2001); and "Funk com Ficha" (Funk with a Police Record) (*Veja*, 5 September 2001, 141).

Whether or not the middle class likes it, the open eroticism and humor are part of popular culture and its lifestyle. Funk music, like other manifestations of popular culture, is not and has never been politically correct. Contrary to expectations of certain feminist groups, young women had a rather playful relationship to "Um Tapinha Não Dói" (A Little Slap Doesn't Hurt), "Eguinha Pocotó" (My Little Mare), and others songs considered offensive to women. As for news about teenagers supposedly getting pregnant during dances, this argument would only make sense to those who are not aware of the reality of Brazilian slums and peripheries.

::: Culture and Anarchy

An article by the poet and literary critic Affonso Romano de Sant'Anna, "Anomia Ética e Estética" (Ethic and Aesthetic Anomie) (*O Globo*, 17 March 2001) is characteristic of the kind of critique directed at postfolkloric popular manifestations such as funk music. The author starts by stressing his authority to discuss the "ethical and aesthetic anomie" of funk music in a literary supplement: After all, didn't he publish, a few years earlier (1986), a book (with structuralist leanings) titled *Música Popular e Moderna Poesia Brasileira*? His invectives against the sound were initially anchored in the analysis (or, rather, the citation) of two obscene lyrics "hyped up on radio and TV, to which even teenagers and children dance." In fact, the two songs in question had little airplay on major media. He was also troubled by reports, later shown to be greatly exaggerated, of a high number of pregnancies and AIDS contaminations during the *dança da cadeira* (chair dance) at the *bailes funk*.

The subtitle of the article, "Porn-Dance Music Brings Back the Worst in Machismo," is highly misleading as to the real focus of his reflection, which leads more toward a reframing of the Arnoldian conservative problematic of culture versus anarchy (Arnold, [1869] 1994) than a feminist theoretical approach. Sant'Anna's targets are both contemporary musical avant-gardes, which took to an extreme artistic experimentation, and the Brazilian culture industry, which looms large in the context of postdictatorial licentiousness and globalizing pressures that turn citizens into mere "consumerist clones" and ratings into the supreme regulator of symbolic goods. What may the relation between the two be? Just as in avant-garde art one can do whatever one wants, today anything can become art and, in his words, "marginality takes the place of the system, the unlettered ones take over the media, quantity unseats quality, and what we used to call culture is now exiled as an authentic counterculture, an alternative culture" (*O Globo*, 17 March 2001).

The ethical and aesthetic anomie and even the "chaos" resulting from it are verbalized "unconsciously" in funk lyrics, as his "literary analysis" clearly demonstrates:

> It is impossible to hear the war cry—"everything is dominated" without recognizing therein the echoes of PCC or the Red Command. It is impossible not to recognize in "A little slap doesn't hurt" a seductive variable of violence against women and children. It is impossible not to hear women being called "bitches" and not see the return of the worst machismo. (*O Globo*, 17 March 2001)

With so many negative ways to interpret the songs, he advises, only demand for the urgent return of order remained. A quick reestablishment of the canon would be a useful weapon against the undermining of values promoted (and reflected) by funk music and artistic avant-gardes.

Sant'Anna's diatribes against funk bring to the surface prejudices, anxieties, and idealizations that mark the intellectual field so often grounded on aesthetic monotheism that becomes a furious attack against cultural pluralism. In the name of the preservation of the values of *Culture* (commonly associated with "great art," the final product of a whole process of aesthetic, intellectual, and spiritual refinement) and the preservation of the critical and subversive potential of modernism's "autonomous" aesthetic production (freed of all ambiguity, all perverse pleasures, all political incorrectness), "Brazilians of spirit" with different ideological affinities, united throughout the twentieth century to subdue the "barbarian noise" of the culture practiced or valued by the masses raised in the chaos of our big cities (Freire Filho 2001). "It is, of course," as Raymond Williams points out, "easier to be respectful and reverent to 'the People, philosophically characterized' than to a Public, which noisily identifies itself" (1983: 34).

::: Citizens of the Periphery? Between Condemnation
      and Expansion in the Media

It would be a caricature, however, to portray the media only as mouthpiece for the political agenda and aesthetic-moral prejudices of the ruling classes. It is undeniable that since the arrastões, funk music has received airtime on the radio and that MCs and DJs have enjoyed success in the phonographic industry. Records by singers such as Latino, MCs like Claudinho & Bochecha or William & Duda, or compilations such as *Funk Brasil* and *Furacão 2000* have had excellent sales numbers. At times during its trajectory, funk has been able to develop its own advertising vehicles: fanzines of reasonable graphic quality, daily FM radio or weekly TV shows devoted to the funk world. In the 1990s, funk became an industry that involved promoting dances and producing and consuming clothes, CDs, dance classes, TV and radio shows, magazines, fanzines, theatrical works, and websites. Just the dances themselves generated, directly and indirectly, 20,000 jobs and 10.6 million reais.

The debate surrounding Rio funk has recently gained a new component: its strong presence in the transnational phonographic industry and its insertion in the electronic music market niche, under the label *world music*. Brazilians discovered, during President Luiz Inácio Lula da Silva's visit to São Tomé e Príncipe in 2004, that the song "Beijo na Boca," by MC Cepakol, is a hit in Africa to the point that an article in *O Globo* suggests that "Brazilian Funks Shakes up the World" (1 September 2004). At the same time, during the 2004 Olympics in Greece, MCS Serginho & Lacraia and the Bonde do Tigrão enjoyed considerable success in Europe: "Do not be surprised if during the Olympics in Greece (2004), some competition takes place to the sound of "Thuthuca" . . . one of the most widely played in the country, having been recorded in Greek by local artists and becoming even a ring tone" (*O Globo*, 1 August 2004).

Taking into account what has been pointed out, it could be argued that the funk market has developed on the margins or interstices of the culture industry. Its situation is similar to the one held by punks and skinheads in England and by the B-boys in the United States, who have occupied a peculiar place in the collective imaginary, allowing it to develop both a market niche (creating jobs, accumulating profit and investment, and also diversifying its activities and products) while thousands of youth associated with it are marginalized and excluded. Funk occupies an ambiguous place in the market and urban space, and in relation to public policies. In a sinuous, conflictive, and negotiated way, it constructs a set of cultural codes (with local and international references) that offers the possibility of elaborating a critical or plural view of the social as well as leads to its mediation and administration by structures that manage the rhythms of spectacle and consumption.

In contrast to what an apocalyptic perspective of old and new media might suggest, there is an enormous potential for struggle within the media for minority groups. This depends on their being able to become a spectacle and perform operations of great symbolic impact (Herschmann and Pereira 2003). Minority and excluded groups must be attentive to these possibilities, exploring in particular the new, still-unregulated interactive media that open a new field for participatory action.

Evidently, we do not ignore the normalizing function held by the media over the social. However, it is important to identify the possibilities of making the Other emerge in the mediatic field. Even though the media is a space with countless limitations and formats, and designed to elaborate regulatory images and disseminate "moral panic," it also produces "breaches" or "gaps," in which the Other emerges, constituting a key space for the perception of differences. Media discourse oscillates, as we have seen, between demonization and a glamorization of the excluded. Insofar as it makes these groups "visible," it allows them to denounce the condition of "banned" subjects and claim citizenship. Members of these groups thereby bring the discussion on the place of the poor, the right to speech, leisure, and city space to the surface in the public sphere. They highlight the contradictions and social tensions of the process of "democratization" of the country.

Beyond the spectacularized discourse of police repression in the territories of poverty, it is precisely this production and this discourse of the local, marginal, or peripheral that ironically have been taken up, with great frequency, by the media and by youth of different social origins who consume cultural expressions such as rap and funk as signs of rebellion and social transgression or as elements of a camp aesthetic (Freire Filho 2003, 2006). Urban polyphony and its diverse "tribes" gain density in territories characterized by social instability—as well as distanced from the state logic of reinforcing borders, enclosure, and apartheid—through the discourses of exclusion and repression that promote fear of the Other. In the analysis of the trajectory of funk music, we note that this cultural universe promotes, to some degree, a kind of politics (not necessarily conscious on the part of social actors) that seems crucial for the recognition and visibility of a minority subjectivity today, one that manifests itself mainly in the terrain of culture.

::: Technobrega, Forró, Lambadão

The Parallel Music of Brazil

Hermano Vianna

::: 8 December 2004

It is the holiday of Our Lady of the Conception in Belém, capital of the Amazonian state of Pará. The festivities occurred last night, when the *umbanda* and *candomblé* (religious) communities made their offerings to Yemanjá on the Outeiro Beach, gathering a crowd that newspapers calculated to be between 30,000 and 70,000 people. Streets are empty today. I head to the Jurunas neighborhood, a central area for the city's popular culture. I follow three documentary makers—Vladimir Cunha, Priscilla Brasil, and Gustavo Godinho—who are producing a film called *Brega S.A.*, about the local, informal commerce of *brega* music. We went to visit DJ Beto Metralha, one of the most important, if not the most important, producer of *technobrega*.

Jurunas is a socially diverse neighborhood. It has rich and poor people living right next to each other. The area we visited is inhabited by a lower middle class—at times rather impoverished—with precarious urbanization; it is considered a dangerous place and a territory of gangs. But it is nothing compared to the Rio de Janeiro slums. It displays that poverty considered full of "dignity" by Brazilian standards. There are no shacks. Most of the houses, however, appear to be in permanent construction, to make room for new people who join the family nucleus, mostly through marriages by sons and daughters. The house where Beto Metralha has his studio is no exception. The studio, located in the back, is indeed undergoing reform in order to hold new equipment and new recording rooms. Many people go from one room to another in the house. I don't know who lives or works there.

Beto receives us with great hospitality. He interrupts what he was doing to show us the novelties of technobrega, including the newest trend, *cybertechnobrega*, or just cybertechno, for the initiated. We talk about the peculiar market strategy that Pará's most popular music has found in order to survive and prosper. I leave with a better understanding of how everything works.

Technobrega is the new electronic evolution of one of the most popular styles ever produced by Brazilian popular music. Its most remote origin, if we don't want to go back further to age-old precursors in the national Romantic tradition, is the 1960s Jovem Guarda (Young Guard), a basic and naive type of rock music, played with guitar, bass, and drums. When Roberto Carlos decided to gear his singing to appeal to an older audience accompanied by orchestras, the music of the Jovem Guarda migrated to the interior, but maintained its faithful audience among the poorest sectors of the population and received the pejorative name of brega, connoting something that is "tacky" or "kitsch"). Brega first flourished in state of Goiás; then it ventured into the northeastern state of Pernambuco, and recently set up its headquarters in Pará.

The first signs of technobrega were heard in the summer, which in Pará happens midyear as in the Northern Hemisphere, of 2002, but it really took over popular parties in 2003. It is the old brega, with a more accelerated beat made up exclusively of computer-produced sounds. It resembles Kraftwerk, but "swampier," that is composed in a stifling tropical heat by folks who have heard lots of *carimbó* (Afro-indigenous music from northern Brazil), *cumbia*, zouk, and Renato e Seus Blue Caps (a popular Jovem Guarda band from the 1960s), and who do not yet fully master the cut-and-paste resources that lie at the basis of musical production software today.

There are five studios that record technobrega in the city. They receive weekly visits of "go-betweens," who stop by to listen to new things. The studios can produce two new songs a day. The go-betweens choose the songs they like better—the ones they feel have more of a chance of being a hit—and take them to the CD makers. The CDs are immediately distributed to the street vendors, who sell to consumers the final product, compilations that include works by various bands, produced in several studios.

They are not really pirated CDs, for the official discs that could really be pirated are more and more rare. These musicians are no longer associated with recording companies; they no longer have to face the costs of pressing records, printing covers, or distributing the product. All these costs are covered by home-based CD makers, street vendors, and their unofficial systems of industry and trade. For authors and producers, the CDs are seen only as ways of distributing the music. Their great hits are often about the media:

songs that praise DJS, TV, and radio shows (such as *Mexe Pará*) or *aparelha-gens* (apparatuses), as they call the sound teams that animate parties in Pará. A new hit was composed in homage to the VW van that goes around the out-skirts of Belém announcing the parties with the Rubi aparelhagens.

A singer-songwriter who was recording at Beto Metralha's studio told me that there is no greater joy than hearing his songs played by street vendors in downtown Belém. He knows very well that he does not make any money from CD sales, but that no longer matters. It's crucial that his music be sold by street vendors so it will become a hit, and his band will be invited to play live shows in the outskirts of the city (in the so-called aparelhagem parties), where he will make money to survive.

The recording studios, in their turn, also donate their production to the street vendor markets, radios, and aparelhagens. They no longer function as recording companies that live off of CD sales. They live from the money that bands pay to record their songs. The more hits they produce, the greater their clientele will be. The technobrega market is thus no longer centralized: there is no longer an element in the production chain with enough power to control all the other stages, a role that the recording industry continues to play in the official pop music market. In Belém's technobrega, money and power are divided among many different partners: musicians, producers, go-betweens, home industries of CDS, distributors, street vendors, radio pro-grams, owners of aparelhagens, and DJS. The hits are produced by the team-work of all these entrepreneurs, almost all of them informal.

If there is a place of prominence in the technobrega circuit, it is the parties with aparelhagens. It is there, in contact with the dancers, and not on radios or best-selling record lists, that hits are defined. Radio plays what the aparelhagens play, not the other way around. Bands are assured of suc-cess when they are hired by the main parties for live concerts.

Aparelhagens are institutions typical of Pará's popular culture and have existed for almost five decades. In this period they have undergone several "evolutions," a native term that designates the yearly changes of equipment that great aparelhagens make in order to maintain the interest of an audi-ence that values the introduction of the latest novelties in light and sounds. These are mobile, gigantic, and powerful pieces of equipment—electronic walls with speakers, amplifiers, TVS, and computers piled up on top of one another. They circulate around the city's ballrooms every weekend.

Fifteen years ago I saw aparelhagens still playing vinyl records. Then DJS then went on to use CDS, then MDS; now they only work with MP3S, mixing the technobrega hits with their mouse and keyboards, controlling everything from their computer screens. They share with the audience the fascination with the latest technology. In this sense they are completely different from Brazilian middle-class DJs of electronic music who organize themselves in provinyl movements that attempt to maintain the analogue tradition of nightclubs. The aparelhagem *people do not hesitate to throw away the old equipment*. They want to be recognized as pioneers, as the first ones to adopt innovations.

The audience values this attitude. The most popular parties are precisely the ones where the aparelhagens show their new "evolutions," the main technological attractions of which are kept as "state secrets" until debut day, to prevent the competition from copying them. The vision is impressive: when novelties are introduced, the aparelhagem fan clubs (yes, the main aparelhagens have fan clubs that go to all parties in uniforms and invent special choreographies to differentiate them from other dancers) become delirious, with their arms up, as though saluting the appearance of a deity, the totem of the electronic tribe of Belém's outskirts.

In Beto Metralha's studio, while talking about these issues and comparing technobrega with other musical universes, I went on to tell—as if this were a novelty that would surprise everyone—that the American band the Pixies, one of the most important of the Indie rock scene, had given up all association with recording companies and had begun to sell their CDs to fans on the Internet. The band developed another line of products that was revolutionary to me: when the audience left a concert, they already found outside the venue a CD for sale with the recording of the show they had just attended. I praised the idea as an important innovation for a phonographic market that looks for alternatives amidst the easy reproduction proper to the digital age of culture: people would buy the CD to keep it as a cherished souvenir, as that was the concert in which they had participated. Beto Metralha looked at me with an expression of disinterest and said that the aparelhagem parties had been doing that for years.

Indeed, right next to the main computer used by the DJ for mixing, some aparelhagens now also feature another computer that records the whole party, and at the end already presses a reasonable amount of CDs for immediate sale. The DJs are smart: they use and abuse the microphone on top of the songs in order to greet the fan clubs, dancers, and other illustrious guests (such as musicians or producers) present at the party. These people end up buying the CD, because in addition to having the musical selection to which they have just danced, it also brings the proof that they are respected by the DJ. It's a bit like buying the newspaper because your photograph has appeared in the social columns. Beto Metralha told me he uses these CDs to advertise his work, while showing how the songs he has produced have made it big and how his presence at the party is valued by the main DJs in Pará.

::: 10 December 2004

I'm already in Manaus. It's still the Amazonian forest, but the local culture is completely different from that of Belém. No one knows technobrega here. The most popular music at the overcrowded parties in the city's outskirts is the *forró* of new bands such as Aviões do Forró, Pipoquinha da Normandia, and Caviar com Rapadura, music usually despised by the Brazilian and Amazonian intellectual elite. It is a style that appeared in Ceará, where local musicians did not hesitate to introduce electric and electronic instruments in their recordings and live concerts, thereby ending the reign of conventional instruments such as the accordion, the triangle, and the *zabumba* (a large bass drum used in the music of northern and northeastern Brazil). The latter are considered the essence of "roots" forró, or true forró, even though Luiz Gonzaga defined the genre, well into the twentieth century, by using the accordion, an instrument that is as alien to Brazil as the synthesizer. This is the reason why this new music has received the most severe and ruthless criticism from traditionalists and defenders of "quality music." But this critical bombardment and the lack of airplay in the media did not prevent the new music from quickly spreading around the country in the parties of the poorest classes (as I always joke, parodying carnivalesque designer Joãozinho Trinta: only rich intellectuals like roots, what poor people really like is technology).

I cannot buy this type of music in record stores in Rio, where I live. But I know it circulates in the Rio forró parties. I found out that it arrived in the city almost by chance. One day, leaving home, I saw a street vendor showing new CDs to the doorman of a neighboring building. This is a parallel market that has nothing to do with the major recording companies, big-audience TV, or radio shows. My rich friends have never heard this music. But as soon as you arrive at a party on the outskirts of any major Brazilian city (above all the ones that attract a large contingent of northeastern migrants), you will hear the hits being sung by the crowd.

As I was in Manaus I decided to stop by the street vendor shopping area downtown (*camelódromo*) to buy a compilation with the new stuff. I wanted a regular CD. In an entire street packed with vendors, I couldn't find one. They only had forró video CDs or DVDs, along with pirated computer games for GameCube2 or PlayStation 2. It was a great surprise to me: I didn't even know that those bands, which do not regularly appear on national TV, had already released DVDs. But I was most impressed when I noted that their audience had DVD players at home to watch concerts by their favorite forró bands. A whole parallel audiovisual market (including countless video producers specialized in recording concerts in the northeastern backlands) was being introduced to me all of a sudden, in the Amazon, distant from the major centers of musical production in Brazil.

I quickly understood what was happening by looking at the bars on the outskirts of the city. For years they have had TVs to entertain their customers. Sound systems for the most popular moments are also common. Today it is cheaper to buy a DVD player that also plays CDs in various formats (including MP3) than a reasonably good sound system. Many bars thus show their own selection of pirated videos—which can be bought at the street vendor for less than 10 reais each—instead of the regular broadcast of network TV. It is in this market that the forró audiovisual operates. This is a market that little by little arrives at homes on the city's periphery, whose inhabitants begin to buy their DVD players and TVs with better sound, thereby retiring their old hi-fis.

This is why the Manaus street vendors did not understand my insistence on "regular" CDs. I felt like a character that had come out of a distant past through a time tunnel. Everyone looked at me with paleontological curiosity. Then a vendor offered: "Is MP3 ok?" It wasn't, but my curiosity was greater: for 10 reais I could buy a disc with 210 songs. It was at that moment that I really was convinced that the phonographic industry such as we know it (even with the iPod and iTunes) was already over. How can you compete with a street vendor who sells songs for less than 2 cents a piece? I even bargained and bought all 210 songs for 7 reais. I have forró for the whole year!

::: 9 June 2004

I come into two official record stores in Cuiabá, the capital of the midwestern state of Mato Grosso. I am trying to do things according to the law. I look for the latest releases of Cuiabá *lambadão*, the most popular music at parties on the urban outskirts of Mato Grosso. I am treated by the vendors with shock or with that expression of superiority of someone who says, "Our establishment does not deal with these lowlifes—please leave." It was almost like trying to buy Coca-Cola at an organic food store.

I realize they are not hiding anything away from me; they really do not have any lambadão to sell. No one buys this kind of music in stores. Of course, I go to the street vendor shopping area (camelódromo) and have a feast, while saving many reais, with pirate CDs of Os Maninhos (volume 6: *Bailão em Mato Grosso*), Banda R Som (*O Melhor do Lambadão de* MT—*Seu Problema é Muito Chifre na Cabeça*), Stillo Pop Som (*Ao Vivo*), Banda Real Som (*Te Amo Demais*), Mega Boys (*A Banda do Momento*), and the sensational compilation by Cabana da Dudu.

Lambada arrived in Cuiabá brought by Mato Grosso folks who had gone to work in the gold mines of the Amazon in the 1970s and 1980s. In the dry prairies of Mato Grosso, it mixed local genres such as *rasqueado* and *siriri* with the Paraguayan polka, which was already electrified, sounding like a swampy rhythm and blues. It thereby generated the lambadão, which continues its mutant trajectory by incorporating influences from the *vaneirão* from Rio Grande do Sul, *axé*, *sertaneja*, and every music that has truly popular success in Brazil. The audience soon understood that it was not exactly (or not just) lambada. They perceived that they were listening to a Mato Grosso creation and began to dance exactly as they would at a traditional siriri party, a "folkloric" dance where the female crowd dominates and women can dance holding each other tight, faces close to one another, spinning ceaselessly around the dance floor.

Because of the ingredients in the mix and the highly unorthodox appropriation of something considered "authentic," even someone who has never studied anything can perceive that the result is not made to please the anti-*brega* movements, which are often simply elitist movements bent on indoctrinating people to appreciate "quality," arbitrarily defined—of course—according to stale aesthetic conceptions. It is a pity, at least to me, that the territory of lambadão is still restricted and regional. It is impossible to buy this music, or even to stay informed about its releases, in Rio or on the Internet.

I have cited these three examples—technobrega from Pará, forró from the Amazonas, and lambadão from Mato Grosso—in order to show how the most popular musics of contemporary Brazil—the ones that are sung in the streets of big cities and that really inspire people to dance at the most exciting parties—are not the ones that play most often on radio, appear on TV shows, or are released by the big recording companies. These hits are generally despised by critics who write for major newspapers. These artists are not invited to the thousands of debates and seminars that discuss "popular culture." It is as if they were too popular to be authentically popular.

I could mention a number of other musical genres that survive in this twilight zone that combines mass success with invisibility in the official mass media: the funk music from Rio (which, despite its momentary success outside the slums, continues to be ignored by the recording industry, radios, and TVs), the pop vaneirão from Rio Grande do Sul, new trends in Bahian music (*arrocha* and hard samba, for example), most sertaneja duets from Goiás and Mato Grosso do Sul, and many others. Furthermore, there are stores in slums in Rio (and all over Brazil) that burn CDs in ten minutes, with downloaded songs chosen by the customer and personalized covers. These are all new markets of cultural consumption that proliferate on the margins of an official culture industry that becomes more and more of a minority.

What remains to be seen, then, is who is in the periphery. It would be enough to pay a visit to street vendors in the official city centers of Rio (next to the Petrobrás, BNDES, and Caixa Econômica Federal buildings) and of São Paulo (next to the most important stock market in the country), which look so much like hundreds of informal markets in other Brazilian cities, to see that the border between center and periphery has been shaking more frenetically than the "Eguinha Pocotó" sung by the Rio funk artist MC Serginho.

The very idea of inclusion—whether digital, cultural, or social—has to be rethought or discarded when confronted with this situation. When we speak of inclusion, we usually start from the assumption that the (included) center has something that is lacking to a periphery that begs inclusion. It is as if the periphery did not have culture, technology, or an economy. It is as if the periphery were to one day have, or hope to have, or be better off if it already had, something that the center already has—something to which the center could presumably lead the periphery, for the latter's own good. It is as if technological or cultural innovations came exclusively through the center, or were created by the center, and then slowly spread out toward the periphery. In the examples given above, we see that the periphery has not waited for the center to present the innovations. Without the center noting anything, the periphery has invented digital cultures that may very well indicate paths for the future of the center, which does not seem to be able to develop, by itself, any consistent "business plan" to deal with the new technological reality.

When I travel around Brazil, beyond the rich and official zones of the Rio–São Paulo axis (though often just a few steps away from its centers of power), I always have the following impression: the culturally official country, even the one depicted in the mass media, looks like a small and claustrophobic spaceship, on a flight route through parallel universes, ever further from the real country, the real economy, and the culture of the majority, and probably heading toward financial disaster or the drying up of creative energy.

Outside (everywhere, in fact), city outskirts invent, at amazing speed, new cultural circuits and new economic solutions, however precarious or informal, to give those inventions sustainability. I pay special attention to the party circuits, which attract multitudes every weekend. Today, almost all of these parties proliferate informally as a consequence of the indifference of public offices and the disdain of self-righteous intellectuals. In sum, the great and real Brazilian hit parade is completely independent of the legal and official culture industry.

Somehow, this informal artistic economy is the product of social inclusion conquered by force. This is when the periphery no longer behaves as a periphery, will not be put "in its place," the place of the one who is always hoping to be included and thinking that its liberation is going to come from the center. Brazil will have to get used to this forced, messy, and bottom-up "inclusion." Meanwhile, the center does not seem to be able to leave aside the perverse nostalgia for a country that we have "lost" when the poor and their brega habits were invisible, except for a book or other by Gilberto Freyre (or Jorge Amado, of course), a movie or other by Glauber Rocha, or a night party at Zicartola.

When I told DJ Marlboro, the main producer of Rio funk, about the new economy of technobrega, he was not surprised at all and simply remarked that when street vendors and go-betweens ally themselves with musicians through exclusive contracts, a new phonographic industry will be emerging. I retorted that but then new peripheries will appear. So on and so forth. There is no containing or controlling the novelties and difficulties that the digitalization of culture bring to the old analogical modes of cultural commerce or to the economy in general.

The aparelhagem parties in Belém, forró in Manaus, lambadão in Cuiabá, funk in Rio, and arrocha in Bahia show the vitality of a national and international, parallel and peripheral, economy that does not appear in the statistics of the Ministry of Labor or the Ministry of the Economy, nor can be domesticated in the ever more fragile agreements of the World Trade Organization.

As the Racionais MCs have sung, a periphery is a periphery anywhere. These lyrics are truer than ever. More and more, the periphery takes everything over. It is no longer the center that includes the periphery. The periphery now includes the center. The center, excluded from the party, becomes the periphery of the periphery.

::: "Tradition as Adventure"

Black Music, New Afro-Descendant Subjects, and

Pluralization of Modernity in Salvador da Bahia

Osmundo Pinho

The site is not the empirical and national Here of a territory. It is immemorial, and thus also a future. Better, it is tradition as adventure.
—Jacques Derrida, *Writing and Difference*, [1967] 1980

I would like to discuss aspects related to the plural constitution of Afro-descendants informed by black discursiveness in Salvador, Bahia. This discursiveness is strongly marked by the role of black music and by the history of Afro-descendant Carnaval. This chapter shows that these subjects are a product of modernization and operate in it, while giving it a specific configuration. Social agents as "reflexive audience" play a decisive role in the review and criticism of such modernity, pluralizing it and pushing the boundaries of democracy and of representation politics, in their demand for recognition and changes. Music, as discursive production and as sociability experience, plays a key part in this process.

::: Narrative of Re-Africanization and
    Unequal Modernization in Salvador

The idea that a new movement in the history of social relations in Salvador could be identified as re-Africanization initially appeared in Antônio Risério's *Carnaval Ijexá*, published in 1981. It proposes that, due to a *jejê-nagô* cultural substrate and to the effects of modernization,[1] Salvador witnessed in the late 1970s a new affirmation of black identity. This version established itself amidst a constellation of discourses, statements, rhetoric, interventions, readings, and performances as the narrative of a new phase in Salvador's cultural life. This new phase would alter the social relations panorama in Bahia, reinterpret black tradition and institutions, transform the identity of Bahia and its residents, and provide other Brazilian cities with models of collective organization and of Afro-descendant subjectivity reconstruction. This new phase was named re-Africanization exactly to highlight a previous Africanization, as described by, among others, Nina Rodrigues, as occurring at the end of the nineteenth century (1977).

As we will see, the setting of this re-Africanization is strongly defined by the particular aspects of the social and economic modernization undergone by Bahia during the course of the twentieth century.

In the history of Bahia, the years between 1930 and 1950 were marked by a "cordial" and hierarchical social organization in which black people "knew their places." This is a period of economic stagnation, the period of elaboration of a specific ideological discourse about identity in Bahia. In the late 1950s, local stability was undermined in a process that has been sufficiently well analyzed by, among others, Francisco de Oliveira (1987, 1980), who describes traditional Bahia, portrayed by Donald Pierson (1942), as a city where the elite lived lavishly thanks to the control of exports and to a few assets. Labor division, relatively simple, gave stability to an arrangement in which a small portion would benefit from economic activities, another small one would benefit from state revenue, and the vast majority would subsist in the fringes of the existing economic order, living for favors or leftovers from accumulated capital.

From this peripheral location of the masses, which in the case of Salvador are formed by slave descendants, Oliveira draws his conclusion about the difficulty of class formation, that is to say, of interests objectified in social subjects. Clientelist relations and the hierarchical favor among classes or color groups flourished in the social structure of Bahia, and the "master" tradition of slavery enabled the accommodation of this contradiction. The entire society appeared unified and signified by a web of personal and hierarchical relations that extended from the richest and whitest to the poorest and blackest, passing through a gradient of colors that would give meaning and legitimacy to basic social organization (Oliveira 1980, 1987).

Due to the modernizing transformations of the economy, the job market was completely changed in Salvador (Faria 1980). This process, however, did not fundamentally alter the racial structure of the job market. Nonetheless, it created new aspirations that clashed, and still do, against a racially structured job market, characterized by noninclusion, underemployment, and structural unemployment. The myth of *baianidade* (Bahianness) (Pinho

1998a) would be the ideological expression of difficulties in identification due to a weak labor market and the legacy of slavery, diluted as rules of social decorum and as "prejudice against prejudice" (Oliveira 1987: 107). The so-called economic miracle of the early 1970s under the military regime, represented an astonishing economic development, but it failed to equally distribute its benefits among the population, and the wealth was concentrated in the hands of those who were better positioned on the social ladder. This period of military rule and industrialization also confirmed the tendency to deepen racial inequalities (Hasenbalg 1985: 32).

Using data from the PED (Pesquisas de Emprego e Desemprego; Employment and Unemployment Survey) conducted between 1987 and 1989, Vanda Barreto and Nadya Castro, as well as other researchers, were able to draw stark conclusions about actual racial inequality in the job market in Bahia. Domestic work is the racial work par excellence. The informal job market, extremely important in Salvador, was composed of 48 percent blacks, 40 percent *mulatos*, and 12 percent whites. White people—who represent 17 percent of the employed—absorb 54 percent of the higher-education level jobs, whereas blacks and mulatos—who represent 83 percent of the employed—have only 46 percent of such jobs (Castro 1998). In Brazil, Afro-descendants represent approximately 45 percent of the population; in Bahia, 70 percent; and in Salvador, 80 percent.

These data reveal the persistence of inequality rates, showing little variation from those found in the previous period of the so-called traditional Bahia. This leads us to believe that industrialization and the "economic miracle," despite improvements in general economic rates, maintained the disparity between blacks and whites. Moreover, the structure of occupations reveals that the social division of labor remains socially marked in this period, in association with industrial development. In this context of structural inequality combined with modernization, new social subjects emerged who were self-identified as blacks or Afro-descendants.

::: Discursive Production of New Afro-Descendant Subjects

In Salvador re-Africanization reproduces collective racial and social identities, new subjectivities that are intersected by Afro-descendant tradition and consumerism, and new subject positions supported by "resistance" discourses. The entire process is shot through with contradictions that contribute to its vitality. Afro-descendant Carnaval in Salvador constituted itself as a field for intertextual reverberations. What has been written about it, both by "external" analysts and by its very agents, has become part of its history and social and political location in many ways, be it through the press or academic commentary. As we go over the literature about Carnaval, we see the repetition of several epigrammatic fragments, which are marks in time and in writing. One of the most notable, from the *Jornal Correio de Notícias*, cites the club manifesto of the Embaixada Africana (African Embassy) from 1897. The published text, in addition to demanding reparation for Africans killed during the 1835 Malê uprising (which involved slaves and free people, Hausas and Islamized Yoruba), described the composition of the procession:

> A very organized band will follow. The band will be organized by the dignified African community of this city to accompany the Embassy. The band will wear distinguished Algerian outfits and will play along the way, marches for Fortunato Santos, Menelik, Makonemm, etc. Six ras (Ethiopian chiefs), bearing swords will form the imperial honor guard. Next, Ambassador Manikus, riding an Alexandrian animal, will march, sided by Muata de T'Chiboco. (Vieira Filho 1998: 45)

Soon after abolition, black people organized themselves in Salvador to play Carnaval in the same molds as the white parades. However, this was done with an explicit reference to Africa and real African characters and used as means to claim a tie to the revolutionary Africans, Yoruba, and Haussa from only forty-two years before. Invoking Africa was a constant in this period, as well as in many other periods of black Carnaval, and so was the suppression of manifestations that were considered "too African," which, nevertheless, the people insisted on repeating perpetually (José Jorge Carvalho 1977, Pinho, 1999; Fry, Carrara, and Martins-Costa 1988; Nascimento 1994; Santos 1998; Tinhorão 1988; Vieira Filho 1995, 1998).

In the cracks created by social and historical circumstances, Afro-descendants were able to create a new tradition of cultural struggle, institutionally materialized in organizations such as *afoxés* (the traditional Afro-Bahian percussion groups) and *candomblé* houses and culturally organized as discursive forms. I would like to develop the idea that this tradition has not been deposited on predefined and determinate subjects, but constituted these subjects in a process with new emphasis and vigor starting in the 1970s.

In order to make this point clearer, I will recap the history of modern *blocos afro* (Afro-Bahia Carnaval groups) in Salvador, notably Ilê Aiyê and Olodum, so that we may understand how re-Africanization has been making way for the constitution of Afro-descendant subject positions as nonreified and reflexively politicized identities. As we examine it as discourse, tradition constitutes its own subject through cultural practices performed in Carnaval. Such performance is a vocalization of the Afro-descendant identity in motion in the arena of racial relations in Salvador.

In the period between the 1950s and the early 1970s, alongside the development of the official Carnaval, other vibrant popular manifestations emerged in the streets. In 1949 Osmar Macedo and Adolfo Nascimento (Dodô), created the *trio elétrico*, which over the years evolved into large, electrified moving sound stages. At that time, the middle class and the local elites were largely absent from the public festivities in the streets and celebrated their Carnivals in private dance clubs. The streets belonged to the people, who were predominately black. In the 1950s and early 1960s, *escolas de samba* (samba schools)—such as Ritmistas do Samba, Juventude do Garcia, Amigos do Politeama, and the Filhos do Tororó—started to make their appearances.[2] All of these organizations coexisted with the afoxés, active in the 1930s and 1940s, and an infinity of more or less organized or mutable ones, in such a way that the complexity of the changing Bahia society reelaborated itself within the structure of Carnaval organizations (Moura 2001a, 2001b).

It's important to remember the sociological context of transformation that took over Salvador at the time involving the passage from a traditional world, marked by status and a relatively simple division of labor, to a world complicated by incipient industrialization. In the 1960s, the middle and upper classes reentered the street Carnaval, following the trios elétricos and forming elite parading groups called *blocos de barão*, such as Os Internacionais (the Internationals) and Os Corujas (the Owls). The first one of these groups was probably Os Fantasmas (the Phantoms), founded in 1957 by residents of the Barbalho neighborhood. Dissidents from this group formed Os Internacionais in 1961 and Os Corujas in 1962 that consolidated themselves as the main elite groups, until the appearance of new groups in the 1980s.

In the late 1960s the *blocos de índio* (Indian groups) contributed to the re-Africanization process by bringing together a large number of working-class black youth. The blocos de índio were connected to the escolas de samba. Members of the Juventude do Garcia, for instance, founded in 1966 the Caciques do Garcia, the first bloco de índio in Salvador. The Filhos do

Tororó also transformed into the Indian group Apaches do Tororó. The Juventude do Garcia evolved from the Filhos do Garcia, which suggests a series of reinterpretations that formed an early basis for the re-Africanized Carnaval (Guerreiro 2000; Moura 2001a; 1996).

Founded in 1974, Ilê Aiyê was the first modern *bloco afro* in Salvador and launched a broad process of re-Africanization. The group was founded by some friends from Curuzu, in the densely populated Liberdade neighborhood in Salvador. Ilê Aiyê means, in a loose translation from the Yoruba, "house of this world." The group was originally to be named Poder Negro, a literal translation of "Black Power," revealing the inspiration that motivated its founders: the radical African American movement. The intention was to form an organization of young black people who sought autonomous representation, entertainment, and expression of content with specific meaning. The first parade of the group in 1975 was advertised by a flier that proclaimed "Ilê-Aiyê: simply an original group THE AFRICANS IN BAHIA," which disturbed white public opinion (Jônatas Silva 1988).

Among several organizations that emerged in Salvador's Carnaval in the late 1960s and early 1970s, Ilê Aiyê stands out precisely for advocating a movement of racial identification as a political subjectivity, similar to what was taking place in other spheres of social life. This movement was marked by intentionality, choosing Carnaval as an area for reflexive discourse that echoes the same claims for justice heard in the Embaixada Africana manifesto of 1897. From the beginning, the group attempted to create an identity as a field of critical identifications:

> When I say we found a way [it means that] black people who participated in the blocos de índio, in the escolas de samba, discovered that we had our own home, Ilê Aiyê. All of these people who sought an identity, a way, realized that they had the home of their ancestors and they joined in. . . . It seems when the drums started to resound with the magical beat of the main *quilombo* (runaway slaves community) people came together. (quoted in Morales 1991: 79)

The construction of this new agenda would identify a home and a way that came about through an appeal to Afro-Bahian tradition constituted throughout the century by multiple agents, including intellectuals, religious leaders, and artists. This process was also determined by a new sociological baseline in which there were mobilized participants, who embraced tradition, while seeking to engage modernity that was transforming Salvador.

It's worth noting how Ilê Aiyê's themes and songs reconstitute the historicity of black people and their struggles in Brazil and the diaspora, as well as the historicity of Carnaval in Salvador. When Ilê Aiyê celebrated the Revolta dos Búzios (an antislavery rebellion of 1798)[3] in their Carnaval parade of 1998, one of their songs "A Esperança de um Povo" (The Hope of a People) proclaimed:

Revolta dos Búzios	Búzios rebellion
História passada	Past history
Deixaram mágoa em Salvador	They left pain in Salvador
E o povo Bahiense	And the Bahian people
Leu o boletim dos revolucionários	Read the revolutionary pamphlets
Homens cidadãos	Citizen Men
Oh! povos curvados e abandonados	Oh! cowered people abandoned
pelo rei	by the king
O rei de Portugal	The king of Portugal
João de Deus, bravo guerreiro	João de Deus, brave warrior
Morreu enforcado, foi esquartejado	Was executed, hung and quartered
Por ser líder negro	For being a black leader

Part of those lyrics transcribed literally a fragment of the rebel manifesto that demanded the end to slavery based on the libertarian ideals of the Enlightenment. In this song, Ilê Aiyê reclaimed history by noting the black identity of the movement's main leader, João de Deus (Mattos 1998).

The way in which the rhetoric of modern blocos afro politicizes culture and history reveals a native appropriation of concepts such as "resistance" that reaffirms the inventive and reflexive character of their practices. As João Jorge Santos Rodrigues, an early member of Ilê Aiyê who later founded the bloco afro Olodum, explained in 1983:

> The songs of Ilê are songs of resistance and an expression of confidence of the black race, the people, in fighting their struggles and finding their own values to express themselves in the present. For this reason the black music of Ilê Aiyê set poor black neighborhoods on fire, reignited their self-confidence, and will do it again in the years to come. The idea of organized black people, leading themselves, and fighting for their space [reveals] a new man. (João Jorge Santos Rodrigues 1983: 248)

The idea of the black man as a new, re-created man is a good way of illustrating what I mean by suggesting that Afro-descendant identity has constituted itself through Carnaval in order to form new subjects or a field in which new subjects will recognize and organize themselves. This process is based on an appropriation of history as means of assigning new meaning to the experience of these subjects and their destinies.

In 1979, five years after Ilê Aiyê appeared, Olodum was founded in Maciel-Pelourinho, the city's historic center. After a crisis that nearly led to the bloco's extinction, it was refounded in 1983 as the Grupo Cultural Olodum with the participation of several dissidents from Ilê Aiyê, such as João Jorge Santos Rodrigues and Antônio Luís Alves de Souza, known as Neguinho do Samba. The latter has been credited as the creator of samba-reggae, a musical genre that would become the aesthetic expression par excellence of the blocos afro (Dantas 1994; Nunes 1997).

If Ilê Aiyê is the guardian of tradition, the purest among the pure, Olodum is the symbol of cultural innovation. As João Jorge has claimed, Olodum represents the *negritude* (blackness) of the twenty-first century, playing a critical role in relation to the traditionalism of other black organizations. Rodrigues is aware of its leading role in the process of re-Africanization and has consciously invested in the reinvention of black people through this process:

> Re-Africanization, even with the prefix "re," was extremely positive as it allowed us to encounter our own history. In this century, the persecution of candomblé and the afoxés produced certain type of black man in Salvador: the one who was afraid, who wore dark clothes so that nobody would notice he was black. The trousers were either navy blue or brown. His hair was as short as possible. No ring on his finger, no bracelets. Candomblé beads were totally hidden. (Rodrigues 1996: 132)

This observation reaffirms the idea of historical reappropriation as reinvention of the self. This process was characterized by subjective emancipation, suggested by the legitimization of "African customs," repressed continuously in the history of the city.

This repression, internalized by blacks themselves, has been addressed by several scholars, such as Roger Bastide, for whom class opposition between blacks and whites in Brazil during the time of slavery was duplicated in the so-called cut principle, which refers to ways in which Afro-Brazilians negotiate their existence between two worlds (Bastide 1971). Bastide was responding to a debate instigated by Florestan Fernandes about the integration of black people into a class society. Will black people, the former slaves, be able to integrate themselves into modern, national, class society and into the competitive social order? By integrating, will black people be de-Africanized, whitened, and forced to abandon their own traditional cultural origin, regarded as inadequate for inclusion in the new order? Bastide suggested that black people, as inhabitants of two worlds, develop almost parallel and nonconcurrent identities that exist insofar as they rest upon defined social structures to maintain themselves. In the case of the black world, the basis is African collective memory as tradition materializes in structures and institutions. In the external white world, class inequality provides the parameters for cultural struggles. The black social agent thus embodies acute contradictions (Bastide 1971; Florestan Fernandes 1978).

These authors were thinking about how a given social group was able to reconcile specific and persistent claims for traditional affiliation connected to the immediacy of social and cultural practice and insertion in the "external" modern Western world. Of course, the question of how to reconcile particularities rooted in ethnic or local traditions and universalism required as the language of modernity and citizenship has been the topic of extensive debate (Arantes 2000; Back 1996; Gilroy 1993). How to be at the same time Afro-descendant, modern, and a citizen?

The discursive formations of re-Africanization emerged as a historical response to this question in that the critical integration of tradition and modernity seems to dissolve both oppositions. In the Afro-Atlantic diaspora, black cultures are reinvented and articulate diverse subject positions that are formed in dialogue with or in opposition to discourses *about* black people. They exist in contexts determined by structural racism made present in daily life. The invention of Afro-descendant tradition takes place in relation to a history that accounts for racial violence and African resistance.

Afro-descendant tradition in Salvador has formed a broad discursive field that through symbolic and material practices has created an image of identity in the Carnaval tradition. Black Carnaval music—its customs, clothes, names of the afoxés and blocos, the yearly ritualized performances, and their institutionalization—forms itself in a discursive, dialogic, and conflicted field around a new subject position.

::: Reggae, Funk, *Pagode*: Modernity and Subjectivity

Re-Africanization takes place in the broad context of Brazilian modernity, a plural and uneven process, determined by the development of collective subjectivities. "The modernization of any given society must be seen in relation to the projects and movements of diverse collective subjectivities that contribute to it" (Domingues 1999: 74). These subjectivities do not predate modernization nor are they effects of it; they are self-constitutive as they modernize society and themselves. From this perspective, racial identities are subjectivities, or what Leonardo Avritzer calls "reflexive publics" (2000: 78), marked by processes of reflexive disassembling and reassembling, anchored in narratives of memory and recuperation of tradition. Collective memory practices "reinterpret and assign new meanings to the past that presents itself in monuments, festivities and celebrations" (Myrian Sepúlveda dos Santos 2000: 92). In this sense, modernization is a process that involves many authors and actors who structure themselves reflexively based on collective resignifications of their own history, as we saw in the case of the blocos afro.

Another determinant in the experience of modernity in this context is related to Brazil's "unequal and combined" development, or what Souza has called "selective modernization," that produces and reproduces "urban and rural pariahs" (José Maurício Domingues 1999; Jessé Souza, 2000). The modernization process in Brazil produces exclusion, poverty, and violence that are not merely legacies from the past, or traditional vestiges, but consequences of the national social development. Both conditioning factors have specific and determinant prevalence in the case of Bahia, as Jeferson Bacelar argues: "In fact, modernization exacerbated inequalities in Salvador, with concentration of wealth in the hands of a small minority, privileged managers of public spaces and services and the perspective of the strengthened middle classes, involved in the presumption of social mobility" (Bacelar 2001: 194). Critical reflection on this inequality has become a constitutive aspect of the very process of local modernization, characterized by the development of Afro-descendant subjectivities, modernized in connection with the world of global consumption (Hall et al. 1976; Hebdige 1989).

As pointed out in the works of Carlos Benedito Rodrigues Silva and Hermano Vianna on soul and funk movements in Rio de Janeiro in the 1980s, dynamic relations involving young Afro-Brazilians, the cultural industry, and elements of global black culture have been long evident (Silva 1984;

Vianna 1988). This relation is expressed in exemplary and reflexive fashion by São Paulo's rap group Racionais MCs in their song "Fórmula Magica da Paz" (Magic Formula for Peace):

Eu era só um moleque	I was just a kid
só pensava em dançar	and only thought about dancing
cabelo black	afro style hair
e tênis All Star	All Star sneakers.

For these new forms of black young identities, clothes and hair management are essential in the constitution of style in consumption-production, that is to say, production formed by consumption practices (de Certeau 1998). This kind of production does not hesitate in appropriating young middle-class dress codes as a sign of the desire for social ascension, as portrayed in Paulo Lins's 1997 novel *Cidade de Deus* (City of God):

> The coolest thing was buying the sports brands, but they were really expensive, and, perhaps for that reason, the sharpest. They dreamed of wealth, and wealth meant living across the road from the beach, having ferns in your living room, wearing designer labels and having a car with tinted windows and wide tires (not to mention a loud Kadron exhaust), having purebred dog to walk on the beach every morning and afternoon, buying 8 pounds of weed in one go so you didn't have to keep making trips to the den all the time. If they were rich, they'd only buy imported skateboards, Caloi 10 bicycles, and waterproof watches; they'd dance on the best dance floor and screw the hottest chicks. (Lins 2006: 157–58)

In Salvador, the formation of the blocos afro was influenced by the consumption of cultural goods, and soul music was central to the repertoire of the new Afro-descendant identities in Bahia (Risério 1981). Several studies have pointed out the importance of image management in the construction of identity among youth who consume funk and reggae (see, e.g., Cunha 1991; Pinho 1998b, 2001; Sansone 1998; Suylan Midlej e Silva 1995). These images frequently circulate as consumer products.

Olívia Cunha, for instance, discusses extensively the importance of dreadlocks in the definition of a true Rasta and in the multiple internal or external interpretations focused on hair. On the one hand, it is a sign of stigma and police persecution, and, on the other, it is an essential element in the "natural" philosophy of the Rasta. As one of Cunha's informers puts it: "Rasta hair is a matter of resistance, a matter of repudiating all that is evil"

(Cunha 1991: 136). We can speak of a politics of visual agency that through cultural consumption strategically produces black images.

In the 1970s, the effects of industrialization and urban development were increasingly apparent in Salvador, where the culture industry acquired a central role in the formation of sensibilities. The process of socioeconomic modernization accompanied the increasing influences of new technologies, allowing for the rapid circulation of images and messages, of which three influences were key. First, at that time, when the news of black rebellions in Africa and in the United States arrived in Salvador, the sounds of soul, funk, and reggae contributed decisively to re-Africanization. Soul music and images of African American musicians such as James Brown interacted with local cultural traditions, producing connections that were key to this process. Second, the Third Worldist discourse of Rastafarianism, reggae music, and the image of Bob Marley were appropriated as elements for affirming a black identity that was at once local and global. Third, the tradition of samba and the style of *pagode baiano*, described later in the chapter, also contributed to the reinvention of musical genres such as samba-reggae. These three musical and symbolic complexes formed a background to cultural reinvention.

To begin, reggae was present not only in samba-reggae, the re-Africanized musical genre par excellence, but was also a point of reference for the bloco afro Muzenza. As a diasporic genre, reggae was disseminated throughout Salvador in an impressive and persistent way, functioning also as a musical marker for organizing space and social participation of young Afro-descendants in Salvador. In addition to the reconstruction of the self and of the body, reggae also enabled the resignification of the city. Starting in the 1980s, amidst Muzenza's discursive reiteration and the introduction of samba-reggae, reggae music and its symbols started to proliferate in Salvador, producing territorial niches such as Bar do Reggae (Reggae Bar) in the historic center Pelourinho (Pinho 1998b, 2001), where pan-African colors and images of Bob Marley became part of the traditional setting of colonial-era buildings.[4]

Rastafarian discourse became part of a field of symbolic and political disputes, primarily through its most performative or spectacular aspects. In the public scene of reggae culture, a certain iconography and embodied visuality gained more visibility, to the detriment of its ideological or religious aspects. Reggae prevailed mostly as a style (Cunha 1991; Veiga 1996, 1998). Cunha has gathered important testimonies on the identity reinvention process, enacted through aesthetic reelaborations and rituals of daily rebellion. One of her informants comments on dreadlocks:

> It is a process. I think the first and most important moment is when one stops straightening the hair. When I see this, I think to myself, "a process has begun there." A process of reassuming identity, which I think Brazilian blacks have lost as they got involved in the community that is not white, but has white values against which it is difficult to fight. (quoted in Cunha 1991: 116)

Reggae enabled the acceptance of black or African cultural values, from a cultural matrix that was not from traditional Afro-Brazilian culture, but was part of the modern African diaspora. Reggae culture developed as self-consciously constructed and elaborated aesthetic-political discourse, not as an archetypal or traditional manifestation.

Another field that has contributed to the modernizing turn in traditional Afro-culture in Bahia is the funk-soul cultural complex. Risério vividly documents the invasion of soul music in the years that immediately preceded the founding of Ilê Aiyê, showing that disco music arrived first in the Liberdade neighborhood. The Sport Club of Periperi, located along the railway line that connected the city to the poor suburban periphery, has held its "Black Bahia" *baile funk* (funk dance) since 1979. These events feature an array of elements identified with funk culture, including clothes, slang, specific break-dance steps, and the organization of permanent dance groups. Those who frequent the bailes funk are motivated by the sheer pleasure of dancing:

> What makes me go to the dance is the funk, the rap, the pure adrenaline that runs in the veins. I'm a *funkeiro*, I'm not going to lie to anyone, and what takes me to the dance is this, the style, funk itself. . . *Funkeiros* go to the dance with the purpose of dancing funk. (Luís Neves, quoted in Midlej e Silva 1996: 103)

Dance expertise that is shown in agonistic rituals among boys, the seductive implications of dancing, and the connection that dance allows between the black body and black history are all recurring features that indicate the importance of corporeality (historicity incarnate in the body) in rituals or gender practices. As Sansone has noted, both in Salvador and in Rio de Janeiro, funk may lend itself "to experimentation with appearance, use of the body, and conspicuous consumption (of clothes, music and transportation)" (1998: 230). These are, again, techniques of style.

The last genre we will focus on is pagode baiano, a style of samba that updates in its own way the contradictions of politics, market, and subjectivity. Contemporary pagode in Bahia has been the target of intense controversy and a certain kind of moral panic that differs from the kind directed at reggae and funk, which were stigmatized by their alleged association with drug use and dealing. Pagode baiano, which grew out of the *axé* music phenomenon—itself an indirect result of the re-Africanization process—has been deemed vulgar, aesthetically poor, excessively sexual and commercial, as if other genres were not (Moura 2001a; Sirleide Aparecida de Oliveira 2001).

The term *pagode* has been used to describe many different ways of playing samba over time. This new version from Bahia is a transformation of *partido alto* from Rio de Janeiro, hybridized with traditional *samba-de-roda* or *samba duro* from the Bahian Recôncavo (the region surrounding All Saints' Bay) from which many public dominion songs and many stylistic themes have been transferred to the repertoires of pagode groups. Pagode is both a commercial musical genre and a popular festive event. The group É o Tchan and others created a media image based on a fixed structure of singers and dancers with skimpy Lycra clothes and an aerobic style of dancing. This phenomenon is fed by and reflects on the experiences of several pagodes that proliferated in all of its poor neighborhoods of Salvador.

Groups that took off in the media as exponents of pagode baiano come from this larger pagode scene oriented toward performance—dancing well, exhibiting the body, and so on. All of these techniques have always had evident sexual content, as we observe in the descriptions of black dances since the colonial period. In other words, it wasn't É o Tchan who sexualized samba. Until recently, pagode in Salvador was seen as degraded, vulgar, and "low class." This changed quickly and unexpectedly for those, myself included, who witnessed the process locally.

Groups such as Gera Samba and Terra Samba, which later spun off more famous groups, performed in popular clubs such as the Cruz Vermelha in the Campo Grande neighborhood, known in the 1980s as the *graxeiras*, or housekeepers' club. Most groups, however, performed in bars, street parties, and religious festivals in Salvador. In addition, pagode has carried the stigma of being nonpoliticized when compared to blocos afro, its closest symbolic opponent, precisely for participating in the same context.

> It was the time for resistance (of the blocos afro), see? People were embarrassed to say, "I'm going to the pagode, I was at a pagode," because the guys would discriminate and would say, "did you have to?" Pagode was for losers, and people

would say things like: "I don't want to see guys wiggling their butts." (Elieser, quoted in Sirleide Aparecida de Oliveira 2001: 66)

Two more important aspects of the pagode universe deserve mention. First, its relation to the market and the music industry is much more brutal than that of other genres analyzed here. Pagode groups are businesses that have owners and no real control over the product of their work, which naturally leads to some tension. As most of the pagode artists are very poor, they cannot make the necessary investments in the band, or quit their jobs, in case they have one, to devote themselves to music. This makes them dependent on people who have money to become professional.

Oliveira tells stories of young men who are in love with music but, with no chance or possibility of managing their own production, end up literally alienating their talent through binding deals with local managers. They saw in music a way of expressing themselves, of feeling like they were someone, or simply of getting girls:

> When I was young, I always had trouble finding a girlfriend because I was considered ugly. I always fell in love but was never loved back. I thought to myself: "if I go to the rehearsal of Barrabas, and if Carina, Patrícia go there and see me singing they will want to go out with me!" I was only thirteen and I went there and bothered the guy who presented the show until he'd let me sing. (Carlos Cabral, quoted in Sirleide Aparecida de Oliveira 2001: 79)

More significant than this, however, is the resentment felt by the artists for managers who interfere in the creative process by dictating how they would have to sing and present themselves. It is ironic that sometimes the managers are credited with the groups' success, for they "believed their potential" and invested money.

The second aspect I would like to highlight in the pagode universe has to do with the presentation of the self and critical reflection focused in the body. Oliveira divides this universe into two areas, the world of production—characterized by the alienation described above—and the world of consumption—where pagode is lived in preeminent space of corporeality and of identity management. At these events *quebrar* (to break) is a central category. "Breaking" in this context means dancing sensuously, with flexions, squats, and choreographed steps that insinuate sexual movements. The *dança da garrafa* (bottle dance), which simultaneously seduced and scandalized the country from north to south, is only one example, turned into a spectacle, of the kind of "breaking" that already existed in pagodes and even the traditional *sambas de roda*.

Sirleide de Oliveira conducted an ethnographic study of the Cruz Vermelha Club pagode. This club used to hold elite Carnaval dances in the early twentieth century, but starting in the 1970s attracted a different crowd, composed of housekeepers, office messengers, people who jumped from job to job, and lower-class students. At this dance, it was possible to witness an embodied gender identity game: "Not only women, but men also may, and should, move without losing their virility, which is actually heightened through a display of muscles and eroticized sensuous gestures, inspired in a choreography led by a woman, the pagode goddess, Carla Perez" (Sirleide Aparecida de Oliveira 2001: 97). The fundamental paradigm in pagode is sensuality and, with its media success, the model for such sensuality has been dictated by the groups' dancers. In Bahian pagode, boys find a model for expressing their own sensuality potential in a woman, the pagode goddess. This happens, however, without any confusion or misunderstanding in sexual orientation or in masculinity performances, which remain as heterosexist as always. Despite the frequent presence of homosexuals in pagodes, their "structural place" is different and well defined (Pinho 1998c).

One of Oliveira's informers has personally experienced these contradictions. His love for dancing had him face the weight of heterosexist normalization, through his neighbors' pressure on his father: "People on my street were always planting doubts in his head: 'Mr. Deraldo, your son will end up a *viado* ["queer"]. All he does is dance samba all the time. Dancing is for queers, dancing is for women. A real man should be involved in hard work'" (Edson, quoted in Sirleide Aparecida de Oliveira 2001: 105). After the pagode explosion, and his father's death, Edson insisted on his dream, and, after having danced in some blocos afro and some pagode bands, has earned his neighbors' respect. Edson is another one of the characters who reveal the differentiated articulations between Afro-descendant tradition and cultural modernization connected to spectacle, commodification, and alienation, as well as the effects of these articulations on the production of subjectivities, themselves modernized and modernizing.

Young reggae singers inspired by the never-ending holy flame of justice, peripheral funkeiros for whom global music and dance constitute their experience with modernity, housekeepers who dream of finding fame—or simply a new boyfriend—as they "break" at Cruz Vermelha, all of these are forms of exercising black self-identification. They are articulated in the new social environment brought on by re-Africanization, an environment marked by the dynamic dissolution and reposition of meanings of tradition and modernity. As we have seen, these fields have very different characteristics, but are also intertwined in the process—whether as a source of images, discourses, or symbolic elements, or as modernized and at times banal extensions of the initial impulse for reinvention of tradition. The adventure of black identities through re-Africanization reveals complex diversity, oscillating between contestation and a sheer desire for fun and recognition.

NOTES

This chapter is an adaptation of chapter 4 of my doctoral dissertation "O Mundo Negro: Sócio-Antropologia da Reafricanização em Salvador" (Black World: Socio-Anthropology of Re-Africanization in Salvador), presented in 2003 at UNICAMP (Universidade Estadual de Campinas).

1. The ethnonym *jejê* refers to the Fon-Ewe people of present-day Benin and *nagô* refers to Yoruba-speaking people.

2. Garcia, Politeama, and Tororó are traditional lower middle-class neighborhoods in Salvador. According to Milton Moura, we can see here the development and transformation process of the same structure that evolved between 1957 and 1959 from a rather undefined organization, as the old *batucadas* (drum groups) used to be, into a structure that is clearly influenced by the samba schools from Rio de Janeiro (2001a).

3. The Búzios Rebellion (1798) is also known as Tailor's Rebellion (Revolta dos Alfaiates).

4. For more references on reggae and Rastafarianism in Salvador and other regions in Brazil, see Janet DeCosmo 2000; Antonio J. V. Dos Santos Godi 2001; and Suylan Midlej e Silva 1995.

::: Modernity, Agency, and Sexuality in
the Pagode Baiano

Ari Lima

In the 1930s, as ideas about nationhood were taking shape, samba stood out among various Afro-Brazilian cultural traditions as a musical genre, cultural product, and focus of racial and identity discourse. Little by little a sector of the elite projected samba as a symbol of identity for a *mestiço* nation. In a context in which the elite advocated the gradual *embranquecimento* (whitening) of the nation, it is curious to note that a stigmatized cultural form so closely associated with African ancestry gained this status. What happened with samba in that period can be understood by reference to the debates over African cultural survivals, miscegenation, and national identity that had been occurring since the late nineteenth century and reaching their apex in the thirties, with the publication (in 1933) of *Casa-Grande & Senzala* (*The Masters and the Slaves*) by Gilberto Freyre (Falcão and Araújo 2001; Munanga 1999; Ortiz 1994; Skidmore 1974; Ventura 1991). Another approach involves displacing the empirical focus from isolated African cultural survivals and search instead for African and Afro-Brazilian *agency* in the streets during the period that samba emerged as a musical genre. It is thus possible to perceive samba, and Afro-Brazilian cultural manifestations in general, as an attempt to demand citizenship, however controversial and incomplete.

The notion of African cultural survivals appears in two key texts: *Os Africanos do Brasil* by Raimundo Nina Rodrigues, written between 1890 and 1905 and published posthumously in 1932; and Freyre's *Casa-Grande & Senzala*. Rodrigues and Freyre share a concern with the future of Brazil from the point of view of race, racial and cultural mixture, and African cultural survivals.

In studying black people as a social problem and object of science, Nina Rodrigues sought to define a new place for them in Brazil. To understand blacks scientifically, morally, and mentally meant to acknowledge, as he put it, "our lowest inferior limits," combat an undesirable ancestry, and compensate for this disadvantage in relation to European civilizations and peoples. He pointed out that blacks had shown throughout history that they were incapable of constituting a civilization and therefore incapable of participating as subjects in the construction of a civilized Brazilian nation. In this way, he regarded the presence of blacks as a negative aspect of national reality; a social problem to resolve and contain.

In *Os Africanos do Brasil*, Nina Rodrigues claimed that as native-born Africans in Brazil disappeared, they would live through *crioulos* (blacks born in Brazil) and their "crude," "bastardized," and "primitive" spiritual practices. These religious, linguistic, artistic, and psychic survivals would be assimilated by the diverse population of the country. In sum, the booming drums, *candomblé* religious ceremonies, and sambas would over time be incorporated into popular festivities and would exercise a "heightened" role in the formation of the artistic taste of the people. These practices would make the country increasingly "black" and erode Brazil's, and especially Bahia's, precarious connection to civilization.

Gilberto Freyre, for his part, never studied samba or addressed the appropriation and transformation of African and Afro-Brazilian culture into symbols of national identity. In his most famous work, *Casa-Grande & Senzala*, Freyre sought to separate race from biology, but reified the idea of culture and interpreted African ethnicities hierarchically in relation to the Portuguese. He uses the concept of culture in order to interpret manifestations such as samba as "residues" "African stains," and "black marks" in a manner that recalled the "African survivals" described previously by Nina Rodrigues.

Freyre observed African survivals from the celebratory angle of racial and cultural mestiçagem, which he did not consider, in the manner of a Nina Rodrigues, as a symbol of degeneration or as an archaic survival that was culturally and socially dislocated. For Freyre, African survivals were not inert residues incapable of transforming African traditions or ideas about Africa, as they were for Nina Rodrigues. Rather, Freyre understood them as contributions to a new social and cultural system that was original due to racial and cultural mestiçagem. Freyre affirmed the presence of blacks not as a picturesque element, but rather as a living and active contribution to national development. Black people were perpetuated by a series of "useful survivals," leading to the peculiar adjustment of traditions and tendencies that would form a part of "modern Brazilian culture" (Freyre 1989a: 159). Blacks were seen not as agents of social change, nor as inventors of traditions; instead, they were valued for practicing racially unmarked "primitive" traditions and customs.

Against critics such as Nina Rodrigues, it is impossible to reflect on Brazilian cultural identity without taking into account black people and their cultural manifestations before and after abolition in 1888. Arguably the most original Brazilian creation, the samba always had great potential to bring together people of different classes and races. On one hand, it emerged as a symbol of national identity in that it was presented as vestigial African heritage and an agent of cultural synthesis. On the other, this musical genre only reached this level of recognition thanks to the agency of Africans and their descendants. Although they could accept samba as a national genre, they had *lived samba* as black music directly related to the social history of Afro-Brazilians.

::: Samba as Black Agency and Identity Discourse

Despite elite efforts at Europeanization, police repression, and the denial of their physical and symbolic presence on the streets, and in the emergent culture industry, Africans and their descendants civilized everyone, by altering, as Nina Rodrigues feared, cultural practices and feelings (José Murilo de Carvalho 1987; Sodré 1988; Vianna 1995). If miscegenation advanced the project of whitening and cultural hybridity, it also allowed for the affirmation of Afro-diasporic culture and, therefore, a parallel civilizing project. Contrary to what Nina Rodrigues thought, Africans and their descendants were aware that, in those particular circumstances, they were dealing with the perspective of a mestiço national identity. By participating, for example, in Carnaval or in popular street festivals—territories formally controlled by whites—they added or juxtaposed different black cultural references. Africa became a social nonplace—a political, cultural, mythic, and religious experiment, rather than an essence (Landes 1967; Sodré 1988; Vieira Filho 1998).

The argument that mestiçagem represented the affirmation of a parallel project of civilization gains more weight when we observe the impact and assimilation of republican ideals in Brazil during the late nineteenth century and early twentieth in Rio de Janeiro, the federal capital and largest city of the time. José Murilo de Carvalho notes (1987) that Rio de Janeiro during the first years of the republic was the Brazilian city in which the best conditions were present, at least in theory, for the development of republican citizenship. As the center of the national political sphere, it was home to a population whose political behavior quickly became reflected in the whole country. In Rio de Janeiro, with about 500,000 inhabitants in the early years of the republic, nearly half of the population was composed of classes that were deemed dangerous or potentially dangerous to the government, the police, and the elites. Among them, there were around 20,000 *capoeiristas*, predominantly black men adept at using capoeira in street fights, who were considered a constant threat to public order. Rio was also associated with sin, cheating, seduction, exploitation, and confidence schemes attributed to the dangerous classes but lived by all (José Murilo de Carvalho 1987). At the same time, Rio de Janeiro was center stage for contradictory ideas of positivism, liberalism, socialism, and anarchism, which elites and workers imported from Europe.

The challenge for the republican government was to govern the country from above; impose a new order and a national project; and control the mentality, expectations, and unrest of the multitude. There was a vast world of popular participation in Rio de Janeiro occurring far from the official world of the politics, habits, culture, and ideas of the elite. Like most large Brazilian cities of the period, Rio de Janeiro had a large population of blacks who influenced profoundly the cultural profile of the city. If Europeanized republican Brazil was constantly at "risk of blackening" itself," the "renegade republics," even as they were under pressure to Europeanize, were always guided by an outlook informed by African civilization that reinterpreted values, moral values, and cultural products of the elites.

In the twentieth century, samba music is exemplary of this phenomenon as it acquired fundamental importance for the articulation of black agency and culture in Brazil. It has always been a genre of music open to European sounds and poetics. It is a "musical experience" (Blacking 1992) that raises extramusical questions pertaining to nationhood, such as tradition, modernity, authorship, race relations, and African heritage. In the 1930s—through deliberate acts of the state, intellectual and economic elites, and samba musicians—an urban, industrialized, and national samba was forged that was neither white nor black, neither of the poor, nor of the elites; it was, rather, Brazilian (Vianna 1995). Yet there also remained and still thrived various types of samba in Brazil, submerged by the "national samba" that was mass-produced since the 1930s by radio and record industries and that was legitimated by samba musicians and singers, the public, and intellectuals.

In nineteenth-century Bahia, before being converted into a symbol of national identity, samba was subjected to constant police vigilance and repression and stigmatized by those regarded as "hardworking and honest." The spaces of sambas belonged to no one: there was no accumulation or constitution of patrimony in them, because they constituted a field of anti-work, or leisure. From the standpoint of law and morality, sambas were a "no man's land," whether practiced in centralized locations or in isolated areas of neighborhoods. As Jocélio Teles dos Santos (1998) suggests, sambas were rather autonomous spaces; they attracted gamblers, prostitutes, the poor and blacks, and "troublemakers."

My recent research on a variation of samba called pagode baiano in several peripheral neighborhoods of the city of Salvador suggests dance parties organized around this genre case provide the context for the affirmation of a racial identity discourse as well as the reterritorialization of "easy women," "dishonest and lazy people," jobless people, homosexuals, and blacks. Although Bahian pagode constitutes a particularly Bahian form of samba, the term *pagode* had been utilized with different meanings, in the universe of black music produced in the states of Rio de Janeiro and São Paulo. Sirleide Aparecida de Oliveira (2001) affirms that in the beginning of the 1970s the term *pagode* reappeared in Rio de Janeiro in order to designate the parties promoted by the sambistas of *partido alto*, a type of traditional samba danced in a circle and originally brought from Bahia to Rio de Janeiro. These events were a reaction to the transformations undergone by samba schools following the arrival of the *carnavalesco*, a general director of sorts who turned them into spectacles at odds with the communitarian world of samba (Ana Maria Rodrigues 1984). These meetings were also a protest against the model of commercialization of samba imposed by the record industry, which disdained the elements considered traditional in samba from Rio de Janeiro and based instead on a standardized samba rhythm. This movement reached its climax when the samba singer Almir Guineto received the title of "King of Pagode" after the sale of 600,000 albums in 1986. There was soon a decline following the astounding success of *música sertaneja*, *lambada*, and *axé* music, styles of music produced with the heavy influence of the recording industry. Since then, *pagode carioca* returned to its original environment, in spite of the fact that a few of its stronger and more emblematic figures, such as the sambista José Bezerra da Silva, succeeded in maintaining visibility through alternative communications and commercialization strategies (Hermano Vianna 1998).

As Sirleide Aparecida Oliveira has shown, the "new pagode" was propelled by two social groups: the "impresarios of the record industry seeking to promote the commercial success of their products"; and the "samba groups, composed of young people, in the majority black and mestiço, originating from their peripheries of Brazilian cities like São Paulo, Uberlândia, Rio de Janeiro, and Salvador" (Sirleide Aparecida de Oliveira 2001: 51). Since then, countless pagode groups have emerged in peripheral and black neighborhoods of Salvador, reproducing the same formula for success: an attractive vocalist who dances well, has good stage presence, and a muscular body; a trio of dancers, normally one black man, a natural or peroxide blond, and a black woman, or *morena*; and finally, a musical accompaniment that includes keyboards, electric guitar, base, *cavaquinho*, drum set, and percussion (*surdo*, congas, *timbaus*, *pandeiro*). Bands have recently tended to include some wind instruments and strip the keyboards of their centrality. All bands have similar repertoires that are easily assimilated, with lyrics that are in turn lascivious, homophobic, sexist, and racist. Various bands emerged in black neighborhoods from the periphery and were transformed by the music industry into successes. Among these, the most important are É o Tchan, Terra Samba, Harmonia do Samba, Pagodart, and Psirico. It is widely suspected, though hard to prove, that when these groups achieve a modicum of popular success, their producers offer *jabá* (payola), a sum of money to radio stations to push their songs on air. From there they are more likely to receive contracts from record companies that also pay jabá, resulting in their groups' appearance on television and play on radio stations throughout the country. At this point, they begin to perform in elite clubs and parade with prestigious blocos of the middle and upper classes during the Carnaval of Salvador. The profile of the fan base changes to include white consumers with higher levels of formal education and buying power.

I attended pagodes in peripheral neighborhoods where emerging bands such as Moleques do Samba, Swing Moleque, and Império do Samba played. In these pagodes, the mode of dress, dances, and bodily self-fashioning suggested patterns associated with a "new ethnicity" (Sansone 1991), based on globalized and commodified identity markers, but also revealed a measure of self-awareness involving the comprehension and reproduction of racialized images and representations.

These pagodes were, by definition, territories for the performance of race, gender, and sexuality. The performative attitude of the adolescent girls and boys was characterized by an apparent informality on stage and in the audience, yet at the same time, specific territories were claimed by heterosexual boys, homosexual boys (called *viados*, or "queers"), girls, and those who merely observed. This apparent informality was manifested in a style of dress that was almost always scanty, or at least comfortable, and with few accessories. This apparent informality, nevertheless, was negated by an abiding concern with appearance—the display of muscles—in the case of straight guys—or of certain body parts, such as legs, hips, waist, belly button, and thighs—in the case of girls—or with the exhibition of complex choreographies in the case of viados and of straight guys who danced in groups. This group of heterosexual and homosexual guys, in general highly competent dancers, stood out in their choice of fashionable clothes and accessories. With plucked eyebrows, dyed and curled hair, they dislocated ideals of manliness and virility attributed to straight white men. This informality was also undone when the masculine, straight performers on stage addressed the crowd, principally the girls, *quebrando tudo* ("giving it up") or calling out well-known phrases, rehearsed and heard in various pagode bands: "Clap your hands if you like it!" "Where are the fans of Bahia [soccer club]?" "And those of Vitória?" "I want to hear the girls scream!" "I want to hear the guys scream!" "*Viados*, raise your hands!"

In pagode baiano, as in other Afro-diasporic musical forms, heterosexual and homosexual men occupy center stage. In the case of pagode baiano, there is gender mobility among the *pagodeiros*, through "simultaneous discursivity" (Henderson 1994), in which gender identity and difference are related to racial identity and difference. Masculine gender and sexuality mobility are reinforced by ideas of femininity that absorb (through performance normally associated with women) black men, both straight and homosexual, who are poor, undereducated, and underemployed. The masculinity of young poor black men thus displaces received ideas about manliness, while reinforcing ideas about race and the black body elaborated by whites.

To further illustrate this point, it's worth examining lyrical passages from the song "Na Baixaria" (Down and Dirty) composed by Dinho Santos and Bola Sete, which was frequently performed by the group Pagodart during the summer of 2002. In popular Bahian vernacular, the word *baixaria* refers to situations in which people lose inhibitions, yell, curse, and even transgress sexual mores.

Eu vou dar um mergulho	I'm going to take a dive
E eu não quero alteração	And I don't want changes
Não tou comendo nada	I'm not eating anything

É suingueira da Bahia	It's the swing of Bahia
Eu vou descendo a zorra	I'm bringing on the chaos
E vou fazer a baixaria	I'm getting down and dirty
. . . .	. . . .
Eu sou samba de roda	I'm from circle samba
Samba de madeira	Samba of wood
Vem na quebradeira	Come and get down
Que eu vou no suingão	I'm getting into the swing
. . . .	. . . .
Olha a coluna tia!	Look at the column, auntie!
Vai mãe, vai mãe, vai mãe!	Go mama, go mama, go mama!
Se pedir eu mexo mais	If you like I'll move more
A baixaria	Down and dirty

The song celebrates baixaria and incites people to partake in it. There are several sexual allusions in the song, such as "I'm not eating anything" (i.e., "I'm not getting sex"). In live performances, the group would substitute the phrase "Se pedir eu mexo mais" (If you ask, I'll move more) with "Se pedir eu meto / deixo mais" (If you ask I'll stick it / let it in deeper). The masculine voice that sings—the subject that speaks—says that he can penetrate ("eat") another man or woman or even allow himself to be penetrated, as suggested in the alternation of *meto* (I'll stick it in) and *deixo* (I'll let you). The song invites everyone to join the *quebradeira* ("get down") and move with the *suingão* ("big swing"), a transliteration of the English word. José Ramos Tinhorão (1991) and Carlos Sandroni (2001) have observed that the verb *quebrar* (to break) was often associated with popular dances such as the maxixe and *lundu*. In the past, the verb was used to encourage the dancers while making reference to the steps that involved shaking hips. In pagode baiano, the verb *quebrar* or *quebradeira* also refers to shaking, but carries an additional connotation emphasizing the erotic movement of the haunches up and down, back and forth, to mimic sexual intercourse. Body language exercises a crucial role in the construction of both gender and race in Brazil (Parker 1991).

In the pagode subculture, young black heterosexual men generally lack steady employment, have limited consumer power, and a low level of education. Their precarious socioeconomic position interferes with their ability to create and sustain stable relationships with women, get married, and constitute families. Even ephemeral relationships with young women often prove difficult because of the men's restricted consumer power and low

Two young men at a pagode in Salvador (Ari Lima).

social prestige. They compensate for reduced access to women by having sex with viados, who usually have more economic means, especially those who are older than twenty. As long as they sexually penetrate their partners without being penetrated themselves and eschew long-term liaisons, these young men can maintain their social identities as heterosexual men. The viados transfer resources to straight guys in the form of consumer items or even money; they may pay their entrance to the dance and buy them drinks, which in turn can be shared with the girls who accompany the straight guys. These affective, sexual, and economic exchanges are always calculated. In the pagode dances, these semidependent straight males often adopt the dance and performance styles of the viados. This performance determines, on the one hand, their emasculation vis-à-vis young, supervirile white men with economic power, social prestige, and distance from the feminine represented by viados and girls. On the other hand, projected and self-elaborated as a phallus, penetrator, and devourer, these young black men become supervirile in relation to these same young white men when they display sexual energy in symbolic or discursive constructions, in sexual roles and categories, in song lyrics and, above all, in performances based on attitude, bodily movement, and dress.

The pagode parties in Salvador are not territories exclusive to heterosexual men, but they do take on the character of events largely determined from a masculine and heterosexual point of view. The critical emphasis on the heterosexual masculine permits an analysis of race or an analysis of the power of the masculine as it is weakened by the vicissitudes of the representation of race and sexuality. It also reveals how irony and sexual ambiguity of heterosexual pagodeiros allow them to feminize themselves and be "a little queer" as long as they adhere to a hegemonic model of black masculinity through the ritualization of violence, sexism, and homophobia. In sum, pagode allows us to think about samba in social, cultural, and aesthetic contexts, taking into account music and lyrics, but also its performance among consumers of this style.

Several musicians confessed to me that they would like to make another kind of music or at least kind of samba that is "better" than pagode. In contrast with other forms of samba, pagode is not completely artisan or communitarian, nor is it exclusively produced and transmitted through institutions, educational programs, and the mass media. It is, rather, a mosaic along the lines of what Roger Bastide (1985) has observed in the "religious syncretism" of candomblé. That is, while there exists, on the one hand, an assimilation and reification, by a white cultural system, of past African cultural diversity, there is also the reconstitution of affective attitudes, a memory, and an insubordinate corporeality that succeeds in curbing white social control and allowing for the search of images, symbols, and instruments of Afro-Brazilian resistance in playful spaces. To the degree that pagode baiano extends samba and responds to its history, we can say that it affirms Afro-Brazilian movements to reinsert blacks into the history of political and cultural interventions. At the same time, it is an experience immersed in paradoxes and responsible for immense frustrations.

::: Final Considerations

Starting in the 1930s, Brazil underwent a long process of modernization in the economic, political, intellectual, cultural, and service sectors. This transformation also required changes in the notion of citizenship in order to recognize a necessarily impersonal and rational attitude focused on universal rights and an egalitarian perspective of educational inclusion, social visibility, and fair access to the labor market. This process of modernization, however, was not generalized as the political elites had promised and the constitution had defended. On the contrary, it was restricted to modern spaces from which poor people, most notably of African descent, were excluded or, at best, included as cultural product, commodity, and fetish. The only opportunity open to the great mass of frustrated blacks in the modern sector, as Jeferson Bacelar affirms (2001), were "jobs created by a failed State," a massive informal economy, and other alternative forms of survival that commodify the black body. Afro-Brazilians have pursued these alternative means of survival since the end of the slavery.

One avenue for social ascension has been the music market, in which blacks have key roles as composers, vocalists, and instrumentalists, though they still have a peripheral role in the music industry. Blacks have throughout the years participated in the modernization of music and its cultural meaning, including the definition of samba as a symbol of national identity. Nevertheless, they tend to be overlooked in the cultural history of samba and experience premodern work relations since they are usually not the beneficiaries of the culture industry with opportunities to build stable and lasting careers.

While pagode is not rigorously modern, it does represent a musical experience that—though not implying an exercise in citizenship—contingently impinges upon the ways in which these poor Afro-Bahian youth are constituted and represented (Hall 1996a). As an alternative framework for the elaboration of an informal economy, pagode also reintegrates aspects of traditional African manifestations found in Brazil, such as dance, call-and-response song, and the emphasis on polyrhythm. It embraces a subaltern gender (feminine) and sexuality (homosexual) and undermines the hegemony of the macho. More importantly, it exists as a musical experience whose feelings are particular and shared amongst certain subjects. Musicians and the public share a language and a way of speaking about themselves and others that reveal an emergent, imperfect citizenship.

::: Candeal and Carlinhos Brown

Social and Musical Contexts of an

Afro-Brazilian Community

Goli Guerreiro

Music in Brazil has been one of the most important modes of social change of everyday life among residents of poor neighborhoods and favelas. The community of Candeal Pequeno in Salvador, Bahia, provides a prime example of the power of cultural expression. Using a strategy that combines music and practices of citizenship, the Candeal community has achieved national and international attention as a place of cultural activism, while experiencing transformations in urban renewal and community development. A leading figure in the process has been the musician, entrepreneur, and cultural activist Carlinhos Brown.

At an early age, Carlinhos Brown was mentored by Osvaldo Alves da Silva, known as Pintado do Bongô, a Candeal percussionist. The relationship with mentors is essential to the learning of percussion. While Pintado was alive, Brown revered him to the point of choosing music over school, an institution that "killed my heroes and the stories I had learned from my family and neighbors . . . and showed people a Brazilian history that was not the one I knew" (Mercante 2004: 31). In addition to introducing Brown to pagode (a form of samba), Mestre Pintado introduced him to Spanish American styles such as bolero and to other samba masters in Bahia, such as Batatinha and Riachão. This musical formation made the difference when, as a popsicle seller, Brown ended up involved in university music festivals, where his songs invariably received prizes. Inspired by the streets, Brown derives much of his sound from his ability to listen to all kinds of city noises. His incursions into neighborhoods such as Pelourinho and Liberdade also played a major part in his development. In the 1970s, the negritude movement arose in Salvador, drawing upon information arriving on records and images from the United States, Jamaica, and African countries such as Angola, Senegal, and Benin. As Milton Moura notes, "The core of the imports came James Brown's soul music, Jimi Hendrix's rock, and the Jackson Five's choreography, with a teenager Michael Jackson. Little by little black role models were constituted" (1987: 14).

The first signs of this process were noticed in Liberdade, the most populous black neighborhood in Latin America and home to the bloco afro Ilê Aiyê, a vigorous expression of black pride in Salvador. An Afro-Bahian Carnaval group, Ilê Aiyê was decidedly countercultural, affirming black pride in a society that was characterized by obvious racism. The Ilê Aiyê song that brought the group to the streets in the Carnaval celebrations of 1975 highlights what the essayist Antonio Risério (1981) has called the "re-Africanization of Bahian Carnaval":

Que bloco é esse?	What is this group?
eu quero saber	I'd like to know
é o mundo negro	it's the black world
que viemos mostrar pra você	we came to show you
somos crioulo doido, somos bem legal temos	we're crazy blacks, we're cool
cabelo duro, somos "bleque pau"	our hair is kinky, we're "black power"

Brown's antennae quickly led him to Liberdade, where James Brown was adored by all, as he recalls: "If your dance was cool, if you brought something new, it was OK, otherwise the guys would say 'you're not *brau* [brown]'" (quoted in Lima 1997: 17). The word *brau* in that context refers to the aesthetics adopted by black people. It was a derogatory form of treatment, denoting "bad taste," used by whites to refer to people from Bahia who acknowledged their blackness. But blacks gave it such a positive meaning that Carlinhos adopted it as his last name.[1]

Brown's artistic experiences in Salvador were linked to the Afro-Bahian musical movement that started to take shape in the outskirts of the city between the late 1970s and early 1980s through Carnaval organizations known as *blocos afro*. The iconic sound of the blocos afro movement was samba-reggae, a genre that exploded nationally in the 1990s and internationalized Afro-Bahian musical production (Guerreiro 2000). Brown composed several songs that became hits through the voices of other singers, but he remained invisible. In 1986 he was invited to be Caetano Veloso's percussionist and was finally acknowledged as a composer for larger audiences with the song "Meia Lua Inteira" (Full Half Moon), on Veloso's album *Estrangeiro* (1989).

Timbalada, the band conceived by Brown in 1992, put Candeal on the musical map of Salvador by making body painting and the use of *timbaus* (a light drum with highly resonant plastic heads) their trademarks. The band, composed of three vocalists and twenty-seven percussionists, released nine albums, all produced by Brown. They quickly achieved international recognition when *Billboard* considered *Timbalada* the best album of 1993 in Latin America. The timbau was not chosen randomly, as Carlinhos Brown attributes a spiritual meaning to it: "The timbau has a soul. It cannot live without its soul. It is phallic, it is movement. It is always pointing to the earth, the ground. The timbau is not the dream of rising, but that of settling down" (interview, Salvador 5 March 2005).

Those who visit Candeal today can hardly imagine how different the place was before the 1990s. A low-income and socially excluded population found its home on mud-covered streets with precarious sanitary conditions and in houses and shacks in terrible states, often leaning on slippery slopes. In the absence of a public transportation system, schools, and health centers, the place had all the characteristics of a slum. A panoramic view suggested some kind of complex and unfinished housing project, with a rough topography that connected the upper and lower parts of Candeal Pequeno. Most houses were made of wood or adobe and built by the owners themselves. There were only a few brick houses. The internal spaces, usually shared by many people, were confused and multifunctional. Living rooms doubled as bedrooms, and kitchens could be spaces to hang clothes to dry. Among the humble pieces of furniture, TV sets had a prominent position. Bathrooms, if there were any, could be separated by a curtain. To this day, there are still no set boundaries between public and private spaces. Household activities take place in streets, paths, alleys, stairways, and squares, which are also places for youth leisure—soccer, bicycle riding, as well as card games and dominos (a favorite pastime for the large unemployed adult population of the area).[2] With little money circulating, local businesses serve only the basic local needs—small markets, grocery stores, barbershops, and bars, often attached to the houses.

Candeal Pequeno is a densely populated subdivision (about 5,500 people within forty acres) of the Brotas neighborhood, located in a large area at the core of the Itapagipe Peninsula, which provides the geographical contour of Salvador. The Brotas neighborhood is divided into areas that are clearly class defined. Vila Laura, Engenho Velho, and Acupe are mostly middle-class areas, while the upper classes live in Horto Florestal. Topographically, Candeal Pequeno is the lowest part of the neighborhood and has the derogatory nickname Ilha dos Sapos, or "Toads' Island." With regard to architecture and urban space in Candeal, a major intervention came in November 1996 with the inauguration of Candyall Guetho Square, a cultural space that houses Carlinhos Brown's production offices, a musical studio, and the Timbalada rehearsal space. A kind of temple for Candeal, referred to as the Guetho, this space held the first meetings to discuss urban development projects. These developments led to a community project named Tá Rebocado, one of the boldest that Carlinhos Brown launched through the NGO known as Pracatum (short for Associação Pracatum Ação Social). Tá Rebocado is an expression with double meaning: *rebocar* means to apply finishing touches to a construction, but it is also a local slang meaning "for sure!"

Before the opening of the Guetho, Timbalada rehearsed on the streets. As they began to attract viewers, the rehearsals were transferred to the local sports court. There was a significant flow of people, but the move to the Guetho stage started bringing around 2,500 young people to Candeal on Sunday afternoons. The public was mostly nonblack, upper-class and middle-class youngsters attracted by the band. The regular events gave informal jobs to street vendors and bouncers, but were also a nuisance to the community. The main streets were paved by the town administration the same year that Guetho was opened, putting an end to taxi drivers' refusals to take passengers to Candeal Pequeno. Timbalada brought journalists, filmmakers, photographers, artists, and researchers from all over the country and the world. They surely helped elevate the local population's self-esteem.

Many in the Candeal community know the history of how the neighborhood was founded in the eighteenth century, when a free African woman bought some land and settled with her children and grandchildren. Legend has it that the family brought from the west African coast a stone that represented Ogum, Candeal's patron *orisha* (Yoruba deity), associated with Saint Anthony in the syncretism with Catholicism. Antônio is Brown's first name and a spiritual son of Ogum. According to Ari Lima, who carried out field research in Candeal in 1995, residents claim a common history and a local tradition that weaves religious universes and family ties (2001). This can be noticed in the care for Ogum's House, a small area surrounded by a low white wall where the orisha's stone is kept. Tradition is also maintained in the relationships that are established near the two water springs that used to supply residents with fresh water before being polluted by industrial waste. Those springs are still an alternative for baths and laundry for those who do not have appropriate spaces at home. The constant presence of children and people doing laundry makes the springs an important space for socializing. These places, as well as the candomblé *terreiros* (sacred compounds for this Afro-Brazilian religion), are sanctuaries to the community. They became widely known due to Carlinhos Brown's "Dandalunda," a Bahian Carnaval hit of 2003 recorded by Margareth Menezes:

Bem pertinho da entrada do Guetho	Very near the entrance to the Guetho
no terreiro de angola e ketu	in the angola and ketu terreiros
Mãe Maiamba que comanda o centro	Mother Maiamba is in charge
Dona Oxum dançando Oxossi no tempo	Dona Oxum dancing Oxossi in time
Lá em cima do tamarindeiro	On top of the tamarind tree
Marinha da pipoca ajoelha	Marinha the popcorn vendor kneels
Em janeiro, no dia primeiro	On January first
Desce o dono do terreiro	The lord of the terreiro descends[3]

The respected Mãe Maiamba, the *ialorixá*, or priestess, who rules the Mutuiçara candomblé and whose ancestors include nations such as Angola and Ketu, has been a spiritual guide for Brown. The sense of community has always played a key role in the Tá Rebocado project under the aegis of Pracatum. The recovery of local traditional practices is one of Brown's goals in his social work, as they reinforce and update the sense of community that echoes throughout the neighborhood. The belief in a common ancestry, the great number of large families that live in adjacent houses, the shared public spaces (sacred or profane) such as the Guetho, the springs, the candomblé terreiros, and the Largo do Tamarindeiro, all strengthen ties and address questions related to urban violence.

The work of the Pracatum—centered on education, urban development, health, and the generation of income and employment—was essential to transforming the community. From December of 1997 to March of 1999, the population was invited to discuss the neighborhood's priorities and to come up with suggestions. The community had to trust strangers who, in their turn, had to translate the technical languages of engineering, architecture, sanitation, and sociology into something understandable to people with little or no formal education. Many previously illiterate adults were taught how to read and write, and youth registered for workshops in art education. There were campaigns for disease prevention and job training. Some residents were hired to work in construction sites, generating income and more business for the area.

In 2001, the first stage of the project was inaugurated. Data from the Pracatum indicate that 122 houses were built for the community, 142 were renovated, and 196 were painted, while sanitary installations were built in 61 units. Other results included the expansion of water, sewage, and lighting systems; the opening of access for cars; improvements to soccer fields; the construction of a community center; the recovery and enlargement of two other community centers; the recovery of degraded areas with the establishment of the Praça das Artes (Square of the Arts), and the construction of a health center. This transformation had an impact on the community. One of the most dedicated activists in Pracatum, the administrator and educator Selma Calabrich, believes that "the pride of being from Candeal reflects a strong historical and cultural identity as well as the sense of belonging to a creative and elegant community that symbolizes resistance and achievement" (interview, Salvador, 2001). Pracatum was recognized by UNESCO, which gave it the Best Practice Award in the youth category, as one of the 100 best social practices in the world. It is among the Brazilian top ten.

Tá Rebocado and the School for Music and Technology are the two projects developed by Pracatum. Designed by Carlinhos Brown, they link art to citizenship. The professionals responsible for the workshops in art education offered to the Candeal youth by the Tá Rebocado project were also in charge of designing Pracatum's pedagogy. The workshops aimed at stimulating creativity and broadening the cultural range of the apprentices. They involved theatrical improvisation, the manufacturing of musical instruments, the audition of eclectic repertoires, singing, musical composition, and debates on topics such as entrepreneurship, social mobilization, and youth involvement. For two years (1997–98), around twenty educators, playwrights, anthropologists, musicians, social workers, and psychologists worked with sixty children and teenagers. The outcome of the workshops was presented at the Guetho. The performances included music and theater equipped with masks and costumes developed by the pupils themselves.

Many current social projects attempt to enact social transformations through art education. Brown also created a group called Lactomia, through which 120 children learned to make percussion instruments out of cans, buckets, and tubes. They participated in Ivaldo Bertazzo's show Stage, Academy, and Periphery in July 1997 at SESC Pompéia in São Paulo. The choreographer, who works with young people excluded from full citizenship, argues that "rhythmic exercise has the ability to discipline and organize the mind, to connect it to the body, thereby providing better psychomotor performance for both body and mind."[4] Through these citizen-artists, children from Candeal got to know the largest city in South America and made direct contact with kids in the Bate Lata Band from Campinas, São Paulo, and in the Funk'n' Lata Band from Rio de Janeiro, as well as with children from the favela Monte Azul in São Paulo, all of whom were also involved in social projects in their hometowns. Music is a powerful link and Pracatum's strategy inserted Candeal residents in a wide network that allowed them to broaden their horizons through the exchange of experiences. The same happened to Timbalada percussionists, who got to visit dozens of countries. Music here deserves the credit for deterring community members from the influence of criminality.

Other peripheral neighborhoods in Salvador, such as Liberdade and Periperi, have had positive experiences with music education. The blocos afro that emerged in these areas strive to improve the quality of their communities' lives and have all founded schools of percussion. Examples are the Ara Ketu School, the Olodum Creative School, and Ilê Aiyê's Erê School. Established in 1974, Ilê Aiyê was the first bloco afro. One of the main differences between the blocos afro, especially Ilê Aiyê, and Pracatum, relates to their positions on miscegenation. Whereas the leaders of Ilê Aiyê have adopted an Afrocentric, black-identified position, Carlinhos Brown has emphasized his mixed heritage.

If, as Simon Frith claims, "music constructs our sense of identity through the experiences it offers of the body, time, and sociability, experiences which enable us to place ourselves in imaginative cultural narratives" (1996: 275), Candeal musical production reaffirms feelings of belonging and differentiation and enables privileged access to the musical market. Carlinhos Brown and Timbalada have become stars who advertise products including jewelry, beer, and mobile phone services, and promote government campaigns to promote citizenship rights. Pracatum has also partnered with the Panorama Percussivo Mundial — Percpan (World Percussive Panorama), which brought together musicians from different parts of the world for alternative activities not taking place at its official site, the Castro Alves Theater, the largest and most important in the city. The Percpan festival is a privileged moment for the world of percussion in Salvador. First organized by Gilberto Gil and Naná Vasconcelos, the festival hosts some of the most important percussionists in the world. It has taken place annually since 1994, with ample coverage from the local, national, and international media, making Salvador "the percussion capital of the world." Although in the last years it has lost some of its power and prestige, guest musicians still hold workshops, as well as concerts, in which an intense exchange of information takes place. These workshops bring together aspiring musicians and great masters of percussion.

Pracatum encourages the participation of Candeal youngsters in these workshops. They have been able to exchange information with masters such as Doudou Rose (Senegal), Savion Glover (United States), Zakir Hussain (India), and Aja Addy (Ghana). The *pangolo*, the emblematic drum of Ghana; the *taiko*, the drum of Japan's Buddhist temples; and the Indian *tabla*, for instance, have been incorporated into youth's musical knowledge. Across from the Guetho, Brown's recording studio, Ilha dos Sapos, subverts the stigma of the neighborhood's old nickname and is a converging point for musicians with different backgrounds. Studio albums are recorded with the artist's label, Candyall Music. The pop stars Marisa Monte and Arnaldo Antunes were regular visitors when they recorded the chart-topper recording *Tribalistas* with Brown. Also present were names such as Cheikh Lô and Manolo Garcia. It was there that the Salvador star Margareth Menezes recorded her album *Afropop Brasileiro*, produced by Brown.

That microcontext reorganizes notions of center and periphery in a constant flow. The three-story building of the Pracatum School is located about a hundred yards from other important sites on Paulo Afonso Street, one of Salvador's most cosmopolitan areas, where a stairway named Bob Marley often becomes a rehearsal stage for local bands. As the writer Zuenir Ventura notes in *Da Favela para o Mundo* (From the Slum to the World)—an account of a successful NGO experience in Rio that gave birth to circus, theater, and dance groups, in addition to bands with international visibility such as AfroReggae—the high standards of these experiences imply a wholly different "professional awareness, sense of responsibility, and notion of labor" (2003: 10).

In order to develop abilities and transform street musicians into qualified professionals able to find their place in a highly competitive job market, the Pracatum school teaches a broad repertoire from the Brazilian songbook, including MPB (Música Popular Brasileira), the eclectic song tradition that emerged in the 1960s. The Pracatum school is one of the few in the country to devote itself to the teaching of MPB, as this was the line of research adopted by the new team in charge of the pedagogical project. Aderbal Duarte (conducting and composition), Sérgio Souto (conducting and composition), Kitty Canário (body and voice), and Eduardo Fagundes (horns) have a long history in common. They created one of the most respected private music schools in Salvador, located in an upper-class neighborhood and attended by upper-class and middle-class youngsters. After twenty years, they closed the school and took on the challenge of educating a new type of clientele: Candeal street musicians. The percussionist Giba Conceição joined a highly qualified team, whose profile could be characterized as academic and research oriented as well as artistic, creative, socially responsible, and active in the market.

The Music and Technology Professional School is a nonprofit organization that invests in the education of young people, providing them with transit and access in society. They are conceived as professionals who utilize the transformational potential of art education in order to produce citizens. The actions of the Pracatum are rooted in previous knowledge and the community's cultural context. Music and citizenship are the conceptual axes of the project, designed to offer a four-year professionalizing course divided into two stages: preparatory and professional. The care with people and their cultural context has guided the general conception of the inaugural pedagogical project led by the school coordinator, the conductor Aderbal Duarte, who says, "When you pull music away from its cultural context, it becomes mechanical, learned simply through theoretical cerebral bases" (Duarte, interview, Salvador, 2002). Comparing the composition process he devised for students of the Pracatum to the method of the UFBA (Music School of the Federal University of Bahia), he says: "At UFBA one learns how to write for an orchestra modeled on a European classical music conservatory. Things are different at Pracatum, as our process starts by gathering elements that feed creativity, sensitivity, and knowledge of popular songs" (Duarte, interview, Salvador, 2002).

The school offers five areas of specialization: guitar, keyboards, percussion, voice, and musical education. The goal of the project is to form citizen-musicians, and students share this expectation. But the ability to form professionals has always been a controversial topic. Among the faculty, there were divergent views on what constituted a professional. There was also some uncertainty as to what competencies should be developed along the learning process. As the number of lectures (highly appreciated by students in general) and other activities especially designed to combine citizenship and music decreased, notions of citizenship began to be passed along in a far more informal way, as pointers and suggestions given in one-to-one interactions with teachers. Despite its great value, this informal procedure was not enough to ensure that the originally set goals would be reached. As the former executive director of the APAS, Caius Brandão, remarks:

> The results obtained by the school are exceptional from the academic standpoint. However, its social results are less than satisfactory, given the school's potential and the community's demand, as well as the institution's wish to accomplish its mission. There is always the danger of becoming an MPB conservatory with no ties to the social work experience. (Brandão, interview, Salvador, 2002)

An institutional crisis took place in the school's third year, 2001, when the first preparatory class entered the professional stage. Many factors set off the crisis that halted classes in 2002. The building was structurally unfit for pedagogical activities. The absence of windows not only blocked natural lighting, but also prevented any immediate connection with the local environment. The space caused a claustrophobic feeling and jeopardized interaction with the neighborhood's daily life. The shape of the building was also detrimental to the interaction that took place in the stairways, requiring repetitive and tiring moves. The spatial inadequacy reached insurmountable proportions when it prevented the development of the originally proposed methodology, based on individual and group classes. Voice lessons, for instance, were quite affected by the use of air conditioning, which affects breathing techniques. Pracatum's lack of didactic resources also made it difficult to maintain a regular school routine. It demanded constant adaptation and established a culture of improvisation, which manifested itself, for example, in the absence of a library or of audio and video material. Students only had some access to materials that teachers, as experienced researchers, brought from their private collections. Besides leading to a work overload for teachers, this solution did not meet students' research needs or create an environment that favored curiosity and discoveries. The lack of a studio prevented students from expanding their ability to experiment with technology.

In addition to structural issues, there was a general need for Carlinhos Brown's presence at the school. His presence, in many instances, could ensure integration. The school expected a more intense exchange with the founding musician, who they saw as playing an important part in the community not only as mentor or role model, but also as the engineer of the institution's social mission. While there was a general feeling that periodical meetings with Brown were necessary, he disagrees: "Pracatum should not be Carlinhos Brown's school. It is a percussion school. It is a school of Brazilian popular music born in this neighborhood" (Brown, interview, Salvador, 2005). There are expectations of Carlinhos Brown that have not been fulfilled. He often finds himself either in the position of myth or employer of students who happen to master the necessary requirements to participate in his musical activities. Students' prospects of insertion into the job market seem to depend on Brown opening doors for them. The market is still seen as a fictitious entity that only materializes with the concrete participation of a few students who operate in this sphere, mainly in shows led by Brown himself. This has produced tension among students, born from the perception that there were different or uneven strata inside the school, as playing with Brown was a sign of status. Besides damaging conviviality, this situation often reinforced the dream of being noticed by an allegedly exceptional talent.

By 2005, the school had become the greatest challenge for its creator. It was necessary to fulfill expectations and maintain the notion of overcoming difficulties in this community's imaginary. Yet if in his own neighborhood Brown is worshiped as a demigod, his position in Salvador has several nuances. His work is quite polemical. Opinions on his work vary from brilliant to banal, from avant-garde to reactionary. His albums sales are insignificant, and he hardly ever has concerts in town as a solo artist. His lyrics incorporate terms from the candomblé liturgy, in addition to stylized descriptions of the Afro-Brazilian religion rituals. This places him at odds with some intellectuals and candomblé followers, who consider the use of symbols and rites as sacrilegious, especially because his songs are played during Salvador's Carnaval, one of the largest profane street parties in the world, where they end up attracting more and more tourists interested in local "exoticism."

Bahian artists' regular references to the Afro-Brazilian religious universe reflect the transit between the sacred and the profane, which is one of the marks of Salvador's culture, noticeable in the extensive calendar of municipal parties. Of the five most widely played songs in Salvador's 2004 Carnaval, four make direct reference to the religious universe and three were composed by Brown. According to date of ECAD (Escritório Central de Arrecadação e Distribuição), which manages musicians' copyright, they are

"Maimbê Dandá" sung by Daniela Mercury; "Rumba de Santa Clara" performed by the group Chiclete com Banana; and "Dandalunda" sung by Margareth Menezes.

Black cultural production is one of the greatest attractions in the city, and music is its major achievement. Local musicians find in candomblé one of its most vigorous sources of inspiration. The rise of Carnaval music produced in Salvador began to take shape in the 1980s through samba-reggae, a genre created by the blocos afro. When they adopted harmonic instruments, they showed all the weight of this style's acoustic percussion in the midst of keyboards, horns, guitars, and basses. The fusion of samba-reggae and Bahian *frevo* gave birth to *axé music*, the best example of a successful form of commercial Afro-pop music that incorporates a sacred term of candomblé into its name.

Wherever it is produced, Brown's music builds an extremely varied musical mosaic where we see the integration and interaction of craft and cybernetics, tradition and innovation, roots and antennas, high technology and tribal impulse. It has an aesthetics of miscegenation that gets more and more attention in the contemporary global scene. One of Carlinhos Brown's recent Carnaval inventions, the *camarote andante* (an exclusive moving skybox for Carnaval revelers), brought 400,000 people to the streets of Barcelona in June 2004 and launched the career of "Carlito Marrón" in the Spanish phonographic market. In order to emphasize the nuances of his miscegenation, he recovers the seeds scattered by Pintado do Bongô, and demonstrates his versatility as a musician while paving his way in the European and Hispanic American markets. Brown's incursions in Spain attracted the film director Fernando Trueba to Candeal.[5] Trueba made a movie that paid homage to the community and won the Goya award for its soundtrack. Candeal's street musicians, its people, and its children saw themselves as protagonists of a movement that brought the city's periphery into the world media.

In 2009, Pracatum was incorporated into the state public education system as one of several Centros de Educação Profissional do Estado da Bahia (Centers of Professional Education of Bahia State) and received a new name: Pracatum: Centro Estadual de Educação Profissional em Artes e Design (State Center of Professional Education in Arts and Design). Candeal can still have quiet days when there are no classes at the music school, events at the Guetho, or artists recording at Ilha dos Sapos studio.

1. Two other American "Browns" inspired Carlinhos to adopt the word as his last name: The escaped slave from Virginia Henry "Box" Brown and the Black Panther H. Rap Brown. This act of naming is not, however, devoid of conflict: "The use of the name 'Brown' interferes with my desire to be recognized as a Brazilian" (Brown, interview, Salvador, 5 March 2005).

2. The UFBA conducted a census in 1997 that provided the following data for the neighborhood: 29 percent were unemployed, 42 percent were salaried workers, 16 percent were informal workers, 18 percent were self-employed, and 11 percent were retired. Of the economically active population, 78 percent earned one minimum salary, and 6.46 percent were illiterate. Only 0.9 percent of that population had a complete college education, and 0.8 percent had an incomplete college education.

3. The religious calendar of the candomblé terreiro has Ogum as a patron and follows the tradition of holding the party devoted to him on 1 January.

4. Ivaldo Bertazzo, program notes to performance "Palco, academia e periferia," São Paulo, 17 August 1997.

5. The Spanish director Fernando Trueba remarks: "When you see the children from Candeal, something changes inside of you. They are happier than those of any European urban area" (www.milagrodecandeal.com.br).

::: Of Mud Huts and Modernity

The Performance of Civic Progress in

Arcoverde's São João Festival

Daniel Sharp

Lula Calixto's public profile shifted markedly during the last decade of his life. In the early 1990s in Arcoverde, Pernambuco, he was principally known as an eccentric candy vendor who taught children to sing *samba de coco*.[1] By the end of the decade, however, the small commercial center on the edge of the northeastern *sertão* (backlands) had begun to celebrate him as a local hero of popular culture—a reservoir of vanishing musical knowledge. When he died of Chagas' disease in 1999, his funeral brought together artists, teachers, politicians, a trade union, representatives of the MST (Movimento dos Trabalhadores Rurais Sem Terra; Landless Rural Workers' Movement), and other sectors of the public sphere. The procession filled the streets with mourners.

Lula was proud of the acclaim that he received near the end of his life as a composer and performer of samba de coco; he once expressed the belief that "with the success of my group came the recognition that I was a citizen" (Micheliny Verunschk, personal communication, 6 November 2003), a sense of belonging he felt he lacked as a member of the working poor. Lula's assessment of his status as bearer of culture offers an entrance into this ethnographic rendering of performance and cultural citizenship at a festival advertised as a posthumous tribute to him: Arcoverde's 2004 São João celebration.

In the mid- to late 1990s, several agendas converged, placing samba de coco on a symbolic pedestal as a valuable cultural tradition believed to be on the verge of disappearing, and naming Lula as a keeper of this cultural memory. Postdictatorship efforts within film and popular music to rediscover an authentic "deep" Brazil distinct from urban, coastal Brazil (Bentes 2003; Labaki 2003) dovetailed with redoubled efforts to promote tourism in the sertão. Media attention turned to previously silenced configurations of identity politics, for instance, markedly Afro-Brazilian cultural practices such as samba de coco in the *mestiço* cowboy culture of the Pernambucan sertão. Samba de coco became the postcard image of Arcoverde, chosen by politicians seeking to portray themselves as being "of the people" and distinguished the city from surrounding areas. Lula's family group, Samba de Coco Raízes de Arcoverde (Coco Raízes), began to travel throughout the state of Pernambuco and perform on festival stages sponsored by the Ministry of Culture and private institutions such as the sesc (Serviço Social do Comércio; Social Service of Commerce Center). The coronation of Lula and his group as celebrated bearers of tradition—representatives of the region's essence—coincided with their entrance into the industries of tourism and culture.

Samba de coco's ascension to the status of Arcoverde's emblematic cultural tradition is intertwined with the career trajectory of Cordel do Fogo Encantado (known as Cordel), a nationally acclaimed art pop group from Arcoverde considered a part of the "diverse estuary" of mangue bit (or mangue beat), a 1990s music scene from the Pernambucan state capital, Recife (see Avelar's chapter in this volume, Galinsky 2002; Sharp 2001; and Teles 1998, 2000). As teenagers, the lead singer, Lirinha, and the guitarist, Clayton Barros, learned samba de coco melodies from Lula Calixto and *reisado* songs from Arcoverde's Reisado de Caraíbas in a kind of musical apprenticeship.[2] By the end of the decade, as Cordel toured throughout Brazil, they constantly paid tribute to their hometown Arcoverde, and cited the influence of samba de coco and reisado in their music. Cordel's popularity inspired their fans to travel to Arcoverde in search of the roots of the band's sounds. Coco Raízes received these visitors, performed for them, and gained recognition in their own right. The São João Festival (Arcoverde's most important annual touristic enterprise) was the event when Cordel, Coco Raízes, and the Reisado de Caraíbas—that is, experimental art pop interpreter and traditional sources—played at the same event.

By 2004, several competing narratives could be discerned within the São João Festival. The municipal government attempted to place a range of performances within an overarching teleological narrative representing certain groups as Arcoverde's past, and others as its present and future. These efforts were evident in the spatial configuration and decorations of various festival zones, each with a contrasting performance venue. The delineation of these zones—from a nostalgic "staged village" reenacting the town's origins, to a contemporary stage with conspicuous state-of-the-art technology—betrayed the administration's mixed feelings toward the marginal-turned-traditional musicians placed on display to prove that the city remembers its cultural roots. Underlying my analysis of the festival's various performances is Jesús Martín-Barbero's formulation that the ambivalence of elites toward popular customs and folklore has led to an uneasy mixture of "abstract inclusion and concrete exclusion" (1987: 15–16). What, at first glance, appeared to be simply a celebration of a place and all of its inhabitants, upon further scrutiny reveals a ascending series of stages, in both senses of the word: stages of development, and scaffolded stages upon which musicians perform.

The spatial organization of the festival revealed a tension between the state-sponsored festival's rhetoric of social inclusion and the persistence of severe social inequality that undercuts the full cultural citizenship of a large portion of the population. Richard Flores's analysis of the "re-membering" and "dis-membering" of a social body through the performance of Los Pastores in San Antonio, Texas, resonates here. Like the Los Pastores troupe, performers in Arcoverde struggle—with varying success—against the performers and the audience becoming "dis-membered from the present" and each other (Flores 1997: 146) by the processes that package a cultural form for touristic consumption. While granting musicians acclaim and remuneration, this process ultimately both helps and hinders the performers' striving for full cultural citizenship.

Cordel and, subsequently, Coco Raízes, have leveraged their success in Recife and throughout Brazil to raise their stature locally within the festival. By 2004, they were performing not just on the smaller, rustic cultural/traditional stage as they had in years past, but headlining on the main stage—now named after Lula—at the festival's height on Dia de São João. But despite this hard-won recognition, both groups continued to struggle against being viewed through a blurred lens of national-cultural nostalgia as fetishes of culture loss, ultimately distanced from the national "here and now."

::: A Museum Made of Mud

During the first week of June, a temporary *casa de taipa* (a house made out of mud) was erected in downtown Arcoverde's main traffic circle. During the ten days of the São João Festival, it would serve as a museum in honor of two samba de coco musicians: Lula Calixto and Ivo Lopes. Once completed, the mud shack resembled those found on the outskirts of town and nearby rural areas. Within the festival area, the mud house was located in the center of a staged village portraying the first settlement of Arcoverde. As workers slapped mud on a frame of wooden slats, poor *arcoverdenses* inquired as to whether the government was building free housing for the poor on such prime real estate. They asked if they could be placed on a waiting list. After the previous year's festival, a family squatted in a mud house in the traffic circle until the municipal government, fearing political fallout from the episode, paid for their bus tickets to return to their relatives' home.

The confusion between the mud house's intended purpose as a temporary museum and the perception that it was a coveted dwelling condenses a tension underlying the festival. The mud house museum plays a role in a narrative of civic progress implied in the spatial layout of the São João Festival. The staged village anchors the festival's epicenter to the city's past, conjuring a caricatured image of the town's origins. This "what came before" constructed of mud and palm leaves serves as a contrast to zones framed as modern and contemporary. By placing a mud house in the center of town and presenting it as an artifact from the past, the city is doing more than merely creating a quaint festival atmosphere: the mud hut can also be seen as a reminder of how far the city has come in its seven decades of existence. The appearance of squatters and waiting list seekers, however, disrupts this attempt to banish mud houses to the past, serving as a reminder that similar shelter persists today on the poorest edges of town.

::: Music and Politics in Arcoverde

During the year that I lived in Arcoverde, politics and music were closely allied. Music enlivened political events and helped delineate constituencies; politics shaped the city's soundscape by structuring events and valorizing or ignoring genres. City-sponsored concerts echoed at high volume from the plaza on an almost biweekly basis, audible in a significant concentric ring around downtown, reaching half of the city until early in the morning. During these performances, announcers declared the concerts to be a service the current administration was offering, placing the cultural events on par with infrastructural projects and other government initiatives.

During the campaign season, trucks flanked with large speakers delivered tape loops of relentless political jingles as they drove through the town's residential neighborhoods. There was a flurry of *showmícios*, a newly coined term combining entertainment—a show—with a *comício*, or political rally. Two main types of showmícios took place during the campaign: a stationary showmício, and an *arrastão*. At a stationary showmício, one side of the temporary stage was crammed with the candidate's family and political allies. A band—usually a *forró estilizado* group[3]—played on the other side of the stage. The candidates then clapped and swayed, to give the impression that they liked the music. The fact that the candidates were willing to dance to the same music as the cheering crowd was used as a display of solidarity with the voters in the audience. The singers, for their part, added rhymes praising the candidates, and led cheers between the songs.

During the São João Festival the nexus of music and politics was not as obvious as it is at the campaign showmícios. There were no cheers for candidates during the São João Festival. Nevertheless, in subtle and not-so-subtle ways, the municipal government's efforts to frame the meaning of the festival permeated its structure and how arcoverdenses understood it. It was not uncommon for performers to recognize politicians and other important figures in the audience, thanking them for their presence or exclaiming, for example, "[The mayor] Doutora Rosa sure likes to dance samba de coco!" São João played a part in what I heard many call the *pastoril político*,[4] meaning that the colors one wore to the festival connoted one's allegiance to a political party and their candidates. Candidates bought matching T-shirts for traditional groups in their party's colors. An internal struggle took place within one traditional group over the colors of their matching outfits.

::: São João Begins: The Downtown Festival Area

On the principal downtown traffic circle, music categorized as "traditional" and "cultural" was played in a *palhoça*, a temporary wall-less shelter with a stage decorated with palm fronds. The principal attractions of the Ivo Lopes stage, night after night, were samba de coco, reisado, and other folkloric groups. This performance venue festooned with markers of rusticity was located next to a staged village advertised as reenacting the town's origins.

In the center of the staged village stood a thatched roof gazebo. Under its canopy, one or two couples danced forró, dressed in exaggerated, clownlike representations of *matutos* (rural "hicks"). The band stood in a closed circle on the pavement next to the thatched gazebo, dressed in the colors of Rosa Barros' political coalition—members wearing matching yellow shirts and red handkerchiefs around their necks—stone-faced as they played for hours at a time.

As I proceeded farther west, past the gazebo, the traditional/cultural area in the center of the festival quickly gave way to a gauntlet of makeshift bars leading to the large open area where the audience stood, their backs to the staged village, and listened to the events at the Lula Calixto main stage. The area outside the staged village was thoroughly plastered with beer ads featuring a nationally prominent spokesmodel dressed as a *matuta*. To the right were two stories of *camarote*, temporarily erected VIP party rooms where people in politics, business, and the press pay for a privileged vantage point of the scene.

::: Samba de Coco Raízes de Arcoverde

Coco Raízes was the most visible group in the São João promotional materials. Tourism magazines and pamphlets carried images of the group. After years of playing a minor role in the annual festival, Coco Raízes' success at Recife's Carnaval and elsewhere raised their stature at home. The main stage of the festival was named in honor of Lula Calixto, and Coco Raízes was the only group performing at São João that performed at both the cultural stage and the main stage.

Coco Raízes were experts at engineering a jubilant mood, succeeding in coaxing even the most hesitant audience to dance. The singer Ciço Gomes and his son Fagner constantly sought eye contact with the audience. Much of the appeal of the group derived from their virtuoso feet, hands, and tongues. Vocal skills came in the form of improvisation, and rapid-fire dexterity. Ciço Gomes was the only singer in the group who improvised verses, but many others sang impressively and quickly. Under layers of interlocking percussion parts, the dancers performed hard-stepping patterns wearing the kind of wooden sandals featured in the festival area's archway.

During their seven festival performances, the dancers were perpetually running back and forth between the stage and the street to coax audience members to dance. Despite these efforts to soften the boundary between performance and audience, however, proximity to and distance from the culture bearers were enacted through samba de coco's two dance steps. A standard samba de coco song is divided into two parts: a verse with overlapping responsorial singing, and a rapid-fire *embolada* section with a solo singer delivering a stream of notes accented on the strong beats of the 3 + 3 + 2 timeline. Two separate dance steps, the *parcela* and the *trupé*, correspond to these two sections. In contrast to the nimble, buoyant steps of urban samba, samba de coco is stomped, the steps contributing to the layers of percussion sounds, and performers wear wooden sandals called *tamancos* in order to generate a clapping sound as the wood slaps against the ground. A section of the stage floor was covered with a piece of plywood to amplify the dance, and a microphone captured the rumbling railroad-like sounds, adding them to the PA system's mix.

The parcela is the initial step that is danced during the verses of the songs. Aligned with the 3 + 3 + 2 timeline, it is not as quick as the trupé, making it easier to learn. When the quicker embolada section begins, the dancers accelerate their total steps per cycle of the timeline from three to eight, stomping continuously with alternating feet (left-right-left-right . . .) on each eighth note, and accenting the triple pulse at the beginning of each measure. In the diagram below, the stressed steps are in uppercase, while the lighter steps are in lowercase. Each letter represents an eighth note, and the periods stand for rests of the same length.

	3	3	2
Samba de Coco timeline	X..	X..	X.
Parcela	R..	R..	L.
Trupé	Rlr	Lrl	rl

When the verse gives way to the embolada, the parcela transitions abruptly into the trupé, and dancers are suddenly required to move their feet almost three times faster than they have been. Visitors most often reacted to the trupé section by attempting to keep up with the steps while smiling or laughing to indicate that they knew they were faking it and would soon fail. Others simply stayed with the slower parcela steps and watched in awe as Fagner and Daiane danced the trupé with ease. Inclusion and exclusion were performed through the two dance steps. While the slower parcela step was relatively simple to learn, welcoming everyone to participate, the trupé sections delineated a line between culture bearer and appreciative, sympathetic audience member. As the groups professionalized, samba de coco tempos sped up. Participation was encouraged, but it was expected that only the culture bearers would be able to do the dance with ease.

Coco Raízes' performances centered on the themes of tradition and family. The lead singer, Ciço Gomes, introduced each member of the three generations of Calixtos and Gomeses, detailing their family relationships.

He made sure the crowd knew that their matching dress was handsewn by Ciço's wife, Dona Maria. The group projected an image of humble families—unified, extended, functional—who celebrated together in musical and social harmony.

The crowd favorite "Barra da Saia" (Skirt Fringe) introduced many of these elements of the group's self-presentation. It is a call for its listeners to come visit, learn to dance samba de coco, and enjoy the group's hospitality. The lyrics evoke old-fashioned skirts so long that one could trip on them; list the group's instrumentation; introduce a difficult but exciting dance that everyone is invited to try, but not everyone does well; announce regular rehearsals that visitors can attend; and lament Lula Calixto's conspicuous absence from the celebration.

::: Reisado de Caraíbas

When the reisado group began to perform at the Ivo Lopes cultural stage, the music sounded terrific from afar—the PA system was crystal clear. As my wife, Laura, and I approached, however, it was difficult to see the performers, who were obscured by the crowd. We squeezed into a decent vantage point and saw that the elderly musicians were nowhere to be found. Suddenly, I realized that the music consisted of selections from a recent field recording session of the ethnomusicologist Carlos Sandroni that I had attended a few months before ("Responde a Roda Outra Vez," Arcoverde, 2005). The recording, which was made as part of a preservationist effort supporting the reisado group, had given the children's dance troupe the independence to perform without the adults. Later that night, I talked to Sandra, who spearheaded the children's reisado while working for the state sponsoring culture. Despondent, she told me that the majority of the adults in the reisado allied themselves with the opposition candidate, and decided for that reason that they could not perform at this year's São João Festival.

The children were tugged along by the unforgiving tempo of the CD. Without the eye contact of the Mestre, or some kind of warning before beginning the song, the dancers took a couple of bars to find the beat after the next CD track unexpectedly began. In between songs, there was little time for applause. A television news camera focused a blindingly bright light on their reflective costumes. In my camcorder recording of the television crew's filming of the event, the dancer closest to their camera dissolves into a glowing ball of light. The dancers' movements are regimented and their faces remain serious as they execute stomping scissor steps to a simple, heavy 3/4 beat.

::: Cordel do Fogo Encantado

Cordel do Fogo Encantado performed their annual homecoming show on the main stage. From my vantage point, not far from the police turret manned with an officer surveying the crowd, I could see across the plaza to the VIP party rooms. A sample of a melismatic *aboio* (cattle-herding song) floated from the left stack of speakers to the right and back again. The band emerged from the fog and colored lights that filled the stage. Three percussionists played layers of *alfaia* (type of bass drum), congas, tom-toms, and cymbals in a thunderous percussion groove. Lirinha launched into a frenzied dance that resembled a marionette desperately trying to break free from the strings that controlled it. Portraying his life as an itinerant musician who missed home, he continued to yell/sing, declaring that he would marry his *saudades* (nostalgia) and that this feeling of loss would become his intimate companion. At one point mid-song, he exclaimed, "My dear city!"

Cordel's music combined the intensity of the local rock scene with an interest in reworking elements of local folkloric traditions. Throughout the performance, Lirinha used gestures and props to contribute to a given song's dramatic impact. As he sang about vengeful justice coming to a favela, bullet sound effects caused him to convulse as if riddled with automatic gunfire. Fog, colored lights, and strobe lights accompanied songs about rain and storms; spinning, flashing lights emulated an approaching police car. As he intoned over relentless percussion, red lights glowed in the centers of the palms of his hands. As he recited a poem, he illuminated his face with a kerosene lantern. While smearing sinister clown makeup onto his face, he screamed that he was a clown in a circus without a future.

The group's most well-known song, "Chover (ou Invocação para um Dia Líquido)" (Rain [or Invocation for a Liquid Day]), exemplifies the band's attempts to rewrite the northeast's folklorized history of charismatic bandits, millenarian preachers, and drought-inspired migrations to the south. Their project is to "burn this story so badly told," as the lyrics phrase it, reinjecting a sense of urgency into figures and events they believed to be mired in layers of sedimented literary and cinematic representations of the region. "Chover," in particular, reverses the plot of Luiz Gonzaga's bleak anthem of the northeast "Asa Branca," which recounts the drought-inspired

Cordel do Fogo Encantado frontman, Lirinha, on stage, Mossoró, Rio Grande do Norte, 2009 (Daniel Sharp).

exodus from the *sertão*. Cordel's response depicts the celebration following a drought-ending downpour.

"Chover" begins with a 12/8 timeline, an .x.x.xx.x.xx bell pattern seldom used outside of *umbanda* and candomblé religious contexts.[5] In this case, rain is called to descend, not the *orixás* and *caboclos*. The pitch and fervor of Lirinha's voice rise as he recites the opening verse establishing the setting of the dry sertão, where it only rains three months a year if at all. These words are an incantation, part of "A heavy mass to make the rain fall" (Um terço pesado pra chuva descer), as one of the lyrics states. As the song begins, the percussion changes to a 4/4 feel combining elements of samba de coco and *maracatu de baque virado* (drum-heavy Afro-Pernambucan carnaval music), while retaining an undercurrent of 12/8. During the first half of the song, a chorus chants "to rain, to rain" (chover, chover) and during the second half, after the euphoric line "the bass drum thundered and the rain fell," this refrain changes to "it rained, it rained" (choveu, choveu). Before the moment in the song where the rain begins to fall, Lirinha implores the people of the sertão not to move away from their home.[6]

Lula Calixto not only influenced the band's music; he also enters the lyrics as a figure embodying folk celebration. Of the many climaxes of this song, the greatest release comes right after the declaration that the rain has indeed fallen. At this moment, the first image described is that of "Lula Calixto becoming Mateus" (Lula Calixto virando Mateus). At the apex of the song's dramatic arc, Lula Calixto is invoked to indicate that with the rain comes the celebration. He is in the process of shedding his everyday identity, and putting on the pointy hat and shiny clothes that indicate his transformation into the protean figure Mateus, the jester of the Reisado. When it rains in the sertão, according to the song, life is turned further upside down: "and abundance hides its sack / because hunger begged for alms" (E a fartura esconde o saco / Que a fome pedia esmola). In a reversal of Asa Branca's depiction of widespread hunger, bountiful crops mean that only hunger personified is forced to beg. At this point, Lirinha flips over his tambourine and mimes begging for alms to the crowd. He looks out into the crowd, pointing to his empty tambourine with anger and resignation.

Near the show's end, the band played a medley of a song they learned from Lula Calixto and a chorus that Reisado de Caraíbas would use to open their performances. The song title, "Foguete de Reis (ou a Guerra)" was derived from the interchangeable local use of the words *foguete* (firecracker), and *folguedo* (celebration), when referring to fast, raucous marches (*foguetes de roda*) in the samba de coco repertoire. Cordel's use of this conflation brought together associations of mass celebration and mass violence, and the song ended with the sound effect of a roman candle exploding. The medley was a remnant of the group's earlier days as a folkloric revue, when a large portion of the evening consisted of interpretations of well-known samba de coco and reisado repertoire. As they attained national recognition, the traditional music that they used as their source material left them vulnerable to lawsuits over royalties. As a result, their overt musical tribute to samba de coco and reisado shrank considerably. By the 2004 festival, the medley consisted of brief excerpts of two songs chosen in part due to the fact that they were so common as to be unclaimable in terms of copyright. In Cordel's travels, Lirinha had heard a variety of different versions of the samba de coco song "O Sol Saiu" (The Sun Came Out) with variations in the lyrics and melodies. The refrain "I saw my love in the cane field" served as definitive proof, Cordel believed, that despite being in local samba de coco repertoire, the song was not written there. On the edge of the arid sertão, the closest cane fields were over two hours away by car.

The reisado excerpt was used by Cordel near the end of their shows to start the process of saying good night to crowds, whose adrenaline was still

Cordel do Fogo Encantado on stage, Mossoró, Rio Grande do Norte, 2009 (Daniel Sharp).

"on high." As the opening words of the reisado, this excerpt is also the most consistently repeated by reisados throughout the neighboring states, thus leaving it less vulnerable to the claim that they had used a specific person's composition. Just as reisados often leave key refrains intact while varying other verses based on the circumstances, Lirinha sings the first three lines verbatim:

Boa noite senhor e senhora	Good night, ladies and gentleman
Eu cheguei agora	I have arrived now
Me preste atenção	Please pay attention

Then, he sings his own lines, a tribute to the "salt of the earth" in a chaotic world:

Nesse mundo de fogo e de guerra	In this world of fire and war
O santo da terra	The saint of the land
Tem calo na mão	Has calluses on his hands

In the cd booklet, these lines are cited as "Opening to the reisado, words adapted by Lirinha." By choosing the most generic, conventional reisado lyrics—the opening—they are able to cite reisado as a form, not mentioning the specific group Reisado de Caraíbas. As mentioned earlier, the risk of conflicts over copyright spurred drastic changes in Cordel's open quotations of samba de coco and reisado repertoire. Contrast Cordel's lines above with what the Reisado de Caraíbas sang at this point in the song during a recording session for Carlos Sandroni's project:

Em Caraíbas, nós somos o reisado	In Caraíbas, we are the reisado
Saindo pra fora	Leaving here for elsewhere
Somos campeões	We are the champions

A busload of members of the Cordel fan club had arrived from Recife earlier that day. The audience was divided between die-hard fans screaming, moshing, and singing along in the area in front of the stage, and the people in the two elevated areas on either side. Facing the stage, to the left were the vip galleries, where local professionals mingled with fairly disinterested, neutral expressions. On the other side were small outdoor bars that charged a fee to reserve groups of tables. This reservation system meant that most of the people sitting at these tables were middle-class and upper-class families from Arcoverde. During the performance, much of this section of the crowd appeared positively stunned. Others looked curious and quizzical, as if trying to fathom how such an unfamiliar treatment of familiar cultural elements had become synonymous with their city elsewhere in Brazil. For these arcoverdenses, Cordel's staged Arcoverde did not resemble their lived Arcoverde.

The bulk of acts playing at the Lula Calixto main stage were elaborately staged forró estilizado groups. Cordel's brooding style starkly contrasted with the manic happiness of most of the other groups sharing this stage for the festival's ten nights. Watching the range of audience members' expressions reminded me of speaking earlier with a clerk at one of the local hotels that hosted Cordel's fans from Recife. When I asked him what performances he was going to attend at the festival, he responded forró estilizado. He liked close forró dancing with his girlfriend, and insisted that forró estilizado was much closer to the local reality. Cordel's fans in contrast, he insisted, were out of touch with reality. From behind the counter in the hotel lobby, he mused that Cordel's fans had probably never even worked a day in their lives, hinting at a class divide between the band's fan base and the bulk of the festival.

Before ending their set, Cordel endorsed the rock band Cobaias (Guinea Pigs), commanding rock fans to go immediately across the street to the circus tent where they were waiting to play.

::: Guinea Pigs

On the other side of the main thoroughfare and outside the cordoned-off festival area was a line of booths proffering foosball, shooting galleries, and concessions. Next to a meager assortment of rickety amusement park rides stood a circus tent with orange, green, and white stripes. Rock bands with names such as Cobaias and Crucificados pelo Sistema (Crucified by the System) played under the big top. I was setting up my equipment to record Cobaias, when a teenager approached me to confirm tonight as the night Pastor was going to sing. His palpable excitement foreshadowed the reverence that Cobaias's congregation of young fans would bestow upon the band's appropriately named lead singer Pastor. With long dreadlocks and a worn Che Guevara T-shirt, Pastor led his flock as they moshed in a circular pattern around the center tent pole.

From the moment the group was introduced, a musical line in the sand was drawn. A friend of the band members stepped up to the mic and roundly criticized forró estilizado, *música sertaneja*,[7] vacuous pop—much of the music played down the street at the main stage. The MC instigated the crowd, who jeered these bands whose fan base—he believed—consisted of people who accepted what television foisted upon them. The tent was situated only a block or two away from the central area of the festival, but because of its placement across a relatively busy thoroughfare, it was isolated from the rest of São João, spatially, as well as in terms of collective mood. The band played heavy rock/punk grooves while Pastor growled lyrics full of righteous indignation toward social inequality, hypocrisy, poverty, and restrictive social roles. In stark contrast to the perpetual celebration within the main festival area, under the circus tent there was the perception that Pastor was singing truth to power, and his followers were listening reverently as they churned around the tent pole.

Introducing the song "Fevereiro" (February) Pastor clarified, "We have never been and will never be against Carnaval. We are against the media that uses popular festivals to cover up the inequality and social ills of this rotten society." After decrying the murder of street children, rape, political corruption, and drug violence over a muscular guitar riff, the entire band added bitter outrage to the chorus that played on alternate meanings of the word *divertido*:

Mas eis que em fevereiro	But in February
Tudo isso é esquecido	All of this is forgotten
É hora de brincar	It's time to play
É o mês mais divertido	It's the month with the most diversion
. . . .	. . . .
Esse é o país do Carnaval	This is the country of Carnaval
Assim é o Carnaval do Brasil	This is the Carnaval of Brazil
Por onze meses o país vai mal	For eleven months the country goes badly
Fevereiro é a nota mil	February is the greatest
Puta que pariu	Fucking hell

Despite the song's references to Carnaval in Rio de Janeiro, it was clear to the audience that its critique of the state's perceived ability to use music as a distraction resonated with the current setting. Strengthening this bridge between urban poverty and Arcoverde, Pastor ended "Fevereiro" by reciting bleak lines from Chico Buarque's "Construção" (Construction). Construção is a song suggesting that the social order during the years of the military dictatorship was more fragile than it seemed.[8] It recounts the story of a construction worker's last day. The protagonist's social invisibility as a member of the working poor means that his fatal fall from the scaffolding does not provoke compassion from passers-by. Instead, drivers only care that the incident caused a traffic jam on their day off:

Amou daquela vez como se fosse a última	He loved on that occasion as if it were his last
Beijou sua mulher como se fosse a última	He kissed his wife as if she were the last
Cada filho seu como se fosso o único	And each of his sons as if he were the only one
Morreu na contramão, atrapalhando tráfego	He died on the wrong side of the street, disturbing the traffic

The threat of violence at the event, however, caused this social criticism to be trumped by the perceived need for physical security. In 2004, the administration had sponsored the rock stage for the first time since it had been shut down four years before after bands used the PA system to scream obscenities at politicians. The performers were acutely aware of how tenuous this support was. Despite their diatribes lobbed at easy targets such as cheesy pop stars, they graciously thanked the mayor's office for their support. They were also outspoken in thanking the security guards for being there for everyone's safety, before the event, and later, when someone threatened to use a knife in the mosh pit. Pastor preached peace, and praised the police for subduing the knife-wielding teen. It was a delicate situation for a band with such strident anti-establishment rhetoric.

::: Up the Hill at the Alto do Cruzeiro

The neighborhood of Alto do Cruzeiro stood uphill, several blocks from the center of town. It was far enough that only fans of Coco Raízes would make the trek. A thatch-roofed palhoça blocked off the cobblestone street lined with rows of small houses. Lula's brother Assis, the main songwriter of Coco Raízes, invited me into his small house. The main room measured approximately six by ten feet. Between the television stand and the couch, there was only room for one person to stand comfortably. Two svelte, tan urban hipsters tentatively came to the doorway. Assis invited them in. They were excited, wide-eyed, and uncomfortable, looking around the small house. The moment betrayed the ambiguity of Assis's social status; recognition of Assis as an artist partially reversed traditional class hierarchies, but had not translated into a significant financial windfall for him. The scene could be seen as an encounter between a revered artist and his doting fans, between poorer people and richer people, between darker-skinned people and lighter-skinned people, or all of the above.

The urban fans' reverence for Assis was predicated on their perception of samba de coco as the embodiment of premodern cultural memory. The preservation of the genre, however, was facilitated not by a rural past located before or outside modernity, but located on its margins, subject to its dangers while excluded from its benefits. Assis and Lula were two of four children who survived out of his mother's twenty pregnancies. They grew up in a thatched-roof mud house in the arid sertão outside of Arcoverde, coming to the city fifty years before when their father found work erecting telephone poles for the electric company. Practices such as samba de coco, ignored or disdained by the middle classes less than a generation before, were now celebrated for their refusal to succumb to mass-mediated consumer culture.

I ventured out under the palhoça and into the Calixtos' bar. Unexpectedly, I recognized two acquaintances from Recife, Daniel and Camila, and sat to talk to them at a table with several of their friends. I asked Daniel why he thought that people came to Arcoverde from Recife for São João, and he responded that the "culture of high-rise apartment buildings" in Recife was cutting off cultural ties between people. As a result, in his view, there simply was not the same kind of strong cultural solidarity that you can find in a place that still has traditional culture such as Arcoverde.

He explained that Arcoverde was becoming the destination for those who were turned off by how stylized they believed the São João festivities had become in nearby interior cities such as Caruaru. Caruaru, halfway between Recife and Arcoverde, has long been the best-known getaway for urban Pernambucans celebrating São João. According to Daniel, there was a demographic of people who found Caruaru's enormous marketplace of handicrafts, quadrilha (square dance) line-dance contests, and quaint bandas de pífano (rural fife and drum bands) to be an inauthentic tourist trap. He believed Arcoverde was capitalizing on this impression by offering a São João Festival more weighted toward samba de coco, reisado, and other traditional music.

A drunken friend of Daniel's insisted that many of the visitors considered themselves superior to those from the small city. He interjected bluntly, "Yeah, well, people from Recife think they're better than people from, for example, Caruaru." Daniel added diplomatically that they had been talking earlier about rivalries between cities in the area. His friend refused to soften his statement: "No. You can just see it on their faces." He gestured to the tall, well-fed, cosmopolitan crowd isolated from the festival's center—"There's just something in their expressions. A lot of the people here think they're better than people from smaller towns."

At the Alto do Cruzeiro, Assis played multiple roles as performer, host, and souvenir salesman. The younger women in the Calixto family—Irã, Iuma, Daiane, and Damaris—also shifted between stations when they weren't performing: tending bar, waiting tables, dancing with visitors, networking, and generally making sure that everyone was in high spirits. They were the stars, the hosts, and the service staff. The smaller children also entertained the crowd, wowing them with their precocious facility at dancing and playing instruments. It was common for an older member of the family to call over three-year-old Luizinho and ask him to show off his dance steps, sing a song, or play a drum. At one performance, Assis and his grandnephew sang a duet in which they sang in harmony "It was a small house, but it was full of love." This, almost without fail, led audience members to comment on how impressive his musical abilities were for his age, and gush about how wonderful it was that they were passing on their traditional knowledge so early, to safeguard the unbroken continuation of the samba de coco tradition in Arcoverde.

::: São João's Stages of Development

The festival's story of civic progress follows a path from the thatched gazebo to the large, fully equipped stage, with its imposing stacks of enormous speakers. In one direction stood the main stage named in Lula Calixto's honor and, in the other, the mud house museum that squatters envied. It was a mud house that unwittingly resembled the kind of shack known to aid the transmission of Chagas' disease, the disease of poverty that took Lula's life five years before. The cracks in the walls and thatch atop these mud shacks harbor an insect that serves as the Chagas' disease vector.[9] The official script suggested by the juxtaposition of the gazebo and mud houses with the main stage's impressive show of technology leaves little room for the messy contradictions of this symbolic gesture of social inclusion. One may surmise, for example, that better public hospital care for Arcoverde's poor may have kept Lula Calixto alive. Instead, he was made posthumously into a hero of popular culture and his portrait hung in the quaint mud house museum at the symbolic center of the festival. The narrative implicitly told to festivalgoers walking through mud house lane to the modern stage is a teleological narrative of modernization—the story of the city's progress. The stages erected for musical performances are framed as stages of development.

The slippage between the rural, the primitive, the traditional, and the local hint that this story is being told on many nesting levels. São João, to residents of larger Brazilian cities, has become a time of year to travel to the sertão and get in touch with the nation's rural roots. To many from the south, the entire northeast suffices as a space of nostalgia. For some *recifenses*, Caruaru is becoming too industrialized in its assembly line approach to celebrating tradition; Arcoverde wins their tourist dollars with a more rustic, more "authentic" product, considered a more effective counterbalance to the alienation of "high-rise apartment building culture." Within Arcoverde proper, the poor are incorporated into a developmentalist vision of the city through the use of traditional musicians for emblematic purposes. The result is an ambivalent mixture of celebration and scorn, homage and appropriation of the marginal-turned-representative.

Cordel is ambivalent about being considered a "mangue beat" band, having come from a sertão town located far from the coastal swamps. Yet the group closely fits Avelar's description in this volume of mangue beat's reestablishment of dialogue between the allegorical engagement with the problem of political violence found in MPB (Música Popular Brasileira), and the visceral enactment of such violence through 1980s Brazilian rock performance. Cordel dialectically reconceived this opposition. The band's turbulent artistic vision adopts hard rock's aura of danger in an attempt to avoid being labeled folklore or celebratory regionalism. One moment, group members enact a hunger riot, and the next, they step back in a Brechtian fashion to sing of the centuries of unequal land distribution in the region that serves as one of the riot's root causes.

Although Cordel attempts a theatrical exorcism of the sedimented stereotypes of the northeastern sertão region, the question remains whether the group's use of traditional styles helps it accomplish this goal. In resonance with the themes of this volume as laid out in the introduction, even the most thoughtful and challenging popular music produces contradictory effects.

The festival performances detailed above suggest that Cordel's constant tributes to reisado and samba de coco traditions result in further distancing these traditional groups from the local here-and-now at the same time that they contribute to opening up performance opportunities for professionalizing traditional musicians. Cordel's popularity arose at a moment when the promotion of cultural tourism arrived deeper into the interior of the state, leading to a complex play of social exclusion and inclusion emblematic of Brazil's disjunctive democracy. These musicians actively participate, with varying degrees of success, in a cultural politics of recognition. At the same time, they also participate in performances that partially erase their modernity, distance them from the contemporary, and, through caricature, threaten to foreclose their cultural citizenship.

Consider, for example, the Reisado de Caraíbas. They did not show up for their show, despite the fact that they were prominently displayed, second only to Coco Raízes, in the festival's promotional literature as an example of the region's cultural riches. Their political opposition to the event notwithstanding, previous stage performances have left them frustrated, contributing to their hesitance. Most of the members are elderly, and at the time they were in a painful moment in their efforts to stage a performance traditionally performed roaming from home to home. This became clear at events where their performances are truncated from three hours to ten minutes. Their discomfort with staging is also evident when they do not have enough microphones, so that certain instruments and certain voices are far too loud while others remain inaudible. Due to their shiny costumes covered in tiny mirrors, and outlandish sequined hats shaped like churches and pyramids, photo-ops with the reisado were more important to city officials and some audience members than actually hearing their performances.

Coco Raízes' place within the 2004 São João festival contrasted with that of the Reisado de Caraíbas. They gained access to both the cultural stage and the main stage (named after their group's founder), and built a tourist destination in their neighborhood. Unlike the Reisado, Coco Raízes had been chosen as the representative traditional group of Arcoverde. Although they gained recognition, however, they continued to feel hemmed in by thatch, mud, and palm fronds. The strictures of the genre of traditional music dictate that they must project the image of musical stability, passed down from generation to generation within a happy family. It is a simulacrum of family and community cohesion, of an imagined premodern time when descent mattered more than consent in human relations. Their uniform dress refers to a romanticized pastoral past, contributing to the discursive distancing of the group, and relegating them to associations of another era. Their percussion and voice arrangements, bereft of any harmonic instruments, also point toward coco in Arcoverde as a variety of proto-samba. They are struggling with, and partially emerging from, folklore's assumptions of anonymity and timelessness.

Cordel inspires fans to travel in search of the roots of the band's sounds. Coco Raízes receives these musical tourists and performs these roots. In order for them to do this, they must maintain their home base in the margins, far enough but not too far from the capital. When Coco Raízes wanted to move either to Recife or the south such as Cordel had done, they were almost universally discouraged from doing so by their Recife fans, reminded that Arcoverde was their place and that they should stay there.

Cordel's sound and career are grounded by the influence of Coco Raízes and Arcoverde's other traditional music. They provide the band with musical uniqueness in a marketplace perceived as increasingly homogeneous. Cordel signifies "today," and samba de coco and reisado signify "what came before." The city's layout of the festival follows a logic of spatial and temporal displacement: the cultural stage could be seen as signifying "here, but not now," the marginalized and controversial rock stage seen as "now, but not here," and Cordel at the main stage projects their stormy version of Arcoverde's "here" and "now" to rebut forró estilizado's saccharine contemporary regionalism. And gaining access to participate in the modern here-and-now—rather than being relegated to a nostalgic past, or dismissed as not Brazilian enough—is fundamental to the recognition of the full cultural citizenship of these musicians.

DISCOGRAPHY

Cordel do Fogo Encantado. *Cordel do Fogo Encantado*. Rec-Beat Produções, 2001.
———. *O Palhaço do Circo sem Futuro*. Rec-Beat Produções, 2002.
Samba de Coco Raízes de Arcoverde. *Godê Pavão*. Via Som, 2003.
———. *Raízes de Arcoverde*. Africa Produções, 2001.
Various. *Responde a Roda Outra Vez: Musica Tradicional de Pernambuco e da Paraíba no Trajeto da Missão de 1938*. Recife, Associação Educação Meio do Mundo. Recife: UFPE; João Pessoa: UFPB, 2005.

1. Coco is a style of music and dance associated with poor blacks from the coastal northeast—the state of Pernambuco and surrounding areas. It consists of layers of percussion with a 3 + 3 + 2 habanera timeline under responsorial vocals and improvised, rapid-fire declamatory embolada sections. Coco is traditionally danced in June celebrating Saint John's day.

2. *Reisado* is a dramatic dance traditionally performed in parts of the northeast during the Christmas season. It is closely related to Folia de Reis.

3. *Forró estilizado*, or "stylized forró," is an ultrapopular style of forró—accordion-based dance music associated with the northeastern sertão but consumed throughout Brazil. Forró estilizado is performed in glitzy pop productions with drum set, horns, electronic keyboards, and large groups of background dancers, as opposed to *forró pé-de-serra*, a style with the ensemble of *zabumba* bass drum, triangle, and accordion standardized by Luiz Gonzaga.

4. *Pastoril* is a folkloric dramatic dance performed during the Christmas season in which dancers and musicians wear brightly colored costumes.

5. Gerhard Kubik (1979) traces the rhythmic timeline of these Afro-Brazilian religions to coastal West Africa.

6. It is interesting to note that Çordel wrote this song imploring inhabitants of the sertão not to leave their home while still living in Arcoverde, but their success, due in no small part to this crowd favorite, led them to move to Recife, and then to São Paulo, in order to make a living as musicians.

7. Música sertaneja typically refers to contemporary commercial country music in which tightly harmonizing male duos sing of heartbreak and longing for an idealized rural life and home.

8. For in-depth analyses of the song "Construção," see Perrone 1989: 24–29; and Béhague 1980: 444–47.

9. See J. Dias, A. Silveira, and C. Schofield, "The Impact of Chagas' Disease Control in Latin America: A Review," *Mem Inst Oswaldo Cruz* 97.5 (2002): 603–12.

:::   Mangue Beat Music and the
Coding of Citizenship in Sound

Idelber Avelar

In mid-1991, an organism/nucleus of research and creation of pop ideas
began to be gestated and articulated in several points of the city. The goal was
to engender an "energetic circuit" able allegorically to connect the swamp's
good vibrations with the worldwide network for the circulation of pop concepts. Symbolic image: a satellite dish stuck in the mud. Or a crab remixing
ANTENNA, by Kraftwerk, on the computer.

Mangueboys and manguegirls are individuals interested in chaos theory,
world music, mass-media legislation, ethnic conflicts, hip-hop, chance, Bezerra da Silva, virtual reality, sex, design, violence, and all the advances of
chemistry applied in the terrain of alteration/expansion of consciousness.

—Fred Zero Quatro, "Caranguejos com cérebro" (Crabs with brains), liner
notes to Chico Science's and Nação Zumbi's album *Da Lama ao Caos* (From
Mud to Chaos), 1994

::: The Performance

New York City, June 1995: a friend tells me that the SummerStage Concert in Central Park, featuring the Afro-Brazilian legend Gilberto Gil, will
be opened by a vocalist with an interesting name, Chico Science, backed
by his band Nação Zumbi (henceforth, CSNZ). By then they were fairly well
known in Brazil, having released their debut *Da Lama ao Caos* (From Mud
to Chaos) in 1994, but in the early days of the Internet it took an expatriate
Brazilian a trip home to have a chance to buy the fresher crop of national
music. At any rate, it was the summer of 1995, and I had not yet heard of
this fellow Chico Science or this scene called *mangue beat*. The fact that I
considered not showing up early enough for Science at all and shooting instead only for the late afternoon Gil concert is a testimony to the segmenta-

tion of Brazilian music at the time, that is, the divorce between northeastern music and the tastes of southeastern middle-class listeners such as myself. I did show up to see the whole thing after all, and little did I know that the CSNZ concert would blow me away as much as anything had ever done. The first thing that hit me was that they were mixing things that had never been mixed before. This element is not, for me, a value in itself, but in that particular instance it surely worked. I was barely aware of how profound their effects already were at that moment.

That afternoon in Central Park, Chico Science led a package of musicians who combined a rock music lineup with the large bass drums used in the Afro-Atlantic coronation dance of *maracatu*. Following the footsteps of their fellow Pernambucan Lenine, who had experimented with the format in his 1983 record with Lula Queiroga, *Baque Solto* (Teles 2000: 229), CSNZ consolidated the dialogue between the powerful beat of maracatu and the guitar, bass, and drum lineup of rock music, where the former contributed to keeping rhythm with power and precision. The band made use of electronic effects, sampling, and scratching. They resorted to language adapted from hip-hop and the Brazilian northeastern verbal art *embolada*. Their sound was no fusion: it preserved the intensity and the rhythm proper to each genre being cannibalized. There was always more than one genre going on at the same time, but they never converged toward a synthesis. The references to different genres succeeded each other in frantic speed and were juxtaposed in ways that turned out to be quite unexpected. From the monochordic music of the Afro-Brazilian martial art of *capoeira*, played over a funk groove, to samba-rock guitar over a maracatu beat, later slowed to a reggae tempo punctuated by electronic effects and fast rapping—not infrequently superimposed with a distorted guitar in heavy metal style, with wah-wah pedals—the music transgressed boundaries hitherto uncrossed. Their lyrics were radical, surrealist, outrageous, protechnology, and furiously cannibalistic of a vast repertoire. They indicated a certain approach to the globalization of cultural flows that dialogued not only with the great tradition of Brazilian lyric writing but also with global trends such as cyberpunk: "The band's style of dress as for example Ray-Ban sunglasses and the straw hats worn by Pernambucan fisherman also embodied a cross-cultural identity" (Galinsky 2002: 2). They crossed so many cultural and musical borders that a newcomer to their sound did not quite know how to classify them: were they a pop band or a folkloric group? Was that sound proper to a region of Brazil? If so, how come it resembled a cannibalization of so

Chico Science and Nação Zumbi perform at Abril Pro Rock in Recife, 1995
(Gil Vicente).

many Anglo-American or Afro-Atlantic genres, or both? If you had enough
musical information, you could tell they were drawing upon a host of different traditions, but what kind of unusual combination was that? Who were
the listeners with enough baggage to know exactly where CSNZ was coming
from?

It would be hard to describe the impression imprinted upon me by
CSNZ's hour-long sonic blast in Central Park. There was something lyrical
about them, but the music was incredibly loud and powerful; their appropriation of cultural icons familiar to me was ironic yet respectful and engag-
ing. As Gilberto Gil got up on stage to play with them, I had the sense that
for the first time in years I was seeing a Brazilian combo of youth music able
to dialogue with tradition without anxieties or excessive reverence. To this
day I consider the summer 1995 CSNZ appearance in the New York Summer-
Stage to be the most impressive performance I have ever seen by a Brazilian
band. I immediately went on to get their *Da Lama ao Caos* CD and anxiously
awaited the release of their second album.

Afrociberdelia appeared in 1996, with a title that combined allusions to
Africa, to cybernetics, and to psychedelia. Having benefited from much
better production, the album was a tour de force that gave testimony to the

band's full maturity. It became a favorite of my son Alex, born that year. Alex was not yet a year old when he fell in love with Science's funk-hop version of a Brazilian classic of the 1970s, "Maracatu Atômico," by the countercultural icon Jorge Mautner. By 1997, mangue beat had accumulated cultural strength unseen in a musical movement in Brazil since the Tropicalist rebellion in the late 1960s. *Village Voice*, *Spin*, and the *New York Times* all ran stories on the "swamp boys." They planned their third European tour. In the frozen winter of 1997, teaching at the University of Illinois, Urbana-Champaign, I hoped to be able to see them again, if not in New York, then for sure mid-year in Brazil.

It was not meant to be. On 2 February, Fat Tuesday, Science chose to take—for the millionth time—a drive from Recife to neighboring Olinda. This time he would go in his sister's compact car, for fears of not finding parking for his 1979 Landau in the crowded Mardi Gras streets of Olinda. Science never made it. He was found dead in his car, crashed into a lamppost in the vicinity of the Escola de Aprendizes de Marinheiros (School of Sailors). The most inventive figure of Brazilian youth music of the 1990s was dead at thirty. For the first time in Recife's Mardi Gras history, all major maracatu nations paraded in silence through the city, followed by a stunned multitude. It was the only time that I sobbed and cursed, inconsolably, for the death of someone other than a friend or a relative. On that same 2 February, the musical legend Gilberto Gil, whose fate had been bound with that of his friend Science, lost his eldest son, also in a car accident. Facing the anger for Science's death I thought of my own son Alex, more than of my musical idol: he would never get to see that amazing spectacle. Nação Zumbi, their contemporaries Mundo Livre S/A, and dozens of other Pernambuco bands have, since then, brilliantly carried the torch, but Chico Science's visionary poetic, rhythmic, and performative art remains the definitive measure of how mangue beat became the most fertile renovation of Brazilian popular music in the past two decades.

::: The Concept

In the struggles around who gets to count as a citizen and how in Brazil, popular music's role has recently proven to be as decisive as it has ever been since the early days of the military dictatorship (1964–85). The debates about art and politics, carried out under the rubric of the national-popular in the 1960s, had centered on the content of the lyrics and on the preservation of the acoustic nature of the music. After the Tropicalist victory over the more purist, nationalist protest music of troubadours such as Geraldo Vandré in that debate, the category of MPB (Música Popular Brasileira), initially associated with that very national-popular imaginary (Napolitano 2001), slowly coalesced into what would become its canonical form: a "sophisticated" set of musics, sanctioned by the canon of good taste and characterized by the preeminence of the singer-songwriter, a certain cleanness of sound, and a distinctive penchant for straddling the "highbrow" borders of popular music, both melodically and harmonically. This set of popular music languages became hegemonic in middle-class taste under dictatorship and was associated with names such as Caetano Veloso, Chico Buarque de Hollanda, Milton Nascimento, and Gilberto Gil.

Following the first major crisis of audience and legitimacy of MPB, in the redemocratization period (1979–85), Brazil witnessed the emergence of what I call a growing *rift between national music* and *youth music*. Most youth listened to Anglo-American rock and formed rock bands, while most of the national music produced by the canonical MPB names was not widely consumed by young folks who, not without reason, began to perceive those national pop stars as representatives of the status quo. It is a contention of this chapter that in the past decade or so we have witnessed a strengthening of the citizenship potential of popular music in Brazil thanks to the bridging of the rift between youth music and national music that characterized the 1980s. The chapter will go on to analyze how Chico Science, his collaborators, and followers have been key agents of that process. After describing the birth and consolidation of mangue beat, the chapter will analyze the conversation it established between "regional" genres that had never acceded to the status of "national" music, and international, mostly Afro-Atlantic youth genres that had never acceded to the pantheon of global (i.e., Anglo-American) rock and pop. The encounters between these two vast collections of traditions made visible the originality of mangue beat. I will then risk a few hypotheses on the impact of these innovations for the coding of citizenship in Brazilian popular music.

::: The Scene

Best described as a fifteen-year-long succession of *scenes*, rather than a "movement," mangue beat is first and foremost the decline-and-rebirth story of the major cultural melting pot of Recife. The city is a river-rich, multicultural capital built on a stiflingly hot swamp in one of the nation's poorest urban areas, but is commonly referred to as "the Brazilian Venice," due to its beautiful estuaries and bridges. It reached its lowest reputation in the early 1990s, when the Population Crisis Committee, an institute based in Washington, ranked the city as one of the five worst urban areas in the world, next to Lagos, Dhaka, Kanpur, and Kinshasa. The ranking generated the phrase "fourth-worst city in the world," later ironically appropriated in mangue beat music. By the early 1990s, the information revolution—e-mail, the Internet, faxes, cell phones—was globalizing the urban areas of northeastern Brazil in ways that the richer center-south was hardly able to measure at first. The freer circulation of information allowed for increasing contact among lower middle-class people from the outskirts, such as Chico Science; white middle-class youth from universities, such as Fred 04, leader of Mundo Livre S/A; and the mostly black musicians from the *mocambos*, the precarious housing units built over the swamp.

The band Lamento Negro, part of the black cultural nucleus known as Daruê Malungo, in the Chão de Estrelas area, became a true school of percussionists for mangue beat. Gilmar Bola 8, Toca Ogan, and Gira—all of whom are from that region—ended up in csnz (Teles 2000: 222). If the originality of mangue beat music could be reduced to one encounter, that would be the one that brought together Afro-Brazilian percussionists from poorer Peixinhos and Chão de Estrelas (who were working both with northeastern maracatu as well as with Bahian-influenced samba-reggae sounds); Chico Science's own experience in African American genres such as funk and hip-hop; and Fred 04's, Renato L's, and other university-educated youth's experiences in the pop-music (particularly punk and postpunk) and journalistic cultures of their time. As testified by Maia, one of the founders of Lamento Negro, the relationship with black international culture was at the heart of the scene from the beginning: "Before Chico ever showed up, André and I already wore black power haircuts. It was a huge mix: rap, soul, and *afoxé*. At home we always bought soul and reggae records" (quoted in Teles 2000: 222).

José Teles's study proposes 1987 as the landmark moment in the constitution of the scene that would explode nationally six years later. Major changes had taken place in the traditional *Jornal do Comércio* newspaper, allowing the emerging scene to have some media space. That was the moment when Mundo Livre S/A had a difficult time convincing audiences that their "synthesis of Johnny Rotten, Jorge Ben, and Bezerra da Silva" deserved to be heard. With lyrics inspired in George Orwell's *1984*, Fred 04 "let the punk anger mature and coalesce into a calculated cynicism." Serviço Sujo (Dirty Work), his earlier band, gave way to Mundo Livre S/A, a "name of clear Malcolm McLarean inspiration, designed to ridicule Reagan's revisiting of the cold war as well as the workings of the record industry" (Zero 04, quoted in Galinsky 2002: 38). For a while Mundo Livre S/A would still be booed off the stage for daring to mix rock music with percussion instruments associated with samba such as the *tamborim* (the Brazilian hand-held frame drum) and the *cavaquinho* (the small Portuguese four-string guitar). Their attempts at a "psychedelic samba" were often ridiculed in their hometown, but they already contained some ingredients of the mangue beat revolution, namely, the production of a sound that dynamited the border between rock music and MPB.

By the time the first edition of the RRS (Recife Rock Show) festival took place, in 1993, fifty-seven bands had signed up and national media outlets such as *Bizz* magazine ran pieces on the "mangue boys." Unusually for a rock festival, RRS featured performances by local folk artists including Lia de Itamaraca and Dona Selma do Coco. By the early 1990s the basic tenets of mangue beat's aesthetic had been formulated by the movements' "organic intellectuals"—DJ Mabuse, the writer and enfant terrible Xico Sá, the journalists Renato Lins and José Teles, in addition to Science and Fred 04. That aesthetic would later coalesce in a manifesto "Crabs with Brains" published in the liner notes to CSNZ's *Da Lama ao Caos*. By then, the mangue boys had eliminated once and for all the reference to the colonial sugar cane as a symbol of regional culture, adopting instead the urban swamp crabs (Leão do Ó 2002: 66). These crabs, in addition to being defined as "brainy" by the movement, were all endowed with antennas to capture global information flows. Therein coalesced mangue beat's definitive image of cultural citizenship.

Whereas globalization intensified social contradictions in megalopolises such as Recife, it also allowed increasing numbers of marginalized youth to acquire the means to depict that crisis and intervene in it through music and videos in ways previously unseen. By 1994, when CSNZ and Mundo Livre S/A appeared on the national scene, it had been fifteen years since Pernambuco music had commanded major national attention at all, either with the electrified approach to the traditional accordion-based dance of *baião* by countercultural figures such as Alceu Valença or the rock-influenced acoustic troubadours such as Paraíba-born and Pernambuco-based Zé Ramalho.

If in the early 1990s it was possible for the local icon Alceu Valença to say that "Pernambuco is old . . . and dying of mold" (Teles 2000: 254), five years later it had become vox populi among music listeners all over the country that the most innovative youth sound in music-rich Brazil was being produced precisely in Pernambuco. Between Valença's interview to the Cultural Supplement of Pernambuco's *Diário Oficial* (Official Daily) in March of 1992 and the establishment of that relative consensus, around 1996–97, mangue beat effected nothing short of a minor revolution in the canon of Brazilian popular music. The movement was epitomized by four major records—CSNZ's *Da Lama ao Caos* (1994) and *Afrociberdelia* (1996), as well as Mundo Livre S/A's *Samba Esquema Noise* (Samba, Noisy Style; 1994) and *Guentando a Ôia* (Putting up with the Vibe; 1996)—but it encompasses a vast production by countless artists who have little to do with each other in strictly musical terms. At the time of writing, in 2010, this effervescence has not subsided, and Recife remains the most creative and diverse laboratory of pop ideas in urban Brazil.

The term "mangue beat" covers a panoply of artists, beginning with the pioneer combos CSNZ and Mundo Livre S/A. It also includes dozens of artists who have either reached national recognition after much-acclaimed debuts or have only appeared on compilations of Recife music. Associated with the scene are bands who have made a creative use of the accordion-based musics of the northeast, such as Mestre Ambrósio; rock bands who have learned the iconoclastic lessons of the movement, such as Querosene Jacaré; musicians who have experimented with the resources of electronics, such as Otto (former drummer for Mundo Livre S/A and signatory to a stellar solo career); a host of different pastiches of national and international genres by Mombojó; the punk rereading of baião by Cascabulho, whose frontman, Silvério Pessoa, left to pursue a solo career; and many others. All of them have taken advantage of the intense freedom to experiment and to combine global with regional forms that has permeated the Recife music since the emergence of mangue beat. Most musical examples in this chapter will be taken from CSNZ's two records, but I will also attempt to say a little about Mundo Livre S/A.

Along with other contemporary forms such as hip-hop, mangue beat has restored the possibility of making collective political and aesthetic statements in popular music, atrophied since the 1960s.[1] It has updated Tropicália by offering another "grand (re)inaugural gesture," with manifestos and the like.[2] Musically, mangue bridged the sounds consumed by the youth with the sounds consumed as "national," having a lasting impact on genres such as heavy metal (Avelar 2003). They systematically combined the *alfaias*, large bass drums of maracatu with the traditional rock music lineup of bass, guitar, and drum set. Perhaps for the first time since the early days of samba, a musical movement drew upon (1) Afro-Brazilian percussionists from the popular classes, (2) *mestiço* and lower middle-class marginalized youth, and (3) white, university-educated young intellectuals. Furthermore, mangue beat mobilized youth musicians nationally around causes such as digital inclusion and the revision of copyright laws. Mangue has not simply been a renewal of the musical canon; it has been a major transformation in the relations between music and politics in Brazil.

As was the case with Tropicália, what characterizes mangue beat is not a particular beat or rhythm, but rather a *certain attitude toward musical mixing*. Mangue beat constituted itself in Recife, making a sound that was distinctively regional, built upon combinations that no one else in the world could have made (maracatu + hip-hop, e.g.), but parallel to that they were also questioning the totality of what was understood as "national music" during the reign of MPB. This is not to say that mangue brings to an end to the relevance of MPB as a category or even that it was "against" MPB in any way. But since mangue's unprecedented mixing of what was understood as "regional" with the "international," the very paradigm of canonization in Brazilian popular music changed profoundly. Mangue is, then, the closest that Brazilian popular music has gotten these days to offering grand inaugural gestures or moments of rupture with tradition. The caveat to that statement is that mangue has been both revisionist (in its revisiting of Tropicalist tenets, for instance) as well as rupturist, as it broke with much of the hitherto dominant ways of thinking about music in Pernambuco and in the northeast as a whole (particularly as emblematized by the nationalist-preservationist perspective held by the doyen of Pernambuco letters and cultural populism, Ariano Suassuna). Mangue presented itself as youth music, but partook of none of the 1980s rockers' misgivings vis-à-vis consecrated acoustic songbooks. It was adamantly "local" in its constant references to Pernambuco culture, but it shared none of the suspicions against international music that "regional" brands of popular music in Brazil have often displayed. Mangue's legacy goes beyond the simple freedom to experiment and points toward the conscious use of that freedom to cross or simply dynamite borders hitherto conceived as identity defining, stable, insurmountable.

Couched "not merely as the recordings of some new bands [but] rather

. . . as a coalition of musicians developing a collective vision, a think tank or association for the research and development of pop music ideas" (Sharp 2001: 37–38), mangue beat was solidly rooted in northeastern musics based in percussion and accordion, but unlike previous "regional" genres it defiantly flaunted its foreign influences. It tapped on the vast resources of international youth musics (reggae, hip-hop, funk, metal), but unlike early Brazilian practitioners of these genres, it shared a strong relationship with local traditions as well. Some of the musicians associated with the scene maintained a commitment to political questions such as digital inclusion and democratization of access to the media, but nowhere did one find the submission of musicianship to politics often seen in sixties-style militancy. Mangue has thus been a unique bird, as it combined things in ways that had not quite been attempted before. It was regionally rooted but ferociously global; radical and rupturist but clearly open to and interested in tradition; visibly political yet painfully aware of the limits of politics in music. In Silviano Santiago's terms, Science, Zero 04, and the like are artists of pastiche, and not of parody.[3]

Black international genres were key mediators that allowed mangue beat to formulate a creative musical response to the encounter between the information revolution and the crisis of nationalism in Brazilian popular music. The repertoire of global pop had inspired the Tropicalists of the late sixties, and Anglo-American punk and postpunk icons had been decisive for the rock generation that came of age in the 1980s. However, the influence of Afro-American and Afro-diasporic music upon the Brazilian youth scene had until then been restricted to circles identified with black music as such—particularly the late 1970s Rio de Janeiro movement known as Black Rio—or yet with giants of MPB such as Jorge Ben, who interpreted and transformed those musics through the lens of samba beginning in the early 1960s. It was only with Chico Science, however, that the repertoire of international black music was made to dialogue with Brazilian youth music tout court in a sustained, consistent way.

Since the 1980s a process of "re-Africanization" of the Carnaval celebrations of the neighboring state of Bahia had been taking place, with the emergence of the blocos afro and the genre known as samba-reggae.[4] Those developments had some impact upon the Pernambuco scene, although perhaps less than Bahian musicians tend to claim. Without a doubt, however, the relationship with black international culture was absolutely essential for the development of the mangue beat aesthetic: Chico Science, particularly, had grown up on heavy doses of James Brown, Curtis Mayfield, Funkadelic, and early hip-hop (Galinsky 2002: 31). In the early 1980s, as the break-dance phenomenon made its way to Recife, "Chico and his inseparable friend Jorge du Peixe joined the Legião Hip Hop, one of the major street break dance groups of the city" (31). Jorge du Peixe later became the lead guitarist for Nação Zumbi and took up the vocals and lyric writing beginning in 1997. After the devastating news of Chico Science's passing, it only took Jorge du Peixe, Lúcio Maia, Bola 8, and so on a couple of years to establish themselves again at the very top among Brazilian pop bands. Over the four records released without Science—csnz (1997—a double-cd homage to Science featuring a number of guest artists), *Radio S.A.M.B.A.* (1998), *Nação Zumbi* (2002), and *Futura* (2006)—Nação Zumbi set more of a foot in hard-rock music, but the band certainly keeps alive the legacy of dialogue between Afro-Atlantic genres from maracatu to hip-hop. Their use of maracatu drums, no doubt, remains a trademark: "Improved microphone placement and amplification of individual *alfaias*, a technique he [Science] saw at concerts of Maracatu Nação Pernambuco in the early 1990s, increased musicians' control over the tone of the rhythm section, providing an important ingredient in csnz's sound" (Sharp 2001: 42–43).

In borrowing both from Afro-Atlantic international genres and from Brazilian northeastern traditions, the mixing present on csnz's *Da Lama ao Caos* and *Afrociberdelia* bypassed the mainstream international rock that had been widely influential in Brazil (Led Zeppelin, Black Sabbath, Pink Floyd, Deep Purple) and did not draw, either, on any of the forms of nationalized Brazilian music, neither bossa nova, nor the singer-centered acoustic mpb—canonized among the country's middle classes—nor even samba, which still held considerably weight amongst the popular classes. Certainly, Science's influences include artists whose work was in relation to samba or mpb (a prominent example being 1980s avant-garde São Paulo band Fellini, pioneers in the creative home use of four-track recorders in Brazilian music). Science's vision of Brazilian culture certainly bore the traces of someone highly steeped in the Tropicalist legacy, but the two main musical ingredients for his work were black international musical genres and a host of Pernambucan musical traditions.

The examples of the forms taken by that encounter are legion. The ceremonial and solemn verses that open *Afrociberdelia* track 1, "Mateus Enter" (concluding with the epigrammatic couplet "Pernambuco underneath my feet / and my mind in immensity"), are recited over a distorted, heavy-metal-style guitar that produces a power chord, while the percussion launches into a maracatu groove. In track 9 of *Da Lama ao Caos*, "Salustiano Song," a maracatu beat on the alfaias dialogues with candomblé-derived patterns on the hand drums. Over that polyrhythmic dialogue we get the droning synthesizer-driven melody, in one of Science's many tributes to electronic music. In "Risoflora" (Laughter Flora) track 8 of the same album, the distorted guitars in heavy-metal style bring with it a speeding up of the tempo of the alfaias, which are phrasing in recognizable maracatu patterns. Track 3, "Rios, Pontes e Everdrives" (Rivers, Bridges, and Overdrives; the original recording of this true classic of mangue beat), explores a number of variations on northeastern genres such as maracatu and baião—in part A—as well as the stunning kinship between hip-hop and embolada, two verbal arts predicated on exploring the rhythmic powers of language—in part A. Track 4, the contagious "A Cidade," became canonical in the mangue songbook, due to its "reinterpretation of the *ciranda* rhythm combined with a rock-funk feel" (Galinsky 2002: 153) and its remarkable lyrics that acerbically describe the pains and hopes of Recife, a city that "won't stop, only grow" (a cidade não pára / a cidade só cresce) and where "the one below goes down / the one above goes up" (o de cima sobe / o de baixo desce).

In complex songs, such as track 2 of *Afrociberdelia*—"Cidadão do Mundo" (Citizen of the World)—the music takes the form of a conversation between the rhythm section and the vocal line: in parts A and A' the rhythm section sets up a funk groove while Science's vocals respond with a maracatu-like, ceremonial melody with a distortion effect. In parts B and B' the maracatu-like melody in the vocals continue, but this time over a maracatu groove in the rhythm section. By the time we come to C the rhythm section has changed back to a funk groove (now played on the *berimbau* [the single-string bow used in capoeira]), and the vocal line has taken off on a frenzied raggamuffin (the electronic sub-genre of reggae/embolada rapping accompanied by distortion effect) (Galinsky 2002: 43–45). In Sciences's vocals in C, it is no longer clear if he is embolando or rapping. The approximation between disparate genres never takes the form of a "fusion" but, rather, offers a sequence of "plays of juxtaposition" that become increasingly complex, as they establish contrasts and also intersections.

Chico Science often combined the most common of the rhythmic cells of maracatu—the pattern consisting of sixteenth note, eighth note, sixteenth note (with the accent on the second beat), with a funk groove coming from

Chico Science and Nação Zumbi on mud flats of Recife, 1995 (Gil Vicente).

the other corner of the rhythm section. While percussion or bass were play-ing funk or maracatu, Science often did not sing in the respective style, as in his songs the vocal line did something else and set up a rhythm pattern of its own. He thus produced an effect of denaturalization and estrangement to the ears of those accustomed to a more "harmonious" marriage of vocals and music that respected certain genre conventions. On top of that particular rhythmic conversation, the chords often went from a distorted heavy-metal solo played with the help of wah-wah pedals all the way to a swinging, elec-trified samba-soul in the Jorge Ben style. The music was often punctuated by various uses of sampling, which came in to mark an abrupt interruption or call attention to a catchy word, a slogan, a tool in the war of words and gestures often depicted in the lyrics. The various tempos of maracatu drum-ming were to become an integral part of Science's shows and continued to be used in his music, as his other influences progressively became even more diverse.

The lyrics to "Cidadão do Mundo" depict a slave fleeing from oppression and confronting the *capitão do mato* (captain of the jungle, a slave catcher): "the dagger spun / flew by my neck." The subject reacts to the scare by gathering "his nation":

Jurei, jurei	I swore, I swore
Vou pegar aquele capitão	I'll get that captain
Vou juntar a minha nação	I'll gather my nation
Na terra do maracatu.	in the land of maracatu.

The ceremony of coronation of the Congo King in maracatu is held up as an image for the gathering of a new nation, *the Zumbi Nation*.[5] The ceremonial tone is broken by the lines "it's all brainy crabs / coming out of this here swamp," which brings together humor and Science's trademark acerbic gaze upon Recife's urban miseries. The closing, rapping stanza describes two quick scenes of small robberies told from the point of view of a narrator who identifies with the petty robbers or is, perhaps, part of them. That identification with the transgressor of law, by definition lived and perceived as unjust and unevenly applied, was one of the features of hip-hop culture that most attracted Chico Science. These scenes of small robberies, conflicts, and gathering of gangs for unnamed upcoming war are common in Science's music. They are set against the backdrop of the fundamental, horrific violence that is reproduced daily in poorer areas of the city. The depiction of these scenes in the lyrics is often accompanied by heightening of the musical tension, through operations on volume, pitch, intensity, and the pace of the music itself.

Along with appropriating attitude, attire, and ideas, Science's music borrows from other genres a certain collection of beats. It is mostly in the realm of rhythm that Science saw how the dialogue between musical genres could provide him with a new metaphor for cultural translation and contact. The creation of channels of communication between Afro-Atlantic genres (ska, reggae, hip-hop, funk, raggamuffin) and Brazilian genres that had never reached the status of national music and continued to be considered "regional" (*coco* [the percussion, vocal, and stomping dancing rhythm from the northeastern backlands], embolada, maracatu, ciranda) altered, profoundly, the canon of Brazilian popular music. Not only did it generate a considerable body of musically rich work; it demonstrated to an ample sector of youth musicians in Brazil that musical cultures previously thought of as antagonistic and mutually exclusive could no longer afford not to dialogue with each other. Science's merit was to have seen the rhythmic, melodic, performative, and political potentials of those encounters.

The obstacles to musical conversation between, say, embolada and hip-hop—two verbal rhythmic arts with considerable formal kinship—had never been properly musical, but rather social and political; that is to say, those obstacles were a product of the unfavorable demographics. The overwhelming presence of a national canon functioned as a filter and ended up preventing musically obvious encounters such as these from happening. It is to the credit of Chico Science's extraordinary intelligence (along with the artistry of his collaborators in Nação Zumbi and friends in Mundo Livre S/A) that these barriers were lifted. Much of the citizenship potential accumulated by mangue beat derives, I would claim, from the dynamiting of those barriers. Mangue often invited its listeners to perform a true act of musical citizenship: in order to process the sound you had to venture into at least one or two genres that you had not yet heard. That transit between hitherto incompatible genres forced the listeners to cross boundaries that were also, invariably, racial, regional, cultural, and political. Mangue beat is first and foremost a major reshuffling and questioning of the social division of listening labor in Brazil.

While samba plays a relatively minor role in the mosaic created by Chico Science and Nação Zumbi, the same cannot be said of their counterparts in Mundo Livre S/A, whose work promotes a true rereading of samba in its various currents. The swinging guitar introduction to "A Bola do Jogo" (The Game Ball) testifies to the influence of Jorge Ben's unmistakable electrification of samba from the early 1960s. Fred 04's famous cavaquinho reaches prominence in the melody of *Samba Esquema Noise*'s third track, "Livre Iniciativa" (Free Enterprise), a song that alternates distorted, heavy metal style guitars with pure cavaquinho-led samba. Mundo Livre's version of the true mangue beat classic song, "Rios Pontes and Overdrives," is a nice counterpoint to csnz's better-known, canonical version. While Science privileges an upbeat, danceable, harder sound, Mundo Livre's version considerably slows the tempo and lends it a meditative quality. In contrast with Science's option for bass drums, Mundo Livre's version juxtaposes samba-swing beats on the guitar later accelerating to a hard-rock pattern, only to slow and "break" its syntax again by shifting to a reggae beat. Mundo Livre can be defined as a psychedelic office of transformation of pop materials, and in that mix urban both samba and new wave rock music have played decisive roles.

As the 1990s evolved, mangue beat became the foremost guerrilla fighter against the violence of intellectual property laws and most especially the anachronistic copyright legislation. Coherent with their ethics of mixing, Mundo Livre S/A was a pioneer in the movement to use the Internet to shake the foundations of copyright law. They have consistently composed songs that are not included on their albums, but remain circulating on the Internet for free. Along with their participation in events such as the Porto Alegre World Social Forum, that political activity has combined to turn from an exclusively mangue beat musical movement into a social movement in its own right. More directly involved in politics than their friends in Nação Zumbi (and even than Chico Science ever was), Mundo Livre S/A have developed international contacts that go from Noam Chomsky to Subcomandante Marcos, and have made a forceful appearance at several editions of the Porto Alegre World Forum, the emblem of the antiglobalization movement.

In short, mangue beat has effected a major reshuffling of Brazilian music by bringing into contact genres considered "regional" with a host of international musics of Afro-Atlantic origin, thereby overcoming the sanctioned, codified filter of the national canon. They overcame a rift that characterized the earlier moment in Brazil, that of the separation between youth and national musics. They have also substituted the urban crabs with antennas—an image of cultural citizenship—for the old iconography associated with northeastern sugar-cane culture and inspired a true "do-it-yourself" revolution in Pernambuco music. Certainly, their legacy in Brazilian popular music remains an open question. But their work has redefined the citizenship potential of popular music in Brazil.

NOTES

1. A previous version of this chapter made an overstated claim as to the primacy and originality of mangue beat in the restoration of political, coherent, and collective statements in popular music. I owe to an excellent question by Jason Stanyek the insight that the initial claim needed to be relativized.

2. For two definitive studies of Tropicália as a "grand inaugural gesture," see Christopher Dunn 2001; and Celso Favaretto [1979] 1996.

3. Silviano Santiago's understanding of *pastiche* (1989) differs from the more widely cited Fredric Jameson definition (1991). While both of them associate the form with postmodernism, for Jameson pastiche is the expression of a "waning of affect" and a fundamental atrophy in historical imagination, a product of late capitalism's inability to think of itself historically. Santiago, on the other hand, strips the concept of any negative connotation and proposes it as a strategy for rewriting the past that does not fall into the binary, oppositional traps of parody. Whereas parody privileges rupture with tradition, pastiche allows for a freer combination of histori-

cal registers that does not necessarily imply antagonism. The question of hybridity in Chico Science's music has been studied by Herom Vargas (2008).

4. See Antonio Risério 1981 for the most thorough study of what came to be called the "re-Africanization" of Bahian Carnaval.

5. Both the name of the band as well as the lyrics of "Cidadão do Mundo" make reference, naturally, to Zumbi, the black hero and the leader of the massive seventeenth-century maroon state in Palmares, northeastern Brazil. I am grateful to my friend and student Alexandre Silva for bringing to my attention an error present in an earlier version of my interpretation of the song.

works cited

Abers, Rebecca Neaera. 2000. *Inventing Local Democracy: Grassroots Politics in Brazil*. Boulder: Lynne Rienner.

Alem, João Marcos. 2004–5. "Rodeios: A Fabricação de uma Identidade Caipira-Sertanejo-*Country* no Brasil." *Revista USP* 64: 95–121.

Almeida, Renato de. 1958. *Música Folclórica e Música Popular*. Porto Alegre: Comissão Nacional de Folclore.

Alvarenga, Oneyda. 1982. *Música Popular Brasileira*. São Paulo: Duas Cidades.

Álvarez, Sonia, Evelina Dagnino, and Arturo Escobar, eds. 1998. *Culture of Politics, Politics of Culture: Re-visioning Latin American Social Movements*. Boulder: Westview.

Amaral, Azevedo. 1941. *Getúlio Vargas, Estadista*. Rio de Janeiro: Irmãos Pongetti.

Anderson, Benedict. 1993. *Imagined Communities: Reflections on the Origin and Spread of Nationalism*. London: Verso.

Andrade, Elaine Nunes de. 1996. "Movimento Negro Juvenil: Um Estudo de Caso Sobre Jovens Rappers de São Bernardo do Campo." Ph.D. diss., Universidade de São Paulo.

———, ed. 1999. *Rap e Educação, Rap É Educação*. São Paulo: Selo Negro.

Andrade, Mário de. [1928] 1972. *Ensaio sobre a Música Brasileira*. São Paulo: Martins.

———. [1933] 1976. *Música, Doce Música*. 2nd ed. São Paulo: Martins.

———. 1984. *Os cocos* [a compilation]. Ed. Oneyda Alvarenga. São Paulo: Livraria Duas Cidades and Instituto Nacional do Livro.

———. 1991. "A Pronúncia Cantada e o Problema do Nasal Brasileiro Através dos Discos." In *Aspectos da Música Brasileira*. Belo Horizonte: Itatiaia.

Arantes, Antonio A. 2000. "Desigualdade e diferença." In *Paisagens Paulistanas. Transformações do Espaço Público*. Campinas: UNICAMP.

Araújo, Paulo César de. 2002. *Não Sou Cachorro, não: Música Popular Cafona e Ditadura Militar*. Rio de Janeiro: Record.

Araújo, Samuel. 1988. "Brega: Music and Conflict in Urban Brazil." *Latin American Music Review* 9.1: 50–89.

Arias, Enrique Desmond. 2006. *Drugs and Democracy in Rio de Janeiro: Trafficking,*

Social Networks, and Public Security. Chapel Hill: University of North Carolina Press.

Aristotle. [350 BCE] 1941. *Politics*. Translated by Benjamin Jowett. *The Basic Works of Aristotle*, edited by Richard McKeon. New York: Random House.

Arnold, Matthew. [1869] 1994. *Culture and Anarchy*. New Haven: Yale University Press.

Artaud, Antonin. 1958. *The Theater and Its Double*. Translated by Mary Caroline Richards. New York: Grove.

Auslander, Phillip. 1992. *Presence and Resistance: Postmodernism and Cultural Politics in Contemporary American Performance*. Ann Arbor: University of Michigan Press.

Avelar, Idelber. 2003. "Heavy Metal Music in Postdictatorial Brazil: Sepultura and the Coding of Nationality in Sound." *Journal of Latin American Cultural Studies* 12.3: 329–46.

———. 2004. *The Letter of Violence: Essays on Narrative, Ethics, and Politics*. New York: Palgrave.

Avritzer, Leonardo. 2000. "Entre o Diálogo e a Reflexividade: A Modernidade Tardia e a Mídia." In *Teoria Social e Modernidade no Brasil*, edited by Leonardo Avritzer and José Maurício Domingues. Belo Horizonte: UFMG.

Ayala, Maria Ignez, and Marcos Ayala. 2000. *A Brincadeira dos Cocos—Alegria e Devoção*. Natal: UFRN.

Azevedo, Fernando de. 1958. *Novos Caminhos e Novos Fins: A Nova Política de Educação no Brasil—Subsídios para uma História de Quatro Anos*. 3rd ed. São Paulo: Melhoramentos.

Bacelar, Jeferson. 2001. *A Hierarquia das Raças: Negros e Brancos em Salvador*. Rio de Janeiro: Pallas.

Back, Les. 1996. *New Ethnicities and Urban Culture: Racism and Multiculture in Young Lives*. London: Routledge.

Baierle, Sérgio Gregório. 1998. "The Explosion of Experience: The Emergence of a New Ethical-Political Principle in Popular Movements." In *Culture of Politics, Politics of Culture: Re-visioning Latin American Social Movements*, edited by Sonia Álvarez, Evelina Dagnino, and Arturo Escobar. Boulder: Westview.

Barbosa, Airton Lima, et al. 1966. "Que Caminho Seguir na Música Popular Brasileira?" *Revista Civilização Brasileira* 1.7: 375–85.

Barbosa, Rui. 1946. *Reforma do Ensino Primário e Várias Instituições Complementares da Instrução Pública: Obras Completas*. Vol. 10. Rio de Janeiro: Ministério da Educação e Saúde.

Barreto, Lima. 2006. *Triste Fim de Policarpo Quaresma*. 23rd ed. São Paulo: Ática.

Barros, Orlando de. 2001. *Custódio Mesquita: Um Compositor Romântico no Tempo de Vargas (1930–45)*. Rio de Janeiro: UERJ.

Bastide, Roger. 1985. *As Religiões Africanas no Brasil: Contribuição a uma Sociologia das Interpenetrações das Civilizações*. 2 vols. São Paulo: Livraria Pioneira.

Becker, Howard. 1963. *The Outsiders*. New York: Free Press.

Béhague, Gerard. 1980. "Brazilian Musical Values of the 1960s and 1970s: Popular Urban Music from Bossa Nova to Tropicalia." *Journal of Popular Culture* 14.3: 437–52.

Bentes, Ivana. 2003. "The *Sertão* and the *Favela* in Contemporary Brazilian Film." In *The New Brazilian Cinema*, edited by Lúcia Nagib. New York: Palgrave Macmillan.

Beverley, John. 1991. "Through All Things Modern: Second Thoughts on Testimonio." *boundary 2* 18.2: 1–21.

Blacking, John. 1992. "Music, Culture and Experience." In *Music, Culture, and Experience: Selected Papers of John Blacking*, edited by Reginald Byron. Chicago: University of Chicago Press.

Bogo, Ademar. "O Papel da Cultura no MST." 1998. Unpublished typescript.

———, ed. 2002. *Gerações: Coletânea de Poesias*. São Paulo: MST.

Bohnsack, Ralf, et al. 1995. *Die Suche nach Gemeinsamkeit und die Gewalt der Gruppe: Hooligans, Musikgruppen und andere Jugendcliquen*. Opladen: Leske + Budrich.

Bohnsack, Ralf, and Bodo Wild. 1997. "Cliquen, Banden und Vereine: Die Suche nach Milieuzugehörigkeit." In *Tatort: Biographie. Spuren, Zugänge, Orte, Ereignisse*, edited by Imbke Behnken and Theodor Schulze. Opladen: Leske + Budrich.

Boito, Armando, Jr. 1982. *O Golpe de 1954: A Burguesia contra o Populismo*. São Paulo: Brasiliense.

Bourdieu, Pierre. 1984. *Distinction: A Social Critique of the Judgment of Taste*. Translated by Richard Nice. Cambridge: Harvard University Press.

———. 1993. *The Field of Cultural Production: Essays on Art and Literature*, edited by Randal Johnson. New York: Columbia University Press.

Branford, Sue, and Jan Rocha. 2002. *Cutting the Wire: The Story of the Landless Movement in Brazil*. London: Latin American Bureau.

Brito, Denise. 2006. "Mano Brown Sem Súvidas," *Folhateen* (20 November).

Buarque, Chico. 1978. *Ópera do Malandro*. São Paulo: Cultura.

Buarque de Hollanda, Heloísa. 1980. *Impressões de Viagem: CPC, Vanguarda e Desbunde 1960/70*. São Paulo: Brasiliense.

Butler, Judith. 1993. *Bodies That Matter: On the Discursive Limits of "Sex."* New York: Routledge.

Calado, Pedro Miguel da Cruz. 2007. "Não Percebes o Hip Hop: Geografias, (Sub)Culturas, e Territorialidades." M.A. thesis, University of Lisbon.

Caldas, Waldenyr. 2004–5. "Revendo a Música Sertaneja." *Revista USP* 64: 59–67.

Caldeira, João Bernardo. 2004. "O Som do Campo." *Jornal do Brasil*, 21 July.

Caldeira, Teresa. 2000. *City of Walls: Crime, Segregation, and Citizenship in São Paulo*. Berkeley: University of California Press.

Caldeira, Teresa, and James Holston. 1999. "Democracy and Violence in Brazil." *Comparative Studies in Society and History* 41.4 (October): 691–729.

Calvino, Italo. 1974. *Invisible Cities*. New York: Harcourt.

Cambi, Franco. 1999. *História da Pedagogia*. São Paulo: UNESP.

Campos, Ires Silene Escobar dos, ed. 1996. *Sem-Terra: As Músicas do MST*. Porto Alegre: Unidade Editorial.

Cançado, Patrícia, and Maria Laura Neves. 2005. "Classe Média no Sufoco," *Suplemento* Época Negócios of the *Revista Época* 395 (14 December 2005): 74–76.

Canclini, Néstor García. 2001. *Consumers and Citizens: Globalization and Multicultural Conflicts*. Minneapolis: University of Minnesota Press.

Carignato, Taeco Toma. 2002. "Por Que Eles Emigram?" In *Psicanálise, Cultura e Migração*, edited by Miriam Debieux, Rosa Carignato, et al. São Paulo: YM Editora and Gráfica.

Carvalho, Daniela de. 2003. *Migrants and Identity in Japan and Brazil: The Nikkeijin*. London: Routledge Curzon.

Carvalho, José Jorge. 1977. "La Música de Origen Africana en el Brasil." In *África en América Latina*, edited by Manuel Fraginals. Mexico City: Siglo Veintiuno.

———. 1994. "Black Music of All Colors: The Construction of Black Ethnicity in Ritual and Popular Genres of Afro-Brazilian Music." In *Music and Black Ethnicity: The Caribbean and South America*, edited by Gerard Béhague. Miami: North-South Center, University of Miami.

———. 1999. "Afro-Brazilian Music and Ritual: From the Traditional Genres to Beginnings of the Samba." *Série Antropologia* 256. Brasília: Universidade de Brasília.

Carvalho, José Murilo de. 1987. *Os Bestializados: O Rio de Janeiro e a República Que Não Foi*. São Paulo: Companhia das Letras.

———. 2001. *Cidadania no Brasil: O Longo Caminho*. Rio de Janeiro: Civilização Brasileira.

Carvalho, Marta Maria Chagas de. 2000. "Reformas da Instrução Pública." In *500 Anos de Educação no Brasil*, edited by Elaine Marta Teixeira Lopes, Luciano Mendes Faria Filho, and Cyntia Greive Veiga. Belo Horizonte: Autêntica.

Castelo, Martim. 1941. "Rádio, VI." *Cultura Política* 6: 329–31.

———. 1942. "Rádio, XI." *Cultura Política* 11: 299–301.

Castro, Nadya Araújo. 1998. "Trabalho e Desigualdades Raciais: Hipóteses Desafiantes e Realidades por Interpretar." In *Trabalho e Desigualdades Raciais: Negros e Brancos no Mercado de Trabalho em Salvador*, edited by Nadya Araújo Castro and Vanda Sá Barreto. São Paulo. Annablume.

Cavalcante, Bernice, et al, eds. 2004. *Decantando a República: Inventário Histórico e Político da Canção Popular Moderna*. 3 vols. Rio de Janeiro: Nova Fronteira.

Cesarino, A. F., Jr. 1942. "A Família como Objeto do Direito Social." *Boletim do Ministério do Trabalho, Indústria e Comércio* 99: 109–33.

Chartier, Roger. 1990. *A História Cultural: Entre Práticas e Representações*. Rio de Janeiro: Bertrand Brasil.

Chaui, Marilena. 1978. "Apontamentos para uma Crítica da Ação Integralista Brasileira." In *Ideologia e Mobilização Popular*, edited by Marilena Chaui and Maria Sylvia Carvalho Franco. Rio de Janeiro: Cedec.

———. 1986. *Conformismo e Resistência: Aspectos da Cultura Popular no Brasil*. São Paulo: Brasiliense.

Chiarelli, Tadeu. 1999. *Arte Internacional Brasileira*. São Paulo: Lemos.

Cicero, Marcus Tullius. [44 BCE] 1991. *On Duties*, edited by M. T. Griffin and E. M. Atkins. Cambridge: Cambridge University Press.

Clifford, James. 1986. *Writing Culture: The Poetics and Politics of Ethnography*. Berkeley: University of California Press.

Cohen, Stanley. 1980. *Folk Devils and Moral Panics: The Creation of the Mods and Rockers*. Oxford: Blackwell.

———, ed. 1971. *Images of Deviance*. Harmondsworth: Penguin.

Cohen, Stanley, and Jock Young. 1973. *The Manufacture of the News: Deviance, Social Problems and the Mass Media*. London: Constable.

Cooper, Carolyn. 1994. "'Lyrical Gun'": Metaphor and Role Play in Jamaican Dancehall Culture." *Massachusetts Review* 35.3–4: 429–47.

Corona, Ignacio, and Alejandro L. Madrid. 2008. *Postnational Musical Identities: Cultural Production, Distribution, and Consumption in a Globalized Scenario*. Lanham, Md.: Lexington.

Costa, André. 2003. *Da Emergência de Subjetividades no Universo Pop Contemporâneo: As Aventuras Subjetivas de Björk*. M.A. thesis, Universidade de Brasília.

Costa, Marcus de Lontra. 2004. "Os Anos 80: Uma Brasileira." In *Onde Está Você, Geração 80?* Exhibit catalogue, Centro Cultural do Brasil. Rio de Janeiro.

Cunha, Olivia Maria Gomes da. 1991. "Corações Rastafari: Lazer, Política e Religião em Salvador." M.A. thesis, Universidade Federal do Rio de Janeiro.

———. 1998. "Black Movements and the 'Politics of Identity' in Brazil." In *Culture of Politics, Politics of Culture: Re-visioning Latin American Social Movements*, edited by Sonia Álvarez, Evelina Dagnino, and Arturo Escobar. Boulder: Westview.

Dagnino, Evelina. 1998. "The Cultural Practices of Citizenship, Democracy, and the State." In *Culture of Politics, Politics of Culture: Re-visioning Latin American Social Movements*, edited by Sonia Álvarez, Evelina Dagnino, and Arturo Escobar. Boulder: Westview.

Dahl, Robert. 1998. *On Democracy*. New Haven: Yale University Press.

DaMatta, Roberto. 1991. *Carnivals, Rogues, and Heroes: An Interpretation of the Brazilian Dilemma*. Notre Dame: Notre Dame University Press.

———. [1978] 1995. "For an Anthropology of the Brazilian Tradition; or 'A virtude está no meio.'" In *The Brazilian Puzzle: Culture on the Borderlands of the Western World*, edited by David Hess and Roberto DaMatta. New York: Columbia University Press.

———. 1997. *A Casa e a Rua: Espaço, Cidadania, Mulher e Morte no Brasil*. Rio de Janeiro: Rocco.

Dantas, Marcelo. 1994. *Olodum: De bloco Afro a Holding Cultural*. Salvador: Edições Olodum.

Davis, Darién. 2008. *White Face, Black Mask: Africaneity and the Early Social History of Popular Music in Brazil*. East Lansing: Michigan State University Press.

Debieux Rosa, Miriam. 2002. "O Não-dito Familiar e a Transmissão de História." In *Psicanálise, Cultura e Migração*, edited by Miriam Debieux, Rosa Carignato, et al. São Paulo: YM Editora and Gráfica.

de Certeau, Michel. 1998. *A Invenção do Cotidiano: As Artes de Fazer*. Petrópolis: Vozes.

DeCosmo, Janet. 2000. "Reggae and Rastafari in Salvador, Bahia: The Caribbean Connection in Brazil." In *Religion, Culture, and Tradition in Caribbean*, edited by Hemchand Gossai and Nathaniel Samuel Murrell. New York: St. Martin's.

Deleuze, Gilles. 1990. *The Logic of Sense*. Translated by Mark Lester with Charles Stivale. New York: Columbia University Press.

Deleuze, Gilles, and Félix Guattari. 2004. *Anti-Oedipus*. Translated by Robert Hurley, Mark Seem, and Helen R. Lane. New York: Continuum.

Dent, Sebastian Alexander. 2005. "Cross-Cultural 'Countries': Covers, Conjuncture, and the Whiff of Nashville in Música Sertaneja (Brazilian Commercial Country Music)." *Popular Music and Society* 28.2 (May): 207–27.

———. 2009. *River of Tears: Country Music, Memory, and Modernity in Brazil*. Durham: Duke University Press.

Derrida, Jacques. [1967] 1980. *Writing and Difference*. Translated by Alan Bass. Chicago: University of Chicago Press.

Domingues, José Maurício. 1999. "Desenvolvimento, Modernidade e Subjetividade." In *Ideais de Modernidade e Sociologia no Brasil: Ensaios sobre Luiz Aguiar Costa Pinto*, edited by Marcos Chor Maio and Glaucia Villas Bôas. Porto Alegre: Universidade Federal do Rio Grande do Sul.

Draper, Jack Alden. 2005. "Redemptive Regionalism in the Brazilian Northeast Forró and the Flows of Popular Culture in a Global Economy." Ph.D. diss., Duke University.

Dunn, Christopher. 2001. *Brutality Garden: Tropicália and the Emergence of a Brazilian Counterculture*. Chapel Hill: University of North Carolina Press.

Enciclopédia da Música Brasileira: Erudita, Folclórica, Popular. 1977. São Paulo: Art Editora.

Enciclopédia da Música Brasileira: Popular, Erudita, Folclórica. 1998. São Paulo: Art Editora.

Enciclopédia da Música Brasileira: Samba e Choro. 2000. São Paulo: Publifolha.

Enciclopédia da Música Brasileira: Sertaneja. 2000. São Paulo: Publifolha.

Falcão, Joaquim, and Rosa Maria Barboza Araújo, eds. 2001. *O Imperador das Idéias: Gilberto Freyre em Questão*. Rio de Janeiro: Topbooks.

Faria, Vilmar E. 1980. "Divisão Inter-regional do Trabalho e Pobreza Urbana: O Caso de Salvador." In *Bahia de Todos os Pobres*, edited by Guaraci Adeodato, A. de Souza, and Vilmar Faria. Petrópolis: Vozes.

Faulks, Keith. 2000. *Citizenship*. London: Routledge.

Favaretto, Celso. [1979] 1996. *Tropicália: Alegoria Alegria*. 2nd ed. São Paulo: Ateliê.

Felix, João Batista de Jesus. 2000. "Chic Show e Zimbabwe e a Construção da Identidade nos Bailes Black Paulistanos." M.A. thesis, Universidade de São Paulo.

Feliz, Júlio da Costa. 1998. "Consonâncias e Dissonâncias de um Canto Coletivo: A História da Disciplina Canto Orfeônico no Brasil." M.A. thesis, Universidade Federal de Mato Grosso do Sul.

Fernandes, Bernardo Mançano. 2000. *A Formação do MST no Brasil*. Petrópolis: Vozes.

Fernandes, Florestan. 1978. *A Integração do Negro na Sociedade de Classes*. São Paulo: Ática.

Fernandes, Sujatha. 2003. "Fear of a Black Nation: Local Rappers, Transnational Crossings, and State Power in Contemporary Cuba." *Anthropological Quarterly* 76.4: 575–608.

Ferreira, Juca. 2003. "Opportunities to Voice, to Communicate, and to Live." In "Living Culture: National Culture, Education and Citizenship Program." Cultural policy press release. Brasilia: Ministry of Culture.

Flores, Richard R. 1997. "Aesthetic Process and Cultural Citizenship: The Membering of a Social Body in San Antonio." In *Latino Cultural Citizenship: Claiming Identity, Space, and Rights*, edited by William V. Flores and Rina Benmayor. Boston: Beacon.

Forman, Murray. 2002. *The "Hood" Comes First: Race, Space, and Place in Rap and Hip hop*. Middletown, Conn.: Wesleyan University Press.

Foucault, Michel. 1990. *The History of Sexuality*. Vol. 1: *An Introduction*. Translated by Robert Hurley. New York: Vintage.

———. 2003. *"Society Must Be Defended": Lectures at the Collège de France, 1975–76*, edited by Mauro Bertani and Alessandro Fontana; general editors, François Ewald and Alessandro Fontana. Translated by David Macey. New York: Picador.

Franco, Jean. 1989. *Plotting Women: Gender and Representation in Mexico*. New York: Columbia University Press.

Freire Filho, João. 2001. *A Elite Ilustrada e os "Clamores Anônimos da Barbárie": Gosto Popular e Polêmicas Culturais no Brasil Moderno*. Ph.D. diss., Pontifícia Universidade Católica do Rio de Janeiro.

———. 2003. "O Rock Está Morto, Viva o Rap! O Rap Morreu: A Nostalgia da Autenticidade na Crítica Cultural Contemporânea." *Ícone* 1.6: 47–77.

———. 2006. "Moda, Estilo de Vida e Distinção Social: Quando o Brega Vira *Fashion*." In *Plugados na Moda*, edited by Nizia Villaça and Kathia Castilho. São Paulo: Editora Anhembi Morumbi.

Freyre, Gilberto. [1933] 1989. *Casa-Grande & Senzala*. Rio de Janeiro: Record.

Frith, Simon. 1996. *Performing Rites: On the Value of Popular Music*. Cambridge: Harvard University Press.

Fry, Peter, Sérgio Carrara, and Ana Luiza Martins-Costa. 1988. "Negros e Brancos no Carnaval da Velha República." In *Escravidão e Invenção da Liberdade: Estudos sobre o Negro no Brasil*, edited by João José Reis. São Paulo: Brasiliense.

Fryer, Peter. 2000. *Rhythms of Resistance: African Musical Heritage in Brazil*. Hanover, Germany: Wesleyan University Press.

Furtado Filho, João Ernani. 2004. "Um Brasil Brasileiro: Música, Política, Brasilidade (1930–1945)." Ph.D. diss., Universidade de São Paulo.

Galinsky, Philip. 1996. "Co-option, Cultural Resistance, and Afro-Brazilian Identity: A History of the *Pagode* Samba Movement in Rio de Janeiro." *Latin American Music Review* 17.2: 120–49.

———. 2002. *Maracatu Atômico: Tradition, Modernity, and Postmodernity in the Mangue Movement of Recife, Brazil*. New York: Routledge.

Galvão, Walnice Nogueira. 1976. "MMPB: Uma Análise Ideológica." In *Saco de Gatos*. São Paulo: Livraria Duas Cidades.

Garcia, Maria Elena. 2004. "The Challenges of Representation: NGOs, Education, and the State in Highland Peru." In *Civil Society or Shadow State?: State/NGO Relations in Education*, edited by Margaret Sutton and Robert Arnove. Charlotte: Information Age Publishing.

Gil, Gilberto. 2003a. "Experimentation, Memory, and Invention" (Inaugural Address delivered by Minister Gilberto Gil, 2 January 2003). In "Living Culture: National Culture, Education and Citizenship Program." Culture policy press release. Brasilia: Ministry of Culture.

———. 2003b. "What Happens When You Set a Bird Free?" In "Living Culture: National Culture, Education and Citizenship Program." Cultural policy press release. Brasilia: Ministry of Culture.

Gill, Lesley. 2004. *The School of the Americas: Military Training and Political Violence in the Americas*. Durham: Duke University Press.

Gilroy, Paul. 1993. *The Black Atlantic: Modernity and Double Consciousness*. Cambridge: Harvard University Press.

Ginzburg, Carlo. 1987. *O Queijo e os Vermes: O Cotidiano e as Idéias de um Moleiro Perseguido pela Inquisição*. São Paulo: Companhia das Letras.

Godi, Antonio J. V. Dos Santos. 2001. "Reggae e Samba-Reggae in Bahia: A Case of Long-Distance Belonging." In *Brazilian Popular Music and Globalization*, edited by Charles Perrone and Christopher Dunn. Gainesville: University Press of Florida.

Gohn, Maria da Glória. 1997. *Sem-Terra: ONGS e Cidadania*. São Paulo: Cortez.

———. 2000. *Mídia, Terceiro Setor e MST: Impactos sobre o Future das Cidades e do Campo*. Petrópolis: Vozes.

Goldemberg, Ricardo. 1995. "Educação Musical: A Experiência do Canto Orfeônico no Brasil." *Pró-Posições* 6.3: 103–9.

Gomes, Ângela Maria de Castro. 1982. "A Construção do Homem Novo: O Trabal-
hador Brasileiro." In *Estado Novo: Ideologia e Poder*, edited by Lúcia Lippi Oliveira,
Mônica Pimenta Velloso, and Ângela Maria de Castro Gomes. Rio de Janeiro:
Zahar.

Goode, Erich, and Nachman Ben-Yehuda. 1994a. *Moral Panics: The Social Construction of Deviance*. Cambridge, Mass.: Blackwell.

———. 1994b. "Moral Panics: Culture, Politics and Social Construction." *Annual
Review of Sociology* 29: 149–71.

Guérios, Paulo Renato. 2003. *Heitor Villa-Lobos: O Caminho Sinuoso da Predestinação*.
Rio de Janeiro: Editora FGV.

Guerreiro, Goli. 2000. *A Trama dos Tambores: A Música AfroPop de Salvador*. São
Paulo: Editora 34.

Guimarães, Maria Eduarda A. 1998. "Do Samba ao Rap: A Música Negra no Brasil."
Ph.D. diss., Universidade de Campinas.

Gustafson, Bret. 2006. "Spectacles of Autonomy and Crisis: Or, What Bulls and
Beauty Queens Have to Do with Regionalism in Eastern Bolivia." *Journal of Latin
American Anthropology* 11.2: 351–79.

Habermas, Jurgen. [1962] 1989. *The Structural Transformation of the Public Sphere:
An Inquiry into a Category of Bourgeois Thought*. Trans. Thomas Burger with the
assistance of Frederick Lawrence. Cambridge: MIT Press.

Hagopian, Frances. 2007. "Latin American Citizenship and Democratic Theory." In
Citizenship in Latin America, edited by Joseph S. Tulchin and Meg Ruthenberg.
Boulder: Lynne Rienner.

Halbwachs, Maurice. 1992. *On Collective Memory*. Chicago: University of Chicago
Press.

Hall, Stuart. 1990. "Cultural Identity and Diaspora." In *Identity: Community, Culture,
Difference*, edited by Jonathan Rutherford. London: Lawrence and Wishart.

———. 1996a. "Identidade Cultural e Diáspora." *Revista do Patrimônio Histórico e
Artístico Nacional* 24: 68–75.

———. 1996b. "New Ethnicities." In *Black British Cultural Studies: A Reader*, edited
by Houston Baker Jr., Manthia Diawara, and Ruth Lindeborg. Chicago: University of Chicago Press

Hall, Stuart, et al. 1976. "Subcultures, Cultures, and Class." *Resistance through Rituals: Youth Subcultures in Post-war Britain*, edited by Stuart Hall and Tony Jefferson.
London: Harper Collins Academic.

———. 1978. *Policing the Crisis: Mugging, the State, and Law and Order*. London:
Macmillan.

Hanchard, Michael. 1994. *Orpheus and Power: The Movimento Negro of Rio de Janeiro
and São Paulo, Brazil, 1945–1988*. Princeton: Princeton University Press.

Hansen, Thomas Blom, and Finn Stepputat, eds. 2001. *States of Imagination: Ethnographic Explorations of the Postcolonial State*. Durham: Duke University Press.

Hasenbalg, Carlos. 1985. "Race and Economic Inequalities in Brazil." In *Race, Class, and Power in Brazil*, edited by Pierre-Michel Fontaine. Los Angeles: University of California Press.

Heater, Derek. 1999. *What Is citizenship?* Cambridge: Polity.

Hebdige, Dick. 1987. *Cut 'n' Mix: Culture, Identity, and Caribbean Music*. New York: Routledge.

———. 1989. *Hiding in the Light: On Images and Things*. London: Routledge.

Henderson, Mae Gwendolyn. 1994. "Speaking in Tongues: Dialogics, Dialects, and the Black Woman Writer's Literary Tradition." In *The Essential Difference*, edited by Naomi Schor and Elizabeth Weed. Bloomington: Indiana University Press.

Herschmann, Micael. 2000. *O Funk e o Hip-Hop Invadem a Cena*. Rio de Janeiro: Editora UFRJ.

———. 2001. "Um Tapinha Não Dói. Funk: Zona de Contato da Cidade do Rio de Janeiro." In *Nas Fronteiras do Contemporâneo*, edited by Nízia Villaça and Fred Góes. Rio de Janeiro: Editora Maud.

———, ed. 1997. *Abalando os Anos 90 — Funk e Hip-Hop. Globalização, Violência e Estilo Cultural*. Rio de Janeiro: Rocco.

Herschmann, Micael, and Carlos Alberto M. Pereira. 2003. *Mídia, Memória e Celebridades*. Rio de Janeiro: Ed. E-Papers.

Homem de Mello, José Eduardo. 1976. *Música Popular Brasileira*. São Paulo: Edusp.

Holston, James. 2008. *Insurgent Citizenship: Disjunctions of Democracy and Modernity in Brazil*. Princeton: Princeton University Press.

Horta, José Silvério Baía. 1994. *O Hino, o Sermão e a Ordem do Dia: A Educação no Brasil (1930–1945)*. Rio de Janeiro: Editora UFRJ.

Irigaray, Luce. 1991. "The Power of Discourse and the Subordination of the Feminine." In *The Irigaray Reader*, edited by Margaret Whitford. Cambridge: Basil Blackwell.

Isin, Engin, and Patricia Wood. 1999. *Citizenship and Identity*. London: Sage.

Jameson, Fredric. 1991. *Postmodernism, or, the Cultural Logic of Late Capitalism*. Durham: Duke University Press.

Jasper, James M. 1999. *The Art of Moral Protest: Culture, Biography, and Creativity in Social Movements*. Chicago: University of Chicago Press.

Jelin, Elizabeth. 2003. "Citizenship and Alterity: Tensions and Dilemmas." *Latin American Perspectives* 30.2: 309–25.

Joseph, Gilbert M., and Daniel Nugent, eds. 1994. *Everyday Forms of State Formation: Revolution and the Negotiation of Rule in Modern Mexico*. Durham: Duke University Press.

Kant, Immanuel. [1795] 2003. *To Perpetual Peace: A Philosophical Sketch*. Translated by Ted. Humphrey. Indianapolis: Hackett.

Kehl, Maria Rita. "Chico Buarque." In *Música Popular Brasileira Hoje*, edited by Arthur Nestrovski. São Paulo: Publifolha.

Kristeva, Julia. 1982. *Powers of Horror: An Essay on Abjection*. Translated by Leon S. Roudiez. New York: Columbia University Press.

Kubik, Gerhard. 1979. *Angolan Traits in Black Music, Games and Dances of Brazil: A Study of African Cultural Extensions Overseas*. Lisbon: Junta de Investigações Científicas do Ultramar.

Kun, Josh. 2005. *Audiotopia: Music, Race, and América*. Los Angeles: University of California Press.

Labaki, Amir. 2003. "It's All Brazil." In *The New Brazilian Cinema*, edited by Lúcia Nagib. New York: Palgrave Macmillan.

Leão do Ó, Ana Carolina Carneiro. 2002. "A maravilha mutante: batuque, sampler e pop no Recife dos anos 90." M.A. thesis, Universidade Federal de Pernambuco.

Leite, Sérgio, and Leonilde Servolo de Medeiros. 2004. *Assentamentos Rurais: Mudança Social e Dinâmica Regional*. Rio de Janeiro: Mauad.

Lesser, Jeffrey. 1999. *Negotiating National Identity: Immigrants, Minorities, and the Struggle for Ethnicity in Brazil*. Durham: Duke University Press.

Lewis, J. Lowell. 1992. *Ring of Liberation: Deceptive Discourse in Brazilian Capoeira*. Chicago: University of Chicago Press.

Lima, Ari. 1997. "A Estética da Pobreza: Música, Política e Estilo." M.A. thesis, Universidade Federal do Rio de Janeiro.

———. 2001. "Black or *Brau*: Music and Black Subjectivity in a Global Context." In *Brazilian Popular Music and Globalization*, edited by Charles Perrone and Christopher Dunn. Gainesville: University of Florida Press.

Linger, Daniel T. 2003. "Do Japanese Brazilians Exist?" In *Searching for Home Abroad*, edited by Jeffrey Lesser. Durham: Duke University Press.

Lins, Paulo. [1997] 2006. *City of God*. Translated by Alison Entrekin. New York: Grove.

Locke, John. [1690] 1988. *Two Treatises of Civil Government*. Cambridge: Cambridge University Press.

Lloyd, David, and Paul Thomas. *Culture and the State*. New York: Routledge, 1998.

Machado de Assis, Joaquim Maria. [1874] 2004. *Helena*. São Paulo: Ática.

———. 1904. *Esaú e Jacó*. Rio de Janeiro: Garnier.

Magalhães, Celso de. *A Poesia Popular Brasileira*. Rio de Janeiro: Biblioteca Nacional, 1973.

Magnini, Jose Guilherme Cantor. 1985. "Espaço e Debates." *Revista de Estudos Regionais e Urbanos* 6.17: 127–30.

———. 1996. "Quando o Campo é a Cidade: Fazendo Antropologia na Metrópole." In *Na Metrópole: Textos de Antropologia Urbana*, edited by J. G. C. Magnini and L. L. Torres. São Paulo: EDUSP.

Mammí, Lorenzo. 1992. "João Gilberto e o Projeto Utópico da Bossa Nova." *Novos Estudos CEBRAP* 34 (November): 63–70.

Mannheim, Karl. 1952. *Essays on the Sociology of Knowledge*. London: Routledge.

———. 1982. *Structures of Thinking: Collected Works*. Vol. 10. London: Routledge.

Marcondes Filho. 1943. "A Senhora do Lar Proletário." In *Trabalhadores do Brasil!* Rio de Janeiro: Revista Judiciária. 51–55

Marshall, T. H. 1950. *Citizenship and Social Class and Other Essays*. Cambridge: Cambridge University Press.

Marshall, T. H., and Tom Bottomore. 1992. *Citizenship and Social Class*. London: Pluto.

Martín-Barbero, Jesús. 1987. *De los Medios a las Mediaciones: Comunicación, Cultura y Hegemonía*. Mexico City: Ediciones G. Gili.

Martins, José de Souza. 2000. *Reforma Agrária: O Impossível Diálogo*. São Paulo: EDUSP.

———. 2003. *O Sujeito Oculto: Ordem e Transgressão na Reforma Agrária*. Porto Alegre: Editora da Universidade Federal do Rio Grande do Sul.

———. 2004–5. "Cultura e Educação na Roça: Encontros e Desencontros." *Revista USP* 64: 29–49.

Massey, Doreen, and N. A. Denton. "A Place Called Home." 1992. *New Formations* 17 (summer): 3–15.

Matos, Claudia. 1982. *Acertei no Milhar: Samba e Malandragem no Tempo de Getúlio*. Rio de Janeiro: Paz e Terra.

Mattos, Florisvaldo. 1998. *A Comunicação Social na Revolução dos Alfaiates*. Salvador: Academia de Letras da Bahia.

McCann, Bryan. 2004. *Hello, Hello Brazil: Popular Music and the Making of Modern Brazil*. Durham: Duke University Press.

McNee, Malcolm. 2003. "The Arts in Movement: Cultural Politics and Production in Brazil's Landless Rural Workers Movement (MST)." Ph.D. diss., University of Minnesota.

———. 2005. "A Diasporic, Post-traditional Peasantry: The *Movimento Sem Terra* (MST) and the Writing of Landless Identity." *Journal of Latin American Cultural Studies* 14.3 (December): 335–53.

Menchú, Rigoberta and Elizabeth Burgos-Debray. 1984. *I, Rigoberta Menchú: An Indian Woman in Guatemala*. Trans. Ann Wright. London: Verso.

Mercante, Renata. 2004. "Carlinhos Brown: Musicalidade na Veia." *Revista Possível* 1.5: 31.

Meyer, Augusto. 1952. *Cancioneiro Gaúcho*. Porto Alegre: Globo.

Midlej e Silva, Suylan. 1995. "Sociabilidade Contemporânea, Comunicação Midiática e Etnicidade no Funk do Black Bahia." In *O Sentido e a Época*, edited by Aristóteles Rocha Filho, et al. Salvador: EDUFBA.

———. 1996. "O Pertencimento na Festa. Sociabilidade, Identidade e Comunicação Mediática no Baile Funk 'Black Bahia' do Periperi." M.A. thesis, Universidade Federal da Bahia.

———. 1998. "O Lúdico e o Étnico no Funk do Black Bahia." In *Ritmos em Trânsito: Sócio-Antropologia da Música Baiana*. Salvador: Dynamis Editorial.

Miller, Toby. 2001. "Introducing . . . Cultural Citizenship." *Social Text* 19.4: 1–5.

Mitchell, Michael J., and Charles H. Wood. 1998. "Ironies of Citizenship: Skin Color, Police Brutality, and the Challenge to Democracy in Brazil." *Social Forces* 77.3: 1001–20.

Moby, Alberto. 1994. *Sinal Fechado: A Música Popular Brasileira sob Censura*. Rio de Janeiro: Obra Aberta.

Moehn, Frederick. 2007. "Listening to Gilberto Gil." Unpublished paper, Society for Ethnomusicology Annual Congress, Columbus, Ohio.

———. 2009. "A Carioca Blade Runner, or How Percussionist Marcos Suzano Turned the Brazilian Tambourine into a Drum Kit and Other Matters of Politically Correct Music Making." *Ethnomusicology* 53.2: 277–307.

Morales, Anamaria. 1991. "Blocos Negros em Salvador: Reelaboração Cultural e Símbolos de Baianidade." *Caderno CRH. Suplemento: Cantos e Toques. Etnografias do Espaço Negro na Bahia* 1: 72–92.

Moriconi, Ítalo. 1996. "Pedagogia e Nova Barbárie." In *Cultura: Substantivo Plural*, edited by Márcia de Paiva and Maria Ester Moreira. São Paulo: Editora 34.

Moser, Walter, et al., eds. 1996. *Recyclages: Economies de l'Appropriation Culturelle*. Montreal: Balzac.

Moura, Milton. 1987. "Faraó: Um Poder Musical." *Caderno do CEAS* [Salvador] 112: 20–39.

———. 2001a. "World of Fantasy, Fantasy of the World: Geographic Space and Representation of Identity in the Carnaval of Salvador, Bahia." In *Brazilian Popular Music and Globalization*, edited by Charles Perrone and Christopher Dunn. Gainesville: University of Florida Press.

———. 2001b. "Carnaval e Baianidade: Arestas e Curvas na Coreografia da Identidades do Carnaval de Salvador." Ph.D. diss., Universidade Federal da Bahia.

MST (Movimento dos Trabalhadores Rurais Sem Terra / Rural Landless Workers Movement). 1996. *Sem-Terra: A Música do MST*, edited by Ires Silene Escobar de Campos. Porto Alegre: Unidade Editorial.

Müller, Rafaela. 2002. "No Ritmo da Viola: Cresce a Demanda por Manifestações Culturais Autênticas." *Problemas Brasileiros* 1: 12–15.

Munanga, Kabengele. 1999. *Redisicutindo a Mestiçagem no Brasil: Identidade Nacional versus Identidade Negra*. Petrópolis: Vozes.

Mussa, Alberto, and Luiz Antonio Simas. 2010. *Sambas de enredo: História e arte*. Rio de Janeiro: Civilização Brasileira.

Napolitano, Marcos. 2001. *Seguindo a Canção: Engajamento Político e Indústria Cultural na MPB (1959–1969)*. São Paulo: Annablume.

———. 2004. "A MPB sob Suspeita: A Censura Musical Vista pela Ótica dos Serviços de Vigilância Política (1968–1981)." *Revista Brasileira de História* 24.47: 103–26.

Nascimento, Regina Célia de Oliveira. 1994. *Trajetória de Uma Identidade*. Campinas: IFCH.

Naves, Santuza Cambraia. 1998. *O Violão Azul: Modernismo e Música Popular*. Rio de Janeiro: FGV.

Nepomuceno, Rosa. 1999. *Música Caipira: Da Roça ao Rodeio*. São Paulo: Editora 34.

Nestrovski, Arthur, ed. 2002. *Música Popular Brasileira Hoje*. São Paulo: Publifolha.

Novaes, Regina, et al. 2002. *Juventude, Cultura e Cidadania*. Rio de Janeiro: ISER.

Nun, José. 1983. "A Rebelião do Coro." *Desvios* 2: 104–18.

Nunes, Margarete F. 1997. "O Turbante do Faraó: O Olodum no Mundo Negro de Salvador." M.A. thesis, Universidade Federal de Santa Catarina.

O'Donnell, Guillermo A. 1996. "Illusions about Consolidation." *Journal of Democracy* 7.2: 34–51.

Oliveira, Francisco de. 1980. "Salvador, os Exilados da Opulência (Expansão Capitalista numa Metrópole Pobre)." In *Bahia de Todos os Pobres*, edited by Guaraci Adeodato, A. de Souza, and Vilmar Faria. Petrópolis: Vozes.

———. 1987. *O Elo Perdido: Classe e Identidade de Classe*. São Paulo: Brasiliense.

Oliveira, Graciete. 1997. "Brown Candealzine: A Influência de Carlinhos Brown na Comunidade do Candeal." M.A. thesis, Universidade Estadual da Bahia.

Oliveira, Sirleide Aparecida de. 2001. "O Pagode em Salvador: Produção e Consumo nos Anos 90." M.A. thesis, Universidade Federal da Bahia.

Oliven, Ruben George. 1987. "A Mulher Faz (e Desfaz) o Homem." *Ciência Hoje* 7: 54–62.

Ortiz, Renato. 1994. *Cultura Brasileira e Identidade Nacional*. São Paulo: Brasiliense.

———. 1996. "Anotações sobre Mundialização e a Questão Nacional." *Sociedade e Estado* 11.1: 36–45.

Oxhorn, Philip. 2007. "Neopluralism and Citizenship in Latin America." In *Citizenship in Latin America*, edited by Joseph S. Tulchin and Meg Ruthenberg. Boulder: Lynne Rienner.

Paiva, Marcelo Rubens. 2000. "Especial para a Folha de São Paulo," *Folha de São Paulo*, 8 December. E13.

Paoli, Maria Celia. 1987. "Os Trabalhadores Urbanos na Fala dos Outros: Tempo, Espaço e Classe na História Operária Brasileira." In *Cultura e Identidade Operária: Aspectos da Cultura da Classe Trabalhadora*, edited by José Sérgio Leite Lopes. São Paulo: Marco Zero: UFRJ.

———. 1989. "Trabalhadores e Cidadania: Experiência do Mundo Público na História do Brasil Moderno." *Estudos Avançados* 3.7: 40–66.

Paoli, Maria Celia, and Vera da Silva Telles. 1998. "Social Rights: Conflicts and Negotiations in Contemporary Brazil." In *Culture of Politics, Politics of Culture: Re-visioning Latin American Social Movements*, edited by Sonia Álvarez, Evelina Dagnino, and Arturo Escobar. Boulder: Westview.

Parada, Maurício Barreto Alvarez. 2003. *Educando Corpos e Criando a Nação: Ceri-*

mônias Cívicas e Práticas Disciplinares no Estado Novo. Ph.D. diss., Universidade Federal do Rio de Janeiro.

Paranhos, Adalberto. 1999a. *O Roubo da Fala: Origens da Ideologia do Trabalhismo no Brasil.* São Paulo: Boitempo.

———. 1999b. "O Brasil Dá Samba? Os Sambistas e a Invenção do Samba como 'Coisa Nossa.'" In *Música Popular em América Latina*, edited by Rodrigo Torres. Santiago de Chile: Fondart.

———. 2004. "A Música Popular e a Dança dos Sentidos: Distintas Faces do Mesmo." *ArtCultura* 9: 22–31.

———. 2005. "A Ordem Disciplinar e Seu Avesso: Música Popular e Relações de Gênero no 'Estado Novo.'" *Lutas Sociais* 13/14: 80–89.

Pardue, Derek. 2004a. "Putting *Mano* to Music: The Mediation of Race in Brazilian Rap." *Ethnomusicology Forum* 13.2: 253–86.

———. 2004b. "'Writing in the Margins': Brazilian Hip hop as an Educational Project." *Anthropology and Education Quarterly* 35.4: 411–32.

———. 2005. "CD Cover Art as Cultural Literacy and Hip Hop Design in Brazil." *Education, Communication and Information* 5.1 (March): 61–81.

———. 2007. "Hip Hop as Pedagogy: A Look into 'Heaven' and 'Soul' in São Paulo, Brazil." *Anthropological Quarterly* 80.3 (Summer): 673–709.

———. 2008. *Ideologies of Marginality in Brazilian Hip Hop.* New York: Palgrave McMillan.

Parker, Richard. 1991. *Bodies, Pleasures, and Passions: Sexual Culture in Contemporary Brazil.* Boston: Beacon.

Pedro, Antonio. 1980. *Samba da Legitimidade.* M.A. thesis, Universidade de São Paulo.

Pereira, Adilson. 2000. "A Lição do Malandro," *Jornal do Brasil*, 27 June.

Perlman, Janice. 1976. *The Myth of Marginality: Urban Poverty and Politics in Rio de Janeiro.* Berkeley: University of California Press.

Perniola, Mario. 2002. *El Arte y Su sombra.* Madrid: Editora Cátedra.

Perrone, Charles. 1989. *Masters of Contemporary Brazilian Song: MPB 1965–1985.* Austin: University of Texas Press.

Perrone, Charles, and Christopher Dunn, eds. 2001. *Brazilian Popular Music and Globalization.* Gainesville: University of Florida Press.

Pichot, Andre. 1997. *O eugenismo: Genetistas Apanhados pela Filantropia.* Lisbon: Instituto Piaget.

Pierson, Donald. 1942. *Negroes in Brazil.* Chicago: University of Chicago Press.

Pimentel, Spensy. 1998. "Microfone Aberto à População," *Caros Amigos* 3.9.

Pinho, Osmundo de A. 1998a. "'A Bahia no Fundamental': Notas para uma Interpretação do Discurso Ideológico da Baianidade." *Revista Brasileira de Ciências Sociais* 13.36: 109–20.

———. 1998b. "Alternativos e Pagodeiros: Notas Etnográficas sobre Territorialidade e Relações Raciais no Centro Histórico de Salvador." *Estudos Afro-Asiáticos* 34: 35–48.

———. 1998c. "The Songs of Freedom: Notas Etnográficas sobre Cultura Negra Global e Práticas Contraculturais Locais." In *Ritmos em Trânsito: Sócio-Antropologia da Música Baiana*, edited by Livio Sansone and Jocélio Teles dos Santos. Salvador: Dynamis Editorial.

———. 1999. "Espaço, Poder e Relações Raciais: O Caso do Centro Histórico de Salvador." *Afro-Ásia* 21–22: 257–74.

———. 2001. "'Fogo na Babilônia': Reggae, Black Counterculture and Globalization in Brazil." In *Brazilian Popular Music and Globalization*, edited by Charles Perrone and Christopher Dunn. Gainesville: University Press of Florida.

Pinto, T. "Fala Tom Zé, o Popular e Erudito Que Pratica a Imprensa Cantada," *Revista Imprensa* 8.137 (1990): 4–10.

Pochmann, Marcio, et al. 2005. *Classe Média: Desenvolvimento e Crise*. São Paulo: Cortez.

Polletta, Francesca, and James M. Jasper. 2001. "Collective Identity and Social Movements." *Annual Review of Sociology* 27: 283–305.

Ponciano, Levino. 2001. *Bairros Paulistanos de A a Z*. São Paulo: SENAC.

Prado, Paulo. [1928] 1997. *Retrato do Brasil: Ensaio sobre a Tristeza Brasileira*. 9th ed. São Paulo: Companhia das Letras.

Raphael, Alison. 1980. "Samba and Social Control: Popular Culture and Racial Democracy in Rio de Janeiro." Ph.D. diss., Columbia University.

Reardon, Christopher. 2005. "The New Favela Beat." *Ford Foundation Report* (Spring–Summer): 18–23.

Rebelo, Marques. 2002. *A Mudança*. 3rd ed. Rio de Janeiro: Nova Fronteira.

Reily, Suzel Ana. 1992. "Musica Sertaneja and Migrant Identity: The Stylistic Development of a Brazilian Genre." *Popular Music* 11.3: 337–58.

Reis, João José. 1993. *Slave Rebellion in Brazil: The Muslim Uprising of 1835 in Bahia*. Baltimore: Johns Hopkins University Press.

Ricardo, Sérgio. 1991. *Quem Quebrou Meu Violão*. Rio de Janeiro: Record.

Ridenti, Buarque de Hollanda. 2000. *Em Busca do Povo Brasileiro: Artistas da Revolução, do CPC à Era da TV*. São Paulo: Record.

Risério, Antonio. 1981. *Carnaval Ijexá*. Salvador: Corrupio.

———. 1993. *Caymmi: Uma Utopia de Lugar*. São Paulo: Perspectiva.

Roach, Joseph. 1996. *Cities of the Dead: Circum-Atlantic Performance*. New York: Columbia University Press.

Robbins, Bruce, and Elsa Stamatopoulou. 2004. "Reflections on Cultures and Cultural Rights." *South Atlantic Quarterly* 103.2/3 (Spring/Summer): 419–34.

Rocha, Francisco. 2002. *Adoniran Barbosa: O Poeta da Cidade*. São Paulo: Ateliê.

Rodrigues, Ana Maria. 1984. *Samba Negro, Espoliação Branca*. São Paulo: Hucitec.

Rodrigues, João Jorge Santos. 1983. "A Música do Ilê Aiyê e a Educação Consciente." *Estudos Afro-Asiáticos* 8–9: 247–51.

———. 1996. *Olodum: Estrada da Paixão*. Salvador: Edições Olodum.

Rodrigues, Raimundo Nina. 1977. *Os Africanos no Brasil*. São Paulo: Companhia Editora Nacional.

Rollefson, J. G. 2007. "Tom Zé's *Fabrication Defect* and the 'Esthetics of Plagiarism': A Postmodern/Postcolonial 'Cannibalist Manifesto.'" *Popular Music and Society* 30.3: 305–27.

Romero, Sílvio. 1954. *Folclore Nacional: Contos e Cantos Populares do Brasil*. 3 vols. Rio de Janeiro: José Olympio.

Rose, Tricia. 1994. *Black Noise: Rap Music and Black Culture in Contemporary America*. Hanover, N.H.: University Press of New England.

Roth, Joshua Hotaka. 2002. *Brokered Homeland: Japanese Brazilian Migrants in Japan*. Ithaca: Cornell University Press.

Rousseau, Jean-Jacques. [1762] 2002. *The Social Contract and the First and Second Discourses*, edited by Susan Dunn. New Haven: Yale University Press.

Rowe, William, and Vivian Schelling. 1991. *Memory and Modernity: Popular Culture in Latin America*. New York: Verso.

Sachs, Céline. 1999. *São Paulo: Políticas Públicas e Habitação Popular*. São Paulo: EDUSP.

Salvadori, Maria Ângela Borges. 1990. *Capoeiras e Malandros: Pedaços de uma Sonora Tradição Popular (1890–1950)*. M.A. thesis, Universidade de Campinas.

Sandroni, Carlos. 2001. *Feitiço Decente: Transformações do Samba no Rio de Janeiro, 1917–1933*. Rio de Janeiro: Jorge Zahar.

Sanford, Victoria. 2004. *Buried Secrets: Truth and Human Rights in Guatemala*. London: Palgrave.

Sansone, Livio. 1991. "A Produção de uma Cultura Negra (Da Cultura 'Creole' à Subcultura Negra. A Nova Etnicidade Negra dos Jovens 'Creoles' Surinameses de Classe Baixa em Amsterdam)" *Estudos Afro-asiáticos* 20: 121–34.

———. 1998. "Funk Baiano: Uma Versão Local de um Fenômeno Global?" In *Ritmos em Trânsito: Sócio-Antropologia da Música Baiana*, edited by Livio Sansone and Jocélio Teles dos Santos. Salvador: Dynamis Editorial.

Sant'Anna, Affonso Romano de. 1986. *Música Popular e Moderna Poesia Brasileira*. Petrópolis: Vozes.

Santiago, Silviano. 2001. *The Space In-Between: Essays on Latin American Culture*, edited by Ana Lúcia Gazzola. Durham: Duke University Press.

Santos, Alcino, et al. 1982. *Discografia Brasileira: 78 RPM*. Vols. 2 and 3. Rio de Janeiro: Funarte.

Santos, Jocélio Teles dos. 1998. "Divertimento Estrondosos: Batuques e Sambas no Século XIX." In *Ritmos em Trânsito: Sócio-Antropologia da Música Baiana*, edited by Livio Sansone and Jocélio Teles dos Santos. Salvador: Dynamis Editorial.

Santos, Milton. 1979. *The Shared Space: The Two Circuits of the Urban Economy in Underdeveloped Countries*. New York: Methuen.

———. 2006. *Território, Territórios: Ensaios sobre o Ordenamento Territorial.* 2nd ed. Rio de Janeiro: DP&A.

Santos, Myrian Sepúlveda dos. 2000. "Teoria da Memória, Teoria da Modernidade." In *Teoria Social e Modernidade no Brasil*, edited by Leonardo Avritzer and José Maurício Domingues. Belo Horizonte: UFMG.

Santos, Wanderley Guilherme dos. 1979. *Cidadania e Justiça.* Rio de Janeiro: Campus.

Schafer, Murray. 1986. *The Thinking Ear: Our Music Education.* Indian River, Ontario: Arcana.

Schiller, Friedrich. [1793] 1954. *On the Aesthetic Education of Man, in a Series of Letters.* New Haven: Yale University Press.

Schmidt, Benício Veiro, Danilo Nolasco C. Marinho, and Sueli L. Couto Rosa, eds. 1998. *Os Assentamentos da Reforma Agrária no Brasil.* Brasília: Universidade de Brasília.

Schwarcz, Lílian. 1993. *O Espetáculo das Raças: Cientistas e Questão Racial no Brasil, 1870–1930.* São Paulo: Companhia das Letras.

Schwarz, Roberto. 1992. *Misplaced Ideas: Essays on Brazilian Culture*, edited by John Gledson. New York: Verso.

Schwartz, Stuart. 1992. *Slaves, Peasants, and Rebels.* Urbana: University of Illinois Press.

Scliar, Moacyr. 2003. *Saturno nos Trópicos: A Melancolia Européia Chega ao Brasil.* São Paulo: Companhia das Letras.

Sharp, Daniel Benson. 2001. "A Satellite Dish in the Shantytown Swamps: Musica Hybridity in the 'New Scene' of Recife, Pernambuco, Brazil." M.A. thesis, University of Texas.

Shimakawa, Karen. 2002. *National Abjection: The Asian American Body Onstage.* Durham: Duke University Press.

Silva, Carlos Benedito Rodrigues. 1984. "Black Soul: Aglutinação espontânea e identidade étnica." In *Ciências Sociais: Compêndio de Comunicações.* Vol. 2. Caxambu: MG.

———. 1995. *Da Terra das Primaveras à Ilha do Amor: Reggae, Lazer e Identidade Cultural.* São Luís: EDUFMA.

Silva, Jônatas. 1988. "História das Lutas Negras: Memórias do Surgimento do Movimento Negro na Bahia." In *Escravidão e Invenção da Liberdade: Estudos sobre o Negro no Brasil*, edited by João José Reis. São Paulo: Brasiliense.

Silva, José Carlos G. da. 1998. "Rap na Cidade de São Paulo: Música, Etnicidade e Experiência Urbana." Ph.D. diss., Universidade de Campinas.

Silva, Marília T. Barbosa da, and Lygia Santos. 1979. *Paulo da Portela: Traço da União entre Duas Culturas.* Rio de Janeiro: Funarte.

Silverstein, Paul A. 2002. "Why Are We Waiting to Start the Fire?": French Gangsta Rap and the Critique of State Capitalism. In *Black, Blanc, Beur: Rap Music and Hip Hop Culture in the Francophone World*, edited by Alain Philippe Durand. Lanham, Md.: Scarecrow.

Skidmore, Thomas. [1974] 1993. *Black into White: Race and Nationality in Brazilian Thought*. 2nd ed. Durham: Duke University Press.

Sneed, Paul. 2007. "Bandidos de Cristo: Representation of the Power of Criminal Factions in Rio's Proibidão Funk." *Latin American Music Review* 28.2 (December): 219–41.

Sodré, Muniz. 1988. *O Terreiro e a Cidade*. Petrópolis: Vozes.

Souza, A. Macus Alves. 1995. *Cultura Rock e Arte de Massa*. Rio de Janeiro: Diadorim.

Souza, Jessé. 2000. *A Modernização Seletiva: Uma Reinterpretação do Dilema Brasileiro*. Brasília: Universidade de Brasília.

Souza, Jusamara Vieira. 1993. *Schulmusikerziehung in Brasilien zwischen 1930 und 1945*. Frankfurt: Lang.

Spivak, Gayatri Chakravorty. 1988. "Can the Subaltern Speak?" In *Marxism and Interpretation*, edited by Cary Nelson and Lawrence Grossberg. Urbana: University of Illinois Press.

Stromquist, Nelly A. 1997. *Increasing Girls' and Women's Participation in Basic Education*. Paris: UNESCO, International Institute for Educational Planning.

Sugimoto, Luiz. 2004. "A classe média está com raiva." *Jornal da Unicamp* 251 (May 10–16): 8–9.

Tatit, Luiz. 2002. *O Cancionista*. São Paulo: EDUSP.

Teles, José. 1998. *Meteoro Chico*. Recife: Bargaço.

———. 2000. *Do Frevo ao Manguebeat*. São Paulo: Editora 34.

Thompson, E. P. 1991. *Customs in Common: Studies in Traditional Popular Culture*. London: Merlin.

Tinhorão, José Ramos. 1966. *Música Popular: Um Tema em Debate*. Rio de Janeiro: JCM.

———. 1988. *Os Sons dos Negros no Brasil: Cantos, Danças, Folguedos. Origens*. São Paulo: Art Editora.

———. 1991. *Pequena História da Música Popular: Da Modinha à Lambada*. 6th ed. São Paulo: Art Editora.

———. 1998. *História Social da Música Popular Brasileira*. Rio de Janeiro: Editora 34.

Treece, David. 1997. "Gun's and Roses: Bossa Nova and Brazil's Music of Popular Protest, 1958–68." *Popular Music* 16: 1–29.

Tsuda, Takeyuki. 2003. *Strangers in the Ethnic Homeland: Japanese Brazilian Return Migration in Transnational Perspective*. New York: Columbia University Press.

Ulhôa, Martha. 1993. "Musical Style, Migration, and Urbanization: Some Considerations on Brazilian *Música Sertaneja* [Country Music]." *Studies in Latin American Popular Culture* 12: 75–95.

———. 1997. "Nova História, Velhos Sons: Notas para Ouvir e Pensar a Música Brasileira Popular." *Debates* 1: 80–101.

Urry, John. 1990. *The Tourist Gaze: Leisure and Travel in Contemporary Societies*. London: Sage.

Vagalume (Francisco Guimarães). 1978. *Na Roda do Samba*. Rio de Janeiro: Funarte.

Valente, Luiz. 2001. "Brazilian Literature and Citizenship: From Euclides da Cunha to Marcos Dias." *Luso-Brazilian Review* 38.2 (Winter): 11–27.

Valente, Rodrigo. 2005. "Assentados e Acampados Mostram e Debatem a Sua Arte." *Revista Sem Terra* 7.28 (January–February): 52–54.

Vargas, Getúlio. 1942. *Boletim do Ministério do Trabalho, Indústria e Comércio* 93.

Vargas, Herom. 2008. *Hibridismos Musicais de Chico Science & Nação Zumbi*. São Paulo: Ateliê.

Vasconcelos, Ary. 1982. "Chegou a hora dessa gente bronzeada mostrar seu valor." Fascículo/LP *Assis Valente*. História da Música Popular Brasileira. São Paulo: Abril Cultural.

Vasconcellos, Gilberto, and Suzuki Matinas Jr. 1984. "A malandragem e a Formação da Música Popular Brasileira." In *História Geral da Civilização Brasileira*. Vol. 3, edited by Boris Fausto. São Paulo: Difel.

Vassberg, David E. 1969. "Villa-Lobos: Music as a Tool of Nationalism." *Luso-Brazilian Review* 6.2 (Winter): 55–65.

Veiga, Ericivaldo. 1996. "Rastafari e Cultura em Salvador." In *Olodum: Estrada da Paixão*, edited by João Jorge Santos Rodrigues. Salvador: Olodum.

———. 1998. "O Errante e Apocalíptico Muzenza." In *Ritmos em Trânsito. Sócio-Antropologia da Música Baiana*, edited by Livio Sansone and Jocélio Teles dos Santos. Salvador: Dynamis Editorial.

Velho, Gilberto. 1994. *Projeto e Metamorfose: Antropologia das Sociedades Complexas*. Rio de Janeiro: Jorge Zahar.

———. 2001. "Biografia, Trajetória e Mediação." In *Mediação Cultura e Política*, edited by Gilberto Velho and Karina Kuchner. Rio de Janeiro: Aeroplano.

Veloso, Mariza, and Angélica Madeira. 1999. *Leituras Brasileiras: Itinerários no Pensamento Social e na Literatura*. São Paulo: Paz e Terra.

Ventura, Roberto. 1991. *Estilo Tropical: História Cultural e Polêmicas Literárias no Brasil*. São Paulo: Companhia das Letras.

Ventura, Zuenir. 2003. *Da Favela para o Mundo*. Rio de Janeiro: Aeroplano.

Véras, Maura Pardini Bicudo. 2003. *DiverCidade: Territórios Estrangeiros como Topografia da Alteridade em São Paulo*. São Paulo: UDUC.

Vianna, Hermano. 1988. *O Mundo Funk Carioca*. Rio de Janeiro: Jorge Zahar.

———. 1996. "O *Funk* como Símbolo de Violência." In *Cidadania e Violência*, edited by Gilberto Velho and Marcos Alvito. Rio de Janeiro: Editora UFRJ.

———. 1998. "Música no Plural: Novas Identidades Brasileiras." *Revista de Cultura Brasileña* 11: 299–311.

———. [1995] 1999. *The Mystery of Samba: Popular Music and National Identity in Brazil*. Translated by John Chasteen. Chapel Hill: University of North Carolina Press.

Vianna, Letícia. 1999. *Bezerra da Silva: Produto do Morro. Trajetória e Obra de um Sambista que Não É Santo*. Rio de Janeiro: Jorge Zahar.

Vicente, Eduardo. 1996. "Música Popular e Produção Intelectual nos Anos 40." *Cadernos de Sociologia* 2: 157–72.

Vieira, Paulo. 1998. "Não vi, não sei, não conheço: Entrevista com Bezerra da Silva." Folha de São Paulo. September 4.

Vieira Filho, Raphael. 1995. "A Africanização do Carnaval de Salvador, BA. A Re-Criação do Espaço Carnavalesco (1876–1930)." M.A. thesis, Pontifícia Universidade Católica do Rio de Janeiro.

———. 1998. "Folguedos Negros no Carnaval de Salvador (1880–1930)." In *Ritmos em Trânsito: Sócio-Antropologia da Música Baiana*, edited by Livio Sansone and Jocélio Teles dos Santos. Salvador: Dynamis Editorial.

Vilhena, Luís Rodolfo. 1995. *Projeto e Missão: O Movimento Folclórico Brasileiro (1947–1964)*. Rio de Janeiro: Funarte.

Walzer, Michael. 1995. "The Civil Society Argument." In *Theorizing Citizenship*, edited by Ronald Beiner. Albany: State University of New York Press.

Waiselfisz, Júlio Jácobo, et al. 2004. *Mapa da Violência IV: Os Jovens do Brasil*. Brasilia: UNESCO.

Waterman, Christopher. 1990. *Júju: A Social History and Ethnography of an African Popular Music*. Chicago: University of Chicago Press.

Weller, Wivian. 2003. *Hip Hop in São Paulo und Berlin: Ästhetische Praxis und Ausgrenzungserfahrungen junger Schwarzer und Migranten*. Opladen: Leske and Budrich.

Williams, Raymond. *Culture and Society, 1780–1950*. 1983. New York: Columbia University Press.

Wisnik, José Miguel. 2004. "Machado Maxixe: O Caso Pestana." In *Sem Receita: Ensaios e Canções*. São Paulo: Publifolha.

Wolford, Wendy. 2004. "This Land Is Ours Now: Spatial Imaginaries and the Struggle for Land in Brazil." *Annals of the Association of American Geographers* 94.2: 409–24.

Wolford, Wendy, and Angus Wright. 2003. *To Inherit the Earth: Brazil's Landless Movement and the Struggle for a New Brazil*. Oakland: Food First Publications.

Young, Jock. 1971. *The Drugtakers: The Social Meaning of Drug Use*. London: Paladin.

Yúdice, George. 2001. "Afro Reggae: Parlaying Culture into Social Justice." *Social Text* 19.4: 53–65.

———. 2003. *The Expediency of Culture: Uses of Culture in the Global Era*. Durham: Duke University Press.

Zé, Tom (António José Martins Santana). 2003. *Tropicalista Lenta Luta*. São Paulo: Publifolha.

Zumthor, Paul. 2001. *A Letra e a Voz: A "Literatura" Medieval*. São Paulo: Companhia das Letras.

contributors

Idelber Avelar is professor of Spanish and Portuguese at Tulane University. He is the author of *The Letter of Violence: Essays on Narrative, Ethics, and Politics* (2004) and *The Untimely Present: Postdictatorial Latin American Fiction and the Task of Mourning* (1999), winner of the MLA Katherine Singer Kovacs Prize and translated into Spanish and Portuguese. He has published numerous essays in scholarly journals in Europe and the Americas and is currently preparing a book on masculinity in Latin American narrative.

Christopher Dunn is associate professor at Tulane University, where he holds a joint appointment in the Department of Spanish and Portuguese and the African and African Diaspora Studies Program. He is the author of *Brutality Garden: Tropicália and the Emergence of a Brazilian Counterculture* (2001), which was translated into Japanese and Portuguese, and is editor with Charles Perrone of *Brazilian Popular Music and Globalization* (2001).

João Freire Filho is the coordinator of the Graduate Program in Communication at the Federal University of Rio de Janeiro. He is author of several books, including *Reinvenções da Resistência Juvenil: Os Estudos Culturais e as Micropolíticas do Cotidiano* (2007); with Silvia Borelli, *Culturas Juvenis no Século XXI* (2008); and *A TV em Transição: Tendências de Programação no Brasil e no Mundo* (2009).

Goli Guerreiro holds a Ph.D. in anthropology from the University of São Paulo. As a postdoctorate fellow at the Federal University of Bahia, she is developing the project "Third Diaspora: Black Cultures in the Atlantic World." She is author of *A Trama dos Tambores: A Música Afro-Pop de Salvador* (2000) and a consultant for the Editora Corrupia of Salvador, Bahia.

Micael Herschmann holds a Ph.D. in communication from the Federal University of Rio de Janeiro (UFRJ) and completed postdoctoral work at the Universidad Complutense University de Madrid. He is co-coordinator of the research group Media and Sociocultural Mediations in the Graduate Program in Communications and coordinator of the Nucleus of Communication Research at UFRJ. He has published several books—including *Lapa, Cidade da Música: Desafios e Perspectivas para o Crescimento* *do Rio de Janeiro e da Indústria da Música Independente Nacional* (2007), and *O Funk e o Hip-Hop Invadem a Cena* (2000).

Ari Lima teaches in the Department of Education and in the Graduate Program of Cultural Criticism at the State University of Bahia (UNEB), where he coordinates the Nucleus of Oral Traditions and Immaterial Patrimony (NUTOPIA). He has published widely about black music, youth culture, and race relations.

Aaron Lorenz holds a Ph.D. from the Stone Center for Latin American Studies at Tulane University. He is a postdoctoral associate in the Department of Romance Studies at Duke University.

Shanna Lorenz is an assistant professor of music at Occidental College, Los Angles. She is currently writing a book about representations of border crossing in theater, film, and music in the post-9/11 era.

Angélica Madeira teaches literature and culture at the University of Brasília. She is the author of *Livro dos Naufrágios: Ensaio sobre a História Trágico-Marítimo* (2005), and with Mariza Veloso, *Leituras Brasileiras: Itinerários no Pensamento Social e na Literatura* (1999).

Malcolm K. McNee is assistant professor in the Department of Spanish and Portuguese at Smith College, where he also serves on program boards for comparative literature and Latin American and Latino/Latina studies. He is editor with Joshua Lund of *Gilberto Freyre e os Estudos LatinoAamericanos* (2006).

Frederick Moehn is an assistant professor of ethnomusicology at Stony Brook University, New York, and a research associate at the Universidade Nova de Lisboa. His publications include articles in *Ethnomusicology*, *Ethnomusicology Forum*, and *Latin American Music Review*. His book on contemporary Brazilian popular music in Rio de Janeiro is forthcoming from Duke University Press.

Flávio Oliveira coordinates policies of social integration for the state secretary of social development of Minas Gerais. He is a research affiliate of the Study and Research Group in the History of Education (GEPHE) of the Federal University of Minas Gerais.

Adalberto Paranhos teaches in the Department of Social Sciences and in the Graduate Program in History at the Federal University of Uberlândia. He is the author of *O Roubo da Fala: Origens da Ideologia do Trabalhismo no Brasil* (2007), and editor of *ArtCultura: Revista de História, Cultura e Arte*.

Derek Pardue is an assistant professor at Washington University, St. Louis, where he holds a joint appointment in the Anthropology Department and the International and Area Studies Program. He is the author of *Ideologies of Marginality in Brazilian Hip Hop* (2008) and editor of *Ruminations on Violence* (2008).

Marco Aurélio Paz Tella teaches urban anthropology at the Federal University of Paraíba (Campus IV, Litoral Norte), where he directs the research group Urban Ethnographies: Differences and Alterities. He is the author of numerous articles about youth and ethnicity.

Osmundo Pinho teaches at the Center for Arts, Humanities, and Letters and in the Graduate Program in Social Sciences at the Federal University of Bahia (Cachoeira Campus). He is the author, with Lívio Sansone, of *Raça: Novas Perspectivas Antropológicas* (2009) and has published numerous articles and book chapters.

Carlos Sandroni is a professor of ethnomusicology in the Department of Music and in the Graduate Program in Anthropology at the Federal University of Pernambuco. He is the author of *Feitiço Decente: Transformações do Samba no Rio de Janeiro, 1917–1933* (2001) and *Mário contra Macunaíma: Cultura e Política em Mário de Andrade* (1988). With Márcia Sant'Anna, he is coeditor of *Samba de Roda no Recôncavo Baiano* (2007).

Daniel Sharp is an assistant professor of ethnomusicology jointly appointed in the Newcomb Department of Music and the Stone Center for Latin American Studies at Tulane University. He is currently working on a book about nostalgia, cultural citizenship, and the musical performance of cultural roots, focusing on Samba de Coco Raízes de Arcoverde and Cordel do Fogo Encantado from Arcoverde, Pernambuco.

Hermano Vianna holds a Ph.D. in anthropology from the Nacional Museum / Federal University of Rio de Janeiro. A cultural activist and administrator, he created the website Overmundo and helped to develop the Cultural Points Program in the Ministry of Culture under the direction of Gilberto Gil. He is the author of *O Mundo Funk Carioca* (1988) and *O Mistério do Samba* (1995), which was published in English in 1999.

Wivian Weller teaches in the Department of Theory and Foundations and in the Graduate Program of Education at the University of Brasília. She is the author of *Minha Voz é Tudo o Que eu Tenho — Manifestações Juvenis em Berlim e São Paulo* (2010), and *HipHop in São Paulo und in Berlin: Ästhetische praxis und Ausgrenzungserfahrungen junger Schwarzer und Migraten* (2003) in addition to numerous articles and chapters.

index

316–17; in liberal school, 2; Marshall on, 3, 111, 127, 209; music as enabler of, 1–2, 6–7, 18–20, 22–27, 31–39, 69–70, 72, 83–94, 109–18, 124–26, 132, 141, 146, 156, 173–74, 179, 181–82, 186–87, 197–204, 210–21, 229–39, 241–49, 277, 283–89, 291–93, 309–11, 319–28; political, 3, 74, 111; race and, 4, 7–8; in republican school, 2, 269; satire of, 79–83; social, 3, 74, 111–12, 115

Claudinho & Bochecha, 229, 237

Cobaias, Os, 304–6

Coco, 25–27, 70–71, 291–311, 312n1

Coco Raízes (Samba de Coco Raízes de Arcoverde), 292–93, 296–98, 306, 310–11

Cohen, Stanley, 223–24

Collor de Melo, Fernando, 20, 98, 233

Conceição, Giba, 286

Conceitos de Rua, 211

Concrete poetry, 93, 102, 122

Cordel do Fogo Encantado, 27, 292–93, 299–304, 309–11

Cozzella, Damiano, 76

CPC (Centro Popular de Cultura), 68, 154n24

CUFA (Central Única das Favelas), 115–19, 127, 129n3

Cunha, Olivia Maria Gomes da, 222n8, 260–62

Cunha, Vladimir, 240

Dagnino, Evelina, 212, 214

DaMatta, Roberto, 5, 81, 110

Daruê Malungo, 318

Deep Purple, 323

DeFalla, 235

Deleuze, Gilles, 101

Desafio, 85

Dicró (Carlos Roberto de Oliveira), 188

DMN, 199–200

Donga (Ernesto Joaquim Maria dos Santos), 11, 184

Duarte, Aderbal, 286

Duprat, Rogério, 42n7, 95n1

Duque (Antônio Lopes de Amorim Diniz), 11

Embaixada Africana, 253, 255

Embolada, 18, 25–26, 296–97, 312n1, 314, 324, 326

É o Tchan, 263, 272

Erundina, Luiza, 212

Escobar, Arturo, 212

Escolas de samba (Samba schools), 13–16, 254–55, 266n2. *See also* Samba

Estado Novo (New State), 28–29, 33, 36, 39

Estilo Negro, 188–89, 197

Eutrópio, José, 49–51

Fagundes, Eduardo, 286

Favaretto, Celso, 328n2

Fellini, 20

Fernandes, Sujatha, 211

Ferreira, Juca (João Luiz Silva Ferreira), 21, 124

Folklore, 17, 35–37, 65–73, 146–47, 223, 235, 246, 293, 295, 299, 301, 309, 311, 312n4, 314

Força Ativa, 205, 210–12, 215–17

Forró, 21, 25, 114, 136–38, 153n13, 240, 244–49, 295, 304–5, 311, 312n3. *See also* Baião

Foucault, Michel, 82–83, 110–11

Fred 04 (Fred Rodrigues Montenegro), 313, 318–19, 327

Freire, Paulo, 212

Frevo, 25, 289, 328

Freyre, Gilberto, 184, 248, 267–68

Idelber Avelar is professor of Spanish and Portuguese at
Tulane University. He is the author of *The Letter of Violence:
Essays on Narrative, Ethics, and Politics* (2004) and *The
Untimely Present: Postdictatorial Latin American Fiction
and the Task of Mourning* (Duke, 1999).

Christopher Dunn is associate professor and chair of Brazilian
literary and cultural studies at Tulane University. He is
the author of *Brutality Garden: Tropicália and the Emergence
of a Brazilian Counterculture* (2001). He is also the editor
(with Charles A. Perrone) of *Brazilian Popular Music and
Globalization* (2001).

: : :

Library of Congress Cataloging-in-Publication Data
Brazilian popular music and citizenship / edited by
Idelber Avelar and Christopher Dunn.
p. cm.
Includes bibliographical references and index.
ISBN 978-0-8223-4884-9 (cloth : alk. paper)
ISBN 978-0-8223-4906-8 (pbk. : alk. paper)
1. Popular music—Social aspects—Brazil. 2. Popular
music—Political aspects—Brazil. 3. Popular music—
Brazil—History and criticism. I. Avelar, Idelber, 1968–
II. Dunn, Christopher, 1964– III. Title.
ML3917.B6B739 2011
306.4′84240981—dc22   2010038072